The Arab World and Western Intelligence

Intelligence, Surveillance and Secret Warfare

Series Editors: Richard J. Aldrich, Rory Cormac, Michael S. Goodman and Hugh Wilford

Intelligence has changed. Espionage chiefs now command secret armies and legions of cyber warriors who can quietly shape international relations itself. Intelligence actively supports diplomacy, peacekeeping and warfare. As traditional inter-state wars become more costly, covert action, black propaganda and other forms of secret interventionism become more important. Meanwhile, surveillance permeates communications to the point where many feel there is little privacy. Intelligence, and the accelerating technology that surrounds it, have never been more salient for the citizen and the state.

This series explores the full spectrum of spying and secret warfare in a globalised world. Books in this series will provide a deeper understanding of modern intelligence, its past, present and future, the manner in which it is gathered and the causes for which it is harnessed. Whether through rich empirical detail, conceptual development and/ or theoretical expansion, they will provoke original questions for researchers and students alike.

www.edinburghuniversitypress.com/series/isasw

The Arab World and Western Intelligence

Analysing the Middle East, 1956–1981

Dina Rezk

EDINBURGH
University Press

Edinburgh University Press is one of the leading university presses in the UK. We publish academic books and journals in our selected subject areas across the humanities and social sciences, combining cutting-edge scholarship with high editorial and production values to produce academic works of lasting importance. For more information visit our website: edinburghuniversitypress.com

© Dina Rezk, 2017

Edinburgh University Press Ltd
The Tun – Holyrood Road,
12(2f) Jackson's Entry,
Edinburgh EH8 8PJ

Typeset in 11/13 Sabon by
IDSUK (Dataconnection) Ltd

A CIP record for this book is available from the British Library

ISBN 978 0 7486 9891 2 (hardback)
ISBN 978 0 7486 9892 9 (webready PDF)
ISBN 978 1 4744 0506 5 (epub)

Contents

Acknowledgements

The personal and intellectual journey that culminated in this book began many years ago. I would like to take this opportunity to express my heartfelt gratitude to colleagues, friends and family who joined, pushed and at times even carried me along the way. I extend thanks also to the team at EUP who have been wonderfully patient and professional.

My doctoral supervisor, Professor Christopher Andrew, clearly saw the potential of this project long before I did, I would certainly not have applied for a PhD without his characteristically gentle but firm encouragement. Since leaving Cambridge, Professor Richard Aldrich has been the best mentor a young scholar could hope to have. I have little doubt that it is to him that I owe my survival in the Hobbesian world of early career academia. Countless others offered valuable comments on embryonic versions of this work, amongst them: Professor David Reynolds, Dr. Patrick Porter, Dr. Kristian Gustafson, Dr. Alastair Reid, Professor John Darwin, Sir Patrick Wright and Sir James Craig. I am particularly grateful to my dear friends Derek and Nadia Plumbly for their hospitality at the British Embassy in Cairo in the spring of 2006, the interviews they facilitated, and the many subsequent dinners, drafts and discussions shared more recently back in London.

My friends and family have provided immeasurable love and encouragement over the years. Gala Riani and Kajsa Westling fuelled my heart and mind upon my arrival in Cambridge in 2002. Tammy Tawadros, Kevin Quinlan, Veronica Massoud and Miki Footman all devoted countless hours helping bring this project to completion. My brother, Tamer Rezk, has been my best friend and the provider of critical pep talks at seemingly hopeless moments. A special thank you to my father, Maurice Rezk, for his unwavering support in so many capacities. Ignoring my relentless protests, his insistence that the Saturday mornings of my childhood were to be spent in Arabic school have stood me in good stead. I would like to dedicate this book to my mother, Laila Rezk, who instilled in me a love of the humanities from an early age and whose determination, resilience and sacrifices taught me the importance of striving for excellence in all endeavours. We miss your smile.

Introduction

On the 6 October 1981, the world watched with horror as the West's most important Arab ally, Egyptian President Anwar el Sadat, was shot dead on live television. It was the first preview of a Jihad that sought to kill for piety. Thirty years later, Islamist militants struck again, this time on American soil, causing death and destruction in the heartland of the world's superpower.

This book addresses a critical question embedded within a heated debate about the 'failure' of American intelligence in a post 9/11 age: have Western experts in some fundamental way failed to understand the dynamics, leaders and culture of the Middle East? Analysing recent history through a series of seminal case studies, this monograph explores whether, how and why the most knowledgeable and powerful intelligence agencies in the world have been so notoriously caught off guard in the region.

The story begins after the tripartite invasion of the Suez Canal in 1956. This momentous event set in motion a ripple of ideological and geopolitical transformations that continue to shape the politics and borders of the modern Middle East. Upheaval marked the two decades that followed: revolutions swept across Syria, Iraq and Yemen; three devastating Arab–Israeli wars ravaged the Holy Lands; and eventually a fraught and contested bilateral treaty bound Egypt and Israel to uneasy peace. The West and the Soviet Union vied for control over the Middle East's destiny through its political centre, Egypt. As the largest and most populous Arab state, Egypt forms the pivot of this book. The transition from Gamal Abdel Nasser to Anwar el Sadat witnessed the decline of an ardently anti-imperialist Arab nationalism, supplanted by a radical quest to realign Egypt's identity towards the Western world.

The background to this story has been well told.[1] The British granted Egypt formal independence in 1922 but decades of indirect rule ensued. A weak and corrupt Egyptian monarchy was personified by the lecherous and indulgent figure of King Farouk. Egypt's brief interwar flirtation with parliamentary democracy saw the dominance of an increasingly discredited nationalist Wafd party. In the years building up to the Egyptian revolution, the Wafd was widely viewed as little more than a British puppet. In 1948, a humiliating Egyptian defeat in the first Arab–Israeli war galvanised both popular and military opposition to the Egyptian regime. In 1952, a group of free officers led a military coup against the government, calling for independence from foreign rule, social justice and the redistribution of land. King Farouk was given a dignified send-off and the new military regime moved to consolidate their hold over the Egyptian state, disbanding political parties, purging universities and the judiciary, while building a formidable security structure. By 1954 the young and personable Colonel Nasser had emerged as the indisputable leader of the Free Officer regime, although he did not officially adopt the title of President until 1956.

British and American attitudes towards Nasser converged somewhat after the Suez Crisis, yet the 'special relationship' was often strained by events in the post-war Middle East. There were certainly stark differences across the Atlantic in how the Egyptian nationalist was viewed in 1952. The British regarded the Free Officer regime with the suspicion one might expect from an imperial power, affronted by the challenge the Egyptian military coup posed to its regional interests and prestige. Meanwhile, the Americans regarded such colonial sentiments as outdated and consequently the CIA played an important role in consolidating Nasser's command. Indeed, head of the CIA's Middle East Division, Kim Roosevelt, was on excellent terms with Nasser and even spearheaded CIA funding to encourage American appreciation of Arab culture within the United States, reflecting what Wilford calls a 'now lost world of secret American Arabism'.[2] Early hopes that Nasser could be courted as an ally of the West were thwarted by tense negotiations over the British evacuation of the Suez Canal base and the Western preoccupation with a regional anti-Soviet alliance, eventually culminating in the ill-fated Baghdad Pact.[3] The Israeli raid on Gaza in February 1955, French arms sales to Israel and Egypt's inability to secure weapons from the United States led to an unprecedented arms deal with the Soviet Union via Czechoslovakia in September 1955. As Nasser ardently advocated 'positive neutralism' with his attendance at Bandung and recognition of the People's Republic of China, the US government withdrew their offer to fund the Aswan Dam.[4] The subsequent nationalisation of the Suez Canal and the invasion that ensued marks a historical 'turning point' over which much ink has been spilled. Scholars have told a tale of woe, of the West's failure to understand Arab nationalism, their neglect of regional opportunities to harness Arab nationalism at the expense of Cold War preoccupations and their fundamental misperceptions of President Nasser.[5]

This book picks up the story after the Suez debacle of 1956. The Suez Crisis was undoubtedly a critical turning point in the West's relations with the Middle East and indeed the Anglo-American 'special relationship'. The British were faced with the humiliating position of being forced to withdraw from Egypt as a result of political and financial pressure from their closest ally. It would not be the last time that Anglo-American policy would be divided by events in the Middle East. It was, however, Britain's last throw of the imperial dice: never again would the United Kingdom's prestige and authority be so directly and publicly challenged on a global scale. In Egypt and the Arab world more broadly, Nasser was elevated to the status of an ideology rather than simply a leader. Nationalism had proven to be a powerful antidote to the humiliation of colonialism and the creeping Westernisation of the Middle East that accompanied the early twentieth century. In the aftermath of the Suez Crisis, American officialdom did not regard Nasser much more benevolently than their British counterparts but they were more inclined to see the benefits that Arab nationalism might offer to the Cold War struggle.

Whilst early histories of this period relied heavily on the retrospective accounts by first-hand participants such as Secretary of State Henry Kissinger, the declassification of government documents on both sides of the Atlantic have more recently allowed

veterans to combine their recollections with official documentation to produce invaluable studies of the period.[6] Nigel Ashton's
monographs provide a detailed analysis of Anglo-American
policy-making towards Egypt, Syria, Iraq and Yemen, exploring their 'competitive collaboration' in the Middle East.[7] Robert
McNamara highlights the mutual 'delusions of grandeur' which
marred relations between Britain and Egypt.[8] Several works have
incorporated the Egyptian perspective based on extensive interviews and an examination of Arab sources, contributing to a
more 'global history' of this formative period.[9] The past decades
have also seen growing scholarly interest in the role of cultural
differences and antipathies in defining the West's relations with
the Arab world.[10] It has become all too clear that 'the activities of
the modern state are shaped by the cultural imagination'.[11]

But much of this literature ignores a vital component. Sparse
attention has been paid to the 'missing dimension' of intelligence
analysis on the Middle East. Though recent declassifications
represent a rich and valuable resource, we know little about the
contemporary 'knowledge' through which the analytical bodies
of the intelligence communities in Britain and America viewed
events of this period.[12] Where the intelligence dimension *has* been
addressed, it is mostly mentioned in passing, recalling for example the 'success' of Anglo-American intelligence in 1967 and the
corresponding 'failure' of 1973.[13]

The remarkable declassification of intelligence assessments
of the most important events of the period provide an unprecedented insight into not only what was known and understood
about the Arab world, but how this information was conceptual-
ised. How was Arab nationalism perceived as it manifested itself
in upheavals in Syria, Iraq and Yemen or the Arab–Israeli wars to
follow? How significant was Arab cultural 'Otherness' in assessments? Did the perceptual prism of the Cold War prevail or were
regional dynamics given their due weight? In essence this work
enables both scholar and practitioner to determine the strengths
and weaknesses of British and American intelligence analyses
of the region in this period. It also sheds light on Western
perceptions of Egypt's most important and contentious 'great
men'. How were Nasser and Sadat perceived by the intelligence

community? Do the respective dichotomies of 'adversary' and 'ally' simplify a more complex repertoire of images?[14] Moreover, how do these perceptions correlate with the available Arab sources?

Thus this book brings to light much new empirical evidence. But it also draws on a novel and interdisciplinary methodology that bridges the existing gap between diplomatic, cultural and intellectual history. James Joll's account of the origins of the First World War marked one of the earliest contributions to an enduring debate among historians as to the role of 'unspoken assumptions' in our study of the past.[15] Since then, 'mindset' has become a keyword in arguably the most popular and fashionable domain of history – the 'New Cultural History'.[16] Reading between the lines or decoding unspoken assumptions (often with a strong postmodernist hue) has provoked some controversial conclusions about the 'Otherness' of the past and a heated discussion about the limits of historical interpretation. As one scholar put it, 'largely unfamiliar with the work of literary and cultural critics, many diplomatic historians have read their documents too literally and assume the events they describe can be understood as unmediated objective realities rather than dynamic historical constructions'.[17] We have learned that the past is another country; that its participants hold a mindset or *mentalité* fundamentally different to ours that must be appreciated, even deconstructed; and that detailed analysis of the text is a central part of decoding unspoken assumptions. The doyen of international history, David Reynolds, persuasively argues that 'in such a text-based area of history as diplomatic history, scholars must therefore be extremely sensitive to language'.[18]

Edward Said's passionate exposé of Western 'Orientalism' in 1978 was one of the most controversial expressions of this new interdisciplinary genre of historical analysis. His subtextual analysis of the 'unspoken' in European literary depictions of the Orient argued that negative Western stereotypes of the Middle East were created by, and provided justification for, a colonial system of political domination.[19] Yet, as Matthew Connelly has observed, 'postcolonial scholars today catalogue the cultures of empire in novels and travel writing, museums and expositions, paintings and postcards – everywhere it seems, but the archives and personal papers of European and US policy makers'.[20]

It should not be surprising therefore that Said's influence, and the 'cultural turn' of which he was a controversial part, has yet to make a significant and visible historiographical dent in the more nascent and specialised 'missing dimension' of intelligence history.[21] Whilst scholars of intellectual or cultural history search for the stated and unstated assumptions of a 'Great Text', or the webs of signification that underlie a particular discourse or ritual, what of the ideas, assumptions and significations of the many 'great texts' used to inform policy-makers? Inspired by fellow cultural, intellectual and postcolonial historians, with their focus on both the spoken and the unspoken, this book advances the proposition that we can use recently declassified political and intelligence documents to unearth how the elite producing 'knowledge' for policy-makers actually thought about the Arab 'Other'. As one scholar puts it, 'information, its analysis and its military and political fall-out are culturally embedded phenomena'.[22] Defining intelligence as 'information' provides a wide and revealing insight into the cultural frames of reference shared by the Anglo-American political elite responsible for analysing the Middle East.

In the absence of accessible Egyptian archival material against which to judge the 'validity' of the ideas and assumptions expressed by Anglo-American political and intelligence assessments, this project relied on interviews conducted by the author with a selection of surviving participants in Egypt.[23] Their interpretation of selected intelligence assessments, and their reference to certain cultural beliefs expressed therein, was both valuable and surprising. Arabic published material has also been used alongside secondary studies which have synthesised the Arab perspective in order to judge the extent to which Anglo-American perceptions of the time corresponded with the 'realities' of their Egyptian counterparts.[24]

This book does not presume to provide a detailed narrative or comparison of policy-making in Britain and America towards the Middle East in this period, nor does it seek to use intelligence documents to draw direct parallels between what they contain and those policies eventually chosen by decision-makers on either side of the Atlantic. The multifaceted nature of policy-making is too complex to be able to draw such direct conclusions and it is perhaps impossible to determine exactly how analysis influenced the policy-making process in Britain and America.[25] Indeed the extent to which 'good intelligence' leads to 'good policy' remains a subject of great contention amongst intelligence scholars.[26] Moreover, the relationship between intelligence analysis and policy-making in Britain and America is substantially different. In the UK, cabinet ministers read the weekly product of the Joint Intelligence Committee (JIC), which serves as the only governmental body of all-source analysis. In America, the executive has a number of competing analytical bodies from which to choose. The Central Intelligence Agency (CIA) provides a daily intelligence summary (usually scattered with snippets of 'raw' intelligence) in the form of the top-secret Presidential Daily Brief (PDB) every morning.[27] Thus the discussion that follows is less concerned with drawing direct causal explanations for Anglo-American policy in the Middle East from intelligence documentation than with exploring the discursive 'habitus' in which the 'knowledge' of policy-makers about the Arab world was constructed.[28]

There are further evidential constraints that have shaped the trajectory of this book. Though there has been much material declassified in recent years, certain documents remain inaccessible. For example, many of the JIC records for 1973 are still classified and almost no signals intelligence (SIGINT) is available. Considering the limitations of the material available and the extent of US/UK intelligence sharing, the book takes a collaborative approach to Anglo-American intelligence rather than a comparative one, highlighting divergences between assessments that will undoubtedly be subject to future revision as further material is declassified. Michael Goodman's *Official History of the Joint Intelligence Committee* describes the growing exchange of assessments and increasingly close relations between the CIA and JIC that characterised the post-war era, notwithstanding differences in policy.[29] Similarly, John Dumbrell makes a persuasive case that together with nuclear information, the 'intimate intermeshing of US and British intelligence . . . formed the essence and beating heart of the Cold War "special relationship"'.[30] Moreover, at various points, both the allies suffered from a break in diplomatic relations with Cairo. Britain had no embassy presence in Egypt after the fall-out from Suez from 1956 until relations were resumed in 1960, only to be broken again in 1965 over British policy towards Rhodesia. Washington experienced a particularly long official diplomatic rupture with Egypt between the Six-Day War in 1967, when America was blamed for supporting the Israeli attack, until after the 1973 Arab–Israeli War, when Sadat began earnestly to court US support. Therefore, it is reasonable to expect that both the allies will have relied even more heavily on their partner's diplomatic and intelligence reporting during these schisms when direct access to Egyptian sources was limited.

Nor does the current distribution of the declassified documents across the Atlantic enable firm comparisons to be drawn between British and American analysis. Although the more comprehensive declassification of JIC reports gives the scholar relatively good access to the 'official mind' of the Committee, the numerous CIA declassifications do not reveal what reports have not yet been declassified. Sir Patrick Dean, head of the JIC, observed in 1958 that 'the United States effort on intelligence was anything from ten to fifteen times as much as ours'.[31] There are thus surely many more American documents still to be released. Furthermore, the reclassification scheme of various 'embarrassing' documents declassified under the Clinton administration some years ago present the historian with the Orwellian predicament that documents once available on the shelves of the American national archives have been quietly removed.[32]

However, the Declassified Documents Reference System (DDRS), National Intelligence Estimates (NIEs) and CIA memoranda online have been well supplemented by American diplomatic reports and the CREST database at the American National Archives in Maryland alongside the most recently declassified material from the Ford Presidential Library. The Foreign Affairs Oral History interviews, a part of the Library of Congress American Memory collection, adds important colour and texture to this official record. An understanding of British perceptions has relied on a rich (if not yet entirely complete) record of JIC papers, diplomatic reports in the Foreign Office files, and interviews and correspondence with surviving British diplomats.[33] The diplomatic reports in particular have proven to be a crucial and valuable spring of 'open-source' intelligence hitherto neglected by intelligence scholars.

With the rising volume of popular and academic attention paid to the 'cloak and dagger' activities of covert operations, it is easy to forget that analysis has always formed the lion's share of intelligence activities on both sides of the Atlantic. In the 1950s, the founding father of intelligence analysis in the US, Sherman Kent, was determined to promote the growth of 'intelligence analysis as a profession'. The rather dreary, but comprehensive all-source National Intelligence Estimates were produced by the Board of National Estimates (BNE) in the Office of National Estimates (ONE), an institution with a reputation as elitist and dominated by Ivy League academics. Kent led both the ONE and the BNE from 1952 until his retirement in 1967. The ONE faced a number of reorganisational initiatives under the Nixon administration until it was dissolved by Director of Central Intelligence (DCI) William Colby. Under Kissinger's influence, the National Security Council (NSC) became increasingly important in producing intelligence assessments from 1973.[34]

In Britain, the main analytic body has always been the Joint Intelligence Committee, operating from the Cabinet Office and providing all-source assessments to policy-makers. The JIC was also something of a 'scholarly' bureaucracy, described by one CIA representative in the Committee as 'rather stiff'. JIC assessments were drafted by Joint Intelligence Staff, which included representatives from the Foreign Office, Armed Services and various other departments that gathered intelligence. The JIC chairman was frequently a high ranking Foreign Office official in this period, rendering this branch of the civil service particularly influential in the Committee. Departmental contributions were gathered into a collective draft, which was reviewed and revised before final JIC approval.[35]

In some ways this study clearly contributes to the institutional, or corporate memory of the Anglo-American intelligence community's analytic bodies. I hope that the historical study of these documents will illuminate the strengths and weaknesses of intelligence analysis in an age when its role is not only significant but all the more urgent in relations between the Western world and the Middle East. Through the various case studies explored in the chapters that follow we interrogate just how accurate this voice of official wisdom proved to be: what did analysts get so wrong and why? More surprisingly: what did they get right? This 'lessons learned' approach forms the first objective of the book.

However, this somewhat positivist endeavour is superseded in import and emphasis by a softer, more literary and critical approach, one that seeks to uncover precisely what role notions of 'culture' played in analytic readings of the region. There is surely nowhere better to test Said's hypothesis that the West's cultural representations of the Middle East were stereotypical, false and static than in the secret archives of those producing 'knowledge' for policy-makers. This investigation into the intellectual library with which analysts approached the Arab world unearths an ongoing debate about controversial ideas such as 'the Arab mind' and the role of 'culture' in understanding the region's politics.

Finally, the book applies this novel methodology to a more traditional focus on the 'great men' of history. In doing so it responds to calls for a 'cultural approach to intelligence history and a more probing evaluation of archival texts'.[36] Indeed I argue that only by playing closer and more critical attention to the language used by analysts can we historians properly mine and exploit the secret murmurings about the two most seminal leaders of the post-war Middle East. As a substantial body of literature explores, Egyptian president Gamal Abdel Nasser was the leader, indeed for many Arabs the embodiment of anti-colonial politics in the Middle East. It is little surprise therefore that he came to be regarded by policy-makers as British 'enemy number one'. By contrast, his successor, Anwar el Sadat, embarked on a quest to redefine Egypt's identity and became one of the West's most important Arab allies. Exposing the intelligence and diplomatic material produced at the time suggests that the respective dichotomies of 'adversary' and 'ally' collapse under the weight of a more nuanced repertoire of images. Examining the detail and complexity of these images thus forms the third objective of this book.

Figure I.1 President Nasser with Cuban Prime Minister Fidel Castro, 1960. US NARA National Archives 2.

We begin by exploring one of the central themes of this study. It is commonly suggested that the major weakness of the American intelligence community in the Middle East stems from its inability to understand the mindset of a fundamentally different culture.[37] How has intelligence conceptualized culture? Exposing a collection of rare documents that deal with the issue of 'national character', this chapter provides striking revelations about the dominant and controversial stereotypes of 'the Arab mind' shared by British and American intelligence in the post-war era. It traces the evolution of ideas about the influence of Islam, Arab 'motivation', the role of rhetoric and the prevalence of 'honour' in the region. Moreover, it demonstrates that these are themes that persist in our understanding of Arab culture and politics to this day. It also contributes to an important and ongoing debate about Orientalist cultural representations expressed by the West. Interviews with high-level Arab diplomats in fact reveal that the indigenous political elite validated many of the cultural assumptions asserted by Western analysts. Indeed, this chapter will argue that this elite often used Western cultural preconceptions about Arab culture to defend, advance or conceal their own strategic objectives.

The formation of the United Arab Republic (UAR) in February 1958 was an unprecedented demonstration of pan-Arab unity. Syria's voluntary sacrifice of its national sovereignty stoked fears that Nasser, Egypt's 'Hitler on the Nile', would stop at nothing to expand his pan-Arab empire. Chapter 2 explores the intelligence community's first encounter with the drive towards Arab unity. It reveals that analysts were initially sceptical about the prospect of any form of political unity, partly due to their perception of Syrian political culture as inherently factional and self-serving. They recognized that a fear of Communist influence in Syria, which had been steadily building throughout 1957, was the primary motivating force behind the union. At the same time, the JIC in particular could not shed the panic of policy-makers that the move was the beginning of Nasser's imperial expansion, potentially absorbing Iraq, Jordan, Kuwait and Saudi Arabia.

The Iraqi revolution that followed in July 1958 brought an unknown nationalist, General Abdul Karim Qasim, to the helm of power and did little to allay these fears. Chapter 3 reveals how analysts reacted to the brutal murder of Nuri al Said, as Britain's most important ally in the Middle East seemed to contract the Nasser 'virus' spreading through the region. General Qasim quickly demonstrated that he was no Nasserist stooge, however. Whilst British policymakers hoped in vain that the new Iraqi leader could be cultivated as a counterweight to Nasser, the intelligence community rapidly realised that Qasim had neither the charisma nor the popularity to compete with his Egyptian counterpart in the Arab Cold War.[38] General Qasim's reliance on Iraqi Communists to counteract the influence of local Nasserites led to widespread fears that Iraq was on the brink of acquiring Soviet satellite status. This chapter brings to light for the first time the JIC's nuanced analysis of the Iraqi Communist Party (ICP), suggesting to policymakers that in fact the Soviet Union was acting as a restraining influence on the rash Iraqi Communists. Qasim came to be increasingly depicted as 'paranoid' and 'irrational', whilst assessments of Nasser took on a new and more complimentary light as a 'moderate' potential ally in the quest to prevent Communist penetration of the Middle East.

Nasser's difficulties in Iraq were compounded by the challenges he faced in Syria. Syria's secession from the UAR in 1961 marked the beginning of the end of pan-Arabism. Chapter 4 thus explores to what extent this dramatic development came as a surprise to the Anglo-American intelligence community, and how they reacted to it. It argues that although analysts had a good sense of the political, economic and cultural challenges of integrating the two regions, Nasser had acquired a 'quasi-invincible' status which precluded serious consideration of secession. Despite initial misgivings about the formation of the UAR, analysts realised that this experiment with Arab unity had rendered Syria more stable than any time since independence was wrested from the French in 1949. Looking to the future, analysts feared how the 'undisciplined' and individualistic people of Syria would manage without Nasser's moderating leadership and how the latter would respond to this unprecedented challenge to his prestige. They presciently warned that Arab–Israeli relations would suffer and that Nasser might seek to restore his status as pan-Arab leader elsewhere.

In September 1962, a group of army officers led by Colonel Abdullah al Sallal overthrew the Hamid'Ud'Din royal family in Yemen. The coup provided just the occasion for Nasser to re-establish his credibility abroad as the vanguard of Arab revolution. Nasser immediately sent Egyptian troops to bolster the republican revolutionaries led by Sallal in the battle against guerrilla royalist forces loyal to the deposed Imamate propped up by Saudi Arabia and the British. The Yemeni conflict quickly became a proxy war between these rival interests, causing a rift in the Anglo-American alliance and symbolising the division between 'traditional' dynasties against the 'progressive' republics in the Arab world. Chapter 5 reveals that analysts demonstrated good strategic and tactical notice of the prospects for revolution although they shared with Egyptians ideas about Yemeni culture as 'backward' and 'unsophisticated'. They recognised that Nasser had no blueprint or master plan for revolution in Yemen and that he had underestimated the commitment the conflict would entail. Bound by his 'face' as the leader of Arab revolution, he was compelled to maintain support for the republicans despite the unassailable stalemate that ensued. Nevertheless, Nasser's determination to capitalise on the protracted British withdrawal from Aden led to a revival of widespread hostility towards the nationalist agenda within the British analytic community. Egypt's withdrawal from the Yemeni conflict would only be achieved as a result of her ignoble defeat by Israeli forces in June 1967.

This 1967 war currently stands as one of the CIA's greatest 'success' stories in the Middle East. Good intelligence is credited with guiding policy-makers in the UK and US to resist Israeli requests for military support and thereby containing a conflict that could have pitted a Western-supported Israel against a Soviet-backed Arab force. What made intelligence so effective in this instance? Chapter 6 argues that analysts recognised the intentions and capabilities of the major players in this conflict, and applied cultural sensitivity to their assessments of Soviet, Israeli and Egyptian actions. They knew that Nasser had no appetite for a war with Israel and acknowledged that he had been goaded by Syria into an aggressive rhetoric that became dangerously self-fulfilling. More importantly, analysts correctly identified that despite the numerical superiority of the combined Arab forces, the Israeli military would prevail. Yet looking beyond the catharsis of military conflict raises important questions about the utility of discourse such as 'success' in describing a war whose tragic legacy remains with us today.

Chapter 7 explores the protracted War of Attrition between Egypt and Israel that ensued along the Suez Canal. In March 1970, this culminated in an unprecedented Soviet military intervention to protect Egypt against Israeli deep penetration raids. This dramatic geopolitical shift forced analysts to question Egypt's commitment to peace and independence and Soviet willingness to escalate the Cold War. The literature published on this issue thus far suggests that analysts 'failed' to predict the Soviet intervention. Contrary to this conventional understanding, the archival material definitively proves that British analysts warned that Arab 'honour' would never accept Israeli use of the east bank of the Suez Canal and that attacks on Egypt's heartland would provoke an intervention by the Soviet Union. Yet policy-makers on both sides of the Atlantic ignored or dismissed the assessments of their analysts. In the aftermath of the intervention, intelligence analysis was critical in counteracting the fears of policy-makers, making it clear that the Soviet Union felt obliged to react to the Israeli offensive and was not seeking to escalate the Cold War. Nor, analysts argued, could Egypt be regarded as a Soviet client state, as the expulsion of the Russian advisors only two years later would aptly demonstrate.

The death of President Nasser marked the end of an era in the Arab world, the subject of Chapter 8. His successor, Anwar el Sadat, was an unknown quantity. Over the course of a decade, Sadat expelled the Russians from Egypt, broke the Arab–Israeli stalemate and radically reoriented Egypt's identity towards the Western world. But what were the first impressions of this enigmatic figure? Intelligence material provides a privileged insight into Sadat that has been neglected in most Western scholarship. The documents reveal that the intelligence communities on both sides of the Atlantic saw Sadat as a temporary figure, an inferior statesman to his predecessor and a man of tactics rather than principles. Thus while analysts were acutely aware of the Soviet–Egyptian tensions that led to Sadat's dramatic expulsion of 15,000 Soviet advisors in July 1972, their negative perceptions of Sadat made it difficult to recognise the strategic considerations behind the move. Not until the October 1973 war did the intelligence community appreciate that Sadat might have been clearing the way for an attack on Israel.

The Yom Kippur War was a game changer in the Arab–Israeli conflict and the politics of the Middle East. Henry Kissinger famously explained the 'intelligence failure' of Yom Kippur thus: 'Our definition of rationality did not take seriously the notion of starting an unwinnable war to restore self-respect.'[39] Chapter 9 suggests that Kissinger's explanation requires some revising. Recently declassified material demonstrates that British and American analysts understood perfectly well Sadat's intentions, specifically his desire for a limited military victory to gain 'face' at home and leverage abroad. Instead analytical weakness lay in assessments of Egypt's military capability where there was a unanimous consensus over Egypt's apparent impotency. Ideas about Arab 'culture' seem to have played a key role in this underestimation: the notion of a fatalistic Islam, for example, prevailed in numerous analyses. In a radical revision of the conventional wisdom about the strengths and weaknesses of Western intelligence agencies, the Yom Kippur War provides a revealing case study whereby the West excelled in understanding the 'mystery' or intentions leading to war, but simply did not believe that Egypt possessed the capability to act effectively, and so perilously dismissed the prospect of an Egyptian attack.

In the aftermath of the 1973 war, analysts grappled with a dramatically different international environment in the Arab world. The Arabs had demonstrated their ability to unite politically and economically to wage a military offensive in pursuit of a political settlement and Sadat declared a transformation in Egypt's orientation towards the Western world. This final chapter thus explores how the 1973 war altered perceptions of Sadat. Was the President finally able to shed his predecessor's legacy? Drawing primarily on documents that, because of their age, have only been made available to the public in the past few years, it will show that intelligence analysts were sceptical about the prospects for peace and the domestic implications of political and economic liberalisation.

Indeed, the JIC predicted the possibility of Sadat's assassination as early as 1975 and the Secret Intelligence Service (SIS) man in Cairo, Mark Allen, warned about the growing threat from the religious right. These most recent declassifications provide a plethora of revealing insights into just how the Anglo-American intelligence community regarded their newest ally in the Arab world until his dramatic assassination by affiliates of the Muslim Brotherhood in 1981.

It is remarkable how frequently intelligence assessments over these two crucial decades anticipated the conclusions of later historical scholarship deprived of these valuable sources. In the growing realism that followed Suez, analysts recognised that Egypt's involvement in Syria, Iraq and Yemen was less to do with Nasser's initiatives than with the 'ideological zeal of his local partisans'.[40] Irrespective of whether their analysis was heeded by policy-makers, the intelligence community's narrative was often, if not always, close to the 'historical truth'.

Strikingly, the assumptions recounted in political and intelligence documents arguably tell a more nuanced story of Anglo-American perceptions of Nasser and Sadat in this period than most current scholarship implies. This book unearths the multiplicity of views evoked about Nasser within the intelligence community, deepening our understanding of the Arab nationalist beyond the images of 'Hitler on the Nile' or Soviet stooge which have dominated Western narratives thus far.[41] Similarly, while Sadat came to be a pro-Western ally courted by Henry Kissinger and received by the Queen, diplomatic and intelligence assessments reveal the evolution of astute and increasingly negative perceptions of this enigmatic figure.

This 'missing dimension' thus tells a story that transcends the narrative of ally or adversary prevalent in extant histories. It is a story not merely of misunderstandings, misperceptions and miscalculations but in fact one which reveals considerable cultural understanding. It is a surprising story lost in a traumatic history that has become entangled in a current debate about the 'failure' of the Western world, and of their intelligence communities, to understand the culture and politics of the Middle East. The declassified documents of the most significant events of this period frequently reveal this understanding. The best of it came from human sources, usually diplomats familiar with the culture and dynamics on the ground and able to penetrate the psychology of the Egyptian political elite with humanity and empathy. Culture, in turn, served as a double-edged sword. It could be a fundamental source of strength in intelligence analysis of the Middle East; illuminating the intentions and mindsets of the West's adversaries and allies alike. However, it could also obscure, mask and simplify Arab objects of analysis as an impenetrable 'other', particularly when Middle Eastern actors used Western cultural preconceptions to advance their own agendas. It is to this problematic 'cultural lens' that we now turn.

Notes

1. See, for example, W. R. Louis and E. Owen (eds), *Suez 1956: The Crisis and its Consequences* (Oxford: Clarendon Press, 1991).
2. H. Wilford, *America's Great Game: The CIA's Secret Arabists and the Shaping of the Modern Middle East* (New York: Basic Books, 2013), p. xx.
3. N. J. Ashton, 'The hijacking of a pact: the formation of the Baghdad Pact and Anglo-American tensions in the Middle East, 1955–1958', *Review of International Studies*, 19: 2, 1993, pp. 123–37.
4. President Sukarno of Indonesia aptly described the Bandung conference of April 1955 as 'the first intercontinental conference of coloured peoples in the history of mankind'. S. Sukarno, Address to the Bandung Conference, 17–24 April 1955. Available at <http://www.bandungspirit.org/IMG/pdf/discours_soekarno_bandoeng_17_24_avril_1955-1-7389.pdf> (last accessed 30 September 2016).
5. See, for example, W. R. Louis, 'The tragedy of the Anglo-Egyptian settlement of 1954', in W. R. Louis and E. Owen (eds), *Suez 1956: The Crisis and its Consequences*. In the same volume Shimon Shamir attributes the failure of 'Project Alpha' to the British 'low awareness of the authenticity, intensity and autonomy of the Arab anti-Western posture'. See S. Shamir, 'The collapse of project Alpha', in Louis and Owen (eds), *Suez 1956: The Crisis and its Consequences*, p. 89. For further examples see S. Yaqub, *Containing Arab Nationalism: The Eisenhower Doctrine and the Middle East* (Chapel Hill, NC: University of North Carolina Press, 2004), p. 8; the Eisenhower doctrine

'rested on a basic misunderstanding of the Nasserist movement, on a drastic underestimation of its power and independence'. See also E. Podeh, 'The United States and the Baghdad Pact', in D. Lesch (ed.), *The Middle East and the United States* (Boulder, CO: Westview Press, 2007), p. 100: 'The greatest mistake of the United States was its failure to comprehend Arab psychology in the postcolonial era and the depth of Arab rivalries.'

6. Official guidelines dictate a thirty-year declassification rule in the UK and twenty years in the US, although in practice there are significant variations on this depending on the material. Recollected histories include: H. Trevelyan, *The Middle East in Revolution* (London: Macmillan, 1970); H. Kissinger, *The White House Years* (Boston, MA: Little, Brown and Co., 1979) and *Years of Upheaval* (Boston, MA: Little, Brown and Co., 1982); W. Quandt, *Decade of Decisions: American Policy Towards the Arab-Israeli conflict, 1967–1976* (Berkeley, CA: University of California Press, 1977). While very valuable, such works are naturally selective and deterministic, influenced both by the evolution of events and the pitfalls of vanity. Works which combine recollections with declassified documents include: R. Parker, *The Politics of Miscalculation in the Middle East* (Bloomington, IN: Indiana University Press, 1992); W. Quandt, *Peace Process: American Diplomacy and the Arab-Israeli conflict since 1967* (Washington: Brookings Institution; Berkeley, CA: University of California Press, 1993); F. Brenchley, *Britain, The Six-Day War and its Aftermath* (London: Tauris, 2005).

7. N. J. Ashton, *Eisenhower, Macmillan and the Problem of Nasser: Anglo-American Relations and Arab Nationalism 1955–1959* (London: Macmillan, 1996), and the same author's *Kennedy, Macmillan and the Cold War: The Irony of Interdependence* (Basingstoke: Palgrave Macmillan, 2002).

8. R. McNamara, *Britain, Nasser and the Balance of Power in the Middle East, 1952–1967: From the Egyptian Revolution to the Six Day War* (London: Frank Cass, 2003).

9. L. James, *Nasser At War: Arab Images of the Enemy* (Basingstoke: Palgrave Macmillan, 2006); K. Beattie, *Egypt During the Nasser Years: Ideology Politics and Civil Society* (Oxford: Westview Press, 1994) and *Egypt During the Sadat Years* (New York: Palgrave, 2000).

10. See Yaqub, *Containing Arab Nationalism;* F. Gerges, *America and Political Islam: Clash of Cultures or Clash of Interests* (Cambridge: Cambridge University Press, 1999); P. Satia, *Spies in Arabia: The*

Great War and the Cultural Foundations of Britain's Covert Empire in the Middle East (Oxford: Oxford University Press, 2008); for the pre-Suez era, see Wilford, *America's Great Game.*

11. Satia, *Spies in Arabia*, p. 5.
12. C. Andrew and D. Dilks (eds), *The Missing Dimension: Governments and Intelligence Communities in the 20th Century* (Basingstoke: Macmillan, 1984). Whereas much of the subsequent focus has been on the 'missing dimension' of operational intelligence, i.e. covert action, the limited number of scholarly works which explore the analysis of the intelligence community include: P. Cradock, *Know Your Enemy: How the Joint Intelligence Committee Saw the World* (London: John Murray, 2002), although Cradock's seminal study of JIC assessments is limited to the Suez Crisis and the Kuwaiti Crisis of 1961 in the Middle East, and J. Vaughn, 'Between Suez and the Six Day War: Israel and the Arabs, 1957–1967', in R. G. Hughes, P. Jackson and L. Scott (eds), *Exploring Intelligence Archives: Enquiries into the Secret State* (London: Routledge, 2008). Other works have utilised a limited number of intelligence assessments in their scholarship: E. Podeh, *The Decline of Arab Unity: The Rise and Fall of the United Arab Republic* (Brighton: Sussex Academic Press, 1999); James, *Nasser at War*; McNamara, *Britain, Nasser and the Balance of Power.*
13. D. Robarge, 'CIA analysis of the 1967 Arab-Israeli War', *Studies in Intelligence,* 49: 1, 2006. For a brief discussion of the American 'failure' in 1973 see Kissinger's account in *Years of Upheaval.*
14. See, for example, H. Eilts, 'Reflections of Suez: Middle East security', in Louis and Owen (eds), *Suez 1956: The Crisis and its Consequences,* p. 356. Despite the general anti-Nasser outlook of most US officials, Eilts refers to the 'residual political mystique' of Nasser. A closer examination of the events in which Nasser was involved and which gave rise to the greatest controversies allows us a deeper and more detailed look into these images. Other important secondary scholarship on Nasser includes: R. H. Dekmejian, *Egypt under Nasser* (Albany, NY: State University of New York Press, 1971); J. Jankowski, *Nasser's Egypt, Arab Nationalism and the United Arab Republic* (Boulder, CO: Lynne Reinner Publishers, 2001); W. R. Louis and A. Shlaim (eds), *The 1967 Arab-Israeli War: Origins and Consequences* (Cambridge: Cambridge University Press, 2012).
15. J. Joll, *Origins of the First World War* (London: Longman, 1984).
16. L. Hunt, *The New Cultural History* (Berkeley, CA: University of California Press, 1989).

17. C. Appy, *Cold War Constructions: The Political Culture of United States Imperialism 1945–1966* (Amherst, MA: University of Massachusetts Press, 2000), p. 4.
18. D. Reynolds, *From World War to Cold War* (Oxford: Oxford University Press, 2006), p. 337.
19. E. Said, *Orientalism* (London: Penguin, 2003).
20. M. Connolley, cited in P. Jackson, 'Pierre Bordieu, the "cultural turn" and international history', *Review of International Studies*, 34: 1, 2008, pp. 155–81.
21. Reassuringly, however, a slim catalogue of recent works suggests that even the most traditional realms of diplomatic, international and military history have been unable to resist the lure of the 'cultural' fever. P. Porter, *Military Orientalism: Eastern War through Western Eyes* (London: C. Hurst and Co. Ltd., 2009), presents a highly nuanced view of Western military encounters with 'the Other' demonstrating the complex ways in which culture can reflect, shape and be manipulated by warfare. J. Vaughn, *Unconquerable Minds: The Failure of American and British Propaganda in the Arab Middle East, 1945–1957* (London: Palgrave, 2005) stands as the first archival based account of British and American cultural propaganda in the Middle East during the Cold War. F. Costigliola, 'Reading for meaning: theory, language, and metaphor', in M. Hogan and T. G. Paterson (eds), *Explaining American Foreign Relations History* (New York: Cambridge University Press, 2003), demonstrates the utility of literary theory to a deeper understanding American foreign policy. Appy, *Cold War Constructions,* provides a revealing insight into the political culture of American imperialism examining the discourses and unspoken assumptions that accompanied imperial adventures after the Second World War. D. Little, *American Orientalism: The United States and the Middle East since 1945* (Chapel Hill, NC: University of North Carolina Press, 2002), attempts to use Said's framework to examine post-war American foreign policy but, with the exception of the first chapter, largely fails to show how ideas about 'the Arab' affected or framed decision-making.
22. Satia, *Spies in Arabia*, p. 5.
23. Those interviewed in Cairo included: Hoda abd-el Nasser (Nasser's daughter and secretary for the last year of his life); Abd-el-Maguid Farid (Nasser's Secretary General between 1967 and 1970); Mohammad Hassanein Heikal (Nasser's confidant and unofficial biographer); Ambassador Shakir (former Egyptian ambassador to the United Kingdom).

24. See, for example: H. M. Heikal, *The Sphinx and the Commissar: The Rise and Fall of Soviet Influence in the Arab World* (London: Collins, 1978); H. M. Heikal, *Autumn of Fury: The Assassination of Sadat* (London: Deutsch, 1983); A. M. Farid, *Nasser: The Final Years* (Reading: Ithaca Press, 1994); M. Riad, *The Struggle for Peace in the Middle East* (London: Quartet, 1981). Arabic sources used include: H. M. Heikal, *1967: Al-Infijar* (Cairo: Markaz al Ahram, 1990); M. Fawzi, *Al-Sadat: Al-Zaim Al-Muftará 'Alayh* (Cairo: Dar al-Nashr Hayih, 1995); M. Gamasy, *Mudhakirrat Al-Gamassi: Harb Uktubur 1973* (Cairo: Al Hayat al 'Ammat l-il-Kuttab, 1998); S. Sharaf, *Sanawat Wa-Ayyam Ma'a Jamal 'Abd al-Naṣir: Shahadat Sami Sharaf* (Cairo: Dar al-Fursan lil-Nashr, 2005–7).

25. P. Cradock, *Know Your Enemy: How the Joint Intelligence Committee Saw the World* (London: John Murray, 2002), p. 297: 'Policy conclusions are often inherent in estimates; but the decisions lie with ministers; they have the privilege of interpreting the facts differently or ignoring them altogether. At this stage the situation and its likely development are not the sole considerations; other factors, party politics, economic interests, public opinion, personal convictions and vanity enter the equation and prove decisive. Nonetheless examining the language and discourse used to discuss a region or problem provides a crucial insight into the frames of reference shared by the political elite.'

26. See, for example: R. K. Betts, *Enemies of Intelligence: Knowledge and Power in American National Security* (New York: Columbia University Press, 2007); R. H. Immerman, 'Intelligence and strategy: historicizing psychology, policy, and politics', *Diplomatic History*, 32, 2008; R. Jervis, *Why Intelligence Fails: Lessons from the Iranian Revolution and the Iraq War* (Ithaca, NY: Cornell University Press, 2010); E. J. Dahl, *Intelligence and Surprise Attack: Failure and Success from Pearl Harbor to 9/11 and Beyond* (Washington: Georgetown University Press, 2013). Whereas Jervis highlights analytic reliance on conventional wisdoms and unarticulated assumptions, Betts holds intelligence consumers rather than producers responsible for most instances of so-called 'intelligence failure'. Meanwhile, Immerman makes a persuasive case that often intelligence is much less important in the formulation of policy than it should be.

27. Declassified PDBs are very rare and often heavily redacted. For a selection see: <http://www.gwu.edu/~nsarchiv/pdbnews/index.htm#pdb> (last accessed 30 September 2016).

28. Pierre Bourdieu defines habitus as a 'system of acquired dispositions functioning on the practical level as categories of perception and assessment or as classificatory principles as well as being the organizing principles of action'. See P. Bourdieu, *In Other Words: Essays towards a Reflexive Sociology* (Stanford, CA: Stanford University Press, 1990), pp. 12–13.

29. M. Goodman, *The Official History of the Joint Intelligence Committee. Volume I: From the Approach of the Second World War to the Suez Crisis* (London: Routledge, 2014), p. 214.

30. J. Dumbrell, *A Special Relationship: Anglo-American Relations in the Cold War and After* (London: Palgrave, 2001), pp. 124–5.

31. Extract from Chief of Staff's 9th Meeting (58), Minute 1, 4 December 1958, TNA, DEFE 25/11. This gives some sense of the disparity in size between the British and American organizations and probably included other forms of intelligence.

32. F. Kaplan, 'Secret again: the absurd scheme to reclassify documents', 23 February 2006. Available at <http://www.slate.com/id/2136480/> (last accessed 30 September 2016).

33. No SIS or GCHQ material has been declassified. Recent scholarship indicates that Egyptian diplomatic reports were decrypted, however. See C. Andrew and V. Mitrokhin, *The KGB and the World: Mitrokhin Archive II* (London: Penguin, 2006), p. 140: 'During the Suez Crisis of 1956 the British Foreign Secretary Selwyn Lloyd, wrote to congratulate GCHQ on both the "volume" and "excellence" of the Middle Eastern decrypts it had produced and to say "how valuable" they had proved to be.' See also R. Aldrich, *GCHQ: The Uncensored Story of Britain's Most Secret Intelligence Agency* (London: Harper Press, 2010).

34. D. P. Steury (ed.), *Sherman Kent and the Board of National Estimates: Collected Essays* (Washington, DC: Center for the Study of Intelligence, 1994), p. 11.

35. R. Cormac, *Confronting the Colonies: British Intelligence and Counterinsurgency* (Hurst: London, 2014), p. 18.

36. Reynolds, *From World War to Cold War*, p. 336.

37. One scholar asserting that the CIA has failed to 'study foreign thought structures' is A. Bozeman, *Strategic Intelligence and Statecraft: Selected Essays* (Washington: Brassey's, 1992), p. 14.

38. M. Kerr, *The Arab Cold War: Gamal Abdel Nasser and his Rivals, 1958–1970*, 3rd edn (London: Oxford University Press, 1971).

39. H. Kissinger, *Years of Upheaval* (Boston: Little, Brown and Co., 1982), p. 465.

40. R. Khalidi, 'The impact of the Iraq revolution on the Arab world', in R. A. Fernea and W. R. Louis (eds.), *The Iraqi Revolution of 1958: The Old Social Classes Revisited* (London: I. B. Tauris, 1991), p. 112.
41. See, for example, W. R. Louis, *The Ends of British Imperialism, The Scramble for Empire, Suez and Decolonisation* (London: I. B. Tauris, 2006), p. 6.

1 Orientalism and Analysis: Ideas of the 'Arab'

Want of accuracy, which easily generated into untruthfulness, is in fact the main characteristic of the Oriental mind . . . Endeavour to elicit a plain statement of facts from any ordinary Egyptian. His explanation will generally be lengthy, and wanting in lucidity. He will probably contradict himself half-a-dozen times before he has finished his story. He will often break down under the mildest process of self-examination.

Edward Baring, 1911[1]

Orientalism was a library or archive of information commonly and, in some of its aspects, unanimously held. What bound the archive together was a family of ideas and a unifying set of values proven in various ways to be effective.

Edward Said, 1978[2]

From the Iranian revolution to the 'Arab Spring', the West has consistently been accused of misunderstanding the culture and politics of the Middle East. In 1995, Samuel Huntington's controversial 'clash of civilisations' thesis revived the argument of controversial Orientalists such as Bernard Lewis that there was a fundamental 'cultural divide' between East and West.[3] Western intelligence communities have borne the brunt of such criticism, yet little historical scholarship has explored how Arab culture has been conceived by the world's most important and powerful producers of 'knowledge' in recent history.

The theoretical underpinning for this chapter is an important and ongoing debate about Western cultural representations and their validity, evoked by Edward Said's seminal work *Orientalism*.

Said's 1978 study raised groundbreaking questions about Western depictions of the Arab 'Other', the purpose and utility of these depictions in justifying European imperial rule and their relation (or lack thereof) to the 'real' Arab world.

This chapter brings to scholarly attention for the first time several recently declassified documents of a different nature to assessments usually produced by the British and US diplomatic and intelligence analytic bodies: those focused primarily on the issue of 'national character'. Unsurprisingly, the declassified documents that deal in length with this issue are few. We can be certain that their authors never imagined that these reflections on Arab culture would ever be available for public consumption. Nonetheless, there are sufficient links between them and repeated reference to their underlying assumptions in more routine diplomatic and intelligence analysis to warrant a critical examination of the intellectual archive or 'library' that the Western political elite compiled about the Arab world. Analysts articulated notions of Arab culture such as the role of Islam, the use of rhetoric, questions of political motivation and the primacy of 'honour' that continue to pervade Western perceptions of the region.

Considering the significance of Said's thesis to Anglo-American relations with the Middle East, why have diplomatic and intelligence historians failed so spectacularly to engage with 'Orientalism'?[4] A recent wave of scholarship has highlighted the intersection of knowledge production and the expansion of American power in the region, emphasising the influence of culture and ideology on US perceptions of, and actions towards, the Arab world.[5] Yet in general, historians have tended to be critical of Said, noting his selective use of sources, polemical rhetoric, verbosity and a marked lack of historical analysis.[6] This post-Orientalism scholarship avers that Said's assertion that by writing about the Orient the author denies agency to, or indeed the existence of, the Oriental subject reflects postmodernism at its most extreme and intellectually nihilistic.[7] His suggestion that the West has a particular axe to grind against the Middle East is clearly disproved by Western stereotypes of other cultures (including of course other Westerners) and rather belies an inherent and universal human inclination to affirm the 'Self' in respect to the 'Other'.[8] There is no inherent 'hostility' in all Western depictions of the Middle East; not all were designed to dominate and empower, as Said claims.[9] More recent works illustrate how depictions of the 'Other' commonly reflect a more deeply rooted anxiety or doubt about the 'Self'.[10] The culmination of this literature has been calls for greater 'intercultural dialogue' in delineating Western relations with the Middle East and a more transnational scholarship that better incorporates Arab perspectives in this genre of history.[11]

A cursory glance at the intelligence material explored in this chapter cannot help but invoke Said's assertion that the West has studied 'the Other' in order to dominate it. However, by applying a more critical approach to both Said's ideas and these controversial documents, we explore with greater nuance the construction of dominant ideas about the Arab 'Other' in this period and how these evolved as the Western world came to terms with the end of empire and the 'winds of change' at home and abroad. Moreover, we examine how these representations of 'the Arab' were received by Arab actors both at the time and retrospectively. The discussion that follows provides an insight into how a history of intelligence can also be a history of culture, ideas and *mentalité*, and sets the stage for the most important cultural assumptions that framed Anglo-American assessments of the Arab revolutions in Syria, Iraq and Yemen, as well as the Arab–Israeli wars, and the perceptions of both Nasser and Sadat as leaders of the most important country in the Arab world.

* * *

A New Terrain: The Challenge of the Middle East

The efforts of the post-war American intelligence community were directed against a clearly defined enemy within the polarised framework of the Cold War. Resources and expertise were allocated accordingly, despite the fact that the parameters of this conflict were increasingly being redrawn beyond the European battleground. The arms deal between Czechoslovakia and Egypt in 1955 marked the beginning of Soviet penetration of the Middle East and signalled a new terrain on which the Cold War was to be fought. Both America and her Western allies sought to establish friendly relations with the Arab world. The intelligence community was thus forced to adapt their analytic capability and resources to understand another culture, a task to which some maintain it is still struggling to rise.[12]

In fact we see that as early as 1959, the CIA's classified in-house journal produced a curious piece of intelligence analysis, entitled 'Intelligence gathering in an unlettered land', that attempted to define the challenges the Middle East posed to the American intelligence community.[13] The author, Francis Hollyman, out-lined problems such as accessing 'open' and 'secret' sources in a closed society, the peculiarities of Arab communication and the 'psycho-cultural' difficulties of recruiting assets in the region. As the document progresses and the perceived challenges move from the practical to the 'psycho-cultural', they become increasingly crude and stereotypical to the mind of the modern reader. As Said insists, it is difficult to dismiss the implicit and explicit assertions of inferiority in such works as they attempt to describe and explain the cultural behaviour of the Middle East. At the same time, this document provides historians with invaluable insight into the challenges the CIA perceived itself to face in the Arab world and the simultaneous if contradictory impulses of ethnocentrism and open-mindedness with which it made sense of this encounter with 'the Other'.

Problems of Access

Few American intelligence officers acquired access to the political elite in the Arab world. Britain's colonial background ensured a steady stream of Arabists with linguistic and cultural expertise in the region but it was only in the 1950s that Ivy League universities recognised a similar need. The American intelligence community therefore relied heavily upon 'open-source' material for its analysis of Middle Eastern political dynamics. CIA analyst Hollyman wrote, 'the official radio and press service, organised efficiently in recent years has become more effective in preventative control of thought rather than informational content'.[14] 'Mirror-imaging' the role of the Middle Eastern press to its Western counterpart, Hollyman dismissed Arab newspapers and radio as mere propaganda rather than a source of information or 'facts'; the notion that this 'preventative control of thought' might *also* be an avenue of useful analysis by American intelligence was at this stage not considered.

A dearth of 'open sources' in the form of media, published surveys, handbooks and statistics also restricted the numbers and quality of human sources 'with access to such knowledge'. This derived 'in part from meagre opportunities for education and in part from traditional restrictions on participation in political and public life'. This non-democratic distribution of political information in many ways paralleled the difficulties of intelligence collection in the Soviet Union, but it was in an unfamiliar social context. In addition to the realities typical of closed societies, such as 'the virtual absence of easy social contacts, the lack of suitable public meeting places, the staggering inadequacy of public communications, and the suspicions commonly aroused among native residents by outsiders attempting to move freely among them', covert operatives had a range of other practical difficulties to overcome. Hollyman sardonically observed that the 'religious requirements of Ramadan, the month of fasting, and of the annual *hajj* or pilgrimage to Mecca, tend to damp down any information collecting activities for considerable periods of time'.[15] Such practical features of political and social interaction within the Arab world exacerbated difficulties already inherent in the agent acquisition process.

Arab Communication

When a source was eventually recruited, his mode of communication was also difficult for the American agent to grasp. Hollyman's analysis presented some of the subtler cultural difficulties that the intelligence officer and analyst might confront in the Arab world. He observed, for example, that in Arab political culture 'an unusual degree of reliance is placed on the spoken word, the personal mission and the personal memory of the minister himself'.[16] The reliance on informal rhetoric as the primary conduit of political communication was, understandably, perceived as strange to a Western political culture fundamentally rooted in the written word and official documentation. The analysis noted that the principal danger of relying on oral communication was the Arab tendency to 'simplify and omit when he has to deal with complicated matters'.[17] Later studies by anthropologists such as Adda Bozeman would observe,

> Writing fixes meaning that in speech tend to be fluid ... stimulates precision and differentiation in both thought and expression, stresses coherence and consistency in the thinking process; guards against drifting from one plane of reflection, or one frame of reference, to another; and promotes detachment and objectivity by disengaging the mind from the immediate experience and directing it, instead, to the level of conceptualisation.[18]

Bozeman's analysis is essentially a more sophisticated and well-articulated explanation of Hollyman's conclusion that oral communication tended to be less precise and, as he correctly ascertains, is considerably more prevalent in Arab political culture than in the Western world. In 1958, the American ambassador to Cairo, Raymond Hare, reported a similar observation in dealing with President Nasser:

> This habit of Nasser's [to] do business in [sic] top of head without record when coupled with obviously defective time sense may indicate that his disconcerting habit of rewriting history which [is] usually interpreted as deliberated distortion, may in fact be due in part and at times at least to confused memory. Consequence is that getting [the] story from [the] horse's mouth in his case many well represent his firm recollection but still be historically defective.[19]

Ambassador Hare was an American Arabist who spent most of the Second World War as an intelligence and liaison officer at the US Embassy in Cairo when Egypt was under attack by the Axis powers.[20] Confident in his cultural expertise, Hare sympathetically reported that what seemed to Western policy-makers to be 'deliberate distortion' could be better explained as the product of a political culture where there was a greater reliance on the spoken word, which in turn rendered inaccuracies more likely. Hare also made reference to the 'instinctive Arab aversion to legalistic engagements as contrasted with informal and unpublicised agreements which are quite congruous with their mental processes'.[21]

Later, Hare recalled his use of flattery and tact to bridge this cultural divide in his lengthy conversations with President Nasser. He would say, 'I know it's not considered normal to be taking notes when talking to a Chief of State, but you talk so interestingly and frankly at some length that I don't want to forget it. I realize that you are not talking just for me; so do you mind if I just take down a few words so that I might better recall your observations?' Apparently Nasser would respond saying, 'No, I don't mind, do you mind if I do the same?'[22]

The work of another anthropologist reviewed by the CIA in 1974 reinforced the notion of greater 'discursive freedom' prevalent in the Arab world.[23] To this day the issue of Arab rhetoric continues to be identified as an important and enduring challenge to the West. As one eminent Arabist argues, 'In the Middle East, rhetoric obscures truth and it reflects different mindsets from those in other areas of the world.'[24] Another agreed that the observations on Arab rhetoric have 'continuing relevance', although he rightly qualified: 'they are also, in varying degrees, capable of being applied to almost any society'.[25] This is indeed the case and yet the enduring and recurring reference to the issue of Arab rhetoric suggests that *this was perceived to be a problem specific to Arab culture.* This early CIA analysis (alongside others in the period) made it clear that Arab rhetoric frequently served a culturally specific function that required decoding. This proved to be a recurring theme in assessments and re-emerges later in this chapter in a curious British diplomatic exchange in the 1970s.

Arab Motivation

If Arab 'rhetoric' demonstrated the 'Otherness' of Middle Eastern culture, the question of Arab 'motivation' proved even more obscure. The 1959 CIA analysis relayed a familiar imperial belief that the Arab suffered from a fundamental inability to understand and practice constructive politics.

> Aside from wanting to be a proper Arab and a good Muslim, he [the potential source] has no strong aims or convictions. His experience is too little, his ignorance too great, to provide a foundation for opposition to Communist imperialism as his motive force. He has no strong

sense of socio-political responsibility, no felt need for thinking, for making a political choice. The idea of subscribing to a positive ideological program or doctrine, except as it incorporates his immediate Arab interests, is beyond him.[26]

This idea of 'the Arab' as devoid of 'social conscience' is present in other intelligence documents that have recently been released by the CIA. In 1952, a draft assessment entitled 'Psychological strategy plan for the Middle East' explained the instability of the region as a result of, in part, a 'lack of social consciousness or a sense of public responsibility on the part of almost all officials'.[27] Similarly the State Department's Office for Intelligence and Research (INR) argued that Soviet attempts to penetrate the Middle East would face the challenge of 'the opportunistic concern of the Arab with his own immediate self-interest, and his poor sense of discipline, self-sacrifice and security consciousness'.[28] There is a policy implication underlying this conclusion – an unspoken obligation on the part of the West to civilise the politics of the region since the Arabs cannot be relied upon to make the right political choices. This perhaps accounts for the reluctance of Western powers to take Arab nationalism seriously, as intelligence insiders have intimated. It may also, among other factors, explain the penchant for covert action and military intervention that marked Western policy towards the Arab world in this period.

In 1957, the CIA conducted an analysis of the regional situation following the tripartite invasion of Egypt. They explained that 'our hesitancy at taking actions favourable to Middle East national aspirations has as its deepest motivations the suspicion that once national aspirations are "satisfied," it will not be in either our power or that of Middle East nations to prevent the forces released from degenerating into anarchy'.[29] Similarly the Eisenhower doctrine, promising military or economic assistance to any Middle Eastern country threatened with communist aggression, was seen to have failed because of the 'Arab reluctance to be committed'.[30] References to 'emotion' in politics or the 'apathy' of the public were other symptoms of the political immaturity of the Arab. Hollyman proceeded to illustrate his point with a specific example:

> At the height of the 1956 Suez crisis he [the source] hoped for nothing more than an immediate end to the fighting; he could not comprehend the international forces at work and he was afraid. He respects force partly because it is simple and within his comprehension.[31]

What Said has described as the 'childish primitive' depiction is clearly discernible – the Arab is too politically young, inexperienced and ignorant to feel bound to a body politic in which he has a voice, an opinion, or even a thought.[32] Hollyman explained,

> It is not uncommon to find that a relatively well educated [BLANK] who occupies an important place in commerce or government cannot read a map, and he may not even be aware that the world is not flat! With this shocking elementary ignorance he cannot begin to comprehend or care about more complex or subtle things like the meaning of the Iron curtain or problems springing from Communist imperialism.[33]

In the eyes of the CIA, the elite of Arab society clearly did not measure up to their Western counterparts. The consequence (and indeed, ultimate demonstration) of this 'shocking elementary ignorance' was that these targets were *not able* to understand or care about the pre-eminent threat from the Soviet Union. The difficulty of recruiting Arab agents to work with Americans against 'the Communist threat' surfaces several times in the text, demonstrating both the priorities of the American intelligence community operating in the Arab world and the conclusions that they drew from the difficulties they faced: the typical Arab recruit was too simple, ignorant or apathetic to appreciate the ominous danger of Soviet designs. This accusation was also frequently directed at Arab nationalist leaders such as Nasser and his Iraqi counterpart Qasim, who sought aid from the Soviet Union.

According to Hollyman, the Arab

> [does] not like to generalise about the world, because all he knows is his home, the marketplace, the desert and the edge of the sea . . . His aims and desires are very simple ones and he does not want to change them . . . He is essentially gentle, not belligerent.[34]

One does not have to go to the extreme of Said's arguably over-gendered analysis of Orientalist studies to observe the feminine adjectives associated with the Arab – 'simple, gentle, non-belligerent'. Note also the romantic associations of the Near East – the desert, the sea, the marketplace, in spite of the fact that most of the natives with whom the American intelligence officer interacted would have been in a predominantly urban context. The undertones of a traditionalist and primitive Near East, unwilling to modernise and move forward, is clearly discernible. Hollyman concluded that 'the cultural differences that wall off Westerners go down to the very roots of motivation and thinking'.[35]

British Conceptualisations of the Arab World

Diplomat and former chair of the JIC Sir Patrick Wright expressed incredulity that such an assessment had escaped the attention of the State Department or the British analytical bodies. They 'would have been howled down', he claimed in correspondence with the author.[36] Yet in a curious coincidence, the British Steering Committee also produced several reports in 1959 that endorsed some of these assertions in an examination of the social and political forces in the Arab world. The Steering Committee was a temporary grouping of Conservative ministers which met without Cabinet Office staff to consider all aspects of government policy, often forwarding colonial matters to the Policy Committee on the Commonwealth and Colonies.[37] Upheavals in Syria and Iraq (particularly the latter) may have prompted this British examination of Arab culture.

The influence of the 1958 Iraqi revolution in the British reports is evident. British analysts were quick to identify the 'violence' of the Arab mob, in notable contrast to the 'essentially gentle' Arab depicted in the CIA piece. The Steering Committee observed that:

> the behaviour of Middle Eastern crowds conforms to the pattern of crowd psychology everywhere; but as Arabs are less restrained and as standards of conduct in the Middle East are generally lower, education less effective and the unremedied social evils greater than in Western Europe, the Arab mob may act with more brutish violence than Europeans are now generally capable of.

The analysis even suggested that the inherent violence of the Arab world explained the political role of Middle Eastern armies since only the military possessed the ability to exert physical control over the unruly Arab masses.[38]

British reports also reinforced the political apathy of the majority. The Committee agreed that despite the impact of improved education and communication,

> it is probable that the peasant . . . has as yet little awareness or comprehension of the world outside his village . . . though he may at times be pertinacious, and even violent, in defence of his local interests, he has never been capable of associating for political ends.

Even the educated and professional were largely 'lacking in judgement and a sense of social responsibility'.[39]

However, British analysis seemed more attuned to the institutional reasons for this prevalent feature of Arab political culture. The nature of education in the Arab world, they explained, focused on 'memorising and reproducing', to the extent that students and officials were 'no longer capable of forming an original thought or an independent opinion, still less of applying their learning to the solution of practical problems'. They also noted that the 'seeds of educational reform' were visible and capable of forming a 'wide educated class able to play an intelligent and responsible part in public affairs', although the process of development was 'likely to be a long one'.[40]

The Committee's findings reinforced the State Department's frustration expressed some years earlier that the Arabs had imported Western ideas but proved unable to apply them. Arab ideas of 'democracy' were 'constantly confused with the social egalitarianism of Arab tradition'. The State Department analysis highlighted the problem of 'formal democratic institutions imposed on a society not prepared for them'. Intrinsic to Western democracy were values unfamiliar to the Arab world, including secularism, 'the free spirit of scientific enquiry, the right of the autonomous individual within a reasonable secure community, and the ability to see political processes in terms of institutions rather than personalities'.[41] The Committee noted that although politically active minorities 'resented the abuse of democracy by their opponents in power, they have behaved in the same way when they had the opportunity'.[42] As Vice President Omar Suleiman echoed in the 2012 Egyptian presidential elections, the Arab world was not ready for democracy.[43]

British analysis agreed also with the deceptive nature of rhetoric in Arab culture. 'The condition of the poor and oppressed inspires the intelligentsia to make political and xenophobic speeches rather than to do anything about it themselves.' But, they noted, 'this is not necessarily hypocrisy. To an Arab, words tend to be ends in themselves, and he sees nothing essentially reprehensible in failing to practice what he preaches.'[44] The report wrote with derision (thinking no doubt of the regimes in the Levant): 'As with social welfare, so with civil liberties; though Arab radicalism passionately champions them in words, it does little practical work in defence of them.'[45] Like many of the assertions above, the gap between rhetoric and action became a conventional wisdom within the intelligence community's analysis of the Middle East.

Conceptualisations of Islam

The Steering Committee also addressed a cultural specificity of the region which the CIA had not explored in its 1959 analysis: the role of Islam in the Arab world. The JIC had, for example, long warned that whilst Muslim 'faith appears superficially to be an effective barrier to Communism we consider that its importance as a stabilising factor should not be over-rated'. On the one hand, they explained that the influence of Islam in the Middle East was 'largely *negative,* in that where the Moslem faith is strong society tends to remain static. On the other hand, where modern civilisation has broken into Moslem strongholds, e.g. through exploitation of oil resources', Islam seemed 'powerless to prevent a rapid demoralisation in the face of materialism'.[46] The State Department agreed that Islam as a religious ideology was on the defensive. Though a powerful force of influence on 'the Arab mind', it had failed to modernise and provide an institutional and philosophical basis for social and political forces in the region.[47]

The Steering Committee reflected upon the relationship between Islam and Arab nationalism. Arab nationalist theory, they wrote, rejected 'the idea of a religious bond', substituting 'for Islamic solidarity a pride of race, which though it is explicit in the Koran and early Arab historians, seems in its modern form to owe more to Hitler than to Mohamed'. However, according to the Committee, the fundamental appeal of Arab unity could ultimately be explained through a reductive recourse to Islam. 'Unity, indeed, is the first attribute of the Deity in Islamic theology and the word has such powerful religious and emotional associations that it is perhaps difficult for any but a few philosophically trained Arabs to consider "unity" analytically and dispassionately in any context.'[48]

In a baffling underestimation of the practical and psychological appeal of pan-Arab nationalism, the Committee concluded that 'most uneducated Arab Moslems feel simply that God is one, therefore Oneness is right'. Analysts asserted that 'the influence of the teaching of Islam for nearly fourteen centuries on the mind, outlook and behaviour of the individual Arab is of fundamental importance'. Beyond the issue of unity, Islam was the driving force behind the 'Arab's conviction of superiority, his resentment of foreign guidance or control and hence the frustrating dilemma of recognising his technical dependence on foreigners, while rejecting their intervention in his affairs.' British analysts maintained that 'Islam will continue strong, as a habit of thought if not as a practised religion.' To an all-encompassing and xenophobic 'Islam' were attributed deeply rooted Arab frustrations towards Western colonial control and exploitation.[49]

The State Department analysis some years earlier had demonstrated some nuance to this depiction of a static and unproductive Islam. Analysts noted that it was 'the *symbols*' of Islam which would 'still, for some time to come, mold the *language* of acceptance and rejection and affect *the motivations of those now in control*'. There was an important qualification reserved for the elite in power: 'rarely', the State Department suggested, 'would Islam affect their decisions to a decisive degree'. If secular solutions failed to solve the region's 'basic intellectual and social crisis' it was possible that:

> Islam or rather a perversion of it, may exercise a decisive influence on political decisions in the Near East. Then emotional rejection of all the West stands for may become the negative content of Islam, and a totalitarian nihilism the Near East's primary defence mechanism.[50]

37

The State Department's report certainly supports the notion that the West viewed the Islamic world with some trepidation.

Deconstructing this Anglo-American analysis suggests two contradictory strains of thought about Islam: the first implied that 'Islamic culture' acted upon the masses in the Arab world and contributed largely to the appeal of Arab unity, to resentment against the West, and effectively nurtured a 'habit of thought' in the region fundamentally opposed to Western culture and civilisation. The second took a less deterministic view of Islam, noting that the influence of Islamic culture was a dynamic rather than static force, altered, for example, by secular education. Moreover, for those in power, Islamic symbols and language could also be used by political actors to justify and explain their ideology and gain legitimacy. The idea of a static, imposing 'Islam' thus existed alongside an Islam that was subject to interpretation and use by its believers.

'"Face" Among the Arabs'

In 1964, the CIA produced a second piece of 'national character' analysis of the Arab world. It was entitled '"Face" among the Arabs'. Its author, Peter Naffsinger, also explored the role of Islam in Arab political culture, affirming the inherent passivity of the religion. The central thesis of the piece was that the primary 'national characteristic' of the Arab world was the predominance of 'face' or honour in society. According to Naffsinger, this commitment to 'face' explained crucial differences between Western and Arab attitudes to personal responsibility, mostly due to the nature of Islam. 'To the Arab, all is from Allah, and if Allah does all, the individual cannot be held responsible.'[51] One cannot help but recall Said's contention that Western assessments of the Arab 'Other' have been conceived primarily to assert the moral authority of the Self. The first paragraph of the analysis exemplifies Said's assertion:

> George Washington, American children are told, having cut down his father's favourite cherry tree, showed his sterling character by confessing to the deed. An Arab hearing this story not only fails to see the moral beauty of such behaviour but wonders why anyone would ever compromise his integrity by admitting thus his guilt. As to Washington's

explanation that 'I cannot tell a lie', the Arab asks how a man could rise to the presidency if he were not suave enough to use a well-concocted falsehood as a tactic in emergency behaviour.[52]

Clearly the CIA's ideas of 'the Other' reflected idealised concepts of the West, juxtaposing the 'objective West' against the 'subjective Arab'. Naffsinger's language is permeated by the discourse of Enlightenment associated with the American with his 'uncompromising willingness to face objective truth and fact'. The American is 'culturally obliged to reconcile his position and his person with truthfully interpreted reality' at 'all times and in all circumstances' but the Arab exists in a contrary cultural setting. He

> manifests his honour and integrity by making a public, outward impression of dignity derived from an ostensible lack of guilt. Even if facts and conditions speak to the contrary, the social veneer of non-guilt must be maintained evident and dominant if he is to achieve the socially demanded face.

Whereas American political culture demanded an honest engagement with the objective realities of 'truth' and 'fact' Arab culture bred merely a façade of dignity, demanded by a society which has 'no place or respect for one whose faults or errors come to public knowledge'.[53] The unspoken implication was surely that American identity and integrity, founded on objective truth and fact, was more 'authentic' or 'real' than that of his Arab counterpart, beneath which lay a plethora of 'faults and errors' that he was socially obliged to conceal. The analysis certainly substantiates the notion that 'America considers itself a morally and politically superior society, a shining city on a hill, with a universal mission informed by a sense of exceptionalism'.[54]

Perhaps the most important aspect of this analysis, and where it was a considerable improvement on its predecessor, was its attempts to explain cultural differences between the Arab world and the West in relativist terms. Naffsinger explained the cultural gap between the Arab and American's approach to 'logic' thus:

> Facts and circumstances can combine in many different ways to reflect unfavourably upon any man, but the Arab cannot afford to

allow accrued facts or logic to impute any flaw or guilt to him personally. In self-defence he must interpret the assembled facts subjectively,
deny them outright, or reject as illogical any construction that leads to
intimations of personal shortcomings. To the American, this defence
is non-objective, a distortion of the truth, and therefore paradoxically
destructive of integrity, unless he can take the Arab point of view and
recognise personal face as having a higher value than fact or logic in
the society.

Ignoring for a moment the historical detail that it was predominantly Muslim scholars who introduced the ideas of Aristotelian
logic to the West, there is an important nuance to this by now
familiar juxtaposition of the subjective, deluded Arab alongside
the objective, enlightened American. The final sentence makes
explicit that the Arab's behaviour only appears in this negative
light 'to the American . . . Unless he can take the Arab point of
view and recognise personal face as having a higher value than
fact or logic in the society'. If the American is able to step out of
his own shoes, look beyond his own values, his own perspective
and culture, he will be able to see that *the definition of integrity
in the two cultures is fundamentally different.* For the American
it rests on a commitment to fact and objectivity; for the Arab it
rests on a commitment to 'personal face' or honour in the eyes of
his society. Naffsinger clarifies early on in the analysis that 'in *our
culturally determined scale of values* the achieving of impersonal
objectivity with regard to facts and truth is more important than
preserving a man's dignity before the world at large'. He makes
explicit reference to 'our culturally determined scale of values', as
if to remind his readers that these American values are not uni-
versally shared. Thus the 'Arab's untruths, half-truths, avoidance
of reply or other ploys that jar Westerners do not spring from any
perverse desire to deceive; they are facets of the need to maintain
that personal dignity and face which in his system of values take
precedence'.[55]
Such efforts to maintain 'face' appeared

almost paranoiac by Western standards. Entertaining delusions of
grandeur, claiming to be persecuted, magnifying faults in others than

one wants to hide in oneself, calling constantly for resurgence of past greatness – all this is behaviour typical of paranoia, but it is manifested in every Arabic political newspaper and among individuals in day to day intercourse. *It cannot be considered abnormal in the Arab cultural setting* . . . The Westerner who, recognising in the Arab the personality traits which in Western culture signify paranoia or inferiority complex, is pleased with himself for being able to 'see through the Arab's attempts at deceit and trickery and his lies' shows his lack of appreciation of the face concept in the Arab culture. It is the Westerner who has learned always to allow the Arab a graceful way to save himself from the implications of guilt when difficulties arise who will make him a friend and avoid many frustrations and impasses in the relationship. [56]

The admission of relative definitions of 'normality' is notable. What is defined as paranoia in a Western cultural setting was recognised by analysts to be acceptable behaviour in Arab culture, a 'socially practical and accepted method' of 'refuting any outside attack on his [the Arab's] identity'. The Westerner imposing his definition of normality upon Arab behaviour was thus gently accused of cultural ignorance. We see yet another (perhaps more constructive) policy recommendation implied: that only the Westerner who recognises the importance of 'face', and allows the Arab an avenue to maintain it, will succeed in political and social interactions with his Arab counterparts.[57] Moreover, analysts were now using the sort of open source material that they had dismissed some five years earlier as propaganda or 'control of thought', to *study* what such thought entailed, how it was perceived by the West, and above all what it reflected about the mindset and different cultural values of the region.

Naffsinger gave the following example to demonstrate that values esteemed highly in the West such as 'fact' and 'logic' were subordinated in the Arab world to the pre-eminent cultural value of 'face' or honour:

In an oil company installation near the Persian Gulf, an American linguist in the training department, after drafting some exercises to be used in instructing American employees in spoken Arabic, gave them to three bilingual Saudi Arabs working for him to check for syntactic and orthographic correctness before publication. The drafts were all tacitly okayed, returned without change but after they had been published several glaring errors in the work were discovered. Distressed, the linguist questioned the three Arabs who reluctantly explained to them that the inaccuracies had of course been obvious to them but they did not feel it would be right to point them out and thereby cause embarrassment to their boss and good friend![58]

Whilst the Western counterpart might prioritise the objective accuracy of the work, this matter was 'of secondary importance to the Arabs'. Rather, it was understood that the Saudi Arabs 'believed in good faith that they had acted with honour as gentlemen in protecting the linguist's dignity above all other considerations'. Unlike the earlier CIA analysis of 1959, Arab behaviour was no longer dismissed as simple or ignorant, but rather subject to a different order of rationale. The author went on to qualify, 'with this subjective processing the facts become what the Arab emotionally wants to believe is true. They can thus be made to mesh harmoniously with criteria which stand higher on the value scale because connected with the maintenance of face.'[59]

Whilst validating earlier ideas about the passivity of Islam and the inferiority of Arab political culture, '"Face" among the Arabs' also formalised an important idea upon which analysts came to rely. 'Honour' was naturally a value found in all parts of the world, but in the Arab world it was perceived to be more deeply rooted and thus likely to affect corollary beliefs and interpretations. In 2009, Sir Derek Plumbly, who served as the British ambassador to Cairo from 2003 to 2007, reflected, for example, that the 'passages on face/objectivity sound familiar in light of the denial with which many in the Arab world greeted 9/11'.[60] Most importantly, however, the piece established that Western values could not be considered as universal and the Western analyst seeking to understand the Arab world in Western terms was likely to founder. Undoubtedly wider intellectual currents prevalent in the 1960s, such as the rise of the social sciences, the civil rights movement and particularly the increasingly frustrating experience of Vietnam, played a part in this increased self-reflexivity, as illustrated in the following section.

Deconstructing the 'Self'

In 1974, the winter edition of *Studies in Intelligence* featured an article entitled 'Re-examining our perceptions on Vietnam'. At its heart, the piece addressed the problem of overcoming cultural 'Otherness' in analysis. In a thorough examination of previous assessments on Vietnam, the author, Anthony Lewis, argued that faulty Western analysis stemmed from insufficient cultural understanding and self-awareness. Detailing some of the cognitive challenges inherent to the analytic process, he wrote that analysts needed 'to overcome unconscious assumptions that our views and convictions about the world, as well as our more basic beliefs, values and norms, are held by reasonable and educated people everywhere'.[61]

Lewis called for a 'process of introspective learning' to deal with this problem. The goal was to allow the analyst to identify the 'subjective elements of his personal perceptions'. As a result, the analyst would build:

> a more solid basis for conscious comparison between his own perspectives and those of people of a different culture. Jogging oneself repeatedly to make such conscious comparisons will root a habit of surfacing perceptual differences. In this way an awareness of the unreliability of one's own perspectives on the world and rationale for action is strengthened.[62]

Lewis suggested concrete ways in which this might be achieved. He cited, for example, a 'behavioural learning technique' called 'Contrast-American' which had been 'used with most Foreign Service Officers at the Foreign Service Institute since late 1972, and was made available for use in CIA in July 1973'. This involved trainee analysts watching a videotaped series of encounters between Americans and non-Americans in order to identify 'the single and typical American cultural characteristic which the American in the videotaped encounter manifests in each scene of a sequence'. The goal of this self-observation was 'to recognise the various subtle ways in which their own thought processes, feelings and behaviour are influenced by cultural factors'.[63]

Lewis also advocated the study of foreign languages rather than relying on translations. Lewis wrote that language 'is both a product and bearer of their culture' and mere translation loses 'the sender's frames of reference – a part of his culture which the receiver does not share. This explains why we must dig hard to grasp what a people's beliefs, values and norms mean to them.' He went on to suggest that 'probing the thought patterns behind the proverbs and aphorisms of a people can be a fascinating and highly productive hobby in the quest for how the mentality of a foreign people differs from ours'. Lewis concluded the piece by urging the intelligence community 'to provide instruction for both intellectual and skill learning for intercultural analysis'.[64]

The timing of these reflections is significant. It was an age of unprecedented global challenge to orthodoxies: from the student protests of the late 1960s and the sexual revolution to the civil rights movement, grave foreign policy failures such as the Vietnam War sat alongside intellectual developments such as the growth of behavioural sciences. The product of these reminders to question conventional wisdoms meant that CIA analysis of 'Otherness' had thus evolved to stress a greater focus on the 'Self'. No longer were analysts merely trying to identify the immutable characteristics of the 'Other', but now they were also questioning the universality of their own logic and in this more self-conscious way, attempting to overcome the analytical challenges of cultural 'Otherness'.[65]

The Arab Response

However, it was not just the West which painted a picture of Arab cultural exceptionalism. In 1973, a remarkable diplomatic exchange between the British ambassador in Jordan, Balfour Paul, and Head of the Near East Division, James Craig, reveals the extent of Arab complicity in perpetuating such ideas about Arab otherness. In a remarkable demonstration of self-orientalising, Balfour Paul relayed the thesis advanced to him by Zaid Rifai, the Jordanian foreign minister, that 'Arabs must be dealt with as children'.[66]

Within this framework Rifai reinforced the importance of several factors which had already been raised by the CIA and British

Foreign Office for many years and cited above: the predominant role of the 'personal' interlocutor and 'verbal' as opposed to written agreements in the Arab world, alongside the distinction between 'the real' and 'the declared' in Arab foreign policy. Whilst the archives rarely reveal so lengthy an exposition of cultural self-criticism, this is certainly not an isolated example. The following chapters repeatedly illustrate how 'Orientalist' depictions of the Arab world were often advanced or at least validated by the Arab political elite themselves.[67]

James Craig, the diplomat who received the memorandum, was quite prepared to endorse Zaid's comments. He wrote that 'one of the most striking characteristics of the vast majority of Arabs, leaders and led, public and private, is their lack of moral courage'.[68] He reflected also upon the disparity between what the Arabs said and what they mean. 'Have we not all been told by the Arabs in private that they love us but cannot say so in public? Have we not all wondered whether the private whisper or the public statement represented the real sentiment of the heart?' Craig qualified that 'though I don't pretend that the verities Zaid was dealing with are eternal, I suspect they may in the end be more useful in working towards an Arab–Israel settlement than all our talk of interim arrangements and demilitarisation'. He concluded his reply with the assertion that upon retirement he would write of his experiences in a book entitled, 'Arabs and the Arab mentality: a study in frustration'.[69]

In 2001, Sir James Craig reflected on his long and eminent diplomatic career to the British Society for Middle Eastern Studies (BRISMES), confirming the endurance of some of these ideas about the Arab world.[70] In an echo of Naffsinger's analysis which suggested that the Greek philosophy of 'know thyself' was unknown in the Arab world, he claimed that the beginning of self-criticism in the region 'has been a refreshing breeze'. He recalled President Bourguiba castigating his fellow Arabs for their lack of realism. 'The Arabs remind me', he cited Bourguiba claiming, 'of a man who because he is angry with his wife and wants to punish her, cuts off his penis'. Craig maintained also that 'there is something seriously discouraging in the system of education' in the region resulting in a belief that the 'pursuit of original ideas will be inhibited by the climate of society'. At the same time he dismissed as 'utterly discredited and risible the idea of a genetically different Arab mind'.[71]

What is the significance of these ideas – do they reveal some 'truth' about Arab culture? The durability of these concepts and interviews with both British and Egyptian diplomats suggests that there must surely be some relationship, however complex, between these ideas and the 'real' Arab world. When presented with excerpts from these controversial analyses, several senior Egyptian diplomats agreed with their findings. 'They are right, it is true', said Nasser's daughter, Hoda.[72] The exception was Hassanein Heikal, who dismissed such ideas of cultural difference as merely encouraging division among nations. British ambassador to Cairo Sir Derek Plumbly expressed 'sympathy' with Heikal's view, as did many other British diplomats understandably uncomfortable with the quasi-racist language of the earlier CIA studies.[73] Others resolutely differentiated between ignorant cultural stereotypes and 'valid' cultural knowledge and understanding, born of exposure to, and immersion in, the Middle East.[74] It is striking that, for the most part, British diplomats were more critical and defensive about these assumptions than their Arab counterparts.[75] As one British diplomat put it, 'Said could justifiably write *quod erat demonstrandum* from the grave.'[76]

* * *

This discussion has sought to reconstruct the challenges the British and American political and intelligence community perceived itself to confront in the Middle East, the beliefs and conceptualisations formulated in order to rise to this challenge and the evolution of thought about dealing with the Arab 'Other'. It shows that in contrast to accusations of 'failure' to do so, attempts were clearly made to understand the 'foreign thought structure' of the Arab world.

By 1959 the political elite on both sides of the Atlantic had made explicit a set of ideas about the 'Otherness' of Arab culture which were to prevail for decades to come. Foremost amongst these were the challenge of Arab 'rhetoric', the problems of Arab 'motivation', the pre-eminence of 'honour' and the role of Islam. Despite many simplistic stereotypes, the practical challenges identified and the relativity of cultural values were important and valid observations. The British Foreign Office, with greater experience in the region, seems to have adopted a more sophisticated and analytical, if less self-reflexive approach. Education and history were rightly identified as crucial determinants in explaining the 'cultural Otherness' encountered, rather than recourse to an inherent and immutable 'Arab mind'.

In many ways it is true that Western evaluations of 'the Arab' appear repeatedly and explicitly to reassert the moral superiority of the West. At the same time, there are also indications of an evolution of thought about the 'Arab Other'. Compared with the CIA study of 1959, which relied on simplistic cultural observations, the 1964 analysis demonstrated a concerted attempt to understand the different value systems upon which decisions in the Arab world were taken, notably the prevalence of honour or 'face'. Moreover, the later 1973 analysis, obviously informed by failures in Vietnam, shifted the focus entirely from an examination of the 'Other' to that of the 'Self'. Thus, alongside continuity in certain beliefs there is also a sense of development in these analyses, a greater self-consciousness and awareness of the complexity of 'culture'. This shift may well have been merely an artefact of growing sophistication at large in thinking about cultures as being more or less superior than one's own – the international version of regarding 'Others' as different but equal, epitomised in the civil rights movement, for example. The expansion of the United Nations to include a significant majority of decolonised states aptly represented this shift towards multiculturalism and multiracialism on an international scale. Certainly the nuances of analysis detectable were embedded in the wider systems of thought and society at the time. Nonetheless, the qualitative development of these assessments clearly challenges Said's contention that 'Orientalism', or the Western gaze upon the Arab world, is by definition static and cannot develop.

At the same time, one cannot help but conclude that there is a profound truth to Said's contention that power relationships have been reified as truths about culture. The legacy of colonisation, and the assumption of Western superiority upon which it relied, is inescapable and permeates the language of these documents. There is certainly a sense that ideas about the Arab national character persisted in the face of independent nationhood in order to prop up the illusion that the Western world was still on top. Perhaps infantilising Arab culture betrayed a denial on the part of analysts of the real relations being played out in the assertion of pan-Arab nationalism. As Said argues, such ideas about the Arab world 'necessarily provokes unrest in one's conscience about cultural, racial or historical generalisations, their uses, value, degree of objectivity and fundamental intent'.[77]

Surely the notion of an immutable, unchanging 'Arab mind' is as deceptive as the idea of a homogenous static 'Western mind'. Yet to deny that geography, historical experience and social conditions create and reflect cultural differences, variations of systems and meanings in society, and thus differences in values and priorities is also patently illusory. It was certainly more difficult for analysts to recognise that Arab culture, like any other, was a 'repertoire' of ideas, constantly and actively constructed, quietly shifting. However, their analysis was formulated in an era where Western superiority was little questioned; one cannot help but feel therefore that these early attempts at relative thinking are worthy of some credit. Whilst these documents read badly to our twenty-first century ears, there is certainly an argument to be made for the virtues of expressing such cultural beliefs explicitly, and thus allowing them to be subject to debate and criticism, rather than informing (or subverting) analysis implicitly.

The alternative to cultural knowledge, for all its pitfalls, appears to be the more worrying state of a falsified universalism of values, doctrines and beliefs by which all are expected to abide. Examples of universal and non-culturally specific definitions of ideas such as 'democracy', 'freedom' and 'rationality' spring to mind. The dangers of such a universalism and its recent political ramifications in international relations only reinforce the importance of further progress in cultural studies by intelligence communities, despite the contemporary inhibitions of political correctness, limited resources and the ever-increasing speed of communications. The perhaps clumsy beginnings by the Anglo-American intelligence and diplomatic community were to make an important, if controversial, contribution to this end.

Notes

1. E. Baring, *Modern Egypt 1908*, 2nd edn (London: Macmillan, 1911), pp. 561–2.
2. E. Said, *Orientalism* (London: Penguin, 2003), p. 41.
3. S. Huntington, *Clash of Civilisations* (London: Simon and Schuster, 1996).
4. One notable exception is H. Wilford, *America's Great Game: The CIA's Secret Arabists and the Shaping of the Modern Middle East* (New York: Basic Books, 2013). Though focused on covert operations, Wilford not only explores how Orientalism affected early CIA attitudes towards the Middle East but also elucidates how British and American intelligence traditions in the region differed.
5. Melanie McAlister was one of the most important scholars in revealing the significance of 'culture' in American involvement in the Middle East. She highlights how foreign policy in the region has contributed to the construction of American nationhood, exploring the various cultural forms in which American Orientalism has manifested and highlighting how the superpower sought to differentiate itself from British Orientalism. See M. McAlister, *Epic Encounters: Culture, Media, and U.S. Interests in the Middle East* (Berkeley, CA: University of California Press, 2005). Subsequent works exploring the influence of Orientalism on American foreign policy include: M. F. Jacobs, *The Building of an American Foreign Policy, 1918–1967* (Chapel Hill, NC: University of North Carolina Press, 2011) and O. F. Khalil, *America's Dream Palace: Middle East Expertise and the Rise of the National Security State* (Cambridge, MA: Harvard University Press, 2016).
6. For a detailed exploration of the intellectual debates sparked by Said see D. M. Varisco, *Reading Orientalism: Said and the Unsaid* (Seattle: University of Washington Press, 2007).
7. Said, *Orientalism*, p. 21: 'the written statement is a presence to the reader by virtue of its having excluded, displaced, made supererogatory any such real thing as "the Orient"'. Indian Marxist literary scholar Aijaz Ahmad eloquently calls Said to account for his denial of Oriental agency in Z. Lockman, *Contending Visions of the Middle East: The History and Politics of Orientalism* (New York: Cambridge University Press, 2004), pp. 195–201.
8. F. Halliday, *Islam and the Myth of Confrontation* (London: I. B. Tauris, 2003), p. 210: 'The claim of a special European animosity

towards Arabs, let alone Palestinians or Muslims does not bear historical comparison.'

9. Said, *Orientalism*, p. 45.
10. P. Porter, *Military Orientalism: Eastern War through Western Eyes* (London: C. Hurst and Co. Ltd., 2009), p. 19.
11. T. Marr, *The Cultural Roots of American Islamicism* (New York: Cambridge University Press. 2006) and U. Makdisi, 'After Said: the limits and possibilities of a critical scholarship of U.S.-Arab relations', *Diplomatic History*, 38: 3, 2014.
12. F. Gerges, *America and Political Islam: Clash of Cultures or Clash of Interests* (Cambridge: Cambridge University Press, 1999), pp. 9–10.
13. F. Hollyman, 'Intelligence gathering in an unlettered land', *Studies in Intelligence*, 3: 3, 1959, Freedom of Information Act Electronic Reading Room (hereafter FOIA Reading Room).
14. Ibid.
15. Ibid. Another practical problem Hollyman identified was the Arab sense of time: 'For him [the Arab], infinity stretches out ahead, contiguous and real. He seldom, perhaps never, feels the pressure of time. The concept of a fiscal year is wholly foreign to him, either as a measure of time or as a means of controlling expenditures. The notion of "production" of political information in certain quantites within a certain period would puzzle him. He does not have our sense of schedule, of a deadline, of a program. Nothing can be done to make him work at a set rate of speed, let alone hurry.'
16. Ibid.
17. Ibid.
18. A. Bozeman, *Conflict in Africa: Concepts and Realities* (Princeton, NJ: Princeton University Press, 1976), p. 70: 'literacy thus invites to the mind a special kind of analytical observation: to be continually conscious of the multiple relationships between signs and sounds on the one hand, and the ideas and objects they represent, on the other; to weigh every word and to verify the particular functions of the word in terms of the idea it is supposed to represent'.
19. Telegram from Ambassador Hare in Cairo to State Department, 18 February 1958, Foreign Relations of the United States (hereafter FRUS) 1958–1960, vol. XIII, no. 197.
20. R. D. Lyons, 'Raymond Hare, 92, State Dept. Official, Encoy and Arabist', *New York Times*, 10 February 1994. Available at <http://www.nytimes.com/1994/02/10/obituaries/raymond-hare-92-state-dept-official-envoy-and-arabist.html> (last accessed 1 March 2017).

21. Telegram from Ambassador Hare in Cairo to State Department, 11 April 1958, FRUS 1958-1960, vol. XIII, no. 204. One perhaps only needs to compare the archival records in any Arab country to those in the West to observe the relative importance of the written word in the latter of the two cultures.

22. Interview with Raymond Hare, 22 July 1987. Available at <http://adst.org/wp-content/uploads/2012/09/Egypt.pdf>, p. 14 (last accessed 1 March 2017).

23. R. Patai, *The Arab Mind* (New York: Charles Scribners and Sons, 1973). Patai's book was reviewed by Lloyd F. Jordan ain the CIA's in-house journal *Studies in Intelligence*, 1974. Available at <https://www.cia.gov/library/center-for-the-study-of-intelligence/kent-csi/vol18no3/html/v18i3a06p_0001.htm> (last accessed 30 September 2016). Patai's work has continued to be influential and controversial. In 2004, investigative journalist Seymour Hersh linked Patai's book to the sexual abuse of Iraqi prisoners after the 2003 invasion of Iraq, describing the book as the 'bible of the neocons on Arab behaviour'. See S. Hersh, 'The gray zone: how a secret Pentagon program came to Abu Ghraib', *The New Yorker*, 24 May 2004. Available at <http://www.newyorker.com/magazine/2004/05/24/the-gray-zone> (last accessed 1 March 2017).

24. R. B. Parker, *The Politics of Miscalculation in the Middle East* (Bloomington, IN: Indiana University Press, 1992), Introduction, p. xii.

25. Derek Plumbly, e-mail to author, 2 January 2009.

26. Hollyman, 'Intelligence gathering in an unlettered land', *Studies in Intelligence*, 1959, FOIA Reading Room.

27. Working Draft, 'Psychological strategy plan for the Middle East', 25 July 1952, CIA Records Search Tool (hereafter CREST), at the National Archives at College Park, College Park Maryland (hereafter NARA II).

28. Intelligence Report, 'Problems and attitudes in the Arab world: their implications for U.S. psychological strategy', 19 May 1952, State Department Intelligence and Research Reports (hereafter OSS/SDIRR), The Middle East 1950-1961, Microfilm, Reel 1, SOAS Library.

29. Memorandum for the DCI, 'Dangers in the Suez situation', 13 March 1957, CREST, NARA II.

30. S. Yaqub, *Containing Arab Nationalism: The Eisenhower Doctrine and the Middle East* (Chapel Hill, NC: University of North Carolina Press, 2004), p. 12.

31. Hollyman, 'Intelligence gathering in an unlettered land', *Studies in Intelligence*, 1959, FOIA Reading Room.
32. Said, *Orientalism*, p. 247.
33. For a particularly sexualised description of 'the Libyan', see T. Leidesdorf, 'The Libyan as agent', in *Studies in Intelligence*, 7: 1, 1963, FOIA Reading Room: 'Befriending a Libyan is much like acquiring a mistress: once the cautious, tentative, defensive sparring is over, the relationship grows progressively deeper, broader, more involving, more consuming, more demanding.'
34. Hollyman, 'Intelligence gathering in an unlettered land', *Studies in Intelligence*, 1959, FOIA Reading Room.
35. Ibid. He qualified that these 'subtler peculiarities . . . would probably not be very apparent if we ourselves did not have definite expectations of a behaviour which fits our requirements in those whom we want to use as sources'.
36. Patrick Wright, e-mail to the author, 8 December 2008.
37. P. Murphy, *Party Policy and Decolonization: The Conservative Party and British Colonial Policy in Tropical Africa, 1951–1964* (Oxford: Oxford University Press, 1999), pp. 162–3.
38. FO Steering Committee Paper no. 13, 'Social and political forces in the Arab Middle East', 1959, FO 487/13. The paper qualified its conclusions at the start thus: 'A handicap in writing a paper of this kind is that little serious sociological research has been done on Middle Eastern countries. There is little evidence on which to base assumptions about the modes of thought of the new men who are coming to power in these countries or who may be influential in the future. Until this field has been more thoroughly explored, any conclusions are bound to be tentative.'
39. Ibid.
40. Ibid: 'Unfortunately little is done in the home to correct the mischief done in the schools. The excessive indulgence shown in Arab families to male children, especially the first born, has a deplorable effect on the character of the young Arab, making him conceited, argumentative, resentful of criticism and scornful (or frightened) of manual work.'
41. Intelligence Report, 'Problems and attitudes in the Arab world: their implications for U.S. psychological strategy', 19 May 1952, OSS/SDIRR, The Middle East 1950-1961, Microfilm, Reel 1, SOAS Library.
42. FO Steering Committee Paper no. 13, 'Social and political forces in the Arab Middle East', 1959, TNA, FO 487/13.

43. Omar Suleiman, cited in P. Martin, 'How will the Arab Spring reshape the Middle East?', 23 August 2012. Available at <http://m.theglo-beandmail.com/news/world/how-will-the-arab-spring-reshape-the-middle-east/article1360507/?service=mobile> (last accessed 30 September 2016).

44. FO Steering Committee Paper no. 13, 'Social and political forces in the Arab Middle East', 1959, TNA, FO 487/13.

45. Ibid.

46. JIC memorandum (54) 72, 'Political developments in the Middle East and their impact on Western interests', 11 November 1954, TNA, CAB 158/18.

47. Intelligence Report, 'Problems and attitudes in the Arab world: their implications for U.S. psychological strategy', 19 May 1952, OSS/SDIRR, The Middle East 1950-1961, Microfilm, Reel 1, SOAS Library: 'The people of the Near East are caught up in a dynami-cally scientific, technologically powerful and dangerously national-ist world. To this world they bring a religiously inspired way of life which, born in a static, pre-scientific, pre-national era, lacks the institutions and perhaps the philosophical premises through which to revitalise its traditions . . . Even now, a politically crucial minority is looking, if not always with adequate understanding, for modern methods which promise success quickly and with the least political dependence of those nations from which such methods are learned.'

48. Annex, 'Arab nationalism: the historical background', to FO Steering Committee Paper no. 8, 'Arab nationalist and radical movements in Egypt, the Levant and Iraq', 1959, TNA, FO 487/13.

49. FO Steering Committee Paper no. 8, 'Arab nationalist and radical movement in Egypt, Levant and Iraq', 1959, TNA, FO 487/13.

50. Intelligence Report, 'Problems and attitudes in the Arab world: their implications for U.S. psychological strategy', 19 May 1952, OSS/SDIRR, The Middle East 1950-1961, Microfilm, Reel 1, SOAS Library [emphasis added].

51. P. Naffsinger, '"Face" among the Arabs', *Studies in Intelligence*, 8, 1964, FOIA Reading Room: 'By definition and by profession, Islam is the surrendering of the self to the will of Allah . . . All of Muslim theology conveys the feeling that God is so all pervading and at the same time so far above and removed from the individual that all human actions and their consequences are but the sequels of God's doing.' Christianity on the other hand emphasized the 'personal God within each man, who enforces an ideal of perfection in behaviour

and in thought', leading in turn to 'a sense of personal guilt and obligation beyond self'. Islam, 'religion, social force, and almost complete way of life', advocated a 'supremely impersonal God, above and beyond rather than within a person' who 'impresses on the individual no requirement to accept guilt or personal responsibility for anything or to develop a conscience differentiating between intrinsic right and wrong'. He noted that attempts to chastise Arab trainees thus met with dismissive responses. 'The Arab is unwilling and unable to accept the idea that he should feel either sorry or responsible for his mistake. He dismisses both blame and censure with a casual "min allah" – "It is from God." To the remonstrance that it had better not happen again he answers "inshallah," "If God wills it," with exasperating nonchalance. In agent work, where supervision cannot be so close, this indifference to personal responsibility and tendency to atomistic thinking will necessarily be even more troublesome.' Thus, 'Man is required to follow the teachings of the Koran and the Hadith and to perform his religious obligations' but in contrast to his Western, Christian counterparts he was 'not answerable to an inner God, a conscience'. As a result, 'instead of a sense of personal responsibility for his acts, the Arab has a deeply inculcated fear of outside forces; he realizes he must answer for his actions to society'.

52. Ibid.
53. Ibid.
54. Gerges, *America and Political Islam*, p. 5. At the same time this self-veneration was not absolute. Naffsinger's analysis cited American sociologist Samia Hamady's account of an 'Arab who caught another man in bed with his wife levelled a gun at them, but instead of shooting he offered to let the man off if he would keep the affair secret. The man promised and was let go. Later the Arab divorced his wife quietly, and the incident was considered closed. The double murder that might have been the outcome in Western cultures would have made newspaper headlines, a result diametrically opposed to the Arab's priority considerations.' The analysis suggested that 'the emotional distress which other husbands might have felt was for the Arab a problem of secondary importance; he could tell himself that Allah determines all and therefore not to trouble himself with the sequels of any acts'. Naffsinger concluded: 'This story illustrates well the principle that the Arab is the reverse of the Westerner in that he feels very strongly the force of public shame in loss of face but is able to slough off the feelings of personal inadequacy which would

be acute in a Westerner.' Whilst much of the analysis stressed the inferior nature of Arab political and social behaviour, this example could also be read as a critique of Western individualism.

55. P. Naffsinger, '"Face" among the Arabs', *Studies in Intelligence*, 8, 1964, FOIA Reading Room [emphasis added].
56. Ibid. [emphasis added].
57. This was a frequent recommendation made by Anglo-American diplomats in the Arab world to policy-makers in their dealings with Arab leaders.
58. P. Naffsinger, '"Face" among the Arabs', *Studies in Intelligence*, 8, 1964, FOIA Reading Room.
59. Ibid.
60. Derek Plumbly, e-mail to author, 2 January 2009.
61. A. Lewis, 'Re-examining our perceptions on Vietnam', *Studies in Intelligence*, 17: 4, 1973, FOIA Reading Room.
62. Ibid: 'In turn, the motivation becomes stronger to acquire the new jogging habit in order to eradicate old habits of misperception which would otherwise continue to limit one's effectiveness.'
63. Ibid.
64. Ibid.
65. It is notable that this was an early precursor to the substantial contemporary literature on different strategic cultures. See, for example, J. L. Johnson, and J. A. Larsen, 'Comparative strategic cultures syllabus', prepared for the Defense Threat Reduction Agency Advanced Systems and Concepts Office, rev. 20 November 2006. Available at <http://www.fas.org/irp/agency/dod/dtra/syllabus.pdf> (last accessed 30 September 2016).
66. Memorandum from Balfour Paul in Amman to Craig in FCO, 27 August 1973, TNA, FCO 93/82.
67. H. Dabashi, *Post-Orientalism: Knowledge and Power in Time of Terror* (New Brunswick, NJ: Transaction Publishers, 2009).
68. Reply from Craig in FCO to Balfour Paul in Amman, 14 September 1973, TNA, FCO 93/82.
69. Ibid. As an example he cited the Sheikh of Dubai 'who for all his power and pelf could not tell a palace driver he was sacked'.
70. For a more recent analysis of Arab culture by a prominent British Arabist, see M. Allen, *Arabs* (London: Continuum, 2006).
71. J. Craig, 'A life with the Arabs', BRIMSES annual lecture, in *British Journal of Middle Eastern Studies*, 28: 2, 2001.
72. Hoda abd el Nasser, interview with the author, Cairo, 2 March 2006.

73. Hassanein Heikal, interview with the author, Cairo, 1 March 2006.
74. James Craig, interview with the author, Oxford, 24 October 2011.
75. Correspondence with Derek Plumbly, Patrick Wright, Roger Tomkys.
76. Roger Tomkys, correspondence with the author, September 2012.
77. Said, *Orientalism*, p. 96.

2 Formation of the United Arab Republic

> No one wanted unity. Even 'Abd al-Nasser didn't want it . . . Who at that hour could dare say we do not want unity? The people would tear their heads off.
>
> *Afif-al-Bizri*[1]

On 11 January 1958, as a self-appointed Syrian delegation of army officers arrived in Cairo to negotiate an unprecedented political union with Egypt, Nasser had his sights set beyond the Arab world, entertaining his friend and ally Indonesian President Sukarno in the temperate climate of Aswan. It took a month of heated negotiations with the Syrians before Nasser was able to exact terms he considered favourable for union, following which he declared: 'Today Arab nationalism is not just a matter of slogans and shouts; it has become an actual reality.'[2] Indeed the formation of the United Arab republic (UAR) marked the first time that a country had voluntarily sacrificed its sovereignty in the name of Arab unity. '*Qawmiyya*' (pan-Arabism) had triumphed over '*Wataniyya*' (nationhood) and decades of unfulfilled Arab rhetoric had finally become a reality.

The Anglo-American intelligence community was all too familiar with the political scene in Syria. Indeed, it was here that the CIA led the first military coup in the Arab world: the 1949 bloodless putsch by Colonel Husni al-Za'im. Za'im only lasted a few months before he was overthrown and executed by rival officers, following which Damascus saw a series of coups and countercoups culminating in union with Egypt in 1958. Due to its strategic position across oil pipelines, connecting the Persian

Gulf with NATO member Turkey, Syria was central to Western calculations in the Middle East. In the enthusiasm for covert action that marked this era, SIS and the CIA conspired to execute a coup in Damascus in 1956 that was foiled by the Syrian intelligence services. In 1957, a second CIA plot, codenamed Operation Wappen, tried and failed to engineer another military overthrow in Syria, eventually forcing the notoriously weak President Quwatly to seek support from the Soviet Union. In turn the Syrian Ba'ath party appealed to Nasser for salvation from Communist infiltration of the Syrian government.[3]

Despite the involvement of Western intelligence services in post-war Syria, few recent works have untangled the perceptions of the intelligence community's assessment of the motivations and implications of this dramatic symbol of Arab unity.[4] Analysts were cynical about the prospects of meaningful cooperation amongst the Arab states. Moreover, they noted the role that Western meddling had played in bringing about this dramatic turning point. The JIC was less level headed about Nasser's intentions in Syria, no doubt reflecting something of an institutional hangover from Suez in which British pride had been so badly damaged by the Egyptian nationalist. The British intelligence community was thus inclined to overstate Nasser's propensity to be influenced by the Soviet Union, whereas American analysts were keen to make the case that Arab nationalism offered the opportunity to fight rather than fuel Communist encroachment of the Middle East.

Historical Background to Arab Unity

Syria was in many ways the birthplace of Arab nationalism and backbone of pan-Arab unity. It had been the focus of ancient rivalry between Mesopotamia (Iraq) and the Nile Valley (Egypt) and since independence in 1949 was beset by political instability. The ideas of Arab unity adopted by Nasser in fact originated with the Syrian Ba'ath (Renaissance) Party formed after the Second World War, inspired by Syrian thinker Michel Aflaq. These ideas were based upon the premise that the Western colonial policy of 'divide and rule' had prevented the Arabs from achieving their former greatness and that there was *'Umma 'Arabiyya wahida dhat risala khalida'* (One Arab Nation with an Eternal Mission).[5] Only if the Arabs combined their political, economic and military forces could they once again rise up against Western domination and its imperial bastion, Israel.

As early as 1954, the JIC raised (and dismissed) the prospect of Arab unity as part of a general consideration of how the region could be mobilised to combat the threat posed by the Soviet Union. The Committee wrote that 'dynastic, political and religious rivalries frustrate attempts to achieve that constructive collaboration between the various countries which would help to strengthen the area against the Soviet threat'. They recognised the potential Cold War advantages of Arab unity, but also noted that 'feuds' in the Arab world could be used 'to our advantage'. Ultimately they judged that 'a unified bloc of Arab countries might be harder to control, more arrogant in its policies and more resistant to Western influence'.[6] The merits of colonial policies of 'divide and rule' were thus implicitly endorsed by the British intelligence community as late as 1954.

The prospect of a specifically Egyptian-Syrian union dated back to October 1955 when a military pact was agreed between the two nations in response to the pro-Western Baghdad Pact designed to protect the Middle East from Communist incursions. Analysts reflected that 'enthusiasm for union was then confined essentially to Syria, and it still is'.[7] In the aftermath of the Suez Crisis, the JIC concluded that despite 'increasing talk of Arab economic co-operation', including an 'Arab League economic council, an Arab airline network, a common rail and road system and even a common currency . . . the Arab league has never proved capable of laying the political basis on which such measures of economic unity could build'. They noted that whilst some further preparations were underway to effect an economic union between Egypt and Syria, 'the rulers and people of the Arab countries have not yet reached a stage where they are able, or indeed willing, to pool their resources and co-ordinate development of the region as a whole'.[8] In the years preceding the formation of the UAR, the prospect of political or economic

Arab unity appeared dim in the eyes of the Western world. As the seasoned British ambassador to Egypt, Sir Harold Beeley put it, despite 'considerable emotional support for the idea' it was merely 'propaganda' and as unlikely as 'other Arab nationalist dreams'.[9] The American NSC concurred that whilst 'the mystique of Arab unity has become a basic element of Arab political thought', in fact 'the tendency' of the area was towards 'fragmentation'.[10]

The question of Syrian (and Arab) political culture clearly played into intelligence analysis on the possibility of unity. In October 1957, the State Department attempted to explain recent Syrian political policies by 'reference to the historical setting, the social characteristics and the international environment which have reacted together to produce the present situation'. The analysis highlighted some familiar beliefs about Arab culture explored in the previous chapter. It raised, for example, the importance of community identity in Syrian culture, the 'frequently wide disparity between the public and private statements of Syrian and other Arab leaders' and 'the tendency of Syrian reactions to be strongly subjective'. Echoing the negative depictions of 'Arab culture', analysts painted a picture of a subjective, untrustworthy and unstable Syrian body politic.[11]

Explaining the 'strong emotional appeal of Arab unity' among the Syrian people was phrased in less contentious and more historical terms. The American ambassador to Syria, Charles Yost, was a mild-mannered and quiet man prone to reflective deliberations.[12] In 1958 he observed that there was 'little distinctive "Syrian patriotism"', and that Syrians had always thought of themselves as 'artificially separated from rest of "Arab nation"'. However, Yost questioned the choice of Egypt as Syria's partner, claiming that immediate neighbours whose 'claim to Arabism' was 'less dubious' might have been preferred.[13] Analysis of Ba'ath Party literature in fact reveals that even those Syrian Ba'athists advocating union had their doubts about the Egyptian partnership.[14] Nonetheless, as the ambassador noted, during the past five years Nasser had 'succeeded [in] imposing himself as Garibaldi on popular imagination'.[15]

Short-term Motivations: Western Meddling and the Threat from Communism

The instability of the Syrian polity was of course not merely the product of 'Syrian culture'. Despite the cultural and historical explanations presented by the intelligence community for and against unity, in the short term it was in fact a series of actions by the West that eventually led to Nasser absorbing Syria. Various covert plots to topple President Quwatly pushed the government into the arms of the Soviets.[16] In turn, the newly elected but increasingly isolated Syrian Ba'ath begged Nasser to save them from a Communist onslaught.

Ultimately, however, it was covert plotting over Suez that had most dramatically radicalised Arab politics. The tripartite aggression in 1956 merely strengthened Arab unity and Nasser's political victory over the 'imperialist' forces gave him an unmistakable aura of invincibility. Immediately after the Suez Crisis, the JIC described Syria as 'politically unstable and buoyed up by Russian support and the promise of further arms'. Surpassing Egypt, Syria had now 'become the main potential troublemaker'.[17] In November 1956, a Special National Intelligence Estimate (SNIE) noted that pro-Western Syrian groups 'were on the defensive even before the British-French action in Egypt' and were now 'increasingly overshadowed by leftist orientated, extreme nationalist, anti-Western politicians and their counterparts in the Syrian army'.[18] By 1957, the JIC took the view that Syria had 'virtually surrendered its policies to Egyptian keeping' and was 'wide open to Soviet penetration'.[19] The CIA concurred that Syria had shown 'less caution' than Nasser in dealing with the Soviets.[20]

In August 1957, Anglo-American fears were reinforced by the signature of a wide ranging economic and technical agreement between Syria and the Soviet Union. This was followed by the humiliating expulsion of three American diplomats and the installation of the left-leaning Afif-al-Bizri as commander-in-chief.[21] On 27 August, Prime Minister Harold Macmillan suggested to the British Cabinet that 'the Soviet Government had substantially increased their hold over Syria and there was a serious risk that the country would soon fall wholly within the influence of the Soviet Union'.[22]

The JIC seemed somewhat divided on the significance of these moves. On the one hand they admitted that it was 'extremely improbable that any elements in Syria can now reverse the movement to deeper involvement with the Soviet bloc', asserting that 'Syria has now become to all intents and purposes a Soviet sphere of influence'.[23] However, they clarified that there was as yet no evidence to show that Russia has had a 'direct hand in recent events'. The Committee suggested that these apparent moves to the left on the Syrian domestic scene seemed to have been 'the product of a purely internal manoeuvre'. They sought to reassure policy-makers that it was unlikely that Russia was 'trying deliberately to set up a Communist regime, even though the acquisition of power by Communists and fellow travellers is a development to her advantage'. Nor did the superpower intend to set up a base in Syria for her own use 'since she would be unlikely to commit Russian forces to a country not contiguous with the Soviet bloc'.[24] This astute picture of a generally cautious Soviet Union was to become a notable feature of JIC assessments and served to temper the Cold War fears of their consumers.

The CIA agreed that it was unlikely that the Kremlin had a 'direct hand in recent events'.[25] They highlighted that the Syrians had often taken the initiative in developing their relationship with the Soviets and that there was 'no clear evidence that these actions were taken in accordance with a prearranged overall plan or that they were carried out on Soviet orders'. They noted that the existing coalition lacked 'common positive goals' and rightly predicted that a Nasserist figurehead by the name of Colonel Sarraj might be able to outmanoeuvre the leftist coalition.[26] In 1957, the British ambassador clarified that 'Syria under communist domination . . . is the policy of a minority in the government' and that Ba'athists were 'concerned to avoid a further extension of Communist influence', reminding Whitehall that (naturally unspecified) 'American actions' in the last year had not helped to 'alleviate suspicions'.[27] Finding themselves increasingly isolated within the Syrian government, the Ba'ath party had appealed to Nasser to save them from Communist domination, hoping in the process to win a more decisive stake in the political system.

If analysts had a fairly good grasp of the Soviet-Syrian relationship, it is clear that the JIC fundamentally underestimated both the extent of Egyptian hostility to a pro-Soviet Syria and Nasser's ability to resist Soviet influence. They felt that Egypt's reactions were 'difficult to predict until we know more about the degree of overtness about the new Syrian government's ties with Moscow'. The Committee judged that:

> Nasser attaches importance to at least an imposing façade of 'positive neutralism'. He will therefore not want to be too closely linked (e.g. by the mooted Egyptian-Syrian federation) with a Government regarded . . . as Communist or flagrantly pro-Communist. Short of that, he will presumably not object to the change of emphasis in Syria; in any case, Russian influence over Nasser's regime must be strong enough to over-ride any objections not shared in Moscow.[28]

The fallout following Suez and particularly the absence of British diplomatic representation in Cairo probably contributed to the JIC's misperceptions of Nasser's relationship with the Soviet Union and his genuine commitment to 'positive neutralism'.[29] Their analysis in the immediate aftermath of the Suez crisis certainly seems to validate the suggestion by JIC chair Sir Percy Cradock that 'the capacity of Arab nationalism to resist Communist persuasions was still much underestimated in the West'.[30] Instead the Committee emphasised that the Suez crisis had increased Egypt's military and economic dependence on the Soviet Union, noting for example the expansion of the Middle East section of the Soviet Foreign Office.[31] The JIC argued that as long as the Soviet bloc was the only source of arms and capital for large investment projects the Kremlin would be able to 'exert strong pressure to prevent Nasser from straying seriously from the Bloc line'.[32]

Interestingly, despite the Cold War preoccupations of the Eisenhower administration, American analysis proved more perceptive at highlighting the limits of Soviet influence over Egypt. In 1957 an intelligence memorandum entitled 'Soviet "presence"

Figure 2.1 Sir Percy Cradock, former chairman of the JIC (1985–1992). Private collection.

in the Middle East' stressed that Moscow would 'almost certainly seek to get into a position in which it can have fuller knowledge of Nasser's plans and activities and influence them to a greater degree', suggesting therefore that they were not *yet* in a position to do so. Analysts noted that 'careful comparison' of Moscow's statements and actions with those emanating from Cairo suggested that 'while Nasser has unhesitatingly accepted and even solicited Soviet aid and advice', he had not felt constrained to support Soviet policy or even coordinate his own with it. Moreover 'in some cases' he had 'not even informed the U.S.S.R. of his actions and intentions'. American analysts sent a clear message to policy-makers that 'if Nasser can make a deal on his own terms with the West he will not be deterred from doing so by Soviet misgivings or charges of ingratitude'.[33] In 1958, the CIA confirmed that, 'we do not believe that Nasser is a Communist or sympathetic to Communist doctrine'.[34]

Despite the exaggerated fears of policy-makers, the intelligence community recognised that the immediate motivation for the union was in fact to *counteract* the influence of communism in Syria and moreover, that Syrian agency drove the union rather than Nasser's ambitions. In April 1958, the JIC reflected that whilst a 'widespread desire for some form of Arab unity has for long existed in Syria', the immediate reason for Syrian President Quwatly's urgent appeal to Nasser was 'the fear that the Communists and their powerful allies . . . would soon be strong enough to seize power'. It was almost secondary that 'extending the Egyptian revolution to Syria fitted in conveniently with Nasser's own conception of Arab unity'.[35] American analysts agreed that Nasser agreed to the proposed union 'because he was convinced that it was necessary in order to forestall a Communist takeover in Syria, as well as because he saw a propitious moment for realisation of long-laid plans on his own terms'. The emphasis of analysis was subtly, but correctly, placed on Syrian fears of Communism.[36]

These analyses thus clearly revise the conclusions of recent scholarship that 'the British generally underestimated the Syrian initiative'.[37] It is perhaps more accurate to say that they overstated Nasser's desire and 'long laid plans' to 'extend the Egyptian revolution'. Arab accounts would later emphasise the extent to which the union was forced upon Nasser.[38] Analysts recognised Nasser's 'reluctance to limit his freedom of action in the area by embracing union with an unstable ally' but wrote that 'it now appears that Nasser has been convinced that his dominant position in Syria can only be maintained by acceding to [union]' . . . and that Nasser had been effectively 'put on the spot'.[39] Their depiction of Nasser backed into a corner was a far cry from allusions to the 'Hitler on the Nile' narrative advanced by policy-makers.

Hitler on the Nile?

The question of 'Nasser's empire' clearly underlay assessments of the UAR. British Foreign Secretary Selwyn Lloyd was a barrister by training who allegedly admitted to Churchill that he knew nothing of foreign affairs, spoke no foreign languages and did not like foreigners.[40] In Lloyd's expert opinion, Nasser was 'following in Hitler's footsteps – embarking on the policy of expansion [outlined in his book]'.[41] To a degree, early JIC assessments shared the paranoid reaction of policy-makers that 'Nasser aims at an Islamic empire based on Arab oil wealth'. The JIC argued that this was backed up by his 'own pronouncements' according to which it was 'fair to say that his long-term aims are that Egypt should control the Arab world'.[42]

Although they recognised that Nasser had not planned or orchestrated union with Syria he was now committed to a pan-Arab dream. The Committee wrote that by 'assuming Presidency of the new Republic, Nasser has now staked everything on the success of the venture'.[43] He had on his side his 'personal prestige' among the Syrian masses and the public of the Arab world and would probably move to 'consolidate his position before popular enthusiasm begins to wane'. He had already begun to do this through, for example, the provisional constitution which, analysts noted critically, 'virtually makes him the Dictator of the Republic'.[44]

The nationalist implications of the union were potentially grave. Nasser was at 'the pinnacle' of his popularity and analysts recognised that even if Arab nationalism had not been the primary motivation in driving the union forward, it had certainly been bolstered by it.[45] American assessments described Nasser as a quasi-messianic figure who 'continued to represent the answer to the prayers of many Arabs, particularly urban elements who have for so long suffered economic, social, political and psychological frustrations'. They were unequivocal that there was 'no pro-Western Arab leader who can begin to match his popular appeal'. Analysts qualified however that Nasser's 'drive for domination' might foster obstacles that would bode badly for the union.[46]

British assessments grudgingly reflected on the reasons for, and impact of, the union on the broader Arab region. They identified a toxic combination of education, technology and foreign domination in fomenting Arab nationalism. The result was 'a conscious or unconscious feeling of inferiority' among the Arabs and 'the attempt to compensate for the feeling of present inferiority by looking back to a person of real or imagined former greatness and a belief that if only the Arabs could unite they could again play a major role in world affairs'. Still denying him the (now two-year-old) title of President, the JIC conceded that 'Colonel Nasser' was the 'personification of Arab dissatisfaction with their old corrupt rulers and with their past inferior status' and that this admiration had received 'a considerable stimulus from the union of Syria and Egypt'.[47]

Perhaps most worrying to the JIC was the notion that Nasser was a dictator with the people on his side. The spectre of 'Nasser the demagogue' was frequently at the surface of analysis in this period. The JIC wrote that Nasser's 'apparently successful union with Syria has, with the assistance of Cairo radio, fired the imagination of the intelligentsia and the mobs throughout the Arab world'. In yet another patronising recourse to 'the Arab national character' the JIC suggested that:

> Nasser well understands that the Arab mind finds it difficult to maintain enthusiasm for long unless it is provided with a constant succession of excitements. Arabs do not take kindly to long periods of consolidation and maintenance. If, when the initial parades, speeches and inaugurations are over, no spectacular results appear, Nasser will have to find other stimuli.[48]

It seems that the popular support which Nasser enjoyed amongst the Arab public was not highly regarded by the intelligence community in part because 'the Arab' was looked upon with a degree of contempt – in a rather circular fashion the 'mob's' lack of political wisdom was demonstrated in their support of Nasser. The analysis also hinted that the union itself could not survive, implying that it was just a matter of time before Nasser's bubble burst.

The JIC somewhat resented American pressure to come to terms with Arab nationalism. They repeatedly resorted to stereotypes of Arab political culture and dictatorial parallels to express their frustration. The following extract reveals the JIC's complicity in the hostility of British policy-makers towards Nasser in February 1958. Whilst the Committee noted that 'Western powers' urged the British government 'to show complaisance' towards 'the demands of Arab nationalism' in the interests of securing their oil supplies, the JIC argued that, 'we do not think this belief justified'. They explained:

> In the absence of U.K. influence ... the oil states might be led by national emotion to the extent of denying oil to the West at least temporarily ... Nor can it be assumed that to relinquish the British special position would lead to the strengthening of pro-Western tendencies in the Arabian peninsula ... Experience elsewhere does not however support the contention that Arab imperialists become satisfied when their immediate ambitions are satisfied.[49]

It is striking that the British intelligence community, the nation's 'official wisdom', relied on the notion that the Arabs were individually and nationally driven by 'emotion' rather than 'rationality' as a justification for maintaining the British special position in the region. Underlying their bitterness was perhaps the belief that the Arabs, respecting strength, had been encouraged to undermine the British position by withdrawal from India. Nasser's role as an 'Arab imperialist' was at this stage clearly endorsed by the British intelligence community, with unspoken mutterings of the dangers of appeasement.

The prospect of expansion of an Egyptian empire over the Arab world seems to have been a genuine fear. Nor perhaps was it entirely as irrational as it now seems. As Syrian Ba'athist Salah Aldin Bitar had put it in 1956, the Syrian-Egyptian union 'could not be solid, strong and lasting if other Arab regions, with their Arab people and their immense material and spiritual capabilities, were not joined to it'.[50] In a speech before the great sultan and military commander Saladin's tomb, Nasser himself pledged to follow the hero's example 'to realize total Arab unity' against Western oppression.[51]

American assessments proved more realistic. They agreed that 'the idea of expansion is inherent in Syro-Egyptian union', although they clarified that 'we do not believe the union leadership is likely to press immediately for the adherence of other Arab countries'.[52] Arab unity was undoubtedly 'the most dynamic political force in the area'.[53] Although they stressed the potent emotional appeal of Arab unity their analysis sought clearly to reassure policy-makers of the unlikelihood of real political union, stating: 'we do not believe that a welding together of the Arab states into a centralised and unitary empire is possible in the foreseeable future'.[54]

Yet there were other more immediate risks. Nasser now had a 'stronghold' on all the main short oil transit routes. The JIC reminded Whitehall that 'quite apart from wishing to destroy his rivals he would obviously like to get his hands on the oil resources of both Iraq and Saudi Arabia. With either of these might easily go Kuwait'.[55] The Committee judged, however, that Nasser would avoid direct military confrontation with the West in pursuit of these goals and rely instead on subversion. They warned that Nasser '*must* be expected to pursue his ambitions by leading the Arabs towards unity in the spirit of the Egyptian revolution'.[56]

Although the Anglo-American intelligence community expressed certainty that the Soviet Union had not collaborated with Nasser in establishing the UAR, analysts nonetheless feared that Egyptian subversion of neighbouring states would render those countries more vulnerable to Soviet influence. Iraq, Jordan and Saudi Arabia were key targets and the JIC judged that the Soviet Union 'may be expected to help Egyptian subversive activities both to further their own objectives and in order to increase their influence in the U.A.R'.[57] Soviet activities would likely be 'hidden behind a cloak of Egyptian nationalism and expansion' though the JIC conceded that there was 'little evidence of planned and concerted collaboration' against Egyptian targets.[58]

The British intelligence community feared that much of the Arab world was in danger of Egyptian machinations. Nasser, they argued, '*must* be expected to try to engineer their overthrow by these and other subversive methods'.[59] Subsequent scholarly studies have suggested that that Egyptian intelligence agencies were indeed engaged in extensive subversion.[60] Jordan, Saudi Arabia and Lebanon were identified as particularly vulnerable. Lebanon was described as possibly 'one of Nasser's primary targets . . . a tempting morsel; a small country, prosperous and comparatively defenceless, and already largely enclosed on its landward side by Syria'.[61] One cannot help but notice the vivid imagery in the usually staid and level-headed JIC reports of Nasser as a beast of giant proportions with an insatiable appetite to conquer the Arab world. With considerably more reservation American analysts also feared that the union would 'facilitate Nasser's dominion of the Arab world'.[62]

'Nasser the Moderate'?

The American ambassador to Egypt, Raymond Hare, was in the habit of enjoying regular and wide-ranging discussions with President Nasser. He recalled that the Egyptian president 'liked to talk about many things . . . if I saw him in the morning about ten o'clock he would breeze in smelling of lotion'.[63] Reporting back to Washington, Hare astutely presented an alternative narrative of the opportunities Syrian-Egyptian unity might present. Whilst the union undeniably had 'disquieting implications' he reminded American policy-makers that Nasser had 'scored his greatest successes outside Egypt as irresponsible champion of Arab nationalism'. He compared Nasser's popularity as 'irresponsible' Arab nationalist with his popularity in Egypt, where he 'had to resume responsibility', and which had consequently 'been much less'. This was the first time, Hare argued, that 'he must assume responsibility outside Egypt and it remains to be seen whether [the] result will be increased prestige or disenchantment'. The ambassador seemed to suggest that the latter was more likely, in which case, it was possible

> to foresee [the] deflation of Nasser's ego to the point where he would be more amenable to reason and impelled [to] deal more constructively with us. This is by no means to suggest that Nasser may suddenly change his spots but merely to foresee the possibility of his coming down a bit from his high horse under [the] compulsion of events and consequently being more tractable.[64]

There was the perceptive hint in early American analysis that the practical experience of union with Syria might serve to 'moderate' Nasser. Combined with earlier indications that Nasser had reacted to events rather than initiated union, that his ambitions for Arab unity were secondary to the battle against Communism, the spectre of a more rational, pragmatic Nasser existed alongside fears of a 'Hitler on the Nile'. Meeting with Nasser a week later, Hare noted, for example, that he had 'refrained entirely from raking over old coals and talked with objectivity and to the point'. Although he warned against 'attaching undue importance to this', the interview had seemed to confirm Hare's thesis that increased responsibility was having a 'sobering rather than inflating effect'.[65]

The Syrian President Quwatly had reputedly warned Nasser that absorbing Syria would be no easy task. Apparently he said: 'You don't know what you're getting into, Mr. President. You have taken a people, all of whom consider themselves politicians, fifty percent of whom think that they are leaders, twenty-five percent of whom think they are prophets, and at least ten percent of whom think that they are divine.'[66] Ambassador Hare agreed that the union provided 'opportunities to undercut him [Nasser] in his newly extended and more vulnerable position'.[67] Redacted paragraphs suggest that Hare might have been alluding to covert action or the cultivation of moderate alternatives such as the Iraqi–Jordanian federation.

The Iraqi Jordanian Federation

Western policy-makers were keen to use their allies to accelerate the challenge to Nasser's leadership. The creation of the rival Arab Union, composed of the British client states Iraq and Jordan, was based on the belief that if 'firmly established', it could act as a 'bulwark against the spread eastward of Nasser's influence and thereby play a vital part in protecting Western interests, particularly oil in the area'.[68]

With the rival unions emphasising the polarisation of the Middle East between 'radical' and 'conservative' forces, analysts recognised from the start that Nasser's union 'almost certainly has a greater popular appeal in the whole area'.[69] The JIC also conceded that even in Iraq and Jordan, 'Nasser's initiative had a great deal more popular appeal than has their own union'.[70] The CIA agreed that 'whatever its policy and behaviour, the federation will be regarded by many inside and outside its boundaries as a Western creation and as basically hostile to the Pan-Arab nationalist cause'.[71] They perceptively recommended that American diplomatic and material support be 'given quietly' and inconspicuously, 'combined with an impression that the U.S. favored Arab unity moves in general' in order to strengthen rather than impede the federation. Relaxing 'current pressures upon Nasser' was identified as key in bringing the latter into 'a more truly neutral position' in light of discreet US support for the Iraqi–Jordanian federation.[72]

The JIC seems to have been more hopeful about the union, highlighting the greater 'practical possibilities' enabled by the geographical contiguity of its components.[73] They recognised that the Arab Union had 'so far gained little public support in the Arab world' where it was seen as a 'defensive grouping of traditional regimes against Nasser', but posited the possibility that 'if the Arab Union is successful, a tendency may well develop for Syria to become less enamoured of her rather unnatural attachment to Egypt and more attracted by some form of closer connection with the Arab Union Area with which she has far more in common'.[74] Evidently disregarding the postcolonial impulses driving Arab nationalism, a strong element of wishful thinking seems to have influenced JIC assessments on the Arab Union.

The CIA was less deluded. It stressed that the federation would not solve the most important domestic problems in either of the states and indeed could make some of them more serious.[75] Even the JIC conceded that only 'strict security measures' were controlling considerable popular preference for the UAR. In a prophetic warning they wrote that 'subversion will remain an acute danger' and that 'assassination of the leaders' was a 'distinct possibility'.[76] Fears of Nuri's violent demise were realised only months later with the announcement of the Iraqi revolution.

*   *   *

Despite the dramatic significance of the Syrian-Egyptian union, analysts had long regarded the prospect of any form of Arab union with a degree of incredulity. Their perceptions of the fissiparous nature of the Arab world and Syrian political culture in particular suggested that these preliminary moves towards unity were unlikely to bear fruit. For the most part, they recognised the past, present and potential contribution of Western action to both extending and limiting Egyptian and Soviet influence in Syria and enhancing Nasser's appeal in the region. On the one hand they clearly tempered the panic of policy-makers regarding Soviet control over Syria and acknowledged that the union was primarily driven by fear of Soviet influence rather than the reverse.

However, the JIC in particular do seem to have underestimated the depth and strength of Nasser's anti-communism. Indeed, the Committee's somewhat hysterical assessments of this event reveal the extent to which this generally level headed bureaucracy was at times complicit in the hostility towards Nasser demonstrated by policy-makers such as Selwyn Lloyd. Relying on flawed historical parallels and a contemptuous view of Arab culture, their assessments were inclined to endorse the 'Hitler on the Nile' interpretation of Nasser's motivations and the likely consequences. American assessments were more balanced: in their assessment of Nasser' relationship with the Soviet Union; the unlikelihood of a real political union between the Arab states; and the suggestion that the union might moderate Nasser's 'irresponsible nationalism'. Both sides of the Atlantic recognised the demagogic appeal of Nasser's nationalism and his role as unrivalled Arab leader. Policy recommendations to avoid explicit Western hostility, which would of course only consolidate support for Nasser, were pertinent and appear to have been heeded. With varying degrees of emphasis, the Anglo-American intelligence communities accurately predicted that the Western backed rival Iraqi–Jordanian federation would pale into insignificance beside its genuine nationalist counterpart.

Notes

1. Afif-al-Bizri, Syria's Chief of Staff, cited in M. Mufti, *Sovereign Creations: Pan Arabism and Political Order in Syria and Iraq* (Ithaca, New York: Cornell University Press, 1996) p. 91.
2. R. McNamara, *Britain, Nasser and the Balance of Power in the Middle East, 1952–1967: From the Egyptian Revolution to the Six Day War* (London: Frank Cass, 2003), p. 117.
3. D. Little, 'Cold War and covert action: the United States and Syria, 1945–1958', *Middle East Journal*, 44: 1, 1990, pp. 51–75.
4. McNamara, *Britain, Nasser*, p. 117. Scholars such as McNamara have identified the union as a 'turning point' in Middle East affairs which seemed to mark the 'complete success of the Nasserite project in Syria', going on to 'unleash a chain of events that were to destroy what was left of Britain's power in the Middle East'. Amongst several contributions to our understanding of this event, Podeh, *The Decline of Arab Unity*, is the first to examine the union based on declassified documents, suggesting that Nasser received an informal green light from Washington before proceeding. Other more general scholarly

works on the Egyptian–Syrian union include: Jankowski, *Nasser's Egypt*, which underlines the pragmatism that underlay Nasser's move towards Arab nationalism; P. Seale, *The Struggle for Syria: A Study Of Post-war Arab Politics 1945–1958* (Oxford: Oxford University Press, 1965) provides an outstanding synthesis of the Union from the Syrian perspective. J. F. Devlin, *The Ba'ath Party: A History of its Origins to 1966* (Stanford, CA: Hoover Institution Press, 1976), examines the Arabic literature produced by the Ba'ath party.

5. R. Khalidi, 'The 1967 War and the demise of Arab nationalism', in W. R. Louis and A. Shlaim (eds), *The 1967 Arab-Israeli War: Origins and Consequences* (Cambridge: Cambridge University Press, 2012), p. 280.

6. JIC memorandum (54) 72, 'Political developments in the Middle East and their impact on Western interests', 11 November 1954, TNA, CAB 158/18.

7. Memorandum from Acting Assistant Secretary of State for Near Eastern, South Asian and African Affairs (Berry) to Acting Secretary of State, 25 January 1958, FRUS 1958-1960, vol. XIII, no. 187.

8. JIC memorandum (57) 107, 'The economic interdependence of the Middle East Arab countries with particular reference to the after effects of the Suez crisis', 10 October 1957, TNA, CAB 158/29.

9. Memorandum from Beeley to Middleton, 13 August 1957, TNA, FO 371/128224.

10. NSC Report 5801/1, 'Note by the Executive Secretary to the National Security Council on long range U.S. policy toward the Near East', 24 January 1958, FRUS vol. XII, no. 5.

11. Intelligence Report, 'Forces shaping Syrian policy', 18 October 1957, OSS/SDIRR The Middle East 1950-1961, Microfilm, Reel 3, SOAS Library. The analysis explains: 'right and wrong or truth and falsehood are not determined by a set of abstract concepts, but solely by the traditional position or the immediate transient interests of this group. Religiously, the concept of truth in Islam has always been highly relative, and has one character for dealings within the fellowship of co-religionists and another for dealing with outsiders . . . The Syrian's relations with outsiders tend to be unreciprocal in nature and essentially a one way street; his alliances tend to be fleeting and unstable. Outside forces are regarded by him mainly as elements to be played against each other for his own advancement or survival . . . he violently resists domination by them since to him domination is the road to assimilation, and this he fears above all because it means the loss of identity for his group. '

12. R. Lyons, 'Charles Woodruff Yost, 73, dies; was Chief U.S. delegate to U.N.', *New York Times*, 23 May 1981. Available at <http://www.nytimes.com/1981/05/23/obituaries/charles-woodruff-yost-73-dies-was-chief-us-delegate-to-un.html> (last accessed 1 March 2017)
13. Telegram from embassy in Damascus to State Department, 8 February 1958, FRUS 1958-1960, vol. XIII, no. 192.
14. Devlin, *The Ba'ath Party*, p. 88.
15. Telegram from embassy in Damascus to State Department, 8 February 1958, FRUS 1958-1960, vol. XIII, no. 192.
16. The most well-known Western plot, 'Operation Straggle' (a joint CIA/MI6 operation), had in fact been planned to take place at the same time as the ill-fated Suez invasion. For a detailed exploration of Western covert intrigues in Syria see D. Lesch, 'The 1957 American Syrian crisis', in D. Lesch (ed.), *The Middle East and the United States* (Boulder, CO: Westview Press, 2007). A. Rathmell, *Secret War in the Middle East: The Covert Struggle for Syria, 1949–1961* (London: Tauris Academic Studies, 1995), also details the covert operations in which the West and the Arab world indulged in Syria, using British, American and Israeli archives. H. Wilford, *America's Great Game: The CIA's Secret Arabists and the Shaping of the Modern Middle East* (New York: Basic Books, 2013), provides the most recent exploration of this story.
17. JIC memorandum (56) 136, 'The extent to which the present state of tension has increased the chances of miscalculation which might lead to global war', 13 December 1956, TNA, CAB 158/26.
18. SNIE 36.7-56, 'Outlook for the Syrian situation', 16 November 1956, FOIA Reading Room.
19. JIC memorandum (56) 133, 'Soviet penetration in the Middle East', 1 January 1957, TNA, CAB 158/26.
20. SNIE 36.7-57, 'Developments in the Syrian situation', 3 September 1957, FRUS 1955-1957, vol. XIII, no. 383.
21. N. J. Ashton, *Eisenhower, Macmillan and the Problem of Nasser: Anglo-American Relations and Arab Nationalism, 1955–1959* (London: Macmillan, 1996), p. 125.
22. Ibid. p. 127.
23. JIC memorandum (57) 86, 'The situation in Syria', 22 August 1957, TNA, CAB 158/29.
24. Ibid.
25. SNIE 36.7-57, 'Developments in the Syrian situation', 3 September 1957, FRUS 1955-1957, vol. XIII, no. 383.
26. Ibid.

27. Annual review for 1957 from Ambassador Middleton in Beirut to FCO, 6 February 1958, TNA, FO 371/134381.

28. JIC memorandum (57) 86, 'The situation in Syria', 22 August 1957, TNA, CAB 158/29.

29. JIC memorandum (56) 20, 'Factors affecting Egypt's policy in the Middle East and North Africa', 4 April 1956, TNA, CAB 158/23: 'HM ambassador in Cairo thinks Colonel Nasser is not a convinced neutralist, but that his inclinations, like those of the majority of his countrymen are still to seek their inspiration and aid from the West.'

30. P. Cradock, *Know Your Enemy: How the Joint Intelligence Committee Saw the World* (London: John Murray, 2002), p. 131.

31. JIC memorandum (56) 97, 'Egypt: economic consequences of the present situation', 19 November 1956, TNA, CAB 158/26.

32. JIC memorandum (58) 21, 'Soviet Egyptian collaboration', 17 April 1958, TNA, CAB 158/32.

33. ONE memorandum, 'The Soviet "presence" in the Middle East', 9 April 1957, CREST, NARA II.

34. SNIE 30-3-58, 'Arab nationalism as a factor in the Middle East situation', 12 August 1958, FOIA Reading Room.

35. JIC memorandum (58) 25, 'The implications of the United Arab Republic and the Arab Union', 30 April 1958, TNA, CAB 158/32.

36. SNIE 30-58, 'Prospects and consequences of Arab unity moves', 20 February 1958, FOIA Reading Room.

37. W. R. Louis, *The Ends of British Imperialism: The Scramble for Empire, Suez and Decolonisation,* (London: I. B. Tauris, 2006), p. 796.

38. Podeh, *The Decline of Arab Unity*, p. 177.

39. Memorandum from Acting Assistant Secretary of State for Near Eastern, South Asian and African Affairs (Berry) to Acting Secretary of State, 25 January 1958, FRUS 1958-1960, vol. XIII, no. 187.

40. G. Bennett, *Six Moments of Crisis: Inside British Foreign Policy* (Oxford: Oxford University Press, 2013). Bennet's chapter on the Suez Crisis gives an excellent flavour of the anti-Nasser sentiments shared by the British political elite.

41. Louis, *The Ends of British Imperialism*, p. 793: 'Most British officials . . . shared the idea of Nasser as a latter-day dictator of 1930s vintage.'

42. JIC memorandum (58) 25, 'The implications of the United Arab Republic and the Arab Union', 30 April 1958, TNA, CAB 158/32.

43. Ibid.

44. Ibid.

45. Memorandum from Rountree to Dulles, 'Assessment of current situation in the Near East', 24 March 1958, FRUS 1958-1960, vol. XII, no. 14.
46. Ibid.
47. JIC memorandum (58) 13, 'Nationalist and radical movements in the Arabian Peninsula', 10 February 1958, TNA, CAB 158/31.
48. JIC memorandum (58) 25, 'The implications of the United Arab Republic and the Arab Union', 30 April 1958, TNA, CAB 158/32.
49. JIC memorandum (58) 15, 'Likely developments in the Arabian Peninsula over the next five years', 11 February 1958, TNA, CAB 158/31.
50. S. Bitar, *Al-Siyasa al-Arabiyah bayn al Mabda aw al Tatbig* [Arab policy in principle and practice] (Beirut: Dar al-Tali'ah, 1960), p. 48.
51. A. Alexander, *Nasser: His life and Times* (Cairo: Cairo University Press, 2005), p. 109.
52. SNIE 30-58, 'Prospects and consequences of Arab unity moves', 20 February 1958, FOIA Reading Room.
53. NIE 36-58, 'Trends in the Middle East in light of Arab unity developments', 5 June 1958, FRUS 1958-1960, vol. XII, no. 17.
54. SNIE 30-3-58, 'Arab nationalism as a factor in the Middle East situation', 12 August 1958, FOIA Reading Room.
55. JIC memorandum (58) 25, 'The implications of the United Arab Republic and the Arab Union', 30 April 1958, TNA, CAB 158/32.
56. Ibid. [emphasis added].
57. Ibid.
58. JIC memorandum (58) 21, 'Soviet Egyptian collaboration', 17 April 1958, TNA, CAB 158/32.
59. JIC memorandum (58) 25, 'The implications of the United Arab Republic and the Arab Union', 30 April 1958, TNA, CAB 158/32 [emphasis added].
60. A. Rathmell, 'Brotherly enemies: the rise and fall of the Syrian-Egyptian intelligence axis, 1954–1967', *Intelligence and National Security*, 13: 1, 1998, p. 235.
61. JIC memorandum (58) 25, 'The implications of the United Arab Republic and the Arab Union', 30 April 1958, TNA, CAB 158/32.
62. Memorandum from Acting Assistant Secretary of State for Near Eastern, South Asian and African Affairs (Berry) to Acting Secretary of State, 25 January 1958, FRUS 1958-1960, vol. XIII, no. 187.
63. Interview with Raymond Hare, 22 July 1987. Available at <http://adst.org/wp-content/uploads/2012/09/Egypt.pdf, p. 12> (last accessed 1 March 2017).

64. Telegram from embassy in Cairo to State Department, 10 February 1958, FRUS 1958-1960, vol. XIII, no. 195.
65. Telegram from embassy in Cairo to State Department, 18 February 1958, FRUS 1958-1960, vol. XIII, no. 197.
66. J. Jankowski, *Nasser's Egypt*, p. 114.
67. Telegram from embassy in Cairo to State Department, 10 February 1958, FRUS 1958-1960, vol. XIII, no. 195. Redacted extracts suggest that Hare may have been advocating covert action, implied by his distinction between 'what we do and what we say'.
68. JIC memorandum (58) 25, 'The implications of the United Arab Republic and the Arab Union', 30 April 1958, TNA, CAB 158/32.
69. SNIE 30-58, 'Prospects and consequences of Arab unity moves', 20 February 1958, FOIA Reading Room.
70. JIC memorandum (58) 25, 'The implications of the United Arab Republic and the Arab Union', 30 April 1958, TNA, CAB 158/32.
71. SNIE 30-58, 'Prospects and consequences of Arab unity moves', 20 February 1958, FOIA Reading Room.
72. Ibid.
73. JIC memorandum (58) 25, 'The implications of the United Arab Republic and the Arab Union', 30 April 1958, TNA, CAB 158/32.
74. Ibid.
75. SNIE 30-58, 'Prospects and consequences of Arab unity moves', 20 February 1958, FOIA Reading Room.
76. JIC memorandum (58) 25, 'The implications of the United Arab Republic and the Arab Union', 30 April 1958, TNA, CAB 158/32.

3 Revolution in Iraq

The victory of the national revolution in Iraq cannot fail – in a profound manner – to disrupt the control of imperialism over all of the Middle East.

Pravda, 1958[1]

The real authority behind the Government of Iraq was being exercised by Nasser, and behind Nasser by the USSR.

John Foster Dulles, 1958[2]

On the 14 July 1958, a brigade of Iraqi army officers marched into Baghdad and declared the end of the Hashemite monarchy established by the British in 1921. Leading members of the royal family were brutally murdered in the courtyard of the opulent Rihab palace. Prime Minister Nuri al-Said escaped disguised as a woman, but was given away by the fact that he was wearing men's shoes; he was captured and shot the next day.[3] Iraq's first republic was established under the leadership of a young and zealous nationalist, General Abdul Karim Qasim. The revolution in Iraq seemed yet another exemplification of the Arab nationalist fervour spreading through the Middle East and destroyed all fledgling hopes for the existence of a conservative counterweight to Nasser. Policy-makers were so alarmed by events in Iraq that on the 15 July 1958, both the British and US governments deployed Marines and paratroopers to bolster pro-Western regimes in Lebanon and Jordan. Ultimately, the Iraqi revolt would transform the basis of the Anglo-American relationship with Nasser.[4]

Most scholars writing about this seminal event have suggested that Western observers fundamentally misunderstood the revolutionary situation in Iraq.[5] Hitherto neglected intelligence documents allows a fresh look at the nature of this 'failure', revealing that analysts were indeed aware of the pressures on the Iraqi monarchy. A detailed examination of the intelligence reports and in-house post-mortems suggest that this was more of a tactical failure than a strategic one.[6] Perceptions of Egyptian influence were also fairly nuanced (after initial panic), noting the similarities in the socio-economic problems in Iraq driving change but also the limitations of Nasser's ability to dictate events in the newly founded republic.

Far from being a Nasserist stooge, General Qasim proved to be a force of nature in his own right. He quickly demonstrated his desire to resist local Nasserists such as Abd al-Salam Arif, utilising the support of the Iraqi Communist party (ICP). The JIC feared the prospect of both a Communist and a Nasserist Iraq but conceded that the latter would be the lesser of two evils. In contrast to their American counterparts, British policy-makers actively (if ambivalently) courted the Iraqi regime until 1960; exploring assessments of General Qasim may suggest why. Increasingly negative perceptions of Qasim echoed a plethora of stereotypes about the deluded Arab 'Other'. At the same time, the trajectory of post-revolutionary Iraq saw a redefining of Nasser's role in the region. The Egyptian President came to be embraced, belatedly and not entirely wholeheartedly by the JIC, as a moderate alternative to the increasingly irrational and erratic Qasim, as well as a bulwark against Communism. In fact, the JIC's pertinent analysis of the ICP in Iraq clearly established the limitations of Communist presence in Iraq, concluding that contrary to the fears of policy-makers, the ICP were probably being restrained rather than encouraged by the Soviet Union. Overall this was a fairly accurate reading of events.

* * *

Strategic Understanding

In 1953, an American intelligence report exploring 'Prospects for the Future' in Iraq presented a prophetic prediction. British decline there was 'destined to be a continuing trend'. The British had failed to cultivate widespread support, depending on 'a narrow segment of Iraqi society', and relying for political influence on a 'group of now ageing leaders' and Nuri's 'ruthlessness' in suppressing oppo-sition.[7] This combination presented:

> Little respectable alternative for politically active young Iraqis, who are driven to extremist groups ... When the ageing Nuri passes, power is likely to fall to a generation whose whole political outlook has been conditioned by the anti-British struggle and whose political life has expressed itself only in negative terms of opposition with-out ever facing the necessities of forming positive and viable policy. British attempts to secure 'short-term internal stability' is serving to harden the attitude of those who will one day be the new ruling group and to make them more suspicious, illogical and intransigent.[8]

The report effectively identified the key issues which would con-tribute to upheaval in Iraq some five years later: lack of popular support, the elite's alienation from the impoverished masses, and the expectations generated by social change. Moreover, the dearth of experienced politicians practicing constructive politics fore-shadowed later criticisms of the Iraqi body politic.

The following year, the JIC undertook a similar assessment, agreeing that Iraq was a 'fertile ground for agitation'. With con-siderable understatement, however, the Committee described the narrow concentration of wealth as an 'unsatisfactory feature'.[9] The British ambassador to Iraq at the time, Sir John Troutbeck, was an experienced Arabist who had served in Cairo for many years prior to his posting in Baghdad.[10] He was sure that the eco-nomic problems of Iraq would eventually provoke revolution.[11] Some analysis at the time clearly presaged the conclusions of later scholars that the social and economic conditions that emerged from the British mandate and Hashemite monarchy created 'such severe social tensions as to make the revolution of 1958 almost inevitable'.[12]

In the more immediate period before the revolution, both the JIC and the CIA recognised the impact that Suez and the fervent nationalism it had nurtured might have on Iraq. In 1957, the JIC noted that the Suez crisis had 'shaken' the position of the monar-chy and Iraqi Prime Minister Nuri Pasha. However, they attrib-uted the turmoil to the Kremlin, citing 'some indications that the Soviet Union will now make determined attempts to secure the removal of Nuri from the Government of Iraq as he is the principal Arab supporter of the Western connection and the Baghdad Pact'.[13] The British ambassador similarly warned that the Suez episode had 'imperilled the continued existence of the regime and the monarchy'.[14]

The CIA agreed that the situation in Iraq was precarious. Despite the Iraqi government's extensive economic assets, the opponents to Nuri's regime were particularly susceptible to the emotional appeal of Nasser as a 'champion of Arab nationalism directed against Israel and "the imperialists"'. Whilst Nuri was widely regarded as a cunning politician, the Agency conceded that he found it 'difficult to show the advantages of Iraq's policies in a way which has equivalent appeal'.[15] The American ambassador concurred just months before the revolution that 'popular dislike for present regime is sufficiently strong so that it is hard for it to do anything which will incur public approval rather than suspicion'.[16]

Postmortems conducted on both sides of the Atlantic confirmed that popular discontent with the monarchical regime was well known. However, it was felt that the lack of a popular base was 'characteristic of Arab governments'.[17]

> There was also general awareness that public resentment and tension had risen somewhat in the aftermath of a bitter and sustained propaganda campaign directed from the U.A.R. capitals at Jordan, Iraq and the Arab Union. In view of the former government's excellent security system and demonstrated capacity for containing such tensions, it was unanimously felt that these symptoms could be disregarded, unless some organized base developed in the armed forces, since there was no organized political vehicle of any importance. Such was indeed the case.[18]

A later postmortem by the JIC also revealed a good understanding of the internal institutional dynamics that contributed to the revolution. They suggested that evidence of dissatisfaction in the army was dismissed by Iraqi intelligence services because of the poor relations between the police and army. The police being 'more directly the creation of the original British administration' were notably less popular than the army which, 'as the principal repository of force and authority, the symbol of national unity and the main prop of the monarchy', lent it a 'special position in the state which to a great extent isolated it from criticism by outsiders'. This in turn led to poor coordination between the Police Director-ate General of Security and the Directorate of Military intelligence (DMI). The JIC in fact suspected that the DMI's performance, if not treasonable, 'may have been culpably passive, even by Arab standards'.[19]

Moreover, the nature of the operation, based on a round of assassinations, was 'one requiring few participants and hence more easily concealed'. The JIC argued that the 'restricted nature' of the conspiracy combined with the fact that 'dissatisfaction was preva-lent among officers' would have made 'effective action difficult' since 'the primary reason' for the collapse of the Iraqi regime 'lay not in organizational or administrative shortcomings' but rather in a more general 'failure to maintain confidence'. They perceptively recognized that security measures could not have 'alone sufficed to counteract the ebb of allegiance'.[20]

The American postmortem also suggested that initial reports had erred in assuming from 'circumstantial evidence' that 'the lines of this plot were laid outside Iraq itself among dissident expa-triates in Cairo and Damascus'.[21] The JIC also questioned whether Nasser had orchestrated the conspiracy though they were sure of his 'support' for the Iraqi revolutionaries.[22] As the following sec-tion explores, the relationship of the Iraqi revolution to Nasser's leadership was a key and immediate concern to analysts.

Extending the Arab Empire?

Initially, the Egyptian influence on the Iraqi revolution seemed a natural, inevitable assumption. In August 1958, the JIC wrote with frustration and perhaps incredulity that Nasser had 'set himself up as the focus of Arab aspirations towards unity and as the champion of the Arabs against Israeli and foreign influence'. They could not help but conclude that Nasser's 'brand of Arab nationalism is now in power in Egypt, Syria and Iraq'. More-over, the JIC feared that Nasser's revolutionary fervour could easily spread to Lebanon and Jordan, highlighting the use of

UAR radio propaganda to persuade the Arab masses to destroy their governments. The 'insidious techniques' of Radio Cairo included

> graphic reporting of imaginary disturbances and acts of violence which is intended as a signal for the audience to translate these imaginary events into reality; another technique is to exaggerate harmless demonstrations in order to stimulate more serious disorder ... the constant reiteration of the hypnotic theme of 'kill' and 'blood' has a dramatic effect, particularly when directed at the mob psychology of the Arab listening public.[23]

The violence of the Iraqi revolution seems clearly to have shaken analysts. Moreover, it reinforced their preconceptions of a politically immature Arab mob manipulated by Nasser's propaganda apparatus. Attached to the JIC analysis was an MI6 report identifying the production of 3,000 surplus Egyptian teachers, who apparently presented 'a grave threat to the future stability of the countries in which they are working and to the Middle East as a whole'.[24] There was a notable sense in British reports that the Nasser virus was spreading through the region.[25]

On the day of the coup, DCI Allen Dulles immediately addressed the issue of Egypt's role. Though an enthusiast of espionage and covert action, Dulles took a rather sanguine view of Egyptian participation and cautioned policy-makers not to overestimate Nasser's control. He conceded that the Iraqi nationalists were 'led by persons some of whom have been clearly identified with the pro-Egyptian campaign' but questioned, however, 'whether the methods and timing of the present coup in Iraq were dictated from Egypt'. Dulles felt that the 'timing seems a little out of gear with what might have been expected, as well as the manner and brutality of carrying out the coup'.[26]

Whilst Nasser was clearly an inspiration to the Iraqi revolution, Dulles almost intuitively dismissed the likelihood that it had been orchestrated from Cairo as part of a master plan to take over the region. He agreed that 'the rebels are in close relations with Nasser and are imitating the general pattern of his policy and outlook' but argued that despite Nasser's position as 'the acknowledged leader of Pan-Arab nationalism', his control over the movement was 'not

Figure 3.1 DCI Allen Dulles. US NARA National Archives 2.

absolute'. He warned, however, that 'further revolts on the Iraqi pattern could occur, either spontaneously or according to plan, at almost any time'. Nasser's role was reactive rather than as orchestrator but if such outbreaks were to occur, 'whether or not Nasser initiates them, he will support them'.[27]

The JIC took slightly longer to come to this conclusion. One month later they admitted that 'revolutionary movements of Nasserist character, supported by Egyptian intrigue, could come to a head without his direct initiative' and subsequently turn to him for support. They accepted that on such occasions he would 'be unable, as the self-appointed leader of Arab nationalism, to refuse his support'.[28] By October they were able to confirm that 'on present evidence the Egyptians did not control this conspiracy, though they probably supported it'.[29] The British ambassador in Baghdad, Michael Wright, was a veteran hand in the Middle East and argued from the outset that the revolution was indigenous rather than driven by the UAR.[30]

In contrast to the alarmist response of policy-makers, contemporary diplomatic and intelligence assessments in fact foreshadowed the conclusions of later scholars that, although 'the Egyptian revolution was an influence [in Iraq], as the fount of pan-Arab feeling and as a model of successful defiance of the West . . . it may be more nearly correct to speak of "convergent development" in closely similar situations'.[31] The distinction between Egyptian influence and control was thus established and perceptions of Nasser came to reflect the realisation that he had no detailed master plan for the takeover of the region, was not in full control and was reacting to events rather than initiating them.

At the same time the precedent of the Egyptian revolution formed an important analytical backdrop to analysts' perceptions of what, at first sight, seemed to be the Iraqi equivalent. The JIC sketched the 'background' in which 'the revolution in Iraq must be considered'. This included an Arab Nationalist Radical Programme consisting of: anti-imperialism, Israel as 'the child and spearhead of imperialism', social reform, Arab unity 'in some form' and neutrality.[32] They wrote,

> a social and political climate has been building up in Iraq for years which in many respects was comparable to that existing in Egypt prior to the Nasser coup of 1952. In Iraq the British occupation had already ended, although much British influence clearly remained, and the government were stronger than Farouk's regime. But enough material for dissatisfaction remained in the country, and full advantage was taken of this by Egyptian propaganda.[33]

The concentration of power in the hands of the few and a growing middle class, 'denied an effective voice in the affairs of their country' created an 'emotional climate' encouraging revolutionaries to 'believe that a successful coup would meet no organised opposition, and would indeed by sympathetically received'. Most importantly, the JIC felt, 'they were able to count on the support of the politically dissatisfied middle ranks of the Iraqi army'. As in Egypt, the coup was organised by a small number of Army officers 'acting with great efficiency and secrecy'. [34]

American analysis even posited the parallels between Qasim and Nasser's predecessor, Muhammad Neguib, as 'figurehead[s]' and estimated that the regime would follow the pattern of Egypt's new order: some measures of social reform, an improvement in governmental efficiency and the repression of opposition. Geopolitically, it was also 'likely to associate formally' with the UAR at an early stage, and assert 'a posture of nationalism, neutralism, and within this context, display a distinct willingness to establish diplomatic relations with the Bloc and to accept aid from it'.[35]

Even the preliminary pro-Western moves on the part of the Iraqi government were paralleled with similar Egyptian moves some years earlier. The JIC dismissed these as 'normal revolutionary tactics . . . it is not unusual for moderate elements to play the leading parts immediately after an insurrection, only to be replaced later by extremists' and warned 'it would be unwise to count on such an attitude continuing indefinitely'. They reminded policy-makers that the Egyptian republic had similarly 'started out with the idea of maintaining good relations with the West'.[36] However, the JIC also articulated a more constructive word of warning to Whitehall: 'it was chiefly their [Egyptian] failure to obtain arms from the West which caused them to seek friendship and support elsewhere. Rebuffs to the new regime in Iraq might have the same effect.'[37]

The parallels between Iraqi and Egyptian nationalism had some limits however. Analysts recognised that the Ba'ath mistrusted Nasser and were 'interested more in making use of his prestige than in accepting his leadership'. They understood that the Ba'ath aim of pan-Arabism was not to be 'under the domination of one country'. The new Iraqi leaders were 'assumed to be admirers of Nasser though not necessarily as yet controlled by him'.[38] There was a striking sense of inevitability to the analysis though – that Iraq would sooner or later fall under Nasser's spell. In fact, the memoirs of Qasim's deputy, Nasserist Abd al-Salam Arif, suggest that Nasser reacted cautiously to suggestions that Iraq accede to the UAR.[39] Although the JIC admitted that:

> there is no evidence to show that the Iraqis are, in any way, taking orders from Nasser . . . it seems certain that they are already sending in advisors of all sorts . . . a natural result of the similarities between the two regimes and of the relative inexperience of the new Iraqi Government but the speed with which the Egyptians are taking advantage of it is alarming.[40]

It was in this spirit of panic that Western interventions in Jordan and Lebanon were conceived to safeguard the TransArabian Pipeline Company against the Nasser fever that seemed to be sweeping through the region. In August 1958, the CIA perceptively warned that 'many makers of the Iraqi revolution may be unwilling to accept Cairo as the ultimate source of authority in Iraqi affairs and conflict between them and the Nasserites may develop'.[41]

The Communist Advance

The first concrete intimations that Nasser's authority in Iraq was in fact circumscribed emerged in the autumn when it became clear that Qasim was relying on the Communists to maintain power. The JIC had mistakenly suggested some months earlier that the Communists 'have been suppressed in Iraq for so long that they are poorly organised and ill-led' and predicted that 'their relations with the new regime can be expected to be on the same lines as in the U.A.R'.[42]

In November 1958, the arrest of the Qasim's deputy, Arif, was identified by the intelligence community to be a 'public slap at Nasser' and confirmed a battle of wills between the Communist and Nasserist factions in Iraq.[43] The American ambassador, John Jernegan, was an old hand in the Middle East with a reputation for 'balanced judgement' and 'a capacity for understanding complex problems'.[44] By January 1959 the Americans were emphasising the limits of Nasser's appeal in Iraq. They described pro-Nasser sentiment as 'largely a part of the reflex' against the Nuri regime suggesting that most Iraqis, 'even nationalists, wish to emulate Nasir rather than to join him'. Nor was it merely the West who feared Nasser's expansionist ambitions. Qasim himself was believed to have similar apprehensions:

> The net result of these early pro-union pressures was, therefore, to tie Qasim even more closely to the (far left) National Democrats and their communist allies who alone offered organised support for his personal position. Of these, the Communists, with better organisation, practiced technique and predetermined goals, are quickly gaining the upper hand.[45]

Drawing once more on Orientalist stereotypes, an American diplomatic report noted that the Communist Arabs 'cannot fit the
molds which have become the clichés to describe Arabs'. Unlike
their non-Communist counterparts, these Arabs were 'not lazy,
not lacking in ability to co-operate, co-ordinate and they obviously are willing to follow directions'.[46] Affiliation with the Soviet
Union had apparently diluted the 'Arabness' of Iraqi Communists.

Qasim, on the other hand, while not a Communist was, like
other inexperienced Arab politicians, 'politically naïve'. He had
allowed the Communists 'various strong positions in government'
and control over propaganda in an attempt to resist Iraqi nationalist demands to unify with the UAR. American Secretary of State
Dulles was informed that 'Communist infiltration probably has
not yet got out of control' but that 'the point of no return may be
reached in a few months should the Qasim regime continue on its
present course'.[47] It was not an overly alarmist analysis but one
which certainly reflected the primacy of the Communist concern
to American policy-makers.

Eisenhower once remarked that choosing between Nasser and
Qasim was 'like choosing between two mobsters – John Dillinger
and Al Capone'.[48] To the JIC, both a Communist or Nasserist Iraq
was a worrying prospect. The former would give the Soviet Union
a foothold in the Persian Gulf, outflanking NATO and splitting the
Baghdad Pact area. The Committee felt that the gradual nature of
the Communist advance would make it 'difficult for any outside
power to recognise the point of no return and decide on direct
intervention, whether political or military'. On the other hand a
Nasserite Iraq would 'tremendously' enhance Nasser's 'prestige'
which alongside threatening Kuwait, Jordan, Israel and Iran, could
endanger oil supplies. If forced to choose between the two the JIC
conceded like their American counterparts, that Nasser would be
the lesser of two evils: 'The establishment of a Communist regime
in Iraq, which would be more likely to come about gradually than
otherwise, would have much more serious consequences for the
West than that of a pro-Nasser regime.'[49]

For the moment, however, the JIC suggested an alternative: that
Qasim might himself emerge to be a strong leader in his own right
capable of managing both the Nasserist and Communist factions.

They thus advised that his request for British arms be positively considered.[50] In February 1959, a SNIE reflected on the reasons for, and likely evolution of, the British position:

> Continuing British hostility to Nasser has prompted the U.K. to hope that Kassim might provide a feasible alternative between a Nasser-dominated and a Communist-dominated regime in Iraq and an effective rival to Nasser for influence in the Arab world at large. The U.K. has been the more inclined to indulge in these hopes because it has received somewhat better treatment from the Kassim regime than has the U.S. There are now indications that at some levels and in some parts of the British Government it has been concluded that these are futile hopes. Further rapid consolidation of leftist forces in Iraq would probably increase U.K. sentiment in favor of a Nasser effort to stop the Iraqi Communists.[51]

Revealing several 'Orientalist' stereotypes explored earlier, assessments of General Qasim gradually evolved from the image of a well-intentioned (if naive) nationalist to a deluded and erratic psychopath.

Assessments of Qasim

Qasim's legacy remains highly contested in Iraq to this day. To many Iraqis he is seen as Iraq's first nationalist leader whose popularity was testified by the media spectacle his enemies displayed upon assassinating him in 1963: presenting his bullet-ridden corpse on national television in order to prove to his followers that he was in fact dead.[52] The British intelligence community initially took a favourable outlook on Qasim. In the immediate aftermath of the revolution the JIC's short biographical sketch described him as: 'Generally interested in Army welfare and extremely popular. Very religious. Sincere and upright idealist but with distinctly fanatical leanings.'[53] Analysts quickly observed 'government changes' which indicated 'a move away from the U.A.R. though not necessarily closer to the Soviet Union'. They saw Qasim as trying to 'steer a middle course between the pro-U.A.R. factions and pro-communist factions'. British analysts expressed hope that this was a man with whom business could be done: 'We do not expect Iraq's relations with the West to deteriorate sharply; indeed there are some reasons for hoping that they may even improve slightly.'[54]

In July 1959, brutal suppressions of Communists in Kirkurk seemed to demonstrate Qasim's 'increased determination and ability to stand up to Communist and other pressure'. The JIC maintained that he was 'increasingly emerging as a factor in his own right'. They were convinced that the 'frequent assertion of his desire to be above parties and to lead Iraq in a policy of neutrality is sincere'.[55]

The American opinion of Qasim was considerably less positive.[56] Reflecting on the Iraqi leader in a later interview Ambassador Jernegan recalled him as 'polite . . . very reserved, basically a little bit shy and a little bit mentally unbalanced I think'.[57] Assessments at the time were more explicitly critical, drawing on the plethora of negative stereotypes associated with the 'Arab national character'. Qasim was a 'man of limited intelligence and neurotic tendencies'. Failing to fulfil the demands of leadership he was 'unable to either make or delegate essential decisions'. Analysts judged that he showed 'little positive leadership' and had 'lost the respect of many of his governmental colleagues, many of whom would resign if allowed to do so'. Moreover, he was unable to 'generate popular enthusiasm for his personal leadership'. One scathing American assessment concluded that 'the poor performance of the entire revolutionary regime – indecisiveness, economic stagnation and bureaucratic chaos, all reaching the point of anarchy' had caused universal 'dissatisfaction and loss of confidence' among the Iraqi people.[58]

The CIA deliberated further on the 'enigma' that was Qasim. Analysts rejected the thesis that he was a Communist 'moving deliberately to advance Soviet control of Iraq'. Rather they explained his behaviour with reference to 'evidence that he is a neurotic and unstable individual . . . lacking in qualities of decisiveness and leadership'. The CIA explained that he feared for his position in the regime and had 'probably been genuinely concerned about the dangers of U.A.R. and U.S. interference in Iraq'. Nor did it help that the Iraqi Communists 'assiduously exploited' Qasim's fears and 'need for support and assurance'.[59] The Agency suggested that the sort of figure needed to counter Communist influence was 'an individual leader more dynamic, assured and competent than Qasim'. He had to be 'sufficiently colourful to command popular allegiance'. Analysts judged that this 'aura of ready-made heroism unimpeded by close relations with the former regime is most likely to be found in the Army'.[60] The underlying if unspoken image of Nasser embedded in this description is perhaps not insignificant.

By the autumn of 1959 there was a greater convergence of opinion between British and American intelligence assessments. In September, the new British ambassador in Iraq, Humphrey Trevelyan, took a less sympathetic view of Qasim and was reporting to Whitehall the 'inconsistency and illogicality, the black rages, the ruthlessness, the naiveté and all the other curious assortment of qualities which make up this extraordinary and not very attractive character'.[61] In October 1959, a group of the Ba'ath party including a young Saddam Hussein made an attempt on Qasim's life. It is claimed that during this ambush, Saddam started shooting prematurely, which ruined the whole operation. Although Qasim's chauffeur was killed, and Qasim was hit in the arm and shoulder, he survived.[62] This event put the Iraqi leader's popularity and sanity into even more serious question. In December, the CIA reflected on the 'crisis of leadership' that followed the unsuccessful attack on Qasim. Analysts wrote that his 'messianic tendencies have apparently been reinforced by his recent near martyrdom'.[63] American ambassador Jernegan recalls that Qasim put the car in which he had been riding with all its bullet holes on a platform outside his headquarters at the Iraqi Ministry of Defence. 'In his office, he had a showcase set up with the bloody clothes, the ones he had been wearing at the time he was shot . . . All visitors were carefully shown this case.'[64]

By 1960, even the JIC could not deny that 'recently there has been more general criticism of Qasim than ever before'. The Committee warned that he was 'increasingly dependent on the Communists for the maintenance of his position although he is no doubt aware of the danger of leaning on them'.[65] In November 1960, the CIA concluded that the regime's 'lack of political dynamism, Qasim's intermittent reliance on the Communists and his failure to make a convincing show of social and economic progress will sooner or later lead to his removal, most likely by nationalist minded army officers', although due to the ineffective nature of opposition they predicted that he would 'remain for the next year'.[66]

American analysts could not help but compare Qasim unfavourably with his rival Nasser. Unlike the Egyptian nationalist, 'Qasim does not appear committed to any particular political system or philosophy and has failed to provide vigorous leadership or to dramatise a program in the way that Nasser has done in Egypt.' The combination of Qasim's 'propensity for ignoring advisers', 'poor grasp of the complexities of government' and 'scant appreciation of economic factors' portended a poor chance of the regime developing a momentum that would allay discontent.[67]

1961 was an eventful year for the Iraqi republic. It saw yet another attempt on Qasim's life, a major split in the Ba'ath party and the collapse of the UAR. The result was a series of erratic and reckless acts that gave rise to 'serious doubts about Qasim's sanity'.[68] Most worryingly, in June 1961, Qasim declared his intention to annex Kuwait. The announcement prompted a British intervention code-named 'Operation Vantage' to defend the newly independent state from Iraqi machinations and protect the flow of oil.

It was enough to turn British official thinking against Qasim once and for all. Even before the Kuwaiti crisis, the JIC painted the picture of a delusional autocrat who had failed both to realize any political or economic reform, and to consolidate a popular following:

> Antagonism to Qasim has become personal and irrational and he is even reproached for things that are in fact not true, such as being the tool of British imperialism. In character, he is brave and capable of cunning, ruthlessness and cruelty. But he is easily susceptible to flattery and often indecisive. He is easily influenced by the last man in. He deludes himself that he has the affection of the mass of Iraqis of goodwill, and that he has a divine mission to lead.[69]

The Committee thus came to share with American analysts what appears to have become a genuine revulsion for Qasim's delusions and revolutionary inefficiency, consolidated by the Kuwaiti crisis, the outbreak of war in the Kurdish region of Iraq and Qasim's nationalisations of Iraqi oil. This was shortly followed by the expulsion of American ambassador Jernegan from Baghdad, despite his considerable efforts to win the trust of Qasim. In June 1962, Jernegan complained to the Iraqi foreign minister, Hashim Jawad, about this most recent insult, and Jawad 'admitted that there was a tendency to go to extremes in Arab countries but asked for understanding on grounds of their political immaturity'.[70] It is notable that Iraqi diplomats themselves advanced the idea of an inferior political culture in order to excuse Qasim's behaviour.

Analysts soon suggested that it was only a matter of time before Qasim would be successfully targeted by an assassin. By 1962, the Americans conceded that Qasim had 'proved more durable than appeared likely a few years ago' but reiterated that 'his position still depends more on the ineffectiveness and mutual antagonisms of his opponents than his own strength'. The wrote that 'plotting is endemic in military circles and assassination is an ever-present possibility'.[71] Analysts observed that 'Qasim is now disliked, hated and privately ridiculed by almost all sections of the Iraqi public including apparently, growing segments of the army.' They attributed discontent in the army to the strains of the Kurdish insurgency and cited an intelligence note that a new Ba'athist attempt to overthrow Qasim was planned for April or May.[72] Indeed in February 1963, a successful coup assassinated Qasim and brought the Ba'ath party to power for the first time in Iraq.

Redefining Nasser's Regional Role

As Qasim increasingly came to be viewed with undisguised contempt by the West, the potential for Nasser to act as the anti-Communist bastion in the region came to dominate American analysis, followed more reluctantly by the JIC. Whilst the latter had emphasised Nasser's role as largely *responsible* for the Communist advance in Iraq, the American intelligence apparatus was much more inclined to see the benefit which might result from having Nasser fight Communism. The CIA suggested that Nasser would 'almost certainly continue to work assiduously to develop and exploit every possible lead to a counterrevolution in Iraq'. Moreover, Nasser had both practical and symbolic 'resources at his disposal. In addition to his own network of agents and friends, he has the authority and influence that stem from his widespread acceptance as a successful leader of Arab nationalism.'[73]

In March 1959, a group of nationalists in the northern city of Mosul began plotting to overthrow Qasim. With Egyptian support, and most likely that of the US administration, the Mosul revolt was the closest Nasser came to eliminating his Iraqi rival.[74] Qasim defeated the Nasser-inspired coup with the help of his Communist allies who rallied their supporters to the streets. The failed Mosul revolt was arguably Nasser's greatest setback thus far. As one scholar puts it, 'never again would he be as close to dominating the Middle East'.[75]

Analysts clearly recognised the significance of this event at the time. DCI Allen Dulles publicly declared Iraq as the 'the most dangerous spot in the world' following the Communist victory in Iraq's second largest city.[76] American ambassador Jernegan described the

> unanimous and savage attack on [the] U.A.R. and Nasser who six short months ago was held by Iraqi people in equal if not greater esteem than Qassim. Today Nasser is a 'Fascist dog' and 'agent of imperialism'. Even taking into account acknowledged Arab volatility and ability [to] change sides almost overnight, this re-moulding of Iraqi public opinion has been masterfully managed by Communists, whose task [has] been made easier by clumsy overconfidence of Nasser's attempts to unseat Qassim . . . Nasser no longer appears to have what it takes to reverse tide of events in Iraq.[77]

The JIC also deduced that the failed Mosul revolt had undermined the moderate forces opposed to Communism. The Committee described these Iraqi groups as 'disorganised and afraid of being accused of being pro-U.A.R'. They concluded that the chance of a pro-UAR coup was now 'much less' and that Nasser's ability to influence internal developments in Iraq was 'greatly reduced'.[78]

For the JIC, the image of a weakened Nasser became strongly associated with the prospect of a more moderate leader. They observed that the 'recent noticeable reduction in the violence of his attacks on Qasim and his surprisingly mild reaction to the news of the United Kingdom decision to offer arms to Qasim' indicated a more pragmatic approach on Nasser's part. They suggested that he 'may have been converted to the view that Qasim is the best, if not the only, defence against the establishment of a Communist regime in Iraq' and perhaps even recognised that 'abusing Qasim was only likely to drive him further into Communist arms'.[79]

Signs that Nasser was taking a stance on Qasim more akin to the British view seemed to make the Egyptian leader more palatable to the JIC. Contrastingly, in the eyes of American analysts, the mere presence of Qasim seems to have rendered Nasser a comparative moderate. Surveying the main currents in the Arab world, the CIA asserted: 'Nasser once considered the most radical advocate of social change, now appears a moderate reformer in comparison to certain elements in Iraq.'[80]

By 1960, Britain was following the lead of its American ally and was working to re-engage Nasser diplomatically. It was a slow and fraught process that bore fruit with the resumption of full diplomatic relations in January 1961. Yet it is notable that while policymakers in Britain were considering a more conciliatory attitude towards Nasser, intelligence reports reveal the JIC's reluctance to accept the argument that Nasser was a leader with whom business could be done.[81] In June 1959, the Committee was sceptical that an Egyptian rapprochement with the British government could be 'any more than tactical'. Whilst noting that 'advantage may accrue to the West' from Nasser's changing attitude to Communist activities in the Middle East, the JIC maintained that 'his basic aims will remain hostile to Western interests'.[82] Moreover, as far as Nasser's broader goals were concerned, the Committee insisted that:

> We do not think that the blows which Nasser's prestige has suffered from the course of events in revolutionary Iraq have caused him to revise his aspirations to the effective control of the Arab world: on the contrary, his hysterical reactions to these events suggest that he regards this as a situation where the leadership of the Arab world may be at stake. As suggested above, we think Nasser may have revised his immediate tactics and may have decided to work for the destruction of the Communist position in Iraq and to postpone further efforts to unseat Qasim until the Communist snake can be scotched.[83]

Their analysis painted a picture of Nasser distracted by the Iraq problem (and by extension Syria) so that his machinations abroad might take a temporary back seat. They conceded that 'Nasser does not appear to want a unitary Arab state but will seek by propaganda, intrigue and subversion to reach a position' that would allow him to 'decisively influence the policies of other Arab States'. Nasser, they felt, was now taking a more careful approach; he would not hesitate to organise subversive coups 'if they seem assured of success' but he would also prefer to let circumstances evolve more gradually in his favour.[84]

These arguments presaged the conclusions of later scholars that it was Nasser's experience in Iraq that 'shattered the psychological impetus to unity'.[85] Ambassador Hare made the interesting distinction between 'Nasser in phases of anticipation as contrasted with realisation'. He suggested that in anticipation Nasser was 'like a man who comes into a restaurant and boisterously orders everything on the menu'. When the promise of the meal was realised, however, and 'served', the man consumed with 'moderation'. In Hare's opinion, Nasser was 'an opportunist, but with principles, if not especially apparent scruples'.[86] By mid-1959 the image of a pragmatic opportunist with more limited goals was slowly coming to replace the 'Hitler on the Nile' narrative of the previous year.

In February 1960, the JIC described an image of Nasser more concretely in decline. His regional role was now '*governed* by developments in Syria and Iraq'. The language here is markedly contrasted with the triumphant and all-powerful Nasser of 1958:

> He will *endeavour* to strengthen further the ties which join Syria and Egypt and to *prevent Syrian discontent from reaching unmanageable proportions*. He will also do *what he can* to prevent his supporters in Iraq *losing heart* and, *if opportunity offers, will try* to extend his influence there. *Nasser is at present unable to act effectively* against Iraq; he is on the other hand suspicious of Qasim's intentions and provoked by the latter's recent statements about the 'liberation of Syria'.[87]

Nasser's machinations were now being described in limited, and aspirational rather than actual, terms. Alongside this more chastened depiction of Nasser, there was a strong association of the nationalist with 'stability' occasioned both by his troubles in Iraq and Syria, and no doubt also his ambitious plans for domestic reform.[88]

From a foreign policy perspective, one of the most important indications of Nasser's newfound moderation was a visibly redefined relationship with the Soviet Union. As the JIC noted, 'the apparent progress of Iraq towards becoming a communist controlled state has been watched with alarm throughout the Middle East'. The Committee observed with some surprise that Nasser had 'reacted very sharply and was now more outspoken against the methods of international communism and the dangers of communist imperialism than would have seemed possible even a few months ago'. They recognised that this was partly to protect his leadership of the Arab world but also, they wrote, stemmed from a 'genuine desire' to resist the spread of Communist influence.[89]

The Americans were less guarded about Nasser's rift with the Soviets. They saw it as 'a move to reaffirm – for the first time to the U.S.S.R. – the political and systemic neutrality of the Arab world'.[90] In a rather patronising analysis the intelligence community posited their hope that 'in the longer run, the term "positive neutralism" may transcend its purely political-nationalist-cold war connotations and come to encompass – the ideological sphere as well, marking a trend away from Arab parochialism'. According to this somewhat triumphalist reading, 'the anti-communist campaign represents in some respects the first beginnings in this field, for implicit and explicit in it is a recognition of the fact that communism is ideologically and not merely politically incompatible with the socio-political aspiration of Arab nationalism'. The analysis went on:

> This in itself may be a sign of *increasing Arab self-confidence and a reflection of Arab political fulfilment*. Thus, it is possible that the future Arab dialogue with the outside world may *begin* to encompass the larger dimensions of society and culture. The point should not be overdone, for the Arabs are still dominated by a sense of political grievance and inferiority. But the point deserves making because the current campaign against communism in the Arab world has never before, in an actively political sense, focussed so squarely on the issue.[91]

With similar condescension, Hare explained Nasser's hostility towards the Communists as the 'typical evolution of his somewhat primitive but nevertheless keen mind which reaches conclusions more by trial and error than by abstract deduction'. Underestimating Nasser's long-standing commitment to non-alignment, he suggested that 'more troubles obviously lie ahead but the trend of events would seem to be toward a point where neutralism which has been largely a policy of words in past will become more nearly one of fact in future'.[92] This idea that only by repudiating Communism could Arab nationalism prove itself mature enough, indeed worthy, to be taken seriously and engaged internationally reveals the patronising Orientalism which all too often shone through analysis of the Arab world. It also reflects the more predictable obsession with Communism that often marked American perceptions of the region.

Other observations by the American ambassador showed more self-reflection and understanding of the nature and implications of Nasser's neutralism. Hare wrote: 'the initial, if pardonable mistake which we made in evaluating the regime here was to judge its position according to unrealistic ideal of full co-operation with West'. He posited that the true guide should always have been the maintenance of 'true neutrality'. He warned consumers in Washington that 'there is always danger that as pendulum moves towards us we may subconsciously move point of judgement with it'.[93]

By 1960 British diplomats agreed that Nasser 'aimed to exclude outside influences from the area, both Western and Sino-Soviet influence, except so far as their financial, technical or psychological assistance may advance his objectives'. As a result, 'in that he also wishes to stem the advance of both Communism and Sino-Soviet influence in the Islamic world and in Africa', they conceded that there was an 'underlying community of interest, however well concealed, between Nasser and the Western powers'.[94] Assessments of the Iraqi Communist Party (ICP) played a key role in this tentative reassessment of Nasser's potential to be an ally of the West.

Assessments of the Iraqi Communist Party

The Iraqi Communist Party was founded in 1934 by Yusuf Salman Yusuf. Rumour has it that Yusuf was introduced to Marxism by a Comintern agent posing as a tailor.[95] The Iraqi monarchy had

vociferously repressed the organisation, punishing the dissemi-
nation of Communist theory among the armed forces or police
with death. This hard-line approach only encouraged the nationalist revolutionaries to regard the Communists as martyrs in the
anti-imperialist cause. Little surprise then that Qasim was quick
to capitalise on the support and benefits offered by a powerful
and resilient ally in the political turmoil that ensued after the Iraqi
revolution.

The JIC made a persuasive case that the Iraqi Communists were
winning a victory by default. Whilst the Communists had played
no role in instigating the revolution, they had been able to take
advantage of the 'temporary eclipse of the established security,
police and intelligence networks' to provide Qasim with 'information of a security nature' as well as 'playing on Qasim's nerves'.
Marxist teaching provided a revolutionary programme whilst their
rivals 'lacked a clear cut policy'. The Committee argued that 'the
apparent strength of the party' was 'deceptive since a large portion
of the support which is given to the ICP derives from a widespread
discontent with local conditions and an enthusiasm for any policy
that appears to promise immediate and tangible benefit than for
Marxism as such'.[96]

Indeed, in the JIC's eyes, one of the most compelling reasons for
the ICP's strength had been the actions of Nasser himself:

> Nasser's ill-judged attacks on Qasim have provoked widespread fear
> in Iraq that he aims at incorporating it in the U.A.R. and the com-
> munists have cashed in on this by representing themselves as the
> champions of Iraqi nationalism and resistance to Nasser's presumed
> ambitions. Much of the support which they enjoy . . . is basically not
> communist but Iraqi nationalist and anti-Nasser . . . The more that
> Nasser and the right wing parties relax their pressure on Qasim, the
> more likely it is that a certain loosening of the cement binding all
> shades of opinion within the ICP will occur.[97]

Even when Nasser was not trying to make trouble he was still
overwhelmingly seen as a source of disruption by the JIC.

Any yet, despite imminent hysteria amongst policy-makers
who repeatedly contemplated military intervention in Iraq to save
it from the red scare, the JIC skilfully distinguished between the

'impression' of Communist control and the reality.[98] They reiterated that there was 'no evidence' that the ICP had 'inspired or had any hand in the direction of the revolution', but that after its success 'the Party, following the usual Communist practice, immediately identified itself with the revolution and even claimed to have taken part in some of the main moves'. They noted that this 'impression' of Communist control was further fostered by tactics such as acquiring advance knowledge of government intentions through infiltration of Qasim's entourage and publishing 'statements of "party policy" so worded as to give the impression that it was they who has inspired new trends in Government policy. By developing these tactics and fostering this impression of influence over Qasim, the party was able to call for public support and exert pressure on the Government for items on its own Party program'. Some ICP goals, such as withdrawal from the Baghdad Pact and army purges, were achieved but they noted that Qasim had also resisted others, such as the execution of traitors and ICP participation in government.[99]

The JIC seemed remarkably level-headed about the threat posed by the ICP, questioning both its internal strength and its backing from the Soviet Union: 'Leaving aside possible serious internal dissension at the top level, the Party as a whole has yet to prove itself to be a well-disciplined, well-knit body, capable of withstanding all forms of pressure and opposition from without.' The Committee noted that prolonged repression gave the party 'little opportunity overtly to practise communist theory on mass organisation and political activity'.[100] Moreover, anticipating the conclusions of future scholars, the JIC suggested that rather than encouraging the ICP, it was more likely that the Soviet Union was acting as a restraining influence.[101] They recognised that whilst the situation in Iraq 'must seem to offer an outstanding and unexpected opportunity to establish a foothold for Communism in an Arab country . . . of great geographical importance to Soviet policies . . . in our view, whatever the long term aim, it is unlikely at present that the Soviet Government will work for the early establishment of an openly Communist regime'.[102] American analysts agreed that 'it is possible that the pace of events in Iraq may be progressing faster than the U.S.S.R. might have wished'.[103]

There were several plausible reasons for Soviet reticence with regards to Iraq. Not only would an explicitly Communist regime decisively alienate Nasser and the rest of the Arab world, it would also embroil the Kremlin in a situation where it might be forced to defend Iraq militarily. Ultimately the JIC judged that the Soviet Union could not 'allow an openly Communist satellite regime to go under because of opposing internal forces or outside interference without great loss of face, whereas a nominally non-Communist government could in the last resort be left to its fate'.[104] The importance of 'face' was, apparently, not just the concern of the Arab world. Ultimately the JIC assessed that the Soviet Union did not perceive Iraq to be ripe for a Communist takeover although it would continue to aspire for 'the greatest degree of indirect control'.

The Committee acknowledged the limits of their knowledge regarding Iraqi–Soviet relations within the ICP. They stressed that there was no direct evidence to show how far the ICP was controlled from Moscow but believed that 'most of the steps taken to date to advance its position have been undertaken in a policy agreed in its broad outlines with the Soviet leaders', though these may have been 'carried out rather over-enthusiastically by the local party'. They were unsure whether the ICP would 'accept Soviet advice to be cautious if its own assessment was that it could seize power and survive'.[105]

Iraqi culture was seen to be a natural antidote to Soviet domination of Iraq. The JIC wrote that due to the 'strongly xenophobic nature of the Iraqi people', the ICP paid 'a minimum of overt lip service to Soviet ideology'. Although the Party was likely to consult Moscow before undertaking major political steps, they argued that Whitehall should account for 'the independent and self-sufficient nature of the Arab', signs that the ICP party leadership was already strained, and 'the fact that at best only a few of the ICP leaders can be regarded as "Moscow trained" and well-disciplined communists'. The real danger, in fact, was that 'the Iraqi communists might carry out a major policy switch without first consulting Moscow'. [106]

The JIC increasingly speculated that the Soviet Union might be restraining the ICP. The Committee suggested that Kremlin leaders would be 'cautious of doing anything which could be construed as direct Soviet interference' and would probably confine their activities to overt channels working through the local Communist parties. This detached approach would ensure that 'in the event of a miscarriage of any plans of Iraqi–Syrian union, Soviet prestige would not be directly involved'.[107] As the ICP indeed faced a series of reversals following the Kirkurk massacre of Communists in the summer of 1959, a JIC report in September suggested that the Soviet Union might have even welcomed the ICP's difficulties.[108]

By 1961, the Committee's assessment of the Soviet relationship with the ICP was more concrete. The JIC wrote that despite increases in official repression of the Communists, 'Soviet interests are probably better served by the Qasim regime than by any likely successor, and we *know* that Soviet influence with the Iraqi communists is in fact being exercised in favour of restraint'.[109] The Soviet Union 'apparently does not consider the Iraqi communists, none of whom is an outstanding figure, ready to assume power as yet'. Nonetheless, they retained the caveat that not all Iraqi Communists would 'agree with this view'.[110]

Whilst their assessment of the ICP and Soviet involvement proved right on the mark, the JIC do seem to have underestimated the Soviet investment in Nasser and the Kremlin's inclination to side with the Egyptian nationalist over Iraq. We now know that this was a key consideration in Moscow's restraint of the ICP. As Soviet archival research has revealed, 'more Soviet hopes were pinned on Nasser than on any other Third World leader outside south America'. Nasser received almost half of all Soviet aid to the Third World between 1954 and 1961.[111] He received a hero's welcome in the Soviet Union in 1958, photographed by Lenin's tomb.[112] The American assessment in October that year perceptively estimated that in the case of a 'showdown' over Iraq, the USSR would 'bow down' to Nasser's wishes.[113]

The JIC were less convinced of Soviet loyalty to Nasser. In May 1958 they wrote, 'it is not altogether clear how whole hearted is Soviet support for the U.A.R. in general', estimating that the Soviet leadership 'may be suspicious of Nasser's Middle Eastern ambitions'.[114] In 1959, sharp Egyptian–Soviet exchanges led the JIC to aver that 'the fundamental contradiction between the objectives of Moscow and President Nasser is coming into the open'.

Whilst the Soviet Union would 'continue the process of healing their rift with Nasser' through aid for the Aswan Dam etc., they estimated that 'if Nasser were to mount a new campaign against Qasim . . . the Soviet Union would be expected to support Qasim, even at the cost of Nasser's goodwill'.[115] In fact research into Iraqi police records shows that the Soviet Union held back the ICP precisely so as not to alienate Nasser.[116] It is possible that this faulty assessment may have partly reflected the JIC's own fairly negative outlook towards Nasser although the Americans also judged after Mosul that the Soviets might be prepared to accept an 'open break' with Nasser in exchange for control in Iraq.[117]

* * *

Although analysts failed to predict the Iraqi revolution, it was a tactical rather than a strategic failure. 'Strategic notice' of sorts existed, revising previous scholarly conclusions of a fundamental misunderstanding of pre-revolutionary Iraq. The revolution proved to be a critical turning point in assessments of Nasser; initial fears that Iraq was the next victim of Nasser's empire were quickly allayed as analysts questioned Nasser's control over, and blueprint for, revolution in Iraq. The prospect of Communist domination of Iraq came to replace fears of Nasser's ambitions and in the process analysts realised (though more slowly in Britain) that Nasser might prove an all too willing ally in the fight against Communism. Whilst the JIC had underestimated Nasser's anti-Communism, the Americans and, notably, British diplomats had long argued that Nasser was no Communist stooge. The initially positive assessments of Qasim reflected the JIC's hopes that a choice would not have to be made between a Nasserite or Communist Iraq, although they recognised that in the event of a takeover, the latter would present a more serious threat.

The Mosul campaign of 1959 consolidated the sense that perhaps Nasser was not an omnipotent 'Hitler on the Nile', that his anti-Communism reflected a newfound 'maturity' and 'moderation' upon which the basis of an alliance might be built. The JIC were more reluctant to come round to this point of view, perhaps because they never viewed the Iraqi Communist Party or Soviet intentions in Iraq with quite the same hysteria as their American counterparts. As the following chapter will demonstrate, Syrian secession would further reinforce the image of a Nasser in decline and yet perhaps more chastened and amenable to cooperation with the West as a result.

Notes

1. Cited in J. Romero, *The Iraqi Revolution of 1958: A Revolutionary Quest for Unity and Security* (Lanham, MD: University Press of America, 2011), p. 162.
2. John Foster Dulles in Memoradum of Discussion, 373rd Meeting of the NSC, 25 July 1958, in FRUS 1958-1960, vol XXII, no. 103.
3. G. Simons, *Iraq: From Sumer to Saddam* (London: Palgrave Macmillan, 2004), p. 218.
4. R. McNamara, *Britain, Nasser and the Balance of Power in the Middle East, 1952–1967: From the Egyptian Revolution to the Six Day War* (London: Frank Cass, 2003), p. 129. Initially it appeared as if Nasser's revolutionary fervour had absorbed the West's most important ally in the region. Iraq was pivotal to the West as a provider of both oil and air transport to the Far East. Subsequent Western interventions in Lebanon and Jordan were thus a direct reaction to the fear of a domino effect in the region.
5. See, for example, R. A. Fernea and W. R. Louis (eds), *The Iraqi Revolution of 1958: The Old Social Classes Revisited* (London: I. B. Tauris, 1991), Introduction, p. xvi. Other works have explored British Anglo-American policy towards revolutionary Iraq: R. Worrall, 'Coping with a coup d'etat: British policy towards post- revolutionary Iraq, 1958–1963', *British Contemporary History*, 21: 2, 2007; S. Blackwell, 'A desert squall: Anglo-American planning for intervention in Iraq, July 1958 – August 1959', *Middle Eastern Studies*, 5: 3, 1999.
6. D. Omand, 'Securing the state: a question of balance', Chatham House transcript, 8 June 2010. Available at <http://www.chathamhouse.org/sites/default/files/public/Meetings/Meeting%20Transcripts/080610davidomand.pdf> (last accessed 30 September 2016). Omand defines strategic notice as understanding the broad range of relevant factors and events to which policy-makers ought to pay attention.

7. Intelligence Report, 'The British position in Iraq', 21 May 1953, OSS/SDIRR The Middle East 1950-1961, Microfilm, Reel 3, SOAS Library: 'British interest in Iraq had been completely identified with the narrow segment of Iraqi society – wealthy feudal landowners and a few businessmen and professional politicians – who comprise the ruling group. This group, although it has dominated Iraqi political life since its inception, has never had broad popular support.'

8. Ibid.

9. JIC memorandum (54) 72, 'Political developments in the Middle East and their impact on Western interests', 11 November 1954, TNA, CAB 158/18: 'Where wealth is concentrated in the hands of a small ruling class the wealthy tend to interest themselves in the more obviously unattractive aspects of Western materialism. This tends to prejudice against the West those who hold the traditional views of the Moslem faith, as well as associating the West with those in the State most likely to be the targets of popular agitation.'

10. M. Cohen, *Strategy and Politics in the Middle East, 1954–1960: Defending the Northern Tier* (Chapel Hill, NC: University of North Carolina Press, 2004), p. 105.

11. W. R. Louis, 'The British and the origins of the revolution', in R. A. Fernea and W. R. Louis (eds), *The Iraqi Revolution of 1958: The Old Social Classes Revisited* (London: Tauris, 1991), p. 37.

12. M. Sluglett and P. Sluglett, 'The social classes and the origins of the revolution', in Fernea and Louis (eds), *The Iraqi Revolution of 1958*, p. 131: 'Much is made in the diplomatic reports of the political dangers arising from Nuri's apparent inability to carry out any kind of social, particularly agrarian reform.'

13. JIC memorandum (56) 133, 'Soviet penetration in the Middle East', 1 January 1957, TNA, CAB 158/36.

14. Memorandum from Ambassador Wright in Baghdad to FO, 'Iraq: annual review for 1956', 8 February 1957, TNA, FO 371/128038. Ambassador Wright clearly held Nuri in high regard. He described him as the 'father of development in Iraq' and praised his 'courage and steadfastness' in the face of the Suez embarrassment.

15. NIE 36.2-57, 'The outlook for Iraq', 4 June 1957, Declassified Document Reference System (hereafter DDRS). See also JIC memorandum (58) 102, 'Reasons for the failure of the Iraqi intelligence services to give warning of the revolution of July 14', 8 October 1958, TNA, CAB 158/34.

16. Telegram from Ambassador Gallman in Baghdad to State Department, 21 February 1958, FRUS 1958-1960, vol. XII, no. 99.

17. Memorandum from Glidden to Cumming, 'Intelligence indications of coup in Iraq', 16 July 1958, FRUS 1958-1960, vol. XII, no. 120.
18. Ibid.
19. JIC memorandum (58) 102, 'Reasons for the failure of the Iraqi intelligence services to give warning of the revolution of July 14', 8 October 1958, TNA, CAB 158/34.
20. JIC memorandum (58) 102, 'Reasons for the failure of the Iraqi intelligence services to give warning of the revolution of July 14', 8 October 1958, TNA, CAB 158/34.
21. Memorandum from Glidden to Cumming, 'Intelligence indications of coup in Iraq', 16 July 1958, FRUS 1958-1960, vol. XII, no. 120: 'important projected steps are known only to Nasir and a small group of intimates around him. Hence unless they [are] divulged by some member of his coterie, or until they become apparent, we are not likely to have much advance notice of important planned actions.'
22. JIC memorandum (58) 102, 'Reasons for the failure of the Iraqi Intelligence Services to give warning of the revolution of July 14', 8 October 1958, TNA, CAB 158/34.
23. JIC memorandum (58) 83, 'Lebanon and Jordan – infiltration and subversion by the United Arab Republic', 8 August 1958, TNA, CAB 158/33.
24. MI6 memorandum in Annex to JIC (58) 121, 'The subversive potential of Egyptian teachers in the Middle East and Africa', 29 December 1958, TNA, CAB 158/34.
25. Memorandum from Glidden to Cummings, 'Intelligence indications of coup in Iraq', 16 July 1958, FRUS 1958-1960, vol. XII, no. 120: 'For some time it has been evident that the drive for change by violent means in Middle Eastern countries was most likely to take effective form from intermediate officer grades in the armies. Especially since the Egyptian revolution, DRN has constantly directed the attention of all reporting agencies to the median officer group and the possibility of Egyptian manipulation of their known nationalist sentiments. This grade-range comprises several hundred officers; it is not surprising that contact could not be established with every one of them. The former Iraqi government maintained a very complete intelligence net within the Army itself which did not discern any questionable contacts on the part of Col. Qasim, even though the Iraqi government was itself aware (as were we) that Col. Qasim had been exposed to Syrian subversive efforts while stationed in Jordan in late 1956.'

26. Briefing notes by DCI Dulles, 14 July 1958, FRUS 1958-1960, vol. XII, no. 110.

27. Ibid.

28. JIC memorandum (58) 77, 'Nasser's probable policy and aims over the next six months', 1 August 1958, TNA, CAB 158/33[emphasis added].

29. JIC memorandum (58) 102, 'Reasons for the failure of the Iraqi intelligence services to give warning of the revolution of July 14', 8 October 1958, TNA, CAB 158/34.

30. Memorandum by Ambassador Wright in Iraq, 'The immediate out-look', 24 July 1958, TNA, FO 371/134201. Wright had also served in Sir Miles Lampson's Cairo embassy in the Second World War.

31. N. Daniel, 'Contemporary perceptions of the revolution', in Fernea and Louis (eds), *The Iraqi Revolution of 1958*, p. 26.

32. JIC memorandum (58) 76, 'The immediate outlook in Iraq', 5 August 1958, TNA, CAB 158/33.

33. Ibid.

34. Ibid: 'We still have little information about its preparation, and the existence of the plot was obviously quite unknown to the Iraq authorities until the last few hours when it was too late to counter it. We have no firm evidence that the U.A.R. were involved in the execution of the coup, although there is little doubt that they have been actively working for the overthrow of the Hashemite regime for over a year and it is quite possible that they helped plan the coup. It may be that they were not actually aware of the details and timing.'

35. Memorandum from the Director of Intelligence and Research (Cumming) to the Under Secretary of State (Herter), 'Intelligence note: the insurgent regime in Iraq', 17 July 1958, FRUS 1958-1960, vol. XII, no. 121: 'There is no common denominator among the governing group thus far identified except a common hostility to the former regime. Older members have long histories of political resistance: two were identified with the pro-Nazi, anti-British coup attempt of 1941. The younger members, both officer and civilian, are of the "young intellectual," nationalist-neutralist-reformist group of which Nasir is hero and prototype. They are superficially Western-ized and several have European or American educational experience. Several are earnest reformers whose political resistance represented real indignation at the graft, corruption and inefficiency of the old regime. They have leadership potential and some political integrity.'

36. JIC memorandum (58) 76, 'The immediate outlook in Iraq', 5 August 1958, TNA, CAB 158/33.

37. Ibid. The JIC also warned that whatever Western policy, it was 'possible that the new leaders, however moderate their intentions, may become prisoners of Iraqi public opinion, worked on by Nasser's propaganda. If this proves to be the case, they may be forced to adopt an increasingly hostile line in order to maintain themselves in power.'

38. JIC memorandum (58) 76, 'The immediate outlook in Iraq', 5 August 1958, TNA, CAB 158/33.

39. A. Alexander, *Nasser: His Life and Times* (Cairo: Cairo University Press, 2005), p. 114.

40. JIC memorandum (58) 76, 'The immediate outlook in Iraq', 5 August 1958, TNA, CAB 158/33.

41. SNIE 30-3-58, 'Arab nationalism as a factor in the Middle East situation', 12 August 1958, FOIA Reading Room.

42. JIC memorandum (58) 76, 'The immediate outlook in Iraq', 5 August 1958, TNA, CAB 158/33.

43. Memorandum from Director of Intelligence and Research (Cumming) to Secretary of State Dulles, 'Intelligence note: significance of the return to Iraq and arrest of Col. Arif', 5 November 1958, FRUS 1958-1960, vol. XII, no. 142. In September it looked as if Arif and his supporters had gained the upper hand when a squadron of UAR planes arrived at RAF base at Habbaniya. Qasim demoted Arif to ambassador to Germany and then upon his arrival in Iraq, arrested him.

44. Biographical sketch of J. D. Jernegan, in JFK Library, Country Files, Box: 117, Folder: Iraq 1961-1962.

45. Intelligence Report, 'Iraq: the crisis in leadership and the communist advance', 16 January 1959, OSS/SDIRR, The Middle East 1950-1961, Microfilm, Reel 3, SOAS Library.

46. R. Barrett, *The Greater Middle East and the Cold War: U.S. Foreign Policy under Eisenhower and Kennedy* (London: I. B. Tauris, 2007), p. 109.

47. Memorandum from the Director of Intelligence and Research (Cumming) to Secretary of State Dulles, 'Intelligence note: the communist threat in Iraq', 25 November 1958, FRUS 1958-1960, vol. XII, no. 144.

48. President Eisenhower cited in D. Ryan and P. Kiely, *America and Iraq: Policy-making, Intervention and Regional Politics* (New York: Routledge, 2009), p. 25.

49. JIC memorandum (58) 114, 'The possible consequences of the early collapse or overthrow of the government in Iraq', 5 December 1958, TNA, CAB 158/34. In early December British policy-makers received

information that Nasser-backed nationalist Rashid Ali was planning to seize power. They informed Qasim of the plot, which their American allies refrained from doing despite possessing the same information. Clearly contradicting the JIC's advice, McNamara concludes that British ministers 'considered that a communist controlled Iraq might be easier to deal with than a pro-Nasser regime'. McNamara, *Britain, Nasser and the Balance of Power,* p. 142.

50. JIC memorandum (58) 114, 'The possible consequences of the early collapse or overthrow of the government in Iraq', 5 December 1958, TNA, CAB 158/34.

51. SNIE 36.2-59, 'The communist threat to Iraq', 17 February 1959, FRUS 1958-1960, vol. XII, no. 161.

52. C. Tripp, *A History of Iraq* (Cambridge: Cambridge University Press, 2002), p. 170.

53. Appendix to JIC memorandum (58) 76, 'The immediate outlook in Iraq', 5 August 1958: 'Biographical notes on some of the main personalities in the Iraqi revolutionary administration', TNA, CAB 158/33.

54. Ibid.

55. JIC memorandum (59) 61, 'Possible trouble spots in the Middle East over the next six months', 7 August 1959, TNA, CAB 158/37.

56. Though the American analytic community agreed that Qasim was not an admirable figure, there was some disagreement on what the best course of action might be, with hardliners in the CIA and Department of Defense advocating American intervention and covert action against those in the State Department suggesting that Western intervention would simply exacerbate tensions within Iraq. This conflict is particularly well detailed in B. W. Honnicut, 'The end of the concessionary regime: oil and American power in Iraq, 1958–1972', unpublished PhD thesis, Stanford University, Stanford, CA, 2011, pp. 40–48.

57. Interview with John Jernegan, 12 March 1969. Available at <http://archive1.jfklibrary.org/JFKOH/Jernegan,%20John%20D/JFKOH-JDJ-01/JFKOH-JDJ-01-TR.pdf>, p. 5 (last accessed 1 March 2017).

58. Intelligence Report, 'Iraq: the crisis in leadership and the communist advance', 16 January 1959, OSS/SDIRR, The Middle East 1950-1961, Microfilm, Reel 3, SOAS Library [emphasis added].

59. SNIE 36.2-59, 'The communist threat to Iraq', 17 February 1959, FRUS 1958-1960, vol. XII, no. 161.

60. Intelligence Report, 'Iraq: the crisis in leadership and the communist advance', 16 January 1959, OSS/SDIRR, The Middle East 1950-1961, Microfilm, Reel 3, SOAS Library.

61. Memorandum from Ambassador Trevelyan to Stevens, 11 September 1959, TNA, FO 371/140922.
62. C. Coughlin, *Saddam: His Rise and Fall* (London: Harper Perennial, 2005), p. 30.
63. SNIE 36.2-5-59, 'Short term prospects for Iraq', 15 December 1959, FRUS 1958-1960, vol. XII, no. 210.
64. Interview with John Jernegan, 12 March 1969. Available at <http://archive1.jfklibrary.org/JFKOH/Jernegan,%20John%20D/JFKOH-JDJ-01/JFKOH-JDJ-01-TR.pdf>, p. 7 (last accessed 1 March 2017).
65. JIC memorandum (60) 12, 'Possible trouble spots in the Middle East over the next six months', 11 February 1960, TNA, CAB 158/38.
66. NIE 36.2-60, 'The outlook for Iraq', 1 November 1960, FRUS 1958-1960, vol. XII, no. 222.
67. Ibid.
68. Sluglett and Sluglett, 'The social classes and the origins of the revolution', in Fernea and Louis (eds), *The Iraqi Revolution of 1958*, p. 82. JIC assessments of the Kuwaiti crisis have been explored by Cradock, *Know Your Enemy*, pp. 202–5.
69. JIC memorandum (61) 10, 'Outlook for Iraq over the next twelve months', 15 March 1961, TNA, CAB 158/42: 'He appears to suffer from a lack of mental balance which makes his actions often unpredictable and gives many who meet him the impression that he is verging on madness . . . [He] lives and works in his office in the Ministry of Defence surrounded by a museum of relics of his attempted assassination, from which he believes he escaped by divine intervention. Since his assumption of power he has only twice left Baghdad, for short visits by air to military headquarters . . . It is in the economic sphere that the inefficiency of the Qasim regime is most manifest. Many experienced civil servants were dismissed in the early days of the regime and there was no one of equal calibre to replace them. At the same time the number of officials has increased. There has been a good deal of wasteful expenditure. Many of Iraq's excellent development schemes, some of the benefits of which would admittedly have been felt only in the long term, were disrupted by the new regime.'
70. Telegram from embassy in Baghdad to State Department, 2 June 1962, FRUS 1961-1963, vol. XVII, no. 286.
71. NIE 36.2-62, 'Iraq', 31 January 1962, FRUS 1961-1963, vol. XVII, no. 183.
72. Memorandum from Grant to McGhee, 3 May 1962, FRUS 1961-1963, vol. XVII, no. 262.

73. SNIE 36.2-59, 'The communist threat to Iraq', 17 February 1959, FRUS 1958-1960, vol. XII, no. 161: 'As Communist power increases in Iraq, non-Communist Iraqi groups – military and civilian – are likely to become increasingly conscious of this threat and ready to compromise with Nasser as the only effective source of help. In the right situation Nasser's propaganda machine could be used to exert a formidable influence upon the Iraqi people and army to turn them against the Kassim regime and their Communist allies.'

74. K. Osgood, 'Eisenhower and regime change in Iraq: the United States and the Iraqi Revolution of 1958', in D. Ryan and P. Kiely (eds), *America and Iraq: Policy-making, Intervention and Regional Politics* (Abingdon: Routledge, 2009), p. 20. Although the documentary record remains incomplete, Osgood concludes that: 'At the very least, the United States gave its tacit approval to the scheme. Knowing of the plot beforehand, the Eisenhower administration did nothing to thwart it and did not alert Qasim to the danger.'

75. McNamara, *Britain, Nasser and the Balance of Power*, p. 150.

76. Allen Dulles quoted in Dana Adams Schmidt, 'CIA head warns of danger in Iraq', *New York Times*, 29 April 1959.

77. Telegram from embassy in Baghdad to State Department, 26 March 1959, FRUS 1958-1960, vol. XII, no. 166: 'On top of all foregoing, very atmosphere of Baghdad almost inescapably forces foreign onlooker (especially American) to conclude that Iron Curtain descending. Many of our Embassy staff recurrently followed by security agents. Embassy office and residential telegrams continuously monitored . . . Embassy complaints on these and other matters are met with mixture of blandness and insolence familiar to anyone who has dealt with satellite officers since World War II.'

78. JIC memorandum (59) 50, 'A re-examination of the likely consequences of military intervention in Iraq', 8 June 1959, TNA, CAB 158/36.

79. JIC memorandum (59) 23, 'Nasser's achievements, aims and future policies', 11 June 1959, TNA, CAB 158/35.

80. NIE 30-59 'Main currents in the Arab world', 25 August 1959, FRUS 1958-1960, vol. XII, no. 71.

81. McNamara, *Britain, Nasser and the Balance of Power*, p. 153.

82. JIC memorandum (59) 23, 'Nasser's achievements, aims and future policies', 11 June 1959, TNA, CAB 158/35.

83. Ibid.

84. Ibid.

85. J. Devlin, *The Ba'ath Party: A History of its Origins to 1966* (Stanford, CA: Hoover Institution Press, 1976), p. 127.

86. Telegram from embassy in the United Arab Republic to State Department, 1 April 1959, FRUS 1958-1960, vol. XIII, no. 235. In another revealing analogy Hare compared the 'hue and cry' of Arab nationalism to: 'no longer existing servitudes in much same way that, according medical theory of "phantom limb", certain persons continue have illusion of suffering pain from previously amputated members'.

87. JIC memorandum (60) 12, 'Possible trouble spots in the Middle East over the next six months', 11 February 1960, TNA, CAB 158/38 [emphasis added].

88. Among the most impressive of these was the Aswan Dam, designed to end to the cycle of flood and drought of the Nile and bring electric power to Egypt's rural areas.

89. JIC memorandum (59) 50, 'A re-examination of the likely consequences of military intervention in Iraq', 8 June 1959, TNA, CAB 158/36.

90. Intelligence Report, 'Nasser and the pan-Arab conflict with communism', 2 March 1959, OSS/SDIRR, The Middle East 1950-1961, Microfilm, Reel 2, SOAS Library.

91. Ibid.

92. Telegram from UAR embassy to State Department, 19 September 1959, FRUS 1958-1960, vol. XIII, no. 244.

93. Telegram from UAR embassy to State Department, 1 April 1959, FRUS 1958-1960, vol. XIII, no. 235.

94. Memorandum from Beith in FO to various Chanceries, 12 May 1960, TNA, FO 371/150912. Ashton attributes the more pro-Nasser policy of the British government from May 1959 as motivated by the goal of protecting Kuwait. Indeed the Kuwaiti crisis was the first time that republican Egypt and Britain had cooperated over a major international crisis. N. J. Ashton, *Eisenhower, Macmillan and the Problem of Nasser: Anglo-American Relations and Arab Nationalism, 1955–1959* (London: Macmillan, 1996), p. 203.

95. T. Ismael, *The Rise and Fall of the Communist Party of Iraq* (Cambridge: Cambridge University Press, 2008), p. 20.

96. JIC memorandum (59) 42, 'The Iraqi Communist Party', 22 July 1959, TNA, CAB 158/36.

97. Ibid.

98. Ibid.

99. Ibid.

100. Ibid.
101. Sluglett and Sluglett, 'The social classes and the origins of the revolution', in Fernea and Louis (eds), *The Iraqi Revolution of 1958*, p. 69. Research into Iraqi police records explained Soviet restraint as the result of 'pressure that the Communist Party of the Soviet Union brought to bear upon the Iraqi Communist leadership' fearing that ties with Nasser would be at risk, and the Soviet policy of peaceful co-existence potentially damaged.
102. JIC memorandum (59) 44, 'Soviet policies in the Middle East over the next two years with particular reference to Iraq', 16 July 1959, TNA, CAB 158/36.
103. Intelligence Report, 'Current trends in Arab unity', 23 June 1959, OSS/SDIRR, The Middle East 1950-1961, Microfilm, Reel 1, SOAS Library.
104. JIC memorandum (59) 44, 'Soviet Policies in the Middle East over the next two years with particular reference to Iraq', 16 July 1959, TNA, CAB 158/36.
105. Ibid.
106. JIC memorandum (59) 42, 'The Iraqi Communist Party', 22 July 1959, TNA, CAB 158/36.
107. JIC memorandum (59) 44, 'Soviet policies in the Middle East over the next two years with particular reference to Iraq', 16 July 1959, TNA, CAB 158/36.
108. JIC memorandum (59) 71, 'Sino-Soviet bloc penetration of Iraq', 9 September 1959, TNA, CAB 158/38: 'The recent reverse which the Communists in Iraq have suffered as a result of stiffening attitude of Qasim and his government may not have been entirely unwelcome in Moscow ... It will have had the result of bringing to the fore those in the ICP who favour a gradualist long term policy. If the leaders of the ICP as a whole can be brought to accept the discipline necessary to carry out such a policy the Soviet government may prefer to play a more unobtrusive role, hoping thereby to avoid any accusation of interfering in the country's internal affairs.'
109. Such decisive language usually indicated that the intelligence was derived from Signals intelligence (SIGINT). See J. Craig, 'The Joint Intelligence Committee and British Intelligence assessment 1945–56', unpublished PhD thesis, Cambridge University, Cambridge, 2000, p. 227.
110. JIC memorandum (61) 10, 'Outlook for Iraq over the next twelve months', 15 March 1961, TNA, CAB 158/42.

111. C. Andrew and V. Mitrokhin, *The KGB and the World: Mitrokhin Archive II* (London: Penguin, 2006), p. 150.
112. Ibid. p. 149.
113. Intelligence Report, 'Soviet UAR differences and related developments in Syria and Iraq', 22 October 1958, OSS/SDIRR, The Middle East 1950-1961, Microfilm, Reel 2, SOAS Library.
114. JIC memorandum (58) 58, 'Likely Soviet reactions to U.K./U.S. military intervention in the Lebanon', 22 May 1958, TNA, CAB 158/32.
115. JIC memorandum (59) 61, 'Possible trouble spots in the Middle East over the next six months', 7 August 1959, TNA, CAB 158/37.
116. Sluglett and Sluglett, 'The social classes and the origins of the revolution', in Fernea and Louis (eds), *The Iraqi Revolution of 1958*, p. 69.
117. Intelligence Report, 'Soviet UAR differences and related developments in Syria and Iraq', 22 October 1958, OSS/SDIRR, The Middle East 1950-1961, Microfilm, Reel 2, SOAS Library.

4 Syrian Secession

Recent events may present us with the best opportunity since 1954 for a limited marriage of convenience with the guy who I think is still, and will remain, the Mister Big of the Arab world.[1]

Robert Komer, 1961

On the 29 September 1961, Nasser announced at a public rally that he would agree to the secession of Syria from the UAR. Admitting that maintaining the union would require the intervention of Egyptian troops, Nasser asserted that 'Arab blood would not be shed by Arab hands'.[2] Scholars would later observe that 'with the exception of the Six-Day War this was the greatest setback of Nasser's political career'.[3]

Political and intelligence assessments of the Syrian secession from the short-lived union have been largely neglected by historians.[4] In fact, analysts demonstrated a long-standing awareness of the difficulties Nasser would face in Syria, although this fell short of outright prediction. They correctly identified the major obstacles to a successful union: the political domination of the regime in Cairo; military rivalry between the Egyptian and Syrian militaries; the role of the unpopular Syrian spy chief Abdul Hamid Sarraj; economic incompatibilities between Egypt and Syria; and contrasting political cultures between the two states. Yet somewhat derisive views of Syrian culture and positive perceptions of Nasser combined with the uncertainty of the secessionists themselves to impede prediction of an outright break-up.

Analysts were more astute in assessing the implications of secession. It is striking that despite fears in 1958 of an 'expansionist' Nasser absorbing Syria into an ever-growing Arab empire, the intelligence community was reluctant to welcome the break up and in fact regarded it as a potentially disruptive force, particularly in inter-Arab relations and the Arab–Israeli conflict. The Americans were particularly pessimistic about the prospect of a stable government emerging in Syria, perhaps reflecting an increasing sense of respect for Nasser. By 1961, the Egyptian President had come to be associated with 'moderation' and 'stability' in the region. As the American ambassador had predicted in 1958, the difficulty of realising the rhetorical ambitions of pan-Arab unity had nurtured a more reasonable and statesman-like Nasser. At the same time assessments perceptively warned policy-makers that such a severe setback to Nasser's pride or 'honour' might provoke an extreme reaction elsewhere.

*   *   *

Anticipating Secession

Both the British and American intelligence communities recognised that in spite of the 'emotional appeal' of Arab unity there would be nationalistic, cultural, commercial and economic interests which would serve as serious divisive factors in any type of federation.[5] From the outset the JIC predicted that 'practical difficulties' meant that the union might be 'doomed to failure' and that 'sooner or later Syria will break away'. However, they warned policy-makers that the 'strength and appeal of the idea of Arab unity' and the 'determination, ingenuity and prestige of Nasser should not be underestimated'. Reflecting a grudging admiration for the leader, they felt sufficiently confident in his abilities to assert that 'as long as Nasser remains in power, the continued existence of the new republic is assured'.[6]

However, analysts appear to have overestimated the caution with which Nasser would approach the process of integration. They suggested that Nasser would endeavour to ensure that the 'governmental institutions of the union avoid any appearance of interference in the domestic affairs of the separate states' and they made explicit the importance of Syrian sensitivities. They predicted that this would be a difficult balance to strike and that whilst Nasser would try to keep his intervention in Syrian affairs 'to a minimum', he would likely become 'involved in matters which many Syrians consider to be of purely Syrian domestic concern'.[7]

Indeed, Egyptian domination of the union was one of the central reasons for the dissolution of the UAR. In early hopes for a rival Iraqi–Jordanian union, analysts had highlighted that 'Syria and Iraq, for example, have more in common, in terms of commercial, economic and various other interests, than either has with Egypt', suggesting that these 'natural affinities' could 'either work against the acceptance of Egyptian primacy or revive fears of Egyptian "imperialism"'.[8] Syrians came to refer to Egyptian behaviour in reproachful terms that had primarily been directed at the West including *'isti'imar'* (imperialism) and *'tassalut'* (dominion).[9]

At the highest political level, this manifested in a split with the Ba'ath party which had advocated the union in the first place. Ba'athist Michel Aflaq later recounted his hopes in the early days of the union that that 'our role would be both practical and theoretical since it was we who began practicing socialist ideas'.[10] The American ambassador to Syria reflected that the Ba'ath 'may well have reasoned that the ideology and the discipline of the regional Ba'ath movement' would furnish the 'political rationale for Nasser's revolutionary regime in Egypt'.[11] The early terms of the union, however, hinted at Nasser's disregard for the Ba'ath alongside other Syrian political parties. Indeed, the JIC's description of Nasser as 'virtual dictator' of both regions foresaw the central problem of Egyptian domination which would plague the UAR. In mid-1959, Ba'athists were purged from the military and reassigned to postings in Egypt where their subversive activity could be limited. One Ba'athist of note was a young airforce pilot named Hafez Al Asad, who formed a 'secret military committee' with other reassigned Syrian military officers. The committee would have an important role in the aftermath of secession and, of course, Asad would eventually rise to the Syrian presidency approximately a decade later.[12]

Analysts correctly identified that Nasser would struggle to eliminate the threat from the left in Syria, which had in fact prompted the union in the first place. He would, they estimated, encounter serious difficulties in obtaining effective control over the army and the faction-ridden political scene in Syria. Despite the agreement of political parties to disband, they estimated that 'jockeying for position would continue along old party lines'.[13]

The establishment of the National Union in mid-1959 was designed to replace the dissolved political parties and respond to Syrian desires for political participation. In what appears to have been an underestimation of the lively (if imperfect) political system enjoyed by Syrians prior to the union, the American ambassador, Yost, wrote just one week after union had been announced that 'western democracy has very frail roots and few loyal followers in Syria'.[14] The Egyptian inspired National Union was a poor compensation for the political activity Syrians had enjoyed since independence in 1949.

Nor was Egyptian domination merely a concern of Syrian politicians. Despite the union's initial popularity, the American intelligence community rightly predicted that minorities, commercial interests and some military groups would increasingly express their dissatisfaction as their special interests were 'encroached upon'. They wrote, 'in the course of time, many Syrian politicians, local notables, officers in the armed forces, civil servants and other persons who have held positions of authority are likely to become increasingly resentful of Egyptian domination of the union government'.[15]

Nowhere was Egyptian–Syrian rivalry more evident than in Nasser's proposals for military integration. In 1958, the CIA assessed that Syrian 'army officers fear ... [that] most of the important positions would go to Egyptians'.[16] A later estimate confirmed this prediction. Analysts noted that 'unification of the military has in practice been implemented by establishing overall Egyptian control and by placing Egyptian officers in key positions in most Syrian units down to the company level', resulting in 'considerable resentment' among officers.[17] British diplomats reported 'the impression that Syrian officers are far more of the military adventurer than the "ideological Free Officer" type, and it is always possible that Army elements might try to stage a separatist coup'. They were sure that Nasser was aware of this, noting 'evidence that the First Army is being systematically penetrated by Egyptian officers'.[18] Indeed, it is thought that four intelligence organisations operated in the union during this period.[19] Contemporary observers agreed that such military grievances were key to prompting the secession.[20]

It was widely felt that the only Syrian with any real power was the young and brutal spy chief Abdul Hamid Sarraj. One journalist described him as a 'sallow, taciturn man with cold eyes and humourless expression . . . "not an ant moves but Sarraj knows it, the people said"'.[21] Analysts accurately regarded Sarraj as critical to Nasser's control of Syria. British diplomats noted that whilst the 'dutiful and reliable caretaker' was loyal to Nasser, Sarraj had aspirations to be 'undisputed master' when the Egyptians were out of the way. An Egyptian source described Sarraj as possessing a 'policeman's mentality'.[22] Analysts recognised that despite his unpopularity, 'Nasser presumably feels that he could not find a better agent to run the Syrian region on his behalf'.[23] Syrian factionalism between left and right continued to plague politics and Nasser was 'compelled to exercise his authority through an opportunistic system of playing factions off against each other meanwhile relying on authoritarian control through his Syrian strongman Sarraj'.[24]

Sarraj's rule served a dual and contradictory function. On the one hand, he clearly contributed to widespread Syrian hostility towards the Egyptians. On the other hand, analysts also identified him as a critical benchmark of Nasser's control of Syria. 'One contingency which would quickly create a crisis for Nasser in Syria would be a falling out with Sarraj and his supporters.' With Nasser's support Sarraj had become the 'most powerful Syrian on the scene'. Analysts recognised that his role was key to Nasser's continued control in Syria.[25] His dismissal just weeks before secession should therefore have been a clear warning to analysts of what was to come. Egyptian spy chief Salah Nasr has suggested in his memoirs that in the weeks preceding secession, the security apparatus had completely disintegrated.[26]

Perhaps the most important arena in which Egyptian domination came to be unduly manifest was in the economy. Whereas the Egyptians could justify military domination on the basis of their clear superiority, the Syrian economy was a different matter. Estimates had highlighted that 'Egypt and Syria do not have complementary economies' and suggested that apart from the union's control of oil transit facilities, there was 'little prospect for mutually advantageous economic co-operation'. Analysts rightly predicted that Nasser's attempts at economic integration would 'probably lead to conflict and criticism of the union'.[27] Moreover the 'wedding of two perennially needy treasuries and underdeveloped economies' was likely to 'create increased political, social and economic problems'.[28] Nasser's economic strategising in both Egypt and Syria only exacerbated the situation. His economic policy during this period was evidently based on the Soviet model of long-range state planning. Despite ambitious five-year strategies to modernise both economies, analysts predicted that the 'growing trend toward nationalization and state control of already existing private enterprise in Syria' would accentuate tensions. Indeed Nasser, had 'encountered the most resistance in the area of economic integration'.[29]

British diplomats agreed that the discernible 'malaise' was due to deeper economic causes. By the time of secession Syria faced a dismal economic situation aggravated by three years of drought. Diplomats cited a Syrian quip circulating at the time: 'There's been no rain since the Egyptians came and there'll be none till they go.'[30] In February 1961, Nasser's announced a Presidential decree that put an end to the free convertibility system of the Syrian pound and imposed new import restrictions that alienated the business community. The nationalisation of seventy-five Syrian companies and confiscation of the shares of seventy-nine firms also served to turn the industrialists against him. The value of the Syrian pound had plunged, cereal exports were down and foreign capital flew to neighbouring Lebanon. All the while, Egyptian policy-makers were considering the possibility of a unified currency. The latter, analysts identified, could be 'the one thing that might cause real trouble'.[31] Podeh concludes that the measures introduced in the first half of 1961 constituted the most significant economic factor leading to the break-up.[32]

Analysts suggested that these tensions reflected fundamentally different political cultures. Scholars have similarly concluded that 'ultimately there was a clash of cultures between the dark-skinned bureaucrats from the Nile Valley and the free-wheeling Syrians'.[33] The Syrians were regarded as 'a people of remarkable commercial enterprise whose traditional way of life is founded upon personal and economic freedom'.[34] Analysts suggested that 'possibly the most pertinent difference' between the two cultures was 'Syrian laissez-faire and zealotry, as opposed to Egyptian submissiveness to state authority', as a result of Egypt's dependence on a centralised irrigation system.[35] As Heikal would later put it, Syria was a '"rain society" and Egypt a "river society"'.[36] The Syrians were noted also for 'a stubborn factionalism, which has always impeded cooperation among Syrians and is no less a troublesome factor in matters of cooperation between Syrians and Egyptians'. The unenviable 'task for Nasser' therefore was 'persuading Syrians to break with the past; to discard their traditional habits of pursuing parochial interests and fragmenting into competing groups'. Analysts doubted whether even Nasser could manage to 'transfer Syrian loyalties from the tribe, sect or other narrow faction to himself and to the larger interests of the nation'.[37]

Analysts also explained Nasser's clash with the Syrian Ba'ath party in cultural terms. They noted Nasser's desire for conservative economic reform in comparison with the Ba'ath's 'extremism, missionary zeal, claims to ideological leadership and initiative'.[38] British reports reinforced the cultural reasons why the union was moribund.

> The very fecundity of the Syrian intelligentsia in political theory and the variability of their enthusiasms have in the past been among the main reasons for their failure to unite with any of their neighbours; and there have been many signs during the United Arab Republic's first 18 months of existence that the independent character of the Syrian is ready to reassert itself. The acceptance by Damascus of permanent subordination to Cairo would be at variance with the independent and restless spirit that Damascenes have shown throughout their history.[39]

The Syrian 'national character' was depicted as something of a wild force that could not be tamed. Retrospective assessments confirmed that alongside the political and economic reforms of July 1961 in which Nasser attempted to further unify the Egyptian and Syrian entities there was a 'general feeling that Nasser was attempting to annihilate the individual personality of Syria'.[40] Though perhaps a melodramatic reading, it reveals much about the importance analysts attributed to incompatibilities in Syrian and Egyptian political cultures in the secession.

By 1961, the diplomatic corps reported a consensus that 'the situation in Syria has deteriorated during the last three months'. People were by now 'speaking openly against the Egyptians and even against President Nasser'. Political unrest was 'nearer the surface'. They reported rumours that former politicians were 'talking openly about loosening the union' and noted unrest in universities. Analysts concluded that the product of Egyptian domination was an 'undefinable psychological unrest . . . Apart from Sarraj (who is doing his best to earn popularity by touring), no Syrian seems to matter, either in Damascus or Cairo'.[41]

Analysts clearly had a keen awareness of the political, economic and cultural obstacles to an effective union. They even identified the contingency scenario in which Nasser's rule would be threatened. Why, however, were analysts unable to predict the act of secession itself? One simple answer is that not even the secessionists were originally intending to separate from the union. Analysts correctly judged that the initial goal of the military was 'to secure from Nasser redress of grievances rather than to break away from the U.A.R. Only when this failed did the rebels decide on secession'.[42]

There was also an underlying sensibility that there was no compelling alternative to Nasser. Analysts wrote complacently that:

> There seems to be no likelihood of serious trouble: there are no leaders, and Syria has nowhere to go . . . the general consensus is that most Syrians remain disillusioned with their dozen years of independence and prefer Nasser to anything else they might get. The general impression is one of political aimlessness.[43]

With some echoes of contemporary discourse about the ongoing Syrian civil war under Bashar al Asad, the idea that Syrian political culture was so wracked with factionalism that the Syrian elite could never get themselves together to oppose a common enemy seems to have taken hold as a conventional wisdom in the intelligence community. Civilian opposition was 'seriously weakened' by disparate ideologies with 'old line leaders of the Populist and Nationalist parties' struggling to get 'together themselves, let alone cooperating with socialist groups like the Baath'. Moreover, the 'sharpening conflict between nationalism and communism' rendered nationalist cooperation with the Communists 'difficult'.

The question of military support was also key: without it, civilian opposition would 'have only limited practical effectiveness in the face of Nasser's prestige among the masses and his authoritarian controls over the instruments of government'.[44]

As the end of this statement shows, the issue of Nasser's perceived power and authority was crucial in contributing to the difficulty of predicting secession. In 1960, analysts argued that Nasser's 'leadership and dictatorial authority have been of the utmost importance in the formation of the U.A.R . . . there is no yardstick with which to measure definitively the limits of the magic of his name or the total effect of his autocratic power on the course of events'.[45] From the start of the union, Nasser had placed himself (and was regarded as being) in a position of supreme authority: just as he had conceded to accept union, it was up to him to determine its dissolution.[46] Assessments of Nasser in 1961 indicate that he was regarded in particularly high estimation by American analysts: 'There is no Arab leader now on the scene, nor as far as we can tell waiting in the wings, capable of matching Nasser's appeal or achieving a comparable basis of power and authority.'[47]

Despite astute awareness and understanding of the tensions existing within the union, a combination of assumptions about Syrian culture together with an unspoken acceptance of Nasser's power and authority fostered a demonstrable reluctance to envisage an alternative leadership for Syria.

Implications of Secession

Western estimations of the likely implications of secession reflected two schools of thought. On the one hand there was the hope that Nasser's acceptance of the situation was indicative of a more mature and statesmanlike attitude. On the other lay the fear that he was likely to strike out if given the opportunity to re-establish his pre-eminence as leader of the Arab world. In fact, both schools of thought to some extent reflected the historical 'truth'. Nasser was indeed chastened by his experience in Syria and initially turned his attention to problems in Egypt, implementing a radical programme of domestic reform. At the same time, when the prospect of revolution in Yemen presented itself, he felt obliged to take the opportunity it afforded to reaffirm his role as leader of Arab nationalism.

Diplomats were initially perplexed as to how Nasser would react to the Syrian secession. It was 'difficult to predict what Nasser will do. The general opinion here is that he does not know himself. Past experience suggests that he will react vigorously and perhaps irrelevantly, to so great a blow to his prestige.' British diplomats in Cairo went on to clarify that although there was no popular pressure on Nasser to take action, 'wounded pride cannot be expected to breed patience in men like Nasser and his colleagues, and I believe they are more likely to take reckless action if an opportunity presents itself'. Moreover, they hinted that such action would 'not necessarily be limited to Syria'.[48]

The JIC confirmed that Nasser's 'immediate reactions to the Syrian coup were violent'. The Committee believed that he had rejected requests for the 'loosening of the U.A.R. into a confederation in the belief that he might retrieve the situation by force or a show of force'.[49] They questioned the role of military calculations in Nasser's decision-making but agreed that he had shown a 'statesmanlike acceptance' of the situation and gained 'some political capital thereby'.[50]

Domestically, the State Department's INR suggested that 'while identifiable anti-regime elements are quietly pleased, there has been no evidence that Nasser's control has weakened significantly'.[51] Scholars have suggested that the Presidential Council, a new executive body instituted in August 1962 to practice collective decision-making, was an effort to offset military (and specifically Egyptian Defense Minister Abdel Hakim Amer's) power.[52] Whilst analysts seemed relatively oblivious to the intra-regime tensions between Nasser and the military occasioned by the secession, they noted that 'since the Syrian revolt there is some evidence that Nasser has been sharing power with former members of the RCC'.[53]

The JIC could not see any serious domestic repercussions from secession within Egypt. Nasser's 'grip remained firm', though he had 'thought it necessary to take stern measures against reactionaries'. They noted that alongside disappointment there was also 'feelings of relief at the termination of the troublesome and expensive Syrian commitment'.[54] During the union Sadat had privately referred to Syria as 'a drag on us and a weight upon our necks'. Nasser also intimated that the secession would allow him to concentrate on Egypt's domestic affairs.[55] It was indeed after secession that the regime began to make its major contribution to Egyptian economic development, putting into effect, for example, an investment programme included in the first five-year plan and the extension of the cooperative system. The National Charter of May 1962 made explicit a new emphasis on Arab socialism, asserting that the 'phase of social revolution has surpassed that superficial concept of Arab unity'.[56]

Economically, the secession with Syria prompted a dramatic shift to the left. It was from this point on that Egypt saw its most wide-ranging nationalisations. Analysts rightly placed the economic moves within the context of the setback in Syria, suggesting that the recent step-up of economic centralization reflected the government's 'frustration and anger following the Syrian break and the fear of a domestic coup in Egypt'.[57] Nasser blamed reconciliation with '*raj'iyya*' (reaction) for the secession and asserted the need for more complete economic reform to remake the ideals and morals of society. British ambassador Harold Beeley had warned some months earlier that whilst there were those who believed that Nasser was 'acting in more or less intimate collusion with the Communist powers' in exchange for Soviet support, Nasser's government was in fact 'positively anti-communist in its domestic politics'. According to Beeley, loans from West Germany and Egypt's export of cotton to 'the free world' demonstrated that the recent 'coincidence of policy' between the UAR and Soviets 'may be explained in terms of an identity of view towards particular problems rather than a derogation from neutrality as it is ordinarily understood in the Western world'.[58] Erstwhile Prime Minister Aziz Sidiqi later confirmed that Nasser 'was neither for capitalism, nor against capitalism: he acquired a pro-socialist position through practice'.[59] With regards to domestic policy, an understanding of Nasser as fundamentally pragmatic lay at the heart of many assessments.

Foreign policy was a greater concern. Although the JIC noted signs that the crisis had nurtured a more moderate Nasser focusing on the domestic sphere, they appeared sceptical that this would last.

> Nasser has in fact been trying in recent months to appear as a restrained and statesmanlike figure and before the *coup* his policy in the Arab world has been marked by an increasing moderation. But he has suffered a serious blow to his prestige. Though for the time being he is concentrating on domestic matters, it is difficult to imagine him remaining aloof from the controversies and possible unrest which the restoration of Syrian independence is likely to create, and he will no doubt assume that General Qasim, King Hussein, King Saud and the Communists will be bent on extending their influence in that country. He will undoubtedly seek to maintain his leading position in the Arab world. In the circumstances he is likely to be tempted to employ whatever means may seem necessary for the purpose.[60]

The greatest significance of the secession was thus judged to be Nasser's role in inter-Arab relations. The State Department's INR wrote that the Syrian defection was a setback 'more serious than the Sinai defeat in 1956 or the failure of Iraq to associate itself with the U.A.R. after the 1958 revolution, because it represents a repudiation of a step towards unity already taken'.[61] Their report suggested that 'the Syrian revolt will have an unsettling effect in the Near East for some time to come. Old rivalries have become inflamed, and conditions have suddenly become favourable again for the expression of *anarchical tendencies inherent in Arab politics.*' The unspoken implication was that, ironically, Nasser had come to play a vital and constructive role in keeping a lid on a political culture that was intrinsically destructive to regional stability.[62]

At the same time the break was perceived to be a denunciation of Nasser personally rather than Arab unity, ultimately 'a reaction against Nasser's idea of the basis and form of such unity'. Nasser had failed to take into account 'the reality of regional national feeling in the Arab world' and instead sought to 'create unity by fiat and compulsion'.[63] Even those most enamoured with Nasser could not deny that his reputation had suffered. The American ambassador, John Badeau, had a memorably cordial relationship with the Egyptian President, indeed Nasser once asked him to smoke his pipe, to which Badeau responded that a pipe was the 'perfect prop' for a diplomat faced with a difficult question.[64] As Badeau put it, his 'aura of invincibility is gone', along with the 'image of Nasser as champion of Arab renaissance'. With the dissolution of the union, Nasser became the tragic hero of Arab unity.[65]

The consequences for the rest of the region could be equally problematic. Consolidating the UAR had forced Nasser

> to play an essentially constructive role. Henceforth, however, his desire to build Arab unity is likely to be offset by the urge to prevent his enemies from profiting from his misfortune and by his need to take revenge on those who seek to do so.

The State Department observed that regional Arab leaders were sensitive to this danger and 'have been careful in this delicate situation not to antagonize Nasser'. Ultimately they concluded that the Syrian issue highlighted 'the growing significance of secession and irredentism as dynamics in inter-Arab relations' in a host of surrounding countries such as Iraq, Kuwait, Saudi, Morocco and Yemen.[66] In accordance with this advice, the responses of Western policy-makers were thus appropriately measured, seeking to assure Nasser diplomatically that they were neither conspiring against him nor rejoicing in his humiliation.

Nonetheless the Arab–Israeli conflict rendered the new Syrian–Egyptian relationship particularly dangerous. In theory the State Department posited that Israel might now feel less threatened by concerted Arab action and hence should be less inclined to pressure the US for support.[67] The JIC agreed that, 'on the surface', the situation for the Israelis was improved, since a coordinated attack from north and south was 'now unlikely'. The analysis went on to clarify that this was 'only part of the story', however.

> The restraining hand of the Egyptians on Syrian military exuberance has been removed. The Syrians have always had the greatest tendency of all the Arabs to aggressive behaviour on the Israel border and it has been reported that, since the renewal of Syrian independence, the number of firing incidents on the Syria/Israeli border has already increased. This tendency . . . can be of no particular comfort to the Israelis.[68]

It was of course Syrian challenges to Egypt's continued commitment to pan-Arabism which would drive Nasser into confrontation with Israel in 1967.

If Syrian foreign policy was more likely to be unstable and hazardous, it was unlikely that Syrian domestic politics would look much better. Despite the right-wing nature of the new government, analysts resorted to their preconceptions of Syrian culture to predict its evolution.

> The Syrians have traditionally been highly individualistic and undisciplined people . . . Syrian political movements, no matter what the coloration or how well unified at the inception, have always degenerated into a dog-eat-dog political jungle, which the communists are better equipped to deal with than we are. We thus cannot take too much comfort from the relatively conservative complexion of the new government.[69]

Indeed, it was likely that new Syrian government would be 'handicapped by its relatively conservative outlook' when trying to 'hold popular sympathy' and control the Communist and socialist political factions. The State Department was not reassured by the regime's assertions that it would 'strive to further the interest of the workers and the small cultivators as well as those of private business and commerce'. They concluded that that the political parties and groups that had been 'suppressed during Nasser's rule all have the overriding aim of acquiring paramount power by one means or another', ensuring that 'the possibility of renewed political turmoil looms again as a major threat to Syria's stability'.[70]

The JIC seemed to take a more positive view of the outlook for Syria, perhaps occasioned by their persistent reticence about Nasser.

> There does not seem to be any immediate likelihood of serious trouble there . . . Although some elements, such as students and workers who received a Nasserite indoctrination, may not be fully content the general feeling in Syria appears to be one of satisfaction at the end of U.A.R. slights to Syrian nationalist feeling and of imposition of economic doctrines better suited to Egypt . . . For the time being, Nasser's prospects of successful subversion in Syria do not appear to be great.[71]

Their suggestion that propaganda and indoctrination was the only explanation for pro-Nasser sentiment belied Nasser's enduring popularity amongst the Syrian masses. They conceded, however, that the new government was unlikely to be popular and was 'vulnerable to certain accusations which can be made against it, namely that it is composed of Right-Wing [sic] politicians, that it is excessively pro-Western, having received immediate support from Jordan, Turkey and Iran, and that it is not wholeheartedly behind the ideals of Arab unity'.[72] In December 1961, the CIA went considerably further, depicting the new Syrian government as ultimately doomed:

> Consisting of second rate politicians, the new cabinet includes rightists and leftists but leaves out representatives of the important Nationalist party as well as the most influential leftist leaders. Many ministers appear to be miscast – an Alawi tribal chieftain is minister of communications; the Ministry of Justice is headed by a professor of Muslim law who is a member of the reactionary Muslim Brotherhood; and the minister of culture's only claim to expertise is his status as an amateur poet . . . the cabinet's life is likely to be short.[73]

In March 1962, the government indeed disintegrated, the army took control in a military coup and the regime shifted to the left.[74] The CIA reported a 'power struggle among military factions' and that Nasser had 'offered his services as mediator' to avoid a civil war.[75] They assessed that the 'military junta do not seem capable of retaining control' and appeared to be 'overconfident regarding the extent of its suppression of the recent pro-Nasir up-surge in the country . . . still paying lip service to the idea of a loose union with Egypt'.[76] Syria was thus not easily able to rid itself of Nasser's influence and despite the Ba'athist seizure of power in March 1963, Syrian politicians were to vie for influence in a series of coups and counter-coups for the rest of the decade until Hafez Al Asad ascended to the presidency in 1971.

* * *

An examination of the declassified record reveals a multitude of cultural beliefs about Syria that informed analysis on the secession: the Syrian as 'entrepreneurial', 'individualistic', 'factional' or 'aggressive'. Analysts identified the factors which later scholars identified as contributing to secession – Egyptian political and military domination, the role of hated spy chief Sarraj and differences in the economies and cultures of the two regions. Their inability to predict outright secession seem to derive partly from the derogatory view they held of Syrian political culture, and partly from perceptions of Nasser as a figure of some invincibility. Perhaps most importantly this case study demonstrates all too well the difficulty of predicting an event, particularly when even those taking action (the secessionists) were themselves not following a concrete plan.

As in Iraq, and as the American ambassador had so perceptively predicted in 1958, the challenges Nasser faced in Syria tempered his ambitions. The spectre of Nasser in decline or difficulty clearly came to be associated with the idea of Nasser as a force of moderation and stability. This seems to have been both an objective and subjective perceptual shift – Nasser was indeed chastened by his experience in Syria but also came to be *regarded* as a more constructive figure. Analysts' advice to avoid demonstrating public satisfaction at this setback to Nasser does seem to have been heeded by policy-makers. In retrospect assessments of the implications of secession appear strikingly prescient and farsighted – the potential for increased Arab–Israeli tensions, the domestic shift to the left as a response to fears of 'reaction' rather than a move of ideological significance and the need for Nasser to re-establish his credibility abroad if the opportunity presented itself. The Yemeni coup would provide just the occasion.

Notes

1. Robert Komer cited in W. Bass, *Support Any Friend: Kennedy's Middle East and the Making of the U.S.-Israeli Alliance* (New York: Oxford University Press, 2003), p. 85.
2. J. Jankowski, *Nasser's Egypt, Arab Nationalism and the United Arab Republic* (Boulder, CO: Lynne Rienner Publishers, 2001), p. 170.
3. R. McNamara, *Britain, Nasser and the Balance of Power in the Middle East, 1952–1967: From the Egyptian Revolution to the Six Day War* (London: Frank Cass, 2003), p. 165.

4. Exceptions include: Jankowski, *Nasser's Egypt, Arab Nationalism and the United Arab Republic*; McNamara, *Britain, Nasser and the Balance of Power*; E. Podeh, *The Decline of Arab Unity: The Rise and Fall of the United Arab Republic* (Brighton: Sussex Academic Press, 1999); L. James, *Nasser At War: Arab Images of the Enemy* (Basingstoke: Palgrave Macmillan, 2006). All these rely on Anglo-American declassified documents and the occasional intelligence report but none has undertaken a comprehensive and analytical deconstruction of the intelligence material available.

5. SNIE 30-3-58, 'Arab nationalism as a factor in the Middle East situation', 12 August 1958, FOIA Reading Room.

6. JIC memorandum (58) 25, 'The implications of the United Arab Republic and the Arab Union', 30 April 1958, TNA, CAB 158/32.

7. SNIE 30-58, 'Prospects and consequences of Arab unity moves', 20 February 1958, FOIA Reading Room.

8. SNIE 30-3-58, 'Arab nationalism as a factor in the Middle East situation', 12 August 1958, FOIA Reading Room.

9. Podeh, *The Decline of Arab Unity*, p. 55.

10. Jankowski, *Nasser's Egypt, Arab Nationalism and the United Arab Republic*, p. 118.

11. Telegram from embassy in Damascus to State Department, 8 February 1958, FRUS 1958-1960, vol. XIII, no. 192.

12. Jankowski, *Nasser's Egypt, Arab Nationalism and the United Arab Republic*, p. 129.

13. SNIE 30-58, 'Prospects and consequences of Arab unity moves', 20 February 1958, FOIA Reading Room.

14. Telegram from embassy in Damascus to State Department, 8 February 1958, FRUS 1958-1960, vol. XIII, no. 192.

15. SNIE 30-58, 'Prospects and consequences of Arab unity moves', 20 February 1958, FOIA Reading Room.

16. SNIE 30-58, 'Prospects and consequences of Arab unity moves', 20 February 1958, FOIA Reading Room.

17. SNIE 30-58, 'Prospects and consequences of Arab unity moves', 20 February 1958, FOIA Reading Room.

18. Telegram from Crowe in Cairo Embassy to FO, 21 June 1960, TNA, FO 371/150902.

19. Podeh, *The Decline of Arab Unity*, p. 180.

20. P. Seale, 'The break-up of the United Arab Republic', in *The World Today*, 17: 11, 1961, pp. 471–9.

21. P. Seale, *The Struggle for Syria: A Study of Post-War Arab Politics, 1945–1958* (Oxford: Oxford University Press, 1986), p. 281.

22. Jankowski, *Nasser's Egypt, Arab Nationalism and the United Arab Republic*, p. 120.
23. Memorandum from Clarke at Consulate General Damascus to Beith at FO, 4 April 1961, TNA, FO 371/158797.
24. NIE 36-61, 'Nasser and the future of Arab nationalism', 27 June 1961, FOIA Reading Room.
25. Ibid.
26. Salah Nasr, cited in Jankowski, *Nasser's Egypt, Arab Nationalism and the United Arab Republic*, p. 166.
27. SNIE 30-58, 'Prospects and consequences of Arab unity moves', 20 February 1958, FOIA Reading Room.
28. Telegram from embassy in Damascus to State Department, 8 February 1958, FRUS 1958-1960, vol. XIII, no. 192.
29. NIE 36-61, 'Nasser and the future of Arab nationalism', 27 June 1961, FOIA Reading Room.
30. Minute from Eden to Beith, 13 September 1960, TNA, FO 371/150190.
31. Note by Arthur, counsellor at Cairo, 'Situation in Syria – January 1961', sent from Crowe to Beith, 28 January 1961, TNA, FO 371/158797: 'the Syrians are said to regard their currency as a precious symbol of their identity: so long as the Syrian pound lives, the union is somehow not quite irrevocable'.
32. Podeh, *The Decline of Arab Unity*, p. 189.
33. T. Ismael, J. Ismael and K. Jaber (eds) *Politics and Government in the Middle East and North Africa* (Miami: Florida International University Press, 1991), p. 196.
34. Despatch from Clarke at British Consulate General Damascus to FO, July 31 1961, TNA, FO 371/158797.
35. Intelligence Report, 'The outlook for the UAR', 11 March 1960, OSS/SDIRR, The Middle East 1950-1961, Microfilm, Reel 2, SOAS Library.
36. H. M. Heikal, *Matar, Bisaraha 'an Abd al Nasir* (Beirut: al-Dar al-Muttahida li al-Nashr, 1972), p. 157.
37. Intelligence Report, 'The outlook for the UAR', 11 March 1960, OSS/SDIRR, The Middle East 1950-1961, Microfilm, Reel 2, SOAS Library.
38. Ibid.
39. FO Steering Committee Paper no. 12, 'Prospects for the unification of the Fertile Crescent', 1959, TNA, FO 487/13. Egypt had ruled Syria during the Mamluk period (1258–1517) and during Ottoman rule for nine years (1831–40).

40. Research memorandum by State Department, Bureau of Intelligence and Research, 'Implications of Syria's secession from the United Arab Republic', 12 October 1961, TNA, FO 371/157387. Podeh's *The Decline of Arab Unity*, p. 181, reinforces this analysis noting, for example, that all major Syrian holidays were erased from the official calendar.

41. Note by Arthur, counsellor at Cairo, 'Situation in Syria – January 1961', sent from Crowe to Beith, 28 January 1961, TNA, FO 371/158797: 'In foreign policy in particular all power rests with the Egyptians: Nasser did not even bother to take a Syrian with him to Casablanca.'

42. Research memorandum by State Department, Bureau of Intelligence and Research, 'Implications of Syria's secession from the United Arab Republic', 12 October 1961, TNA, FO 371/157387.

43. Note by Arthur, counsellor at Cairo, 'Situation in Syria – January 1961', sent from Crowe to Beith at FCO, 28 January 1961, TNA, FO 371/158797.

44. NIE 36-61, 'Nasser and the future of Arab nationalism', 27 June 1961, FOIA Reading Room.

45. Intelligence Report, 'The outlook for the UAR', 11 March 1960, OSS/SDIRR, The Middle East 1950-1961, Microfilm, Reel 2, SOAS Library.

46. NIE 36-61, 'Nasser and the future of Arab nationalism', 27 June 1961, FOIA Reading Room.

47. Ibid.: 'Nasser remains the prime leader and symbol of Arab nationalism. No other leader has so consistently and forcefully expressed its essential sentiments and no other leader has enjoyed such concrete successes in its name.'

48. Telegram from Arthur in British Embassy Cairo to FO, 1 October 1961, TNA, FO 371/158789.

49. JIC memorandum (61) 75, 'Short term effects of the Syrian situation on the Middle East', 26 October 1961, TNA, CAB 158/44: 'His objective was probably to win over a firm base in Syria with Syrian Armed Forces' backing, in the hope of eventually regaining control of the whole country.'

50. Ibid.

51. Research memorandum by State Department, Bureau of Intelligence and Research, 'Implications of Syria's secession from the United Arab Republic', 12 October 1961, TNA, FO 371/157387.

52. K. J. Beattie, *Egypt During the Nasser Years: Ideology Politics and Civil Society* (Oxford: Westview Press, 1994), p. 160.

53. Memorandum from Secretary of State Rusk to President Kennedy, 'Action program for the United Arab Republic', 10 January 1962, FRUS 1961-63, vol. XVII, no. 159.
54. JIC memorandum (61) 75, 'Short term effects of the Syrian situation on the Middle East', 26 October 1961, TNA, CAB 158/44.
55. Jankowski, *Nasser's Egypt*, p. 171.
56. Podeh, *Decline of Arab Unity*, p. 192.
57. Airgram from the embassy in Ethiopia to the State Department, 21 February 1962, FRUS 1961-1963, vol. XVII, no. 195.
58. Telegram from Ambassador Beeley to FO, 18 July 1961, TNA, FO 371/158786.
59. Aziz Sidiqi cited in Beattie, *Egypt During the Nasser Years*, p. 157.
60. JIC memorandum (61) 75, 'Short term effects of the Syrian situation on the Middle East', 26 October 1961, TNA, CAB 158/44.
61. Research memorandum by State Department, Bureau of Intelligence and Research, 'Implications of Syria's secession from the United Arab Republic', 12 October 1961, TNA, FO 371/157387.
62. Ibid. [emphasis added].
63. Ibid.: 'Syria now advocates a federation rather than a union of Arab states . . . A principal point of weakness in the Arab federation concept however, will continue to be the compulsive tendency of one faction or leader to dominate the others. Nasser himself is the prime example of this tendency.'
64. Bass, *Support Any Friend*, p. 85.
65. Ambassador Badeau cited in Podeh, *The Decline of Arab Unity*, p. 191.
66. Research memorandum by State Department, Bureau of Intelligence and Research, 'Implications of Syria's secession from the United Arab Republic', 12 October 1961, TNA, FO 371/157387.
67. Ibid.
68. JIC memorandum (61) 75, 'Short term effects of the Syrian situation on the Middle East', 26 October 1961, TNA, CAB 158/44.
69. Memorandum from State Department Executive Secretary (Battle) to the President's Special Assistant for National Security Affairs (Bundy), 30 September 1961, FRUS 1961-1963, vol. XVII, no. 114.
70. Research memorandum by State Department, Bureau of Intelligence and Research, 'Implications of Syria's secession from the United Arab Republic', 12 October 1961, TNA, FO 371/157387.
71. In fact Egyptian subversive activities became so troublesome that the Syrian government called a special Arab league summit to complain

in August 1962. See Rathmell, 'Brotherly enemies' *Intelligence and National Security*, p. 240.

72. JIC memorandum (61) 75, 'Short term effects of the Syrian situation on the Middle East', 26 October 1961, TNA, CAB 158/44.
73. Current Intelligence Weekly Summary, 29 December 1961, FOIA Reading Room.
74. Current Intelligence Weekly Summary, 30 March 1962, FOIA Reading Room.
75. Current Intelligence Weekly Summary, 6 April 1962, FOIA Reading Room.
76. Current Intelligence Weekly Summary, 13 April 1962, FOIA Reading Room.

5   Civil War in Yemen

Mr. President [Nasser], there's one thing to remember about Yemen. Everybody, including the Romans, who went into Yemen got burned doing it. If I could give you any advice, stay out of there!

Ambassador Raymond Hare recalling a conversation with President Nasser, 1987[1]

In September 1962, a group of Yemeni army officers led by Colonel Abdullah al-Sallal overthrew the *Hamid'Ud'Din* royal family. Sallal was a high ranking officer of humble origins – rumour has it that at the age of thirty, Sallal had never slept in a bed and was so confused by the first pair of trousers he owned that he wore them as a shirt.[2] On the night of the coup, one of Sallal's men botched an attempt to shoot Imam Badr in the back, the rifle's trigger jammed and he shot himself in the chin as a guard moved to arrest him. Less than an hour later, however, tanks moved to close in on the royal palace, holding Badr under siege for twelve hours before, having run out of cigarettes and ammunition, he managed to escape disguised as a common soldier.[3]

The farcical nature of the Yemeni revolt would later be a popular topic of conversation between Nasser and his political colleagues at home and abroad. But the experience took its toll on the Egyptian republic and it was the last of the Arab revolutions in which the Egyptian nationalist was to become enmeshed. In an effort to sustain the republican revolutionaries, Nasser sent over a third of his army to help fight guerrilla royalist forces loyal to the deposed Imam together with his uncle, Prince Hassan, propped up by Saudi Arabia and the British in what became known as Egypt's 'Vietnam'. The Yemeni conflict became a proxy war between these rival interests and a powerful if increasingly futile symbol of the Arab division between 'traditional' dynasties versus 'progressive' republics. It was not the first Middle Eastern conflict to place Anglo-American allies on opposing sides.

Scholars have explored this conflict from many perspectives.[4] Anglo-American political and intelligence assessments of Nasser's final Arab revolution add valuable detail to this picture of the Yemeni revolution thus far constructed.[5] There was good strategic notice of a possible coup in Yemen and analysts recognised that Nasser had supported but not orchestrated this Arab revolution. British policy towards Yemen was notoriously divided between Foreign Office mandarins advising recognition of the revolutionary status quo alongside top secret covert operations designed to support the Yemeni royalists.[6] The American administration was inclined to side with the 'progressive republicans' despite the misgivings of their Saudi allies and wider fears beyond the Yemen.

In retrospect it is clear that the Americans (along with Nasser) underestimated royalist resistance and overestimated the republican ability to effect political change in Yemen's 'medieval society'. It quickly became obvious that Nasser faced a stalemate in Yemen with neither side able to penetrate the other's stronghold. For the British, a preoccupation with Aden in southern Arabia, their last remaining imperial outpost, surpassed all other considerations. Despite the hysteria of some policy-makers, the JIC took a generally measured and progressive outlook amidst the notable absence of an 'East of Suez' policy. At the same time, we see the 'troublemaking' face of Nasser rise to the forefront of the JIC's analysis, particularly after diplomatic relations between the UK and Egypt are broken in 1965.

Overall, it is a relatively astute and accurate narrative that stands up well against scholarship written with the benefit of hindsight. The discussion below perhaps revises the conclusions of historians that 'British intelligence as a whole remained woefully ill-informed regarding the situation inside Yemen'.[7] It also reveals a greater repertoire of images the West held of Nasser than has been emphasised in previous Western studies. The Yemeni revolution overwhelmingly revealed the spectre of a pragmatist limited by his concern for 'face', together with a troublemaker not entirely in control. It was an image which would certainly resurface in subsequent crises involving Nasser.

* * *

Notice of a Coup

Yemen was something of an anachronism in the Middle East. Not only was it the poorest Arab state but also it was uniquely unexposed to the outside world. Iman Ahmad was a 'fat and frogeyed man' known in the Western press as the 'Old Devil' and famous in Yemen for murdering four out of his nine brothers. His worldview was aptly captured in an interview his son gave to *Life* magazine: 'My father distrusted the 20th Century', Badr remembered.[8] The Imamate's lack of interest in the modern outside world was somewhat reciprocated. As Robert Komer, the CIA officer seconded to the White House to advise on the Yemeni crisis, put it: 'Nobody knew very much about Yemen, about what went on in the back country and how you could control Yemen.'[9] Chester L. Cooper, the liaison officer to National Security Council staff from the CIA, recounts the following conversation with DCI Allen Dulles in the late 1950s, betraying just how low on the American administration's list of priorities the peninsula was. Apparently Dulles asked,

> 'What's the Yemen?... A country?... Never heard of it. Where is it?' The expert pointed with a shaking finger to a small speck on the edge of the Red Sea. 'There, Mr. Dulles.' 'I can't see it. But what's happening there that's so important?' 'It's the Imam sir.' 'Imam? Never heard of that either.' 'It's a person, sir. A religious person. He's the head of the government – the Imam of Yemen.'[10]

Notwithstanding this self-proclaimed ignorance, in fact there was good strategic notice of the Yemeni coup, despite the not insubstantial distraction of the Cuban Missile Crisis brewing simultaneously. On 13 September 1962, the Director of Intelligence and Research in the State Department reported that a group of Yemeni Army officers were 'conspiring "perhaps shortly" to assassinate the Imam, arrest Crown Prince Badr, and establish a republic'. The note suggested that the plotters had Nasser's support and had 'gained the adherence of important tribal leaders'.[11]

In fact, the elderly Imam was spared assassination and died a natural death. The intelligence community had long recognised that a crisis of succession could trigger revolt. As early as 1958, the JIC predicted that 'a more radical regime might be established as a result of the dynastic struggle', providing 'ample opportunity for Soviet or Egyptian intrigue in favour of an extremist candidate who would rely on their support'.[12] American analysis concurred that the death of the Imam Ahmed 'might prove to be the spark setting off severe internal disturbances in Yemen'.

> The Imam had controlled successfully an explosive situation: the low level of economic activity, frustrated pretensions to the Aden Colony and protectorates, the impecunious state of the treasury, the Islamic sectarian schism, reformist discontent, and tribal restiveness are built-in factors which have long threatened internal stability. The U.A.R., the U.S.S.R. and the U.K. have fished in these troubled waters. The Imam barely managed to keep the lid on by force of personality, a ruthless policy of divide and rule, clever manipulation of various factions in the country, and a repressive police and legal system.

In contrast, the Imam's son and appointed successor Badr was not perceived to have the 'stature of the Imam' nor the 'internal following' or 'qualities of leadership'. Insiders described him as 'weak, and fearful of opposition'. Just one week before his overthrow, analysts reported their fears that Badr might all too soon face a threat to his leadership.[13]

The Imam had clearly prevailed somewhat precariously over a simmering pot of domestic and foreign tensions. The London *Times* provided the following epitaph for the leader's death: 'Imam Ahmad will be remembered for his success in preserving his kingdom virtually intact against all the political and social ideas of the twentieth century.'[14] The JIC referred in 1957 to the 'semi-feudal isolation in which the national life of the Yemen is conducted'.[15] Contemporary observers struggled to comprehend that this was a country in the twentieth century with no currency and 'not a single ministry capable of performing a public service function'.[16]

Figure 5.1 Yemeni volunteers parading before Premier Abdullah al Sallal in the centre window, 1962. Egyptian National Library.

CIA analysts concluded that government had an altogether different meaning in Yemeni culture. It was 'essentially a balance of forces among powerful, armed, semi-autonomous tribes, urban centres and the central government'. The role of government was essentially negative, 'exploiting inter-tribal rivalries to prevent any one tribal group developing enough power to threaten the capital'. According to the CIA, the Yemeni people expected little from their governments beyond 'rudimentary public order, Islamic law administered by jurists educated in the traditional pattern and a crude system for collection of revenue'.[17]

Notwithstanding his conservatism, the Imam Ahmad was the first Yemeni leader to expose the peninsula to foreign influence, inviting both Soviet and Egyptian power in the region. Soviet offers of military and economic assistance saw the threat of communism spread to even this remote outpost. The JIC regarded such moves ominously, writing that 'it is true that the Yemen has a tradition of distrust of all foreigners, including Egyptians and Communists'. However, they warned, 'the isolation of the Yemen has already broken down and it would be folly to rely on this national characteristic to neutralise the powerful political and physical forces of penetration at the disposal of the enemies of the U.K.'[18]

Perversely but predictably, British control over Aden only bolstered Egyptian influence in Yemen. In 1959 the State Department seemed to chastise their allies, claiming that Yemeni fear of 'British efforts to consolidate control of the Aden protectorate brought it closer to Egypt' and was in fact responsible for a loose federation with the UAR.[19] The JIC conceded that 'even the remotest corners of the Peninsula' were being infected by the influence of Arab nationalism, 'the most powerful emotional force in the area'.[20] Egypt was the obvious target of blame but the JIC were careful to point out that although 'fed and strengthened by propaganda from Radio Cairo and elsewhere', the appeal of Arab nationalism 'exists independently of such propaganda and can be expected to increase'.[21] Despite their early hostility to Nasser the JIC established as early as 1958 that Arab nationalism in the Arabian Peninsula was by no means simply a product of Nasser's manipulation.

Unlike Iraq, in Yemen, Nasser was considered a greater risk than even the Soviets. Nasser had been 'working closely' with the ailing Imam's son, Badr, to supplant Soviet influence in Yemen for Egyptian military advisers, all the while giving covert assistance to his opponents.[22] In 1960, the JIC had estimated that that the UAR probably intended 'to create a perhaps nominally independent Yemen wholly submissive to Cairo' and that Nasser was 'better equipped to dominate the Yemen than any other power'.[23] They correctly predicted two years before the revolution that 'a prolonged dispute over succession might lead to a revolutionary situation and the establishment of a republican regime'.[24]

As analysts had feared, Syrian secession in 1961 provoked a more 'activist' attitude on Nasser's part to perceived reactionaries. After the Imam attacked Nasser's 'socialism' , Cairo withdrew from a nominal federal union with Yemen and condemned 'the reaction, ignorance and backward mentality of the Yemeni rulers'.[25] Whilst Nasser's hostility to the Imamate was evident, his role in the revolution remained unclear.

Nasser's Role

This question of precisely what Nasser wanted to achieve in Yemen is one that baffled the intelligence community and continues to plague historians. As a recent study notes, there is 'still considerable disagreement among historians regarding Egypt's role . . . Did she know about the revolution in advance; did she provide moral or actual support; was she the principal driving force?'[26] 'Principles and nothing else induced us to go to Yemen', Nasser himself insisted in a public address to the Palestinian National Congress in 1965.[27]

Beneath Nasser's disingenuous professions there were clearly tangible and important interests at stake. Interviews with Arab sources reveal that Nasser believed access to the Bab-al-Mandab strait could give Egypt control over both ends of the Red Sea, potentially allowing him to deny Israel access to the Iranian oil that reached her from Eilat. Others have suggested that access to Aden's oil was a more direct incentive.[28]

American analysts aptly recognised the relationship between the Syrian secession and Nasser's support for 'revolution' over 'reaction'. They wrote that 'in the wake of his continued failure to stage a comeback in Syria, Nasser probably feels the need for some concrete victory in the war he declared against the "reactionaries" following the breakup of the U.A.R. and the U.A.S. at the end of 1961'.[29] Egyptian accounts emphasise the degree to which Nasser considered the Yemeni revolution to be a 'counter-response' to the separation from Syria.[30]

Yet the question of Nasser's exact involvement remains obscure. Interviews with Egyptian and Yemeni officials suggest that the Egyptian regime 'was at least informed in advance of the Yemeni revolutionaries plans, promising to provide support after the coup had been accomplished' and that it 'seems probable' that Nasser was also aware of the timing.[31] American intelligence reached the same conclusions: Nasser, they wrote, was 'probably aware of rebel intentions and may well have supported the movement'.[32] The American embassy in Cairo reported that 'completely reliable sources' indicated 'some U.A.R. responsibility for liaison with [the] Yemen coup'.[33] The deposed Imam al-Badr himself chronicled Nasser's machinations as early as 1958, backing Badr's plan to depose his father with two cases of pistols and £50,000 sterling.[34]

To the JIC, the Yemeni revolt only underlined the symbolic appeal of Nasserism. With a tone of resignation, the Committee reported that 'despite various setbacks, Nasser remains the leader of Pan-Arabism. His doctrine is that Arab socialism will inevitably sweep away reactionary regimes and that this progress is to be encouraged at every opportunity.' However, they were keen to point out that the Egyptians, had 'so far shown no sign of wanting political union with the Yemeni republic; moreover such a union would not be wanted by the Yemenis'. Whilst Nasser did not have imperial ambitions for Yemen, the JIC believed that 'Egypt will be able to exercise considerable control over the policy of the Yemeni government'. The wider consequences of Egypt's involvement were not clear, however: if the revolution succeeded, 'the resulting encouragement to revolutionary elements in other Arab countries might well lead to further upheavals and could create further openings for Egyptian interference'. Nevertheless, the JIC observed, 'should Nasser remain heavily committed in the Yemen, he may be less able to take advantage of such opportunities'.[35]

The narrative of Nasser as opportunistic troublemaker was thus re-emerging in the discourse of the JIC – associated almost naturally with 'pan-Arabism', though now with considerably more reservation than their earlier assessments of Syria and Iraq. The prospect of a domino effect sweeping through the Middle East in 1961 seemed considerably less likely in contrast to similar fears in 1958; they had no illusions of a grand master plan. American diplomats defined the Egyptian position even more accurately, suggesting that Egypt was 'deeply concerned lest it be drawn into military adventure', yet at the same time was 'really determined' to prevent the collapse of Yemen regime 'due to outside forces'.[36] It was clear that this was not a conflict that Nasser had designed.

Fears beyond Yemen

The reality is that the outcome in Yemen itself was not of great importance to British and American policymakers. Rather, Anglo-American analysis revealed a predictable coterie of fears relating to the interested parties enmeshed in this conflict, including the Soviet Union, Saudi Arabia and most of all, Aden.

As always, Cold War considerations were paramount. As early as 1957, the JIC had warned that Soviet influence in Yemen was increasing and was likely to continue to do so unless Western powers took action.[37] Yemen was strategically significant to the USSR because of its proximity to Aden, the Horn of Africa and the southern entrance to the Red Sea. The Yemeni revolution meant that aid was 'likely to continue and may be increased', serving also 'a made-to-order opportunity for the Soviet Bloc to identify itself with a revolutionary cause'. The poverty stricken government was obliged to accept this aid partly out of desperation but also as 'a counter to the overwhelming Egyptian influence'.[38]

There was a clear sense, therefore, that Egyptian influence would limit Soviet influence in Yemen and analysts generally took a measured view of what the USSR was capable of achieving in the conflict. The Office of National Estimates qualified to DCI McCone that in fact the republican revolt was unlikely to be 'particularly conducive to the spread of Communist influence in the area'.[39] Moreover, analysts noted that notwithstanding military and economic assistance, 'the activities of local Yemeni Communists are strictly curtailed'.[40] They suggested that although 'Soviet and U.A.R. interests in the Yemen coincide at the moment: both wish to protect and secure the revolutionary regime and they are cooperating toward that end', this was unlikely to last.

> If and when the republican regime is consolidated in the Yemen, the Soviets will almost certainly attempt to play a more independent role and this will bring them into conflict with Egyptian interests. Nasser is unlikely to be willing to permit any challenge to his predominant position of influence in the Yemen. He can be expected to pressure the Y.A.R. to curtail Soviet and Bloc activities to the extent necessary to maintain this position.[41]

Secondary sources have confirmed that 'the Soviets may have had an interest in the Egyptian presence in Yemen, but there are no other indications that they dictated it'. Egyptian diplomat Mourad Ghalib 'expressly denies that they influenced Cairo's policy'.[42]

In a bid to win the US government to the royalist camp both British and Saudi governments attempted to taint Yemeni republicanism with the Soviet brush. But American intelligence demonstrated a keen awareness that increasing Soviet influence in Yemen was likely to be offset by Nasser. The CIA made subtle distinctions between the three levels of Soviet 'penetration': prestige, influence and control. In Yemen, they argued, there existed only the lowest level of Soviet presence due to the bulwark of Egyptian influence and traditional Yemeni xenophobia. Although 'Soviet prestige will probably remain high for a long time to come, converting prestige into influence for specific end is another matter'. The UAR would 'guard its position against Soviet encroachments' combined with the 'xenophobic tendencies of the country', which would 'frustrate anyone trying to dominate the whole, be he Westerner, Egyptian or Russian'. Despite 20 million dollars' worth of military equipment and Soviet construction of a large airfield north of San'aa, the greatest prospect for influence was thought to be 'air support for clandestine operations in nearby areas'. Even the 'unsophisticated Yemeni republic' shared 'the Arab world's emotional reaction to foreign dominance' and thus would resist supplying military base rights to, or accepting direction from, the USSR.[43]

For the British, the question of Aden lay at the forefront of the JIC's analysis. The Committee conceded that:

> hitherto the United Kingdom's position in Aden has in part rested on the fact that the Yemen has been too weak and backward to command any loyalty or respect from her neighbours. The problem with a Yemeni republic, especially if it should assume the appearance of an established and, in an Arabian context, progressive regime, is that it would encourage the nationalists in Aden to prosecute with greater vigour their campaign of opposition to the retention of the British base and to the merger of the Colony with the South Arabian Federation [SAF].[44]

At the same time the JIC made clear that a republican government in Yemen would have 'its hands full at home for some time'. Analysts poignantly made the point to policy-makers that the Yemen's 'attitude to Aden will depend to some extent on the circumstances in which the Egyptians and others disengage from military operations in the Yemen' and the manner in which the United States and British governments addressed the republican government's call for recognition.[45]

Thus initial assessments of the likely impact on Aden put the onus of responsibility on Anglo-American policy-makers, correctly suggesting that their recognition (or non-recognition in Britain's case) would in turn determine Nasser's response towards Aden. American analysts made this link more explicitly, arguing that UK 'recognition of Y.A.R. [Yemen Arab Republic] would mute Y.A.R. opposition to Aden Federation' and reduce the likelihood of an 'aggressive Y.A.R. policy in Aden'.[46] It was a sensible, if discreet, policy recommendation.

The third crucial concern beyond Yemen for both Britain and the US revolved around their oil rich ally Saudi Arabia. The prospect of a revolutionary Yemen had potentially serious implications for the stability of Saudi Arabia. Fear of what might ensue within the Kingdom of Saud drove the critical role the latter came to adopt in backing the royalists. The JIC recognised that the Saudi administration 'remains largely feudal and corrupt. Although she has oil revenues of about £130 m[illion] a year, there has been little economic development . . . and Saudi Arabia remains among the most backward of the Arab countries.' There was discontent with the slow pace of reforms and thus the possibility of a 'palace revolution', or more worryingly 'the possibility of a revolution with Egyptian assistance'. After a power struggle, King Saud's brother, the Crown Prince Feisal, was installed as Prime Minister in 1962. The more enlightened Prince Feisal had 'promised reforms which might stave off rebellion'; but there was also the risk that 'any real liberty might help it on'. The JIC recognised that conservative leaders faced a catch-22: both resisting and promoting reform ran the risk of revolution.[47]

The Saudi regime was convinced that the Egyptians were using Yemen as a springboard to overthrow the Kingdom. Nonetheless, the JIC were not convinced about alleged Egyptian plans to destabilise Saudi Arabia. They suggested that Nasser was not ready to prompt a rebellion 'because he has no organisation there ready to assume power'. The risk was that his supporters 'might forestall him', encouraged by events in Yemen. The potential overthrow of the Saudi regime would in turn place 'the existing order' in the Persian Gulf under 'very severe strains'.[48] State Department analysts agreed that the conflict had increased the domestic pressures on the Saudi Kingdom but they were not convinced by the argument that the latter was a target. Egyptian military assaults on Saudi territory near the Yemeni border were seen as reactive and limited. The attack, they suggested, was a response to 'stepped up' Saudi supplies of the Royalists. The republicans had hoped that peaceful declarations of intent and US recognition of Yemen would have led to a suspension of Saudi aid to the royalists. The bombings were designed to pressure the Saudi regime 'to move rapidly towards cessation aid and/or to stimulate U.S.G into increased efforts' to persuade their Saudi allies accordingly.[49]

The Americans initially took a rather hardline view as to how Saudi and Britain could best protect themselves against the 'infection' of nationalism. NSC advisor Robert Komer was a bright and passionate 'intellocrat' who enjoyed the nickname of 'Blowtorch Bob' because arguing with him was 'like having a blowtorch aimed at the seat of your pants'; his frank approach established him as President Kennedy's main advisor on Yemen.[50] As Komer put it, 'instead of fiddling around in Yemen Faysal needs to shore himself up domestically as the chief means of protecting himself against Nasser virus'.[51] He made the case to Kennedy that, 'we won't save oil just by giving Faysal a blank cheque on us. Nor will we necessarily lose it if we let Faysal get bloodied a bit.'[52] The Assistant Secretary of State for Near Eastern and South Asian Affairs, Philip Talbot, agreed that major Saudi military participation in the Yemeni conflict was 'likely to lead to violent repercussions at home, very possibly even the demise of the Royal Family. Included in the ultimate results would be the weakening of the very position in the area the British seek to preserve by their support of Hassan.'[53] This American position was clearly expressed in an appeal at the highest level from President Kennedy to Prime Minister Macmillan:

> We are equally worried over the effect of Faysal's unpopular war in Yemen on his own domestic position. He and Hussein [King of Jordan] think they're defending themselves against Nasser in Yemen, but we think they're making themselves more vulnerable to Nasser-inspired revolution at home. At the least, they are diverting badly needed attention and effort from domestic reforms. A revolution or serious disturbance in Saudi Arabia would hardly strengthen our position in Aden and the Gulf. On the other hand, once Nasser is deprived of an excuse to maintain a heavy presence in Yemen, natural Yemeni distaste for what is really an alien occupation should soon reassert itself. We doubt that Nasser will find the Yemenis willing tools, any more than he found the Syrians or Iraqis so. But if we force the U.A.R. to reinforce rather than reduce its presence in Yemen, and give the Soviets the chance to do so too, we may end up with a situation far more threatening to us.[54]

The JIC agreed that the Saudi support for the royalists was a dangerous gamble, but took a slightly more ambivalent tone than their American counterparts, suggesting that Saudi intervention in Yemen was 'unpopular' and that the Saudi government was showing 'great nervousness' about its position as a result.[55]

Despite the JIC's advice, the British government not only backed Saudi support for the royalists but sent covert British mercenaries to Yemen in support of their campaign. The head of MI6, Dick White, shared the view of his American counterparts across the Atlantic and was also resistant to the idea that the British secret service engage in 'cloak and dagger' operations in Yemen.[56] In understanding why the British chose to back the Saudi government and royalists against their most important ally scholars have advanced many suggestions, including the influence of the 'Suez group' (a number of Conservative politicians who had pushed for intervention in Suez) and the pre-eminence of 'competition' over 'collaboration' in the Anglo-American relationship.[57] Yet, according to intelligence assessments, who was most likely to win?

Military Predictions, Stalemate and Attempts at Peace

Initially, the analytic community on both sides of the Atlantic believed that ultimately, the republicans stood a better chance of success. They were likely influenced by early Egyptian optimism about the conflict. The Egyptians regarded the Yemeni tribes as 'backward and incapable of holding their own in modern warfare without external intervention'.[58] Moreover they enjoyed a fervent conviction that 'revolutionary right was on their side'.[59] Initially, the intelligence assessments (particularly American) seemed to agree on both counts. Although they predicted a stalemate of sorts, American analysts believed that 'in time the advantages will lie with Nasser and the republicans'.[60] They estimated that the new Yemeni regime was 'firmly in the saddle' and that the UAR was 'committed to keep it there'. They expressed doubt that, even with British and Saudi support, Prince Hassan could restore the old Imamate which, even if restored was 'too discredited to last for long'.[61] There was a sense in which a republican victory was inevitable despite the increasing support for the royalists by their allies.

Neither in fact was the JIC much more confident about the prospects of their government's attempts to overthrow the Sallal regime. In October 1962, the chairman of the JIC presented his assessment that the Republicans probably controlled some three-quarters of the population.[62] The Committee stated:

> We have previously assessed that although some of the border tribes in the north and east are likely to maintain their dissidence indefinitely, it will be extremely difficult for the Royalists to make any serious inroads into the republican position, particularly as Nasser is unlikely to withdraw his direct military support of the republican regime until he is confident of its survival.[63]

In March 1963, the CIA suggested that an impending Egyptian victory 'was nearly assured' and warned that 'with the Saudi Government nevertheless persisting in supporting the Yemeni royalists', Nasser was 'stepping up pressure' on the Saudi regime.[64]

However, the summer of 1963 saw a marked deterioration in the republican military position. In July, the ONE estimated that 'the prolongation of the civil war has gradually eroded the support initially enjoyed by the republicans' as a result of conflicts between the Zaydi and Shafi ethnic populations. Sectarian tensions between the two groups stemmed from continued Zaydi dominance under the republican regime. Analysts critiqued 'the regime's inability to carry out any of its promises to provide a better life' and the lack of progress on the part of the republicans in forming a 'reliable and effective military force' independent of the Egyptians. Consequently, the intelligence community judged that the Yememi government's position appeared to be 'slowly deteriorating' and assessed that 'a halting rather than reversal of this trend was the best the republicans could realistically hope for in the near future'. Further worrying signs included reports of an 'upsurge of plotting' and 'an attempted coup'.[65] Some months later, the CIA scathingly critiqued the 'low order' of the republican government's administrative capability, 'even by Yemeni standards'. Though there was a widespread 'let down feeling' with the republican government, they maintained that 'to most Shafis and some Zaydis it still looks preferable to the archaic regime of the Imamate'.[66]

It became clear that both the Egyptians and the West had underestimated the royalists. The ONE was forced to concede that 'the royalist forces have shown considerably more staying power than their adversaries anticipated'.[67] Later scholars were to confirm that the combination of Saudi money and the 'unexpected recalcitrance of the royalist tribes' perpetuated Nasser's symbolic intervention.[68] However, analysts maintained that whilst royalist advances had raised their 'confidence and led to new Egyptian apprehensions, we do not believe they portend a decisive change in the conflict'.[69]

By the first anniversary of the revolution, the Egyptians had approximately 30,000 troops in Yemen (nearly one third of Nasser's entire army), reorganised for a long-term occupational role, holding key towns and lines of communication.[70] In September 1963, Komer admitted that 'the Yemen regime we recognise is a non-government . . . the U.A.R. has to run the whole show. If the U.A.R. pulled out precipitately we'd have chaos.'[71] There is a hint in Komer's comment that Nasser's presence in Yemen might have been regarded as necessary, if not quite welcome.

However, the winter of 1963 saw the souring of US–Egyptian relations with disagreements over arms supplies to the royalists and the Gruening Amendment which denied American aid to Egypt.[72] In November 1963, the CIA reported to policy-makers that Nasser was 'overcommitted' with 'little likelihood of the smashing victory he once hoped for'. Analysts estimated that whilst 'Nasser recognises the difficult situation he is in [he] does not see a solution. So far his thinking has apparently not gone beyond a broadening of the present government, which hopefully would give it greater strength' and would in turn allow him to make the troop withdrawals without sacrificing Egypt's 'predominant influence'. They assessed that Nasser had not yet recognised that 'a drastic reduction of the Egyptian influence and presence' would be required to achieve a political settlement.[73]

So why did Nasser insist on remaining in Yemen? Analysts recognised that there was a 'face' aspect to Nasser's decision-making about this crisis compounded with pressure from the republicans and fears that 'reaction' and 'imperialism' were attempting to humiliate him. The stalemate presented Nasser with 'a serious dilemma'. He had 'committed his prestige to the success of the republicans' and the conflict had already absorbed 'Egyptian resources and blood'. The ONE estimated that failure would be a 'major blow' to Nasser's 'standing in the Arab world, and would probably cause widespread disgruntlement within Egypt'.[74] Moreover pressure from the republicans would 'urge Nasser not to withdraw any troops'.[75] Research from the Egyptian side has revealed that knowledge of British support for the royalists and the perceived threat from Saudi Arabia certainly impeded disengagement.[76] Heikal cites private correspondence from Nasser to his Defense Minister Amer indicating his genuine belief that the Saudis were bent on the destruction of the republican government.[77] Komer agreed that Nasser's suspicions were bona fide: 'the U.A.R. probably thinks we're either being hoodwinked by Faysal or conniving with him behind the screen of disengagement'. They warned, 'Nasser cornered is a dangerous animal, and we want to be mighty careful how we handle him.'[78] Later scholarship has confirmed that Nasser's suspicions were indeed sincere, rather than merely an excuse to expand Egyptian influence.[79]

The year of 1964 thus began with a stalemate reinforced. In the spring, chairman of the JIC Bernard Burrows urged the Committee to reassess its own assumptions on the threat of the UAR.[80] They concluded that the Egyptians 'cannot militarily defeat the tribesmen in their mountains. Conversely the Royalists cannot take the Egyptian garrison towns and hold them in the face of Egyptian heavy equipment and air support.' This state of affairs seemed likely to remain unchanged.[81]

> Despite disillusionment, economic difficulties, the financial drain, the bad effect on the morale of the U.A.R. forces, over-extension in relation to Israel and possible international disadvantages, Nasser seems at present determined to sit it out in the Yemen in order to ensure the survival of the Yemeni Republic. The effect of evident defeat for the U.A.R. sponsored Republic would be a major loss of face for him. We have no clear evidence to what extent Nasser would concede on realities if the appearance of Republican survival could be preserved. He has so far opposed all attempts on the Republican side to seek a broader base for the Republican Regime or to compromise with elements opposed to it.[82]

The issue of 'face' recurs in analysis and perhaps even offered some hope for a resolution of the conflict. The assessment above hinted that some way might be found to preserve the 'appearance' of victory for the republicans even if the reality was different.

There were some signs of diplomatic progress. In January 1964, Cairo hosted the first Arab summit, soon followed by the resumption of diplomatic relations between Egypt and Saudi Arabia and significantly, Nasser's first trip to Yemen in April. He was profoundly disappointed with what he saw, privately expressing disgust at the so-called 'revolutionary' government.[83] In September, a second summit in Alexandria instigated talks between Yemeni royalists and republicans resulting in a brief ceasefire. The deposition of King Saud for his more progressive brother Feisal even seemed to portend a meeting of minds between the Egyptian and Saudi regime. Ultimately the ceasefire agreement broke down following tensions between the various Yemeni factions.[84]

Nasser's patience was waning. Egyptian losses were increasingly difficult to justify to his constituency at home. One American diplomat recalls that at the beginning of the conflict the Egyptian regime 'brought back the dead for burial by their families, but soon stopped, for so many bodies were being returned that protests had broken out in the mosques and processions to the cemeteries'.[85] Nasser's frustrations increased further with political developments in the Yemeni republic. In 1965, a dissident group of republicans emerged known as the 'Third Force', led by the new Yemeni Prime Minister Ahmed Mohammed Nu'man. Their attempts to reconcile with Feisal led Nasser to cut off support and threaten an immediate withdrawal from Yemen. In February 1965, Sherman Kent provided a cultural explanation of why 'the Egyptians seem unable to visualise assisting a Yemeni regime which is not entirely dependent on them'. In a footnote he suggested that:

> This is not only intransigence on Nasser's part: it is a reflection of a political characteristic of the Arab world, namely, that power is indivisible. A leader only has supreme power or he doesn't, and, if he shows in some specific instance that he doesn't then doubts arise as to his power in general . . . [hence] the almost universal tendency toward authoritarian government – whether by King, president or prime minister – in the Arab states.[86]

Yet the significance of the 'Third Force' was more substantial than a mere challenge to Nasser's political authority. Scholars would later observe that 'the two client factions assumed independent attitudes and proceeded to impose various constraints on their patron's policies'.[87] After a substantial royalist advance in July 1965, the JIC observed that Nasser went to Saudi Arabia 'determined to reach a settlement which would permit him to withdraw his troops from the Yemen regardless of any undertakings' he had given to the Yemeni Republican government. They noted 'evidence that he had lost patience with Sallal and other Republican leaders'. The JIC were aware of the restrictions the clients were imposing on their patrons: 'Republicans of all shade are apprehensive of Egyptian betrayal.' Moreover republican 'fear of reprisals' by royalists might lead those 'publicly identified with the U.A.R. to try to bring about a breakdown in the agreement in order to keep the Egyptians in the Yemen'.[88] In November 1965, Nasser joked with American ambassador Lucius Battle that 'there was no real revolution in Yemen. It was only a plot. But I just found that out lately.'[89]

The JIC recognised this pragmatic side of Nasser as dominant in his policy towards Yemen. He had evidently reached the conclusion that the Egyptian military presence was 'never likely successfully to impose a Republican regime and that the time had come for him to cut his losses'. The agreement to withdraw his troops, and abandon the puppet regime in San'aa, was 'bound to damage his prestige in the Arab world'. Yet they correctly guessed that he 'may have calculated that in the long run the loss of prestige would be greater if he allowed the stalemate in the Yemen to drag on'.[90]

It was a typical manifestation of this pragmatism that Nasser had simultaneously guarded his military position, whilst ruminating on a compromise political solution. The JIC noted that 'without breaking the agreement he can retain until the late summer of 1966 sufficient forces to threaten Saudi Arabia. With each month that passes his position relative to the Royalists will be likely to improve as the latter's tribal forces disperse.' They went on to explain that the 'best hope for the success of the Agreement lies in the fact that it should suit the two principal protagonists'.[91]

These tentative moves towards disengagement were quickly foiled. In December 1965, King Feisal and the Shah of Iran called for an Islamic conference, a move that Nasser took to be a direct challenge to his authority in the Arab world. Moreover, Britain and America announced a major arms deal with Saudi Arabia. Most importantly, however, Nasser found a new resolve to persevere in Yemen after the British government announced in February 1966 that they were leaving Aden. This news, combined with Nasser's fears of conspiratorial planning against him, culminated in a declaration in March 1966 of a 'Long Breath' strategy to reduce friction with the Saudis in northern Yemen while maintaining pressure on the British in the South.[92] In May 1966, the State Department considered the prospect for conflict between Egypt and Saudi Arabia. INR took a relatively sanguine view of Egypt's intentions and maintained that Nasser's military posture in Yemen was 'basically more defensive than offensive and could not lend itself to more than isolated strikes'.[93] Saudi Arabia was not in any real danger – Nasser's intentions and capabilities in Aden, however, were a different story.

Aden

The question of Aden had plagued the British intelligence community for some time and was undoubtedly the central focus of their interest and activities in Yemen. In 1958 Aden became home to the British military's Middle East Command and was central to British plans to defend the oil fields of the Persian Gulf. It thus played a crucial role in the execution of 'Operation Vantage', supporting the newly independent state of Kuwait against Iraqi territorial claims in 1961. A republican Yemen threatened to strengthen the nationalist People's Socialist Party (PSP) in Aden who demanded union with Yemen and the expulsion of the current rulers, widely regarded as 'puppets' of London. In January 1963, the crown colony of Aden became the State of Aden and joined with the sheikhdoms and sultanates of the East and West Aden Protectorates to form the South Arabian Federation. Yet the British position came under increasing international criticism. In November 1963 the U.N. passed a resolution demanding elections in South Arabia, British withdrawal from the base and an early date to be set for independence.[94]

In 1964, what became known as the 'Aden insurgency' began in earnest, though it took a rather amateur form initially. That year, one insurgent destroyed himself in an empty club room by incorrectly wiring his explosives, another mistakenly threw the pin of his grenade instead of the weapon itself and consequently blew his feet off. However, by the end of the year the Adeni insurgents had upped their game – in December 1964 the teenage daughter of a British air commodore was killed by a hand grenade at a Christmas party. The Marxist and Egyptian backed National Liberation Front (NLF) became increasingly active in Aden, distributing training manuals for insurgents titled: 'How to Disrupt the British'. Their techniques were simple but effective: pouring sugar in the petrol tanks of cars or disabling their air conditioning.[95]

The Anglo-American intelligence community were aware that Nasser's brand of Arab nationalism had significant appeal in Aden. One American diplomat remembers 'walking through the streets of the Bazaar in Aden, and when Nasser was giving a major speech you could walk from place to place in town and not miss a word because every radio in the town was tuned in'.[96] The JIC conceded that similarly, the republicans 'embodied fashionable nationalist ideas'. Lacking 'the handicap of the Imam's reputation for tyranny, their espousal of pretensions to the Arab South was favourably received by many in Aden and the Protectorate, who would have feared an Islamic takeover'. The JIC described 'the coincidence' of the revolution in Yemen with constitutional reform in Aden and the revised treaty between Britain and the Federation as 'unfortunate, especially as many felt, and the Republicans could harp on this, that the people of Aden Colony had not been fully consulted over the new arrangements'. They admitted that the 'manifest weakness' of the Adeni government 'encouraged waverers to fall for Republican blandishments', although they noted that the 'subsequent failure of the Republicans to establish a stable regime' had served to offset this 'to some extent'.[97]

The explicit criticism of the 'manifest weakness' of Aden's government was reinforced by the JIC's subtler but discernible critique of British policy to withhold recognition of the Republic. The JIC made the case that, 'once the Republicans lost hope of British recognition, they also lost any inhibitions about following policies hostile to the Federation'. Moreover, the Republicans 'concluded, rightly, that the Federation's leaders were hostile to them and working against them'. This compounded with 'frustration within the Yemen; confidence of U.A.R. preservation of the Republican regime; a feeling that they had nothing to lose vis-à-vis the British, the lack of Imamic caution; a desire to impress by demonstration of militant "nationalism"', all of which encouraged the Republicans to 'make what trouble they could for the British in Aden by any means at hand including gun running and subversion'.[98]

Ambassador Badeau was inclined to defend Nasser somewhat. The American embassy reported back to Washington that Cairo's leadership regarded attacks on Aden as a 'means' rather than an 'end', placing Egyptian action clearly in the context of Nasser's

Figure 5.2 British paratroopers stationed in Aden, 1964. Parachute Regiment Museum Aldershot.

'impasse' in Yemen.[99] American analysts made explicit their belief that the British were sabotaging their own interests. They cited a 'report just received from Cairo' stating that the Egyptian secret service had 'documentary evidence' that forty-two European mercenaries had so far been recruited and organised by a British reserve officer for service with Yemeni royalists.[100]

The JIC's early reports also indicated that British policy towards Aden was problematic and misguided. The Committee questioned the fervent contentions of the High Commissioner in Aden that Nasser was engaged in a deliberate and concerted campaign of subversion and terrorism. Of course it could not be denied that Arab nationalism was 'the most potent force for change throughout the Arab world'. In Aden, the JIC argued that its 'emotional appeal' combined with 'anti-feudal sentiment to which fresh impetus was given by the impact of the Yemeni revolution and with the anti-colonialist feeling' which continued British presence in Aden was 'bound *in any case* to arouse'.[101] They made clear that there was no evidence of a systematic Egyptian campaign suggesting that 'before initiating a major subversive campaign against the British . . . Nasser would need to feel able to risk at least a major row with the West'.[102] The implication was that this point had not yet been reached.

Rather than imposing a strategic impetus upon Egyptian policy towards Aden, the JIC suggested that UAR policy was 'largely short term and pragmatic'. They highlighted that it was 'necessary to recognise that Nasser is not in full control of events either in the Yemen or elsewhere in Arabia'. Notwithstanding his ideological commitment to anti-imperialism, the JIC opined that:

> Nasser would not want early confrontation with the British if this could be avoided . . . there have been indications of Nasser's tacit acceptance of the fact that the British base is useful to him in the short term in safe-guarding things he cannot grab and does not wish others to seize e.g. the Persian Gulf oil fields.[103]

At the same time, they recognised that the 'general hostility' of the UAR to the Federation of South Arabia was 'unquestionable; so is its complicity in political subversion'. Yet they reminded policy-makers that 'evidence of direct U.A.R. complicity in the organisation of sabotage' in the Federation was 'comparatively recent'. They identified the date of 28 November 1963 when UAR forces in Sana'a began despatching mines and grenades to the border 'for retaliation against "the British" over sabotage around Sana'a in which U.A.R. casualties had been caused and for which the British were held responsible'. The question of British covert action re-emerged in assessments: 'The U.A.R. and Y.A.R. suspect British complicity in the supply of arms to the Royalists from federation territory and the U.A.R. claim to know the location of alleged British mercenaries with the Royalists.' The JIC clearly seemed to be suggesting that UAR sabotage of Aden only began *after* British involvement in support of the Yemeni royalists. They wrote:

> it remains in our view an open question whether the U.A.R. sponsorship of sabotage of which we have increasing evidence represents a decision to adopt a more forward policy or, rather, the reaction of Egyptians frustrated in the Yemeni deadlock against those they regard as partly responsible for that deadlock . . . Pressure on the Federation is popular in pan-Arab circles and takes the eye off the ball of Egyptian inability to gain popular support in the Yemen as a whole or suppress the Royalists. It might stop either if pressure effective enough to discourage it could be brought to bear on the U.A.R.; or alternatively if the U.A.R. concluded that help to the Royalists from Federal territory had ceased or greatly decreased.[104]

In a perhaps overly tentative manner the JIC nonetheless effectively placed doubt on the assumption of policy-makers that Nasser was engaged in a proactively hostile mission in the Federation, suggesting instead that he was responding reactively to British and Saudi machinations. On 1 May 1964, the Egyptian daily *Al Ahram* published documents definitively proving British involvement in covert action.[105] Once more we see a policy recommendation buried in this analysis: the British government should cease their aid to the royalists in order to encourage Nasser to ease pressure on the British position in the Arabian Peninsula. The JIC thus established early on that the initiative lay with their own government.

That is not to say that the Committee regarded Nasser benevolently. A more hostile attitude to Nasser clearly appears in the JIC reports around 1965. There are several possible reasons for this shift. After the Labour Party victory in 1964, the British government and federation leaders agreed at a constitutional conference in June that SAF independence would take place no later than 1968. In September 1965, five British school children about to fly back to the UK from Aden after their summer holiday, were seriously injured in a grenade attack.[106] Repeated acts of terrorism by the NLF led to the suspension of the Aden constitution and the declaration of a state of emergency.[107] Tensions between the British and the Nasser regime were no doubt accentuated by Ambassador Beeley's departure in June 1964, shortly followed by the breaking of diplomatic relations between Britain and Egypt in 1965 over British policy towards Rhodesia. Such developments almost certainly affected the tone of JIC reports. Nasser's aggressive speech at Port Said in December 1964, infamously retorting that the West could 'drink from the Mediterranean', did little to enamour the US with him either.[108] Disputes over Egyptian support for the nationalists in the Congo and food aid also contributed to less sympathetic American assessments of Nasser's intentions.

In March 1965, the JIC assessed that any republican regime was likely to wish to undermine the Federation. However their 'capability and determination to do so depend much less on the Yemen than on the U.A.R'.[109] Moreover Nasser's pronouncements to 'drive "British imperialism" out of the "Arab South" and liquidate British bases were not necessarily going to be implemented in accordance with public statements'. In accordance with his familiar pragmatism they estimated that Nasser was 'likely to vary his timing and tactics according to what he considers U.A.R. interests to be, and to other pre-occupations such as the U.A.R.'s financial situation and the state of its relations with East and West'.[110] Indeed after the declaration of independence for South Arabia in 1964, Nasser had hinted that he would accept a staging post at Aden.[111] The JIC intimated that the familiar cultural gap between 'the declared' and 'the real' combined with Nasser's pragmatism might mean that in the short term at least, the British position was not necessarily quite as gloomy as it seemed.

By 1965, American assessments on the security situation in Aden increasingly reflected a more hostile attitude toward Nasser. The CIA now expressed sympathy with the Adeni High Commissioner's view of the 'psychological importance of not giving the impression that the prize will shortly fall to Nasser'. In an apparent reversal of earlier reports, likely fuelled by the realisation that their most important ally was considering a serious regional retrenchment, American analysts argued that in fact British restraint in dealing with the security problems in Aden was putting at risk 'one of Britain's most valuable assets'.[112] Their concerns about British withdrawal went unheeded. As financial pressures and the prospect of alternative staging posts in the Indian Ocean impressed themselves upon British policy-makers, the 1966 February White Paper revealed that the British would withdraw entirely from Aden by 1968, irrespective of the security situation they left behind.

The JIC were rightly concerned about the impact the announcement would have on Nasser. There were several options. It was possible that since

> Nasser and most of his immediate advisers genuinely wish to extricate Egyptian forces from their involvement in the Yemen ... an early announcement of a British withdrawal from South Arabia might help them to do so, since they would be able to conceal the extent of their failure in the Yemen by exploiting the success of their policy in South Arabia.

There was also the 'remote possibility that they might attempt to strike a bargain by reducing terrorism in return for some British concession, though we cannot at present envisage what they might expect to gain from such a deal which they would not prefer to achieve by other means'. The JIC suggested that this course of action would depend on the readiness of the United States to bring pressure to bear as a condition of continued aid to Egypt.[113] The more likely option was that the Egyptians 'will be tempted to continue and even increase subversion and terrorism in the Federation until independence in order to demonstrate that the British are being forced to withdraw as a result of persistent nationalist pressures'.[114] As Egyptian Foreign Minister Riad later put it, 'since they are leaving we might as well fight'.[115]

Ultimately the JIC discounted the argument that there might be a propitious time for announcing departure from Aden:

> An announcement of a British military withdrawal, whenever it is made, will be seen as a weakening of the British position in the Middle East, even though this impression could be offset to some extent by a declaration that the British military presence in the Persian Gulf was to be reinforced and that steps would be quickly taken to carry this out.[116]

Thus, on the eve of the February White Paper, they were cautious to remind policy-makers not to expect too much.[117]

Some weeks later the JIC reported Nasser's reactions to the announcement of British withdrawal: They noted that 'U.A.R. opposition to Western and particularly British influence anywhere in the Middle East is most unlikely to change, even though the British departure from South Arabia will in practice meet the principal Egyptian demand.' There was a discernible frustration with Nasser's double standards in this regard. The JIC wrote that although, 'as an Arab socialist, Nasser disapproves of the type of hereditary ruling families whose members make up the present Federal Government' he was nonetheless 'prepared to work through any of them whose allegiance he can acquire'. By this point Nasser's primary tool for disruption in Aden was the Front for the Liberation of the occupied South Yemen (FLOSY). The JIC described the group as including 'the majority of the extremists who made up the former National Liberation Front'. They were sure that Nasser would 'doubtless prefer to see a firmly pro-Egyptian government established' before the British withdrawal. However, 'since it was still fairly unlikely that he will achieve this object, he will concentrate on preventing the appearance of any alternative government, and try to ensure that the British withdrawal takes place in as much disorder as possible'.[118] The spectre of Nasser 'the trouble-maker' was increasingly visible in JIC reporting.

Nasser was clearly taking advantage of the opportunity to humiliate the British. Egyptian covert operations increased following the White Paper, but analysts do seem to have resisted the tendency to regard his actions as indicative of imperialist expansion. Although evidently frustrated with what they described as the 'hypocrisy' of Nasser's 'Arab socialism' and his determination to cause disruption during British withdrawal, they seemed not entirely convinced about the possibility of direct Egyptian intervention south of Yemen. The JIC conceded there was 'a risk that President Nasser might find it difficult to refuse a public appeal for Egyptian intervention in a chaotic situation' in South Arabia.[119] In spite of the political and military risks, 'Nasser would in the last resort be forced to intervene militarily in Aden' if called upon to do so by his friends 'since the political cost of failing to respond . . . would be unacceptable'.[120] Yet their language clearly put Nasser in the role of reacting to local demands rather than desiring such Egyptian intervention *per se*. Their analysis effectively anticipated the conclusions of scholars that, considering

> the weight of the burden Egypt already bore, it is unlikely that Nasser planned to extend the Egyptian military occupation of Yemen southward. He hoped instead to bring about an anarchic situation whereby his local supporters could take over as soon as the British left, enhancing his own regional status.[121]

In September 1966, the American embassy in Yemen reported their 'suspicion that U.A.R. [is] keep[ing] its forces here for day of "liberation" South Arabia until 1968 in anticipation of new opportunities'.[122] The CIA reminded anxious policy-makers that Adeni nationalist leaders were not 'working to hand Aden over to Egypt but to free it from foreign domination'.[123]

British experience in Aden seemed to indicate critical lessons for the future. As Sherman Kent had predicted a year earlier, the British were indeed eventually forced to hand power over to the very extremist forces they had sought to exclude.[124] Moreover they had badly compromised their standing in the international arena. The *Sunday Times* published an eyewitness account of a British soldier beating an Adeni 'about the head and prodding him in his midriff and genitals, a second soldier hitting him with a tin mug' before a third used his fists to knock him out. The article drew the attention of the Red Cross and Amnesty International, poignantly alerting the British government to the moral high ground they could no longer defend.[125] Focusing on the more practical lessons learned for the future, the JIC warned, 'only if the British Government can persuade the Rulers [of the Gulf] to adopt a gradual policy of liberalisation, and to spend more of their revenues on development, can the political threat to their own and to the British position be contained'.[126]

Paradoxically, the JIC regarded Saudi Arabia as the natural successors to British influence. Despite noting the Saudi government's autocratic and feudal nature the JIC wrote,

> there is no doubt that we and the Saudi regime enjoy a strong common interest in the exclusion of revolutionary forces from the peninsula, and in the encouragement of political and economic progress through the area by peaceful evolution. An extension of Saudi influence to the Gulf States after a British withdrawal would be a natural development.[127]

The Committee seemed to endorse passing over the mantle of British influence to yet another dubious ally, to whom they entrusted the goals of political and economic progress despite only limited signs that the Feisal regime was itself interested in such reform.

* * *

The record of intelligence assessments on the Yemeni conflict is relatively plentiful, particularly on the British side. They reveal a narrative of the conflict that was reasonably accurate, revising the most recent scholarship which suggests that misperceptions and misunderstanding dominated British policy towards Yemen. From the outset, analysts demonstrated good strategic and tactical notice of the prospects for revolution, although they shared with the Egyptians ideas about Yemeni culture as 'backward' and 'unsophisticated'. Their judgements of Nasser's intentions were astute, recognising that Nasser had no blueprint or master plan for revolution in Yemen, that he had underestimated the commitment required and that bound by his 'face' as Arab revolutionary leader, was compelled to maintain support for the republican government despite the unassailable stalemate that ensued. Early assessments stressed that Soviet influence would be offset by the Egyptian presence and Yemeni xenophobia and that revolution in Saudi Arabia was more likely to come about from domestic conditions and the unpopular intervention in Yemen than from

Nasser's policies. Assessments of Aden initially highlighted the reactive nature of Nasser's actions, exacerbated by the British policy of non-recognition and 'covert' support for the royalists. They emphasised Nasser's pragmatism and the gap between Nasser's anti-imperialist rhetoric and his *realpolitik* interest in British presence in the Gulf. After 1965 the image of Nasser the troublemaker rose to the surface of JIC assessments as it became evident that despite fulfilling nationalist demands, he was determined to extract the maximum political benefit from British withdrawal. Dubious terms such as 'rabid nationalists' only occasionally permeated what appears to have been a relatively progressive and self-critical analysis by the JIC. They could certainly have shouted louder about the negative impact of British action in Yemen but their caution perhaps stemmed from the absence of a discernible East of Suez policy. Overall their images of Egypt's president were multiple and nuanced, reflecting the many faces of Nasser: the shrewd pragmatist, the sometimes misguided ideologue, the nationalist not entirely in control and, of course, the long-standing opportunist. Many of these images were to be reinforced by the tragic debacle of the Six-Day War.

Notes

1. Interview with Raymond Hare, 22 July 1987. Available at <http://adst.org/wp-content/uploads/2012/09/Egypt.pdf>, p. 12 (last accessed 1 March 2017).
2. V. Clark, *Yemen: Dancing on the Heads of Snakes* (New Haven, CT: Yale University Press, 2010), p. 63.
3. Ibid. p. 67, pp. 89–90.
4. N. J. Ashton, *Kennedy, Macmillan and the Cold War: The Irony of Interdependence* (Basingstoke: Palgrave Macmillan, 2002), pp. 90–108, explores the policy rift across the Atlantic which the conflict occasioned and argues that at the heart of this rift lay different attitudes to Nasser alongside a spirit of 'competitive collaboration'. C. Gandy, 'A mission to Yemen', *British Journal of Middle Eastern Studies*, 25: 2, 1998, reveals the extent to which the British government was divided on the issue of Yemeni recognition. L. James, *Nasser At War: Arab Images of the Enemy* (Basingstoke: Palgrave

Macmillan, 2006), uses numerous interviews and Arabic sources to explore the Egyptian perspective and how Nasser's actions in the conflict were driven by perceptions of his enemies such as Britain, Saudi Arabia and increasingly the US. This builds on much earlier works such as A. I. Dawisha, 'Intervention in the Yemen: an analysis of Egyptian perceptions and policies', *Middle East Journal*, 29: 1, 1975, who explores the transformation of Nasser's perceptions of the conflict in an attempt to answer why he remained embroiled for so long. A. Rahmy, *The Egyptian Policy in the Arab World: Intervention in Yemen: 1962–1967: A Case Study* (Washington: University Press of America, 1983), provides an account by an Egyptian army officer who served in North Yemen during the intervention, marking an early contribution to a more 'international' historiography of this important conflict. S. M. Badeeb, *The Saudi-Egyptian Conflict over North Yemen, 1962–1970* (Boulder, CO: Westview Press, 1986), provides a more subjective defence of Saudi policy in Yemen. The minister writes, for example, that 'it is well known that the Kingdom does not intervene in the domestic policies and affairs of other nations' (p. 109). Abd al-Ghani Mutahhar, one of the organisers of the revolution and a member of the Council of Revolutionary Leadership in the republican government founded after the coup, provides a Yemeni narrative of the revolution in A. Mutahhar, *Yauma Walada al-Yaman Majadahu: Dhikrayat' 'an Thaorat Sibtambir 1962* (Sana'a: Dar Nobal lil-tiba'a, 1990).

5. The intelligence dimension has been explored in more recent years by a selection of scholars. The most comprehensive accounts can be found in C. Jones, *Britain and the Yemen Civil War, 1962–1965: Ministers, Mercenaries and Mandarins: Foreign Policy and the Limits of Covert Action* (Brighton: Sussex Academic Press, 2004), and S. Mawby, *British Policy in Aden and the Protectorates 1955–67* (London: Routledge, 2005). See also R. Aldrich, *GCHQ: The Uncensored Story of Britain's Most Secret Intelligence Agency* (London: Harper Press, 2010), p. 164: 'SIGINT not only gave a detailed picture of troop deployments, but also revealed tensions between republican ministers and the Chief of Staff of the Egyptian armed forces.'

6. Jones, *Britain and the Yemen Civil War*, provides the best account of this rift within the British government.

7. Jones, *Britain and the Yemen Civil War*, p. 42.

8. Badr cited in G. De Carvlaho, 'Yemen's Desert Fox', *Life Magazine*, 19 February 1965.

9. Robert W. Komer, Oral History Interview – JFK #2, 16 July 1964. Available at <http://www.jfklibrary.org/Asset-Viewer/Archives/JFKOH-ROWK-02.aspx> (last accessed 1 May 2017).
10. C. Cooper, *In the Shadows of History: Fifty Years Behind the Scenes of Cold War Diplomacy* (Amherst, NY: Prometheus, 2006), p. 182.
11. Memorandum from Director of Intelligence and Research (Hillsman) to Secretary of State Rusk, 13 September 1962, FRUS 1961-63, vol. XVIII, no. 38.
12. JIC memorandum (58) 13, 'Nationalist and radical movements in the Arabian Peninsula', 10 February 1958, TNA, CAB 158/31.
13. Report by Seelye, 'The implications of the death of Imam Ahmed of Yemen', 20 September 1962, FRUS 1961-63, vol. XVIII, no. 51.
14. S. Guldescu, 'Yemen: the war and the Hardah conference', *Review of Politics*, 28: 3, 1966, p. 320. The article also hints at the enduring comparisons with Hitler in open sources at the time: 'the Saudi monarch has come to the conclusion that he cannot do business with Nasser any more than European governments could with Hitler in the pre-1939 era', p. 331.
15. JIC memorandum (57) 87, 'The effect on the Yemen of recent events in Syria and the Arabian Peninsula', 20August 1957, TNA, CAB 158/29.
16. W. Brown, 'The Yemeni dilemma', *Middle East Journal*, 17: 4, 1963, p. 387.
17. SNIE 36.7-63, 'Situation and prospects in Yemen', 6 November 1963, FOIA Reading Room.
18. JIC memorandum (58) 15, 'Likely developments in the Arabian Peninsula over the next five years', 11 February 1958, TNA, CAB 158/31.
19. Intelligence Report, 'Political dynamics and trends in the Yemen', 21 July 1959, OSS/SDIRR The Middle East 1950-1961, Microfilm, Reel 3, SOAS Library.
20. JIC memorandum (58) 13, 'Nationalist and radical movements in the Arabian Peninsula', 10 February 1958, TNA, CAB 158/31.
21. Ibid.
22. Intelligence Report, 'Political dynamics and trends in the Yemen', 21 July 1959, OSS/SDIRR The Middle East 1950-1961, Microfilm, Reel 3, SOAS Library.
23. JIC memorandum (60) 22, 'The outlook in Yemen', 19 May 1960, TNA, CAB 158/39.
24. Ibid.
25. James, *Nasser at War*, p. 56.

26. Ibid.
27. G. A. Nasser, Address by President Gamal Abdel Nasser at the Palestinian National Congress, 31 May 1965 (Cairo, 1965).
28. James, *Nasser at War*, p. 62.
29. Memorandum from Director of Intelligence and Research (Hillsman) to Secretary of State Rusk, 13 September 1962, FRUS 1961-63, vol. XVIII, no. 38.
30. M. Gamasy, *The October War* (Cairo: AUC Press, 1993), p. 18. See also A. Sadat, *In Search of Identity* (London: Collins, 1978), p. 163.
31. James, *Nasser at War*, p. 58.
32. Memorandum from Brubeck to Bundy, 'Implications of the revolution in Yemen', 5 October 1962, FRUS 1961-63, vol. XVIII, no. 69.
33. Telegram from embassy in the UAR to State Department, 1 October 1961, FRUS 1961-63, vol. XVIII, no. 63.
34. Jones, *Britain and the Yemen Civil War*, p. 33.
35. JIC memorandum (62) 90, 'The implications of the Yemeni revolt', 30 November 1962, TNA, CAB 158/47.
36. Telegram from the UAR Embassy to State Department, 10 October 1962, FRUS 1961-63, vol. XVIII, no. 77.
37. JIC memorandum (57) 87, 'The effect on the Yemen of recent events in Syria and the Arabian Peninsula', 20 August 1957, TNA, CAB 158/29.
38. Memorandum from Glass in DIA to Bundy, 'Soviet/Soviet Bloc activity in Yemen', 21 June 1963, FRUS 1961-63, vol. XVIII, no. 278.
39. Draft memorandum from CIA's ONE to DCI, 'The situation in Yemen', 8 October 1962, FRUS 1961-63, vol. XVIII, no. 74.
40. Memorandum from Glass in DIA to Bundy, 'Soviet/Soviet Bloc activity in Yemen', 21 June 1963, FRUS 1961-63, vol. XVIII, no. 278.
41. Memorandum from Glass in DIA to Bundy, 'Soviet/Soviet Bloc activity in Yemen', 21 June 1963, FRUS 1961-63, vol. XVIII, no. 278.
42. James, *Nasser at War*, p. 71.
43. SNIE 36.7-63, 'Situation and prospects in Yemen', 6 November 1963, FOIA Reading Room.
44. JIC memorandum (62) 90, 'The implications of the Yemeni revolt', 30 November 1962, TNA, CAB 158/47.
45. Ibid.
46. Telegram from State Department to embassy in UK, 28 February 1963, FRUS 1961-63, vol. XVIII, no. 171.
47. JIC memorandum (62) 90, 'The implications of the Yemeni revolt', 30 November 1962, TNA, CAB 158/47.
48. Ibid.

49. Telegram from State Department to embassy in the UAR, 18 January 1963, FRUS 1961-63, vol. XVIII, no. 134. Only some months later the CIA expressed concern that Nasser was considering a ground strike into Saudi Arabia although this was dismissed by State and DIA. See memorandum from Komer to Bundy, 1 March 1963, FRUS 1961-63, vol. XVIII, no.173.

50. John Jernegan, Oral History Interview, 12 March 1969. Available at <http://archive1.jfklibrary.org/JFKOH/Jernegan,%20John%20D/ JFKOH-JDJ-01/JFKOH-JDJ-01-TR.pdf>, p. 30 (last accessed 1 March 2017).

51. Memorandum from Komer in NSC to President Kennedy, 21 February 1963, FRUS 1961-1963, vol. XVIII, no. 160.

52. Ibid.

53. Memorandum from Talbot to Rusk, 'Analysis of the situation in Yemen and recommendation for course of action', 9 October 1962, FRUS 1961-63, vol. XVIII, no. 76.

54. Telegram from President Kennedy to Prime Minister Macmillan, 'Exposition of U.S. views on disengagement agreement in Yemen', 26 January 1963, FRUS 1961-63, vol. XVIII, no.142.

55. JIC memorandum (63) 29, 'The outlook for Jordan and Saudi Arabia in 1963', 11 April 1963, TNA, CAB 158/48.

56. Jones, *Britain and the Yemeni Civil War*, p. 36.

57. Ashton, *Cold War: The Irony of Interdependence*, p. 94.

58. James, *Nasser at War*, p. 66.

59. Ibid.

60. Draft memorandum from CIA's ONE to DCI, 'The situation in Yemen', 8 October 1962, FRUS 1961-63, vol. XVIII, no. 74.

61. Memorandum from Talbot to Rusk, 'Yemeni situation and its implications', 9 October 1962, FRUS 1961-63, vol. XVIII, no. 76.

62. Jones, *Britain and the Yemen Civil War*, p. 30.

63. JIC memorandum (62) 90, 'The implications of the Yemeni revolt', 30 November 1962, TNA, CAB 158/47.

64. Current Intelligence Weekly Review, 15 March 1963, FOIA Reading Room.

65. ONE memorandum, 'The Yemeni revolution: disengagement or continued conflict', 2 July 1963, CREST, NARA II.

66. SNIE 36.7-63, 'Situation and prospects in Yemen', 6 November 1963, FOIA Reading Room.

67. ONE memorandum, 'The Yemeni revolution: disengagement or continued conflict', 2 July 1963, CREST, NARA II.

68. James, *Nasser at War*, p. 68.

69. ONE memorandum, 'The Yemeni revolution: disengagement or continued conflict', 2 July 1963, CREST, NARA II.
70. James, *Nasser at War*, p. 69.
71. Paper by Komer in NSC, 'The next round in Yemen', 20 September 1963, FRUS 1961-63, vol. XVIII, no. 329.
72. This amendment by Congress denied aid to countries (such as Egypt) attacking countries (such as Saudi) receiving US assistance.
73. SNIE 36.7-63, 'Situation and prospects in Yemen', 6 November 1963, FOIA Reading Room.
74. ONE memorandum, 'The Yemeni revolution: disengagement or continued conflict', 2 July 1963, CREST, NARA II.
75. Ibid.
76. James, *Nasser at War*, pp. 72–4.
77. H. Heikal, *Sanawat al Ghalyan* (Cairo: Al Ahram, 1988) p. 651.
78. Paper by Komer in NSC, 'The next round in Yemen', 20 September 1963, FRUS 1961-63, vol. XVIII, no. 329.
79. James, *Nasser at War*, p. 75.
80. JIC minutes (64) 17th Meeting, 2 April 1964, TNA, CAB 159/40.
81. JIC memorandum (64) 32, 'Developments in the Arabian Peninsula and their implications for Aden', 17 March 1964, TNA, CAB 158/52.
82 Ibid.
83. D. M. Witty, 'A Regular Army in counter-insurgency operation: Egypt in North Yemen, 1962-1967', *Journal of Military History*, 65: 2, 2001, p. 246.
84. James, *Nasser at War*, p. 79.
85. Interview with Richard E. Undeland, 29 July 1994. Available at <http://adst.org/wp-content/uploads/2012/09/Egypt.pdf>, p. 232 (last accessed 1 March 2017).
86. ONE Special Memorandum no. 9-65, 'Nasser's problems and prospects in Yemen', 18 February 1965, FOIA Reading Room.
87. Dawisha, 'Intervention in the Yemen', *Middle East Journal*, 29: 1, 1975, p. 56.
88. JIC memorandum (65) 59, 'Implications of the U.A.R./Saudi Arabian agreement to end the war in Yemen – a preliminary assessment', 31 August 1965, TNA, CAB 158/59.
89. James, *Nasser at War*, p. 80.
90. JIC memorandum (65) 59, 'Implications of the U.A.R./Saudi Arabian agreement to end the war in Yemen – a preliminary assessment', 31 August 1965, TNA, CAB 158/59.
91. Ibid: 'Nasser should be able to extract himself from an unsuccessful adventure with the minimum loss of face owing to the length of

time given him. Feisal should succeed both in removing the Egyptian pressure from southern Arabia, and avoiding the establishment of a revolutionary regime on his immediate borders.'

92. James, *Nasser at War*, p. 84.

93. Research memorandum from Hughes at INR to Secretary, 'Prospects for a direct Saudi-UAR armed conflict over Yemen', 9 May 1966, DDRS.

94. D. French, *The British Way in Counter-Insurgency, 1945–1967* (New York: Oxford University Press, 2012), p. 240.

95. Clark, *Yemen*, p. 83.

96. Interview with Michael Sterner, 2 March 1990. Available at <http://www.adst.org/OH%20TOCs/Sterner,%20Michael%20E.toc.pdf>, p. 8 (last accessed 1 March 2017).

97. JIC memorandum (64) 32, 'Developments in the Arabian Peninsula and their implications for Aden', 17 March 1964, TNA, CAB 158/52.

98. Ibid.

99. Telegram from Ambassador Badeau in Cairo to State Department, 4 May 1964, DDRS. In this insightful cable Badeau stressed both the importance of dealing with Nasser in a pragmatic manner, and applying diplomatic pressure 'without publicity'.

100. Memorandum from Read to Bundy, 'Rising tensions among officials in Aden and latest report on European mercenaries fighting with Yemeni "Royalists"', 8 May 1964, FRUS 1964-1968, vol. XXI, no. 58.

101. JIC memorandum (63) 80, 'The threat to Aden', 3 January 1964, TNA, CAB 158/50 [emphasis added].

102. Ibid.

103. JIC memorandum (64) 32, 'Developments in the Arabian Peninsula and their implications for Aden', 17 March 1964, TNA, CAB 158/52.

104. Ibid: 'We cannot say how far this UAR sponsorship may persist. As however it represents little effort for the Egyptians; as it is much easier for the Y.A.R and U.A.R. to stimulate traditional dissidence and to organise sabotage than to counter it; and as it is relatively easy for the Egyptians to promote it without their direct participation on the territory of the Federation, we should expect it to continue.'

105. McNamara, *Britain, Nasser and the Balance of Power*, p. 198.

106. Clark, *Yemen*, p. 84.

107. JIC memorandum (64) 77, 'The threat to South Arabia', 8 March 1965, TNA, CAB 158/54. The JIC regarded the NLF as 'a "front" organisation created and financed by the U.A.R to provide a nationalist cover for the UAR's activities directed at South Arabia'. They also noted that in Aden, NLF 'terrorist activity and sabotage have increased recently and show a new sophistication, both in technique and execution, reflecting the specialised training given by the Egyptians at a camp near Taiz'.
108. McNamara, *Britain, Nasser and the Balance of Power*, p. 212.
109. JIC memorandum (64) 77, 'The threat to South Arabia', 8 March 1965, TNA, CAB 158/54.
110. Ibid.
111. McNamara, *Britain, Nasser and the Balance of Power*, p. 201.
112. Intelligence memorandum OCI no. 1812/65, 'The security situation in Aden', 9 June 1965, FRUS 1964-68, vol. XXI, no. 61.
113. JIC memorandum (65) 92, 'The effects in the Middle East and Africa of an announcement of a British withdrawal from South Arabia in 1967 or 1968', 23 December 1965, TNA, CAB 165/60. While critical of their own government, the JIC also reserved criticism of the Americans for not wanting to pressure Nasser in this regard.
114. Ibid.
115. James, *Nasser at War*, p. 86.
116. JIC memorandum (65) 92, 'The effects in the Middle East and Africa of an announcement of a British withdrawal from South Arabia in 1967 or 1968', 23 December 1965, TNA, CAB 165/60. This report also makes reference to 'rabid nationalists'.
117. JIC memorandum (65) 60, 'The outlook for the United Arab Republic over the next two years', 2 February 1966, TNA, CAB 158/59.
118. JIC memorandum (66) 37, 'The outlook for the Persian Gulf and South Arabia up to the end of 1968', 25 May 1966, TNA, CAB 165/63.
119. JIC memorandum (66) 64, 'The possibility of an Egyptian military occupation of Aden after independence', 10 October 1966, TNA, CAB 158/ 64.
120. JIC memorandum (67) 20, 'The likely situation in South Arabia in 1968 and the implications for British interests', 3 March 1967, TNA, CAB 158/66.
121. James, *Nasser at War*, p. 87.

122. Telegram from embassy in Yemen to State Department, 4 September 1966, FRUS 1964-68, vol. XXI, no. 408.

123. NIE, 'Soviet actions in respect of possible successor regimes in South Arabia', 12 October 1966, FRUS 1964–68, vol. XXI, no. 78.

124. Special memorandum prepared in the CIA, no. 26-65, 'Outlook for Aden and the federation of South Arabia', 5 November 1965, FRUS 1964-68, vol. XXI, no. 67.

125. Clark, *Yemen*, p. 85.

126. JIC memorandum (66) 37, 'The outlook for the Persian Gulf and South Arabia up to the end of 1968', 25 May 1966, TNA, CAB 158/63: 'Nevertheless Egyptian opposition will build up over the period and may manifest itself overtly through the United Nations ... In the absence of colonial relationships and with very limited military force, present and future British position in the Persian Gulf depends on the confidence of the Rulers in British ability to protect them and assist development. This confidence could be gravely affected by a failure to establish a viable independent state in South Arabia and to carry out an orderly withdrawal. Any considerable increase in subversion and terrorism in their own States might also lead them to the view that this was to some extent due to the British presence attracting the unwelcome attentions of the U.A.R. and Iraq, and to begin to question the advantages of British protection.'

127. JIC memorandum (65) 90, 'The outlook for Saudi Arabia until 1970', 9 May 1966, TNA, CAB 158/60.

6 Six-Day War

It had all the smell to me of a Guns of August kind of situation. People had blundered into a situation none of them really wanted. I don't, to this day, believe Nasser wanted a war. He wanted the fruits of victory without having to fight the war.

Roy Atherton, 1990[1]

The Arab–Israeli War of 1967 marked a fundamental turning point in international relations. The state of Israel absorbed three times its former territory and the spectacular Arab defeat signalled the failure of pan-Arabism as an ideological force in the Middle East. The cult of Nasser as the leader of Arab nationalism would never be restored to its former glory. Scholars would later identify this ideological vacuum as the primary motivating force in the turn to Islamic fundamentalism.[2] From the perspective of the outside powers, it signalled the 'last moment' of prominent British influence in the Middle East, the consolidation of Soviet influence in Egypt and the affirmation of a 'special relationship' between Israel and the US.[3] Diplomatic relations between Egypt and America were instantly broken and not resumed until 1974, following false Egyptian accusations that the Israeli victory could not have been possible without American support. A junior member of the American diplomatic corps recalls the demonstrators attacking the American consulate in Alexandria. Apparently one of the more courageous consular staff went downstairs from the vault where they were hiding to try to defuse the situation. He remembers that the leader of the Egyptian mob 'politely asked to borrow the American's cigarette lighter so he could burn the American flag which he had just taken down'.[4]

Notwithstanding the damage done to Egyptian–American relations, the CIA portrays this crisis as a resounding intelligence success. In his memoirs, DCI Richard Helms cites it as one of the
most important achievements of his career, concretely proving the
worth of intelligence to a sceptical President Lyndon Johnson.[5]
Though Helms maintained a low profile as DCI, after the Six-Day
War he was regularly invited to attend President Johnson's Tues-
day lunch meetings with his closest advisors. Intelligence analysis guided policy-makers to resist alarmist fears that Israel was
about to be driven into the sea, enabling a 'hands-off' approach
that minimized the impact of the crisis on Western interests in
the Arab world and contained the confrontation that might have
polarised a Western supported Israel against a Soviet supported,
unified Arab force.[6]

Figure 6.1 DCI Richard Helms with former CIA heads Allen Dulles
(left) and William Rayborn, 1966. US NARA National Archives 2.

Nonetheless, it is only recently that we have been able to ask a set of more complex questions from a first-hand examination of the sources.[7] In what sense did this crisis constitute an intelligence 'success' and what were the features which made it possible? Ultimately, the strength of Anglo-American intelligence derived from its ability to look beyond the 'facts' and into the cultural dynamics of the key players in the region in order to determine their capabilities and intentions. In regards to their primary Cold War enemy, analysts correctly assessed that whilst the Soviet Union stood to gain from general Arab–Israeli tensions, its role in this crisis was constrained by the limited nature of patron–client relations with Egypt, and its reluctance to be drawn into superpower confrontation.

With Israel, analysts faced a slightly different set of considerations. The agenda of the Israeli intelligence community and pro-Israeli feeling on both sides of the Atlantic, together with the vehemence of Arab rhetoric, put significant pressure on policymakers and analysts to ensure the survival of the still relatively nascent Israeli state. The Anglo-American intelligence community established beyond doubt that Israel was in the superior military position, and placed likely Israeli actions within the familiar context of Israel's political culture.

On the final, and perhaps most important player, Western intelligence analysts faced their greatest challenge. Diplomat and former head of the JIC Patrick Wright recalls, 'Nasser's behaviour over the Tiran Straits appeared to all of us to be totally illogical . . . he was one of those who could actually believe what he knew to be untrue.'[8] Yet the Anglo-American intelligence community accurately applied its conceptual analysis of Arab cultural 'Otherness' to quell international fears that Nasser was the next Hitler intent on, and capable of, exterminating the state of Israel as Arab nationalistic rhetoric threatened. Instead they identified the pre-eminent role of 'face' in contributing to an unintentional escalation of tension and aptly distinguished between what Arab leaders said and the 'facts' of what they were capable of achieving militarily. Relying on a controversial intellectual archive of the behaviours typical of Arab culture amassed during the previous decade, analysts managed to resist 'mirror-imaging' Western rationale to explain Nasser's motivations and actions.

That is not to say the intelligence process worked perfectly; this notion of 'success' obscures important weaknesses in intelligence analysis of this crisis, namely the inability to look beyond the 'fog of war' to what would follow. Nonetheless, in the prelude to and immediacy of the 1967 war, an application of cultural knowledge proved crucial to accurate Anglo-American intelligence assessments of this regional and geopolitical crisis point.

* * *

The Soviet Union

The intelligence community had no dearth of data on the Soviet threat to the Middle East. As the vast majority of the analytic products in this region were devoted to assessing Soviet intentions and capabilities, it is not surprising that a framework for estimating likely Soviet policy in the Middle East was well established.[9] Analysts recognised that the Arab–Israeli conflict presented a critical opportunity for the Soviet Union to expand its influence in Egypt. The CIA believed that 'one almost certain objective of the Soviets is to see the US more firmly and publicly identified with Israel'. This would serve the purpose of 'making the entire Arab world – including in an ambivalent way even the more conservative states – convinced that the U.S. is irrevocably committed to their common enemy'. As a result, the American position would be weakened, its oil interests threatened, and the Soviet position 'as friend and protector of all Arabs against their imperialist foes' significantly strengthened. [10]

Just days before the war, American analysts asserted that that the Soviet Union 'sees the Arabs, in consequence of their numbers and revolutionary nationalism, as the best long term bet' and that 'Moscow has clearly decided that it has more to gain by taking sides'. Although the Soviets 'would not run high risks of an East–West confrontation for the sake of an Arab cause', analysts assessed that they had no 'basic objection to an Arab resort to violence' and might seek to support their clients 'at some fairly high level of risk short of actual intervention'.[11]

Fear of Soviet machinations was exacerbated by intelligence received indicating that a KGB officer had falsely informed Egypt that Israel was concentrating brigades on the Syrian border. This was the trigger prompting Nasser to move troops into Sinai. In the build-up to war such alarmist fears seemed to be emanating from various sources. On 28 May the American ambassador to the Soviet Union relayed a panicked warning from the Egyptian Embassy's political counsellor that Nasser had a 'larger commitment from [the] Soviets than anyone (presumably including the source) had realized'. He feared that Moscow sought to 'transform Arab–Israeli struggle into showdown between Communists and anti-Communists for control of Middle East'. The Egyptian source warned that the Soviets were 'succeeding. If Nasser wins this one, monarchies and Western oil interests will go.'[12] The danger was, of course, what type of 'showdown' this would be. If the Soviet Union backed the Arab war effort, the US would have no choice but to stand by Israel, thereby transforming a regional battle into a global war.

The strength of the intelligence community's analysis derived from its ability to contextualise such fears of Soviet involvement within their knowledge of Soviet–Egyptian relations. Analysts recognised that the Soviet role in this crisis was constrained by two factors: firstly, its limited capability to dictate or influence Egyptian decision-making and secondly, its desire to avoid superpower confrontation.

The JIC had long observed that despite effective Soviet penetration of the Middle East it was 'doubtful whether the Russians are in a position to dictate Egyptian policy since we would expect Nasser to react as sharply to any direct pressure from the Soviet Union as from the West'.[13] American analysts also judged that Egyptian nationalism would militate against any Soviet strategic initiatives in the Middle East, and suggested that:

> It has not been so clear that these actions were governed by any systematic strategic conception, apart from the general proposition that the area offered considerable opportunity for damaging U.S. interests ... In part the growth of Soviet presence and activity in the area has been a response to forces operating within the region, it has not all been Soviet design.[14]

The role of Egyptian agency in the relationship was evident. Nor was it clear that the Soviets wanted a greater role in the region. Analysts suggested that even the Kremlin sought a 'cautious Soviet policy towards the Arab-Israeli dispute' not least because 'armed conflict would inevitably lead to a call from the Arabs for increased Soviet arms supplies' and perhaps 'even in the last resort for a more direct form of Soviet intervention; this in turn would give rise to the danger of escalation and direct confrontation with the United States'.[15] The Cuban Missile Crisis had likely set an important precedent in recognising that despite what was perceived by the West to be inflammatory action, the USSR was probably not seeking direct confrontation.

Both the JIC and the CIA deployed a little positive 'mirror-imaging' when considering the Soviet role in this crisis. Their sensitivity to the nuances of the relationship between the Soviet Union and Egypt perhaps derived from America's experience with its own quasi-client state in the Arab–Israeli conflict. As they could not control every action of the Israelis, so the Soviet Union could not be held responsible for Egypt's actions. Moreover, like its corollary superpower, America was determined to prevent a regional conflict from escalating into superpower confrontation.

The first issue to reckon with was the rumour that Soviet intelligence had prompted Nasser to take provocative action against Israel. Surely this indicated a Soviet plan of sorts? An analyst from the NSC put forward a plausible scenario intimating that this was more likely to be an error than intentional deception. They suggested that:

> Soviet agents actually picked up intelligence reports of a planned Israeli raid into Syria. I would not be surprised if the reports were at least partly true . . . Intelligence being an uncertain business, the Soviet agents may not have known the scale of the raid and may have exaggerated its scope and purpose.[16]

Knowledge of the disparate transmission of information that characterised Soviet political culture was also useful. With some two decades of experience interpreting Cold War developments, analysts understood that the Soviet leadership was unlikely to have been informed of, least of all approved, such meddling at this level.

It was also regarded as unlikely that the Soviets had been much consulted as to the Egyptian response. The CIA suggested that the Soviet Union 'may not have known in advance about the closing of the Strait', concluding that 'we do not believe that they desire a Middle Eastern war or that they have planned with Nasser the destruction of Israel at this juncture'.[17] Heikal confirms that Nasser's decision to close the Strait was met with surprise by the Soviet Ambassador to Egypt.[18]

That is not to say that Soviet influence was negligible, as retrospective accounts have verified. On 19 May, the Novosti Press Agency asserted that the USSR would not stand idly by if Israel attacked Syria.[19] The CIA were careful to remind consumers that the crisis could not be considered a Soviet plan. Nor did they think that the Soviets had 'urged' Nasser to his present course of action, but they were sure that the Soviet 'attitude must have been sufficiently permissive' to allow Nasser to count on political and logistic support as the crisis developed.[20] Subsequent memoirs and rare instances of Egyptian documentation have confirmed that this was precisely the case. Heikal provides a badly photocopied memorandum revealing a categorical assurance from the Soviet Defence Minister Grechko to Egyptian War Minister Shams Badran as he left Moscow for Cairo on 28 May: 'I want to make it clear to you that if America enters the war we will enter it on your side.'[21] After Badran boarded, Grechko apparently told the Egyptian ambassador in Moscow: 'I just wanted to give him one for the road.'[22] Without knowing the above details, the Anglo-American intelligence community correctly anticipated the conclusions of future scholars that 'the Soviets were too free with their apparently unequivocal statements of support'.[23]

The central question in the minds of policy-makers, however, was how far would this support reach? Would the Soviet Union militarily intervene on behalf of its client state, thus forcing the United States to do the same for Israel? The CIA accurately predicted that whilst the Soviet Union was theoretically capable of using bomber and missile forces against Israel in defence of the Arabs,

They would be very unlikely to do so, though they might threaten it. They do not have the capability of introducing lesser kinds of forces (ground troops, or volunteers) in this area with sufficient speed to be decisive, and we do not think they would try to do so. They would be cautious about the risk of armed confrontation with U.S. forces. And they would probably count upon the political intervention of great powers, including themselves, to stop the fighting before Nasser had suffered too much damage.[24]

Once war had begun, analysts correctly observed that the Soviets would be 'anxious to forestall a disastrous Arab defeat' that would leave Moscow vulnerable to the accusation 'in Arab capitals of not having done what it could to defend the Arab cause'. They rightly anticipated that 'following the end of hostilities the Soviets are likely to weigh in very heavily on the Arab side to repair the damage already done to their standing'.[25]

The Soviets continued to play a delicate balancing act as the conflict progressed. They pressured the Egyptians to accept an agreement but following Israeli violations of the ceasefire, also made token gestures of support towards their Arab allies. The Directorate of Intelligence speculated that the Soviets had circulated reports of Soviet military preparations days into the conflict as 'an attempt to scare the Israelis into stopping their advance into Syria'.[26] Ultimately, however, the Moscow/Washington Emergency Communications Link was put into action for the first time since the Cuban Missile Crisis and over twenty messages were exchanged between President Johnson and Premier Kosygin in which a series of potential crisis points between the superpowers was effectively defused.

Israel

Western powers had a more direct, if not entirely candid access to Israeli thinking. Intelligence on Israel's capabilities and intentions was readily available but the US intelligence community was keenly aware of the prospect for politicisation that such close contact entailed. Analysts were conscious of, for example, the close relationship between the Israeli intelligence agency Mossad and James Angleton, chief of CIA counterintelligence.[27] Most importantly, it was no secret that Israel desperately wanted an American declaration of support in this crisis, a move that analysts in the State Department feared would only further jeopardise American interests in the Middle East. Michael Sterner, the Arab–Israeli desk officer during the crisis, recalled that:

> no one at the time that this thing was brewing had any assurance that the Israelis could win this war in six days' time. The Egyptians seemed very confident and for all we knew could give the Israelis some real trouble and we saw emerging out of that a very serious possibility of U.S.-Soviet confrontation, the Soviets being committed to Egypt at that time and ourselves to the Israelis.[28]

A crucial assessment was tasked by policy-makers to determine whether the US could afford to leave Israel to 'go it alone' in the face of a united Arab attack.

Analysts responded definitively in the affirmative. Israel could 'defend successfully against simultaneous Arab attacks on all fronts . . . or hold on any three fronts while mounting successfully a major offensive on the fourth', argued the CIA.[29] Mossad challenged this assessment, asserting that in fact the Israeli military were badly outgunned by a Soviet-backed Arab war machine.[30] DCI Helms thus tasked the ONE to prepare an appraisal of the Mossad assessment. They stated in no uncertain terms that:

> We do not believe that the Israeli appreciation . . . was a serious estimate of the sort they would submit to their own high officials . . . it is probably a gambit intended to influence the U.S. to . . . provide military supplies . . . make more public commitments to Israel . . . approve Israeli military initiatives, and . . . put more pressure on Nasser.[31]

Informed by these assessments, President Johnson declined to airlift special military supplies to Israel or even to support it publicly. He later recalled bluntly telling Israeli Foreign Minister, Abba Eban, 'All of our intelligence people are unanimous that if the U.A.R. attacks, you will whip hell out of them.'[32]

Contact with the Israeli elite was thus more useful in discerning how and when war might begin. In April 1967, the CIA had reported on internal political disputes within the Israeli government over policy towards the Arabs, noting that the Israeli military were calling for harsher retaliation on the familiar Orientalist premise that 'force is the only thing the Arabs understand'.[33] On 1 June, DCI Helms met with a senior Israeli official who hinted that Israel could no longer avoid a decision. Restraint thus far was directly on account of American pressure, the official claimed, the delay had cost Israel the advantage of surprise. Helms interpreted the remarks as suggesting that Israel would attack imminently. That morning, according to published accounts, Helms wrote a 'For your eyes only' letter to President Johnson, forewarning that Israel would start a war within a few days.[34] Analysis clearly reflected a strong awareness of the political culture within which policy-making in Israel was operating. Helms accurately assessed that the 'decision' to which the official referred could only mean an Israeli attack. The British air attaché in Tel Aviv cited the dictum of Brigadier General Ezer Weizman, creator of the modern Israeli Air Force, that: 'the only way to defend Tel Aviv is over Cairo'.[35] The Board of National Estimates had drawn a similar conclusion,

> To acquiesce in the permanent closing of the Strait of Tiran would constitute an economic and political setback from which no early recovery would be foreseeable. The Israelis would expect, correctly we believe, that the Arabs over the long run would be encouraged to undertake new and still more dangerous harassments.[36]

For a nation encircled by enemies whose avowed purpose was her elimination by any means, the notion of pre-emptive attack as a form of defence was the most natural, if not only, option from the Israeli point of view and consistent with how Israel had previously confronted threats to its existence.

From Israel's perspective, there was a frightening unity within Arab ranks. On 1 June, Nasser and King Hussein of Jordan exchanged a historic and public reconciliatory 'kiss', after which Israeli defence minister Shimon Peres commented that Israel was 'now surrounded by a sort of banana filled with Russian weapons'.[37] The following day an Israeli cabinet reshuffle signalled the ascendency of the 'hawks' over the more moderately inclined Prime Minister Eshkol. Nasser himself allegedly concluded that war was now certain, informing his military that an attack on the air force would take place on 5 June.[38] A PDB on the morning of the war confirmed that the signs pointed to an Israeli initiative and that the Israelis had become 'increasingly convinced that time was running against them'.[39]

The reading of Israeli capabilities and tactical moves was near perfect. The problem lay in looking beyond the 'fog of war' and predicting what might follow an Israeli victory. Although analysts correctly recognised Israel's territorial objectives they fundamentally misread the possibility of a political settlement emerging from an Arab defeat. On 6 June, the CIA reported that 'the Israelis probably have begun to see a major Arab defeat looming, which would give Israel the opportunity to dictate terms of a semi-permanent peace'. They correctly predicted that Israel hoped to take the West Bank and old Jerusalem as well as the Golan Heights. Nonetheless, in a basic misreading of the impact of an Israeli military conquest on a settlement acceptable to the Arabs, analysts concluded that 'to the degree they succeed in humbling the Arabs, they will so dictate a settlement'.[40] In fact the opposite was true: analysts patently failed to recognise that despite Israel's best efforts, military superiority would not produce a political solution.

Egypt

The real test to intelligence analysts came with the most important and yet enigmatic player in the conflict. To this day scholars remain undecided about Nasser's intentions in provoking this tragic war. Similarly, analysts grappled to understand Nasser's actions and rhetoric although interestingly recent scholarship suggests that in fact the CIA had a good relationship with Egyptian intelligence in the period prior to and immediately after the crisis.[41] Indeed the CIA station chief, Bill Bromell, was 'declared' to the Egyptian government and played an important role in managing the impact of the crisis.[42]

Analysts had long seen Nasser's relationship with Israel as essentially pragmatic. As early as 1960 British diplomats argued that Israel provided 'a useful theme with which to whip up unified Arab sentiment'. They empathised with Nasser's belief that Israel was 'a pistol held by the West at the head of the Arab world' but concluded that he was 'sufficiently a realist to know that Israel has come to stay'.[43] In 1964 the American intelligence community reminded policy-makers that acceptance of Israel's right to exist 'remains basically a private and reluctant one'. Referencing their theoretical conceptualisations of the 'Arab national character', analysts opined that 'Arab political leaders customarily adopt verbal positions considerably stronger than what they know the facts or the possibilities of the situation to be'.[44] Just one month before the crisis the JIC accurately noted that:

> President Nasser has intimated that the U.A.R. itself would not be ready to take on Israel before 1970. The United Arab Command (UAC) based in Cairo has not made any progress towards developing an effective Arab military entity . . . We consider a deliberate attack on Israel by the forces of the U.A.R. and Syria on the one hand and of Jordan on the other is most unlikely in the period under review.[45]

Indeed, with over one third of his army tied down in Yemen, Nasser had stated both publicly and privately that Egypt and the Arabs were not ready for war. However, in the last two weeks of May 1967, Nasser decided to move troops into Sinai, to request the withdrawal of the UN forces stationed there since the Suez Crisis, and to close the Strait of Tiran to Israeli shipping. In an unprecedented show of Arab unity, a mutual defence agreement was signed with former enemy King Hussein, binding Egypt, Syria and Jordan to use all means at their disposal to repel an attack. Intelligence analysts were thus faced with a baffling question: what had motivated Nasser to shift his position from avoiding confrontation to provoking it, after clearly stating that his armed forces could not withstand an Israeli attack?

Despite Nasser's long-standing pragmatism, analysts were forced to confront the possibility that there had been a tangible shift in inter-Arab dynamics, presenting a real threat to Israel. The international community questioned the actions and rhetoric of Arab states bound by a newfound unity and verbalising an anti-Semitic determination not unlike that which the world had witnessed only a quarter of a century before in Nazi Germany. President Atasi of Syria was a member of the more radical, 'neo-Bath' faction which had just come to power, advocating a form of socialism based on the Eastern European model. The new Syrian

President pursued an equally radical foreign policy, proclaiming to troops in the Golan Heights the previous year, 'We have resolved to drench this land with our blood, to oust you [*sic*] aggressor and throw you into the sea for good.'[46] The American embassy in Cairo conceded that 'if Nasser's and Heikal's words are to be believed, Egyptians have been prepared for this moment for some time. In retrospect it may have been as long ago as last summer.'[47] A student at Oxford University during the crisis recalled widespread fears that a second holocaust was in the making and his attempts to persuade his Jewish roommate 'that perhaps it would be a good idea not to skip his final exams and go off to volunteer in Israel'.[48] British diplomats speculated that although Arab 'unity' in the past had proven to be of a fleeting and somewhat ineffective nature, there was 'agreement' amongst their sources that recent moves had 'been extremely well orchestrated' and 'acquired sufficient momentum to carry it for some time certainly weeks'.[49] The military and political position was dependent almost wholly on the leaders and armed forces and there was 'little likelihood of "battle fatigue" among either of these in the near future'.[50] As US Undersecretary of State Walt Rostow put it:

> There is considerable legitimate argument as to whether Nasser is now postured as a Hitler, determined at all costs to exploit temporary Arab unity to crush Israel once and for all, or whether he is a shrewd operator, working off a weak base, willing to settle for as much as he can get from this crisis.[51]

The Hitler analogy was of course a familiar one in the public sphere on both sides of the Atlantic. As the war erupted, Foreign Secretary George Brown made a speech asserting Britain's condemnation of hostilities and commitment to peace. The responses that echoed within the political elite reveal the extent to which the Arabs were perceived as serious aggressors with real military potential and the resultant fear that Israel would not survive their onslaught. Anglo-American reluctance to intervene on behalf of Israel met with vigorous condemnation not least because, as representatives in Parliament reminded the Foreign Secretary, the 'citizens of the State of Israel are composed largely of a remnant of those who were exterminated as a result of the ineffectiveness of international action'. When Brown responded that the Arabs too had a 'case which has not only plausibility, but legality and force', he was met with the following: 'When he says that an Arab aggressor may have something to be said for him, does he also remember Neville Chamberlain saying that there was something to be said for the Sudeten case . . . Does he realise that I have horrible memories of the 1930s coming back to me?'[52] A string of anti-Israel summits and water diversion schemes in the 1960s accentuated such fears. Israel perceived itself, and in turn reflected itself to the international community, as a 'Biblical David surrounded by the modern equivalent of Goliath'.[53]

Analysts were thus forced to question whether Nasser's actions in this crisis were the product of a Hitler inspired master plan. Did he intend to unify the surrounding Arab nations in order to squash the nascent state of Israel? More importantly, could these intentions be realised? Analysts recognised the importance of 'face' over fact in Nasser's calculations, the role of rhetoric in creating a semblance of Arab unity and the dissonance between what Arab propaganda espoused to the world, and what they were actually able and willing to do.

The issue of 'face' tied in concretely with the role of Arab nationalism and rivalry in potentially escalating tensions. The intelligence community had already warned policy-makers that that 'rivalries and disputes amongst the Arabs' would create 'a danger of precipitating crises from which large scale hostilities could develop'.[54] The combination of 'face' and inter-Arab nationalism provided some answer as to why Nasser had apparently abandoned his long-standing avoidance of military confrontation with Israel. In May 1967, the CIA reflected that 'Nasser was probably prompted to initiate these manoeuvres by Israeli threats against Syria. He probably felt that he had to identify himself with Arab nationalist interests and that some action on his part would refurbish his image in the Arab world.'[55] A top secret PDB also identified the role of Nasser's identity as the vanguard of Arab nationalism, suggesting that Nasser 'must be hoping desperately that there will be no need for him to fight the Israelis. He probably feels however, that his prestige would nose-dive if he stood idly by while Israel mauled Syria again.'[56] The new Syrian junta was determined to prove its revolutionary credentials by espousing aggressive anti-Israeli rhetoric, in the process challenging Nasser's position as leader of the Arab world. In May 1967 one regional radio station goaded Nasser further, asking 'will Egypt restore its batteries and guns to close its territorial waters in the Tiran Strait to the enemy? Logic, wisdom and nationalism make it incumbent on Egypt to do so.'[57]

In fact, 'logic' and 'wisdom' in the Western understanding of the words suggested that closing the Tiran Straits would be a clear *causus belli* in Israeli eyes and almost certainly provoke an unwanted attack. However, instead of interpreting Nasser's actions according to Western logic, analysts proved remarkably astute at gauging how this escalation had come about. The CIA accurately estimated, for example, that Nasser, 'probably did not expect such a speedy departure of UN forces from Sharm el Sheikh'.[58] This has now been confirmed by a range of Egyptian sources, thoroughly synthesised by Richard Parker, who concludes that 'no thought seems to have been given in advance to the possibility that a request for partial withdrawal would be unacceptable to the U.N. Secretariat'.[59] The most recent research has revealed that Nasser himself was concerned about the wording of the missive: 'Wanting to clarify that UNEF could remain in Sharm-el Sheikh and the Gaza strip, Nasser asked the Marshall [Amer] to change "withdraw" to "redeploy" and remove "all" before "these troops".' Amer responded that it was impossible because the letter was already being delivered.[60] Other Egyptian accounts, such as General Murtagi's memoirs, reinforce the improvised nature of the decision-making process and confirm analysts' conclusions that the Egyptians were not following a master plan.[61]

At some stage, however, Nasser must have realised that his actions would lead to war. What of his previous admission noted by the JIC that even united Arab forces would not match their Israeli counterparts? Analysts perceptively recognised that in this crisis, 'face' took precedence and the relevant 'facts' were interpreted accordingly. It was justly accepted that Nasser's primary concern was to demonstrate to the international Arab community that he was not 'hiding behind the skirts of UNEF', as his rivals taunted. The American embassy in Cairo made explicit reference to the role of 'face' in making it difficult for Nasser to back down, speculating:

> The crisis could probably be defused if [a] way could be found to put Aqaba issue on ice for a few weeks. However, this would presumably require either U.A.R. temporarily permitting oil to pass or Israel temporarily acquiescing in oil being excluded. We doubt Nasser could tolerate [the] former without unacceptable loss of face.[62]

Analysts empathised that there may have been 'some element of desperation in Nasser's attitude'. Several factors contributed to this sense of anxiety, including 'the parlous condition' of the Egyptian economy, worsening US–Egypt relations, 'a belief that some sort of U.S.-Israeli plot against him existed, and perhaps a fatalistic conclusion that a showdown with Israel must come sooner or later, and might best be provoked before Israel acquired nuclear weapons'.[63]

The result was that Nasser had bound himself to a path which he knew would provoke an Israeli attack, despite knowing that even the united Arab military forces would not be ready to withstand the onslaught. The CIA conceded that Nasser's processing of 'reality' was subject to an entirely different set of considerations to those that might govern Western decision-making. Desperation to save face and 'a large element of accident' backed Nasser into a corner in which he was forced to re-evaluate the military facts in the absence of a diplomatic alternative.[64] As later scholarship put it: 'the Cairo regime had blinded itself . . . ignoring or reinterpreting all contrary evidence'.[65]

The Egyptian defence establishment was particularly culpable. Field Marshall Amer was a charming socialite entirely unsuited to his role as Defence Minister. Soviet military attaché in Cairo, Sergie Khrakhmalov, recalled Amer to be a man with 'exceedingly primitive' views. According to Khrakhmalov, he seemed, 'not the supreme commander of a state's armed forces, but rather an infantry battalion commander of mediocre capacities'.[66] Amer had told the army the previous year that: 'We are capable of defeating Israel at any time, for we are superior to it in arms and morale.' Prior to the war he assured Nasser that 'everything's in tip-top shape'.[67] It is difficult to know definitively how convincing Amer's

assurances were to Nasser. Other Arabic accounts certainly reinforce the intelligence community's belief that Nasser knew that
Egypt was not prepared to fight and win a war with Israel.[68]

Despite Nasser's pronouncements that Egypt was 'ready for
war', Egyptian deployments were rightly seen by American intelligence as defensive.[69] The distinction between the rhetoric of Arab
unity and its implications for concrete action was astutely noted.
The CIA critiqued the Israeli appraisal, arguing that, 'the steps
taken thus far by Arab armies do not prove that the Arabs intend
an all-out attack on Israel'. They noted that 'there have been no
coordinated manoeuvres by the various Arab states' and suggested
that 'it would be difficult if not impossible for the various Arab
units cited in . . . the Israeli estimate to be used in concert'.[70]

Moreover, the JIC had previously estimated that whilst the
numerical superiority of the Arab forces would have some utility
in a long protracted war, Israel's vastly superior air force would
render this numerical advantage useless.

> Despite some numerical and material inferiority Israel would have
> the best of any conflict with the U.A.R., owing to its greater fighting
> efficiency and higher morale of the armed forces, who are maintained
> at a high state of readiness and backed by an efficient intelligence
> organisation, and who would have the advantage of operating on
> interior lines.[71]

Their analysis effectively foreshadowed the conclusions of scholars that 'high-flown Arab rhetoric gave the impression of a closely
coordinated Arab military front ready to strike at Israel while the
reality was of divided armed forces whose leaders hardly understand their own capabilities, let along those of their allies'.[72] The
CIA felt compelled to remind policy-makers that: these were
'merely gestures which all Arab states feel compelled to make in
the interests of the fiction of Arab unity, but have little military
utility in a conflict with Israel'.[73] A week later the British Foreign
Office reported 'signs that the Egyptians were already tending to
modify their application of the blockade'.[74] Even after the onset of
war analysts wrote that 'when the crisis began, the Arabs hoped
for a political victory short of war'.[75] Perhaps the Suez precedent
was prevalent in Nasser's thinking that a show of force might be

sufficient. Either way, Anglo-American analysts felt sure that political posturing formed a large component of Nasser's escalatory behaviour.[76]

They could also rely on long-standing assessments of Arab nationalism which identified that inflammatory rhetoric against Israel was an integral part of an ideology challenging post-colonial Western influence in the Middle East. It was not indicative of military strength or unity in the Eurocentric experience of nationalism – indeed the Syrian secession was the clearest demonstration of the limits of inter-Arab cooperation. Rather it was an assertion of moral strength, rising against the colonial oppressor and demanding the right of the Arabs to political and economic self-determination. Nasser's intentions and motivations in the crisis were analysed with an understanding of these regional sentiments and a 'hands-off' policy by both Britain and the US was directed accordingly.

* * *

Western intelligence assessments of the main players were both important and accurate in the prelude to, and course of, the 1967 crisis. They were able to posit Soviet actions within the analytical framework of Soviet political culture and the limitations of Arab nationalism, suggesting that the Soviet Union would provoke tensions to the 'brink' of what was within their interest and capability, but de-escalate at the prospect of confrontation with the West. Whilst the Soviet Union had and would support their client state to the point even of careless reassurance, they employed neither the capability nor the will to categorically provoke or intervene in a full-scale Arab–Israeli war. Intelligence analysis on Israel's role was appropriately cautious of the political pressure from Mossad and pro-Israeli sentiment, yet confident in its assessment of overwhelming Israeli military superiority and aware of the pre-emptive strategy of defensive attack which characterised Israeli political culture. Finally, analysts proved sensitive to the nuances and complexities of Arab nationalist behaviour. They recognised the existence of a different value system in which 'face' took precedence over both 'fact' and 'logic'. Nationalist rhetoric had developed an escalatory momentum that overwhelmed Nasser's pragmatic realisation that even the Arab forces combined could not defeat Israel. Analysts interpreted his actions with empathy and within the nationalist context in which he was bound. Such pertinent assessments of the main players enabled intelligence to serve as a crucial means of arbitration in this crisis.

And yet the limits to this notion of success must also be considered. As William Quandt recalled, 'no one seems to have thought through the full implications of Israel's going to war, especially the problems this might cause in the long run'.[77] Certainly intelligence must be credited with cutting through the hazy 'fog of war', yet what of the aftermath? In September 1966 a British 'Intelligence Methods' Conference had unknowingly prophesised this shortcoming. The introductory address posited 'whether we were doing all possible to identify comparable problems, perhaps now only beginning to take shape, which might at some future time develop into a threat, not necessarily direct or directly military to our interests'.[78] Was intelligence able to rise to this challenge, to look beyond the immediate catharsis at what the implications of a stunning Israeli victory against the united forces of the Arab world might be? In his memoirs Dean Rusk put forth the dilemma posed for future US policy in the Middle East.

> For twenty years, since the creation of Israel, the U.S. had tried to persuade the Arabs that they needn't fear territorial expansion. Throughout the sixties, the Arabs talked continuously about their fear of Israeli expansion. With the full knowledge of successive governments in Israel, we did our utmost to persuade the Arabs their anxieties were illusory. And then following the Six-Day War, Israel decided to keep the Golan Heights, the West Bank, the Gaza strip and the Sinai, despite the fact that the Israeli Prime Minister Levi Eshkol on the first day of the war went on Israeli radio and said that Israel had no territorial ambitions. Later in the summer I reminded Eban of this, and he simply shrugged his shoulders and said, 'We've changed our minds'. With that remark . . . he turned the United States into a twenty-year liar.[79]

Not only were Israel's long-term territorial ambitions underestimated but American policy-makers clearly overestimated their ability to influence Israeli policy-making in the aftermath of a crisis in which they had been left to 'go it alone'.

This myopia was to have profound implications in the Arab world. The helplessness that accompanied a bitter defeat and Israeli intransigence laid the seeds for the decay of Arab nationalism. Intelligence analysts had acquired some understanding of its symbolic power in the Middle East yet they did not estimate that its death would create an ideological vacuum in which an alternative had to be found. The legacy of this vacuum remains with us; Ayman Al-Zawahiri, Al-Qaeda's chief strategist, made the migration to Islamic militancy after the 1967 war.[80] The inability to look beyond the immediacy of military conflict is one that some identify as an inescapable feature of crisis management and others as characteristic of the Western way of war. The subordination of the strategic to the tactical plagues intelligence services to this day.

Finally, it is a cruel irony that the relatively successful analyses of the main players in this crisis set the stage for later intelligence failures. Accurate predictions of Israeli success and the sheer scale of the Arab defeat set in motion a dangerous mythology of Israeli superiority in the minds of Western analysts.[81] An idea had been born in the West, in Israel and even amongst the Arab states that by the very nature of its statehood, a political culture built upon isolation and in a perpetual state of readiness, Israel would always be one step ahead of the game. The Arabs, on the other hand, had proven that despite their deluded rhetorical self-aggrandisement, they could not effectively unify and certainly could not inflict but a dent on their principal enemy around which Arab nationalism had for so long rallied. David had defeated Goliath with an invincible military and intelligence community on his side. Only months later, however, an intelligence estimate perceptively warned that:

> in the long run, the frustration of the Arab states would almost certainly drive them to seek military means of compelling Israeli withdrawal . . . they will build up their forces and, in time will probably seek to avenge the 1967 defeat. The Egyptians, in particular may come to believe that they could win a limited victory over the Israelis, for example, dislodging them from the East Bank of the Suez Canal.[82]

As the following chapters will show, it was not an isolated warning.

Notes

1. Interview with Alfred LeRoy Atherton, summer of 1990. Available at <http://adst.org/wp-content/uploads/2012/09/Egypt.pdf>, p. 310 (last accessed 1 March 2017).
2. See, for example, R. B. Parker, *The Politics of Miscalculation in the Middle East* (Bloomington, IN: Indiana University Press, 1992), p. 4, and D. Reynolds, *One World Divisible: A Global History since 1945* (London: Allen Lane, Penguin Press, 2000), p. 240.
3. For the most recent examination of the crisis see W. R. Louis and A. Shlaim (eds), *The 1967 Arab-Israeli War: Origins and Consequences* (Cambridge: Cambridge University Press, 2012). Other important scholarly works include: J. Bowen, *Six-Days: How the 1967 War Shaped the Middle East* (London: Pocket books, 2003); M. B. Oren, *Six-Days of War: June 1967 and the Making of the Modern Middle East* (Oxford: Oxford University Press, 2002); R. B. Parker, *The Six-Day War: A Retrospective* (Gainsville, FL: University Press of Florida, 1996); I. Abu-Lughod, *The Arab-Israeli Confrontation of June 1967: An Arab Perspective* (Evanston, IL: Northwestern University Press, 1970).
4. Interview with Robert Mark Ward, 27 May 1998. Available at <http://adst.org/wp-content/uploads/2012/09/Egypt.pdf>, p. 479 (last accessed 1 March 2017).
5. R. Helms, *A Look Over My Shoulder: A Life in the Central Intelligence Agency* (New York: Random House, 2003), p. 295.
6. The most thorough exploration of the American intelligence assessments of the Six-Day War is Robarge's 'CIA analysis of the Six-Day War', *Studies in Intelligence*, 49: 1, 2005. The British intelligence dimension has been relatively unexplored. See, for example, F. Brenchley, *Britain, the Six Day War and its Aftermath* (London: I. B. Tauris, 2005), p. xxii: 'in general terms it can be said that policy-makers in the government quite often had valuable information about the policies and intentions of Middle Eastern governments deriving from the Special Intelligence Services and Government Special Headquarters'.
7. Material from this chapter derives partly from earlier research. See D. Rezk, *British and American Political and Intelligence Assessments of the Nasser-Sadat Transition*, unpublished MPhil thesis, University of Cambridge, Cambridge, 2006.
8. Patrick Wright, e-mail correspondence with author, 8 December 2008.

9. JIC memorandum (67) 11, 'Soviet policies in the Middle East and North Africa and their likely development', 21 March 1967, TNA, CAB 158/ 66: 'The importance of the area to the Soviet Union is illustrated by the fact that it has received or been promised more aid, both economic and military, than any other region in the non-communist world. The UAR alone has been allocated one fifth of the total aid offered by the Soviet Union to non-communist countries and, if military aid is added, has been the largest recipient of Soviet aid.'

10. Memorandum from Kent in CIA's Board of National Estimates to DCI, 26 May 1967, FRUS 1964-1968, vol. XIX, no. 79.

11. NIE 11-6-67, 'Soviet strategy and intentions in the Mediterranean Basin', 1 June 1967, FOIA Reading Room.

12. I. Ginor, 'The Russians were coming', *Middle East Review of International Affairs*, 4: 4, 2000. Based on a selective use and exploitation of limited sources Ginor argues that the Soviets intentionally orchestrated the war in order to implant themselves more concretely into the Middle East. The thesis fails to consult any Arabic sources in order to substantiate the argument.

13. JIC memorandum (67) 26, 'Comparison of the armed forces of Israel and those of certain Arab states up to the end of 1967', 17 April 1967, TNA, CAB 158/66.

14. NIE, 'Soviet strategy and intentions in the Mediterranean Basin', 1 June 1967, FOIA Reading Room.

15. JIC memorandum (67) 11, 'Soviet Policies in the Middle East and North Africa and their likely development', 21 March 1967, TNA, CAB 158/ 66.

16. Memorandum from Davis of the NSC Staff to the President's Special Assistant Rostow, 'A scenario of the Soviet role', 2 June 1967, FRUS 1964-1968, vol. XIX, no. 136.

17. Memorandum from the Acting Chairman of the CIA's Board of National Estimates, Smith to DCI, 9 June 1967, FRUS 1964-1968, vol. XIX, no. 240.

18. H. Heikal, *1967: Al-Infijar* (Cairo: Al Ahram, 1990), p. 522.

19. Intelligence report by the Directorate of Intelligence, 'Soviet policy and the 1967 Arab-Israeli War', 16 March 1970, FOIA Reading Room.

20. Memorandum from the CIA's Board of National Estimates (Kent) to DCI, 26 May 1967, FRUS 1964-1968, vol. XIX, no. 79.

21. Heikal, *Al-Infijar*, p. 625.

22. H. M. Heikal, *The Sphinx and the Commissar: The Rise and Fall of Soviet Influence in the Arab World* (London: Collins, 1978), pp. 179–80.

23. Parker, *Politics of Miscalculation*, p. 31.
24. Memorandum from the CIA's Board of National Estimates (Kent) to DCI, 26 May 1967, FRUS 1964-1968, vol. XIX, no. 79.
25. Unattributed CIA memorandum, 'Objectives of the Middle East combattants [*sic*] and the USSR', 6 June 1967, DDRS.
26. Intelligence report by the Directorate of Intelligence, 'Soviet policy and the 1967 Arab-Israeli War', 16 March 1970, FOIA Reading Room.
27. T. Mangold, *Cold Warrior: James Jesus Angleton: The CIA's Master Spy Hunter* (New York: Simon and Schuster, 1991), pp. 49, 362. Angleton had run the Israeli account out of his counterintelligence staff, without involving the Directorate of Plans Near East Division for years.
28. Interview with Michael Sterner, 11 March 1990. Available at <http://adst.org/wp-content/uploads/2012/09/Egypt.pdf>, p. 196 (last accessed 1 May 2017).
29. Robarge, 'CIA analysis of the Six-Day War', *Studies in Intelligence*, 49: 1, 2006, p. 2.
30. Ibid. p. 3.
31. ONE, 'Appraisal of an estimate of the Arab-Israeli crisis by the Israeli Intelligence Service', 25 May 1967, FRUS 1964–1968, vol. XIX, no. 61.
32. L. B. Johnson, *The Vantage Point: Perspectives on the Presidency, 1963–1969* (New York: Holt, Rinehart and Winston, 1971), p. 239.
33. NIE, 'Arab-Israeli conflict: current phase', 13 April 1967, FOIA Reading Room.
34. Robarge, 'CIA analysis of the Six-Day War', *Studies in Intelligence*, 49: 1, 2005, p. 5.
35. Memorandum by air attaché in Tel Aviv, 'Activities of the Israeli Air Force during the Arab-Israeli War, 5th-10th June 1967', 9 August 1967, TNA, DEFE 13/851.
36. Memorandum from the CIA's Board of National Estimates to DCI, 26 May 1967, FRUS 1964-1968, vol. XIX, no. 79.
37. R. S. Churchill, *The Six-Day War* (London: Heinemman, 1967), p. 60.
38. A. Sadat, *In Search of Identity: An Autobiography* (London: Collins, 1978), p. 174.
39. Presidential Daily Brief, 5 June 1967, FOIA Reading Room.
40. Unattributed CIA memorandum, 'Objectives of the Middle East combattants [*sic*] and the USSR', 6 June 1967, DDRS.
41. L. James, *Nasser At War: Arab Images of the Enemy* (Basingstoke: Palgrave Macmillan, 2006), p. 96.

42. Interview with David Nes, 28 April 1992. Available at <http://adst.org/wp-content/uploads/2012/09/Egypt.pdf> pp. 464–6 (last accessed 1 March 2017). Nes was Deputy Chief of Mission in Cairo from 1965 to 1967.
43. Memorandum from Stevens to Crosthwaite, 8 September 1960, TNA, FO 371/150931.
44. NIE 36-64, 'Main trends in the Arab world', 8 April 1964, FOIA Reading Room.
45. JIC memorandum (67) 26, 'Comparison of the armed forces of Israel and those of certain Arab states up to the end of 1967', 17 April 1967, TNA, CAB 158/66.
46. Parker, *Six-Day War*, p. 127.
47. Telegram from embassy in Cairo to State Department, 1 June 1967, FRUS 1964-1968, vol. XIX, no. 119.
48. Parker, *Six-Day War*, p. 255.
49. Telegram from embassy in Cairo to State Department, 1 June 1967, FRUS 1964-1968, vol. XIX, no. 119.
50. Ibid.
51. Memorandum from the President's Special Assistant Rostow to President Johnson, 4 June 1967, FRUS 1964-1968, vol. XIX, no. 144.
52. Extract from Hansard, 8 June 1967, TNA, PREM 13/1620.
53. Parker, *Six-Day War*, p. 119.
54. W. C. Matthias, *America's Strategic Blunders* (University Park, PA: Pennsylvania State University Press, 2001), p. 222.
55. Memorandum from the CIA's Board of National Estimates to DCI, 26 May 1967, FRUS 1964-1968, vol. XIX, no. 79.
56. Presidential Daily Brief, 16 May 1967, FOIA Reading Room.
57. James, *Nasser at War*, pp. 111–12.
58. Ibid.
59. Parker, *Politics of Miscalculation*, p. 71.
60. James, *Nasser at War*, p. 108.
61. Ibid. p. 74.
62. Telegram from embassy in Cairo to State Department, 1 June 1967, FRUS 1964-1968, vol. XIX, no. 119.
63. Memorandum from the CIA's Board of National Estimates to DCI, 26 May 1967, FRUS 1964-1968, vol. XIX, no. 79.
64. Ibid.
65. James, *Nasser at War*, p. 122.
66. J. Ferris, *Nasser's Gamble: How Intervention in Yemen Caused the Six-Day War* (Princeton, NJ: Princeton University Press, 2013), p. 40
67. Ibid. p. 98.

68. M. Fawzi, *Harb al Thalath Sanawat 1967–1970* (Cairo: Dar al-Mustaqbal al Arabiyy, 1983), p. 53.
69. James, *Nasser at War*, p. 113.
70. ONE, 'Appraisal of an estimate of the Arab-Israeli crisis by the Israeli Intelligence Service', 25 May 1967, FRUS 1964–1968, vol. XIX, no. 61.
71. JIC memorandum (67) 26, 'Comparison of the armed forces of Israel and those of certain Arab states up to the end of 1967', 17 April 1967, TNA, CAB 158/66.
72. A. Rathmell, 'Brotherly enemies: the rise and fall of the Syrian-Egyptian intelligence axis, 1954–1967', *Intelligence and National Security*, 13: 1, 1998, p. 245.
73. ONE, 'Appraisal of an estimate of the Arab-Israeli crisis by the Israeli intelligence service', 25 May 1967, FRUS 1964–1968, vol. XIX, no. 61.
74. James, *Nasser at War*, p. 116.
75. Unattributed CIA memorandum, 'Objectives of the Middle East combattants [*sic*] and the USSR', 6 June 1967, DDRS.
76. James, *Nasser at War*, p. 119.
77. W. Quandt, *Decade of Decisions: American Policy towards the Arab-Israeli Conflict, 1967–1976* (Berkeley, CA: University of California Press, 1977), p. 70.
78. Summary of opening address to the 'Third Intelligence Methods Conference', 19 September 1966, TNA, DEFE 13/923.
79. Parker, *Six-Day War*, p. 243.
80. Y. A. Enein, 'The Heikal Papers', *Strategic Insights*, 4: 4, 2005.
81. Memorandum by British air attaché in Tel Aviv, 'Activities of the Israeli Air Force during the Arab-Israeli War, 5th–10th June 1967', 9 August 1967, TNA, DEFE 13/851: 'The Israeli Air Force had been continually planning for the past 19 years to defeat its principal adversary, the Egyptian Air Force. It was not therefore an ad hoc arrangement. Over the years detailed target folders had been built up as a result of Israeli intelligence and each pilot knew where he was to go and what he had to do. Only the issue of a single code-word was necessary to put the plan into operation.'
82. NIE 35-68, 'Israel', 11 April 1968, FOIA Reading Room.

7   War of Attrition

After the Six-Day War, Israel was no longer the object of sympathy and compassion, but rather an important strategic asset to be reckoned with.

Simcha Dinitz, 2000[1]

Peace does not mean surrender . . . There is no other way for us but force, we have no alternative to safeguard our honour.

President Nasser, 1969[2]

Egypt's humiliation in 1967 had a visibly dramatic impact on President Nasser. His associates recall that his hair 'turned white' and he lost the 'spark' in his eyes, subsumed as he was with the bitterness of defeat.[3] In the context of frayed diplomatic relations, American policy-makers increasingly viewed Nasser as the 'villain' of the war and a 'Soviet client'.[4] As Arabist Richard Parker put it, 'We had no particular interest left in Egypt. All the Americans had been kicked out . . . [It was] very hard to get anybody to pay any attention to Egypt. Very hard to get anybody to take Egypt seriously.'[5] Against this increasingly adversarial relationship, the British assumed the more neutral role of 'honest broker' in the Arab–Israeli dispute, authoring, for example, the United Nations Security Council Resolution 242 which called for Israeli withdrawal from occupied territories in exchange for peace. The protracted War of Attrition on the Suez Canal, culminating in the unprecedented Soviet intervention of 10,000 men to protect Egypt against Israeli deep penetration raids, raised important questions about Egypt's commitment to peace and independence and Soviet willingness to escalate the regional conflict.

An examination of the diplomatic and intelligence assessments of these events provides a more nuanced view of the War of Attrition than that which exists in the current literature. The historical record thus far has emphasised Western miscalculation and the West's broad misunderstanding of Nasser's intentions in launching the War of Attrition.[6] One study, for example, asserts that 'the Americans were still unable to assess Egypt's motives correctly or the logic behind its military actions' during this period.[7] Similarly, Richard Parker attributes the failure to predict Soviet intervention in 1970 to a 'lack of imagination'.[8]

In fact, Anglo-American analysis was not as one-sided as such studies presume. Certainly, the illogicality of Nasser's behaviour during the 1967 crisis seems to have permeated analysts' comprehension of likely Egyptian calculations in the War of Attrition. 'Posturing', 'rhetoric', 'miscalculation', 'irrationality' and 'fatalism' were all identified as contributing factors to Nasser's decision-making. However, there was also a strong sense of Nasser's realism underlying many assessments, alongside the cultural precondition of 'dignity' in war and peace. At the same time the most astute analysis observed an internal logic to Nasser's actions, suggesting that Nasser could not allow the Israelis to make themselves comfortable on the east bank of the Canal and that a degree of military strength would be the only way to exact a just political settlement.

The Soviet intervention in the summer of 1970 was appropriately judged to be a response to Israeli deep penetration raids rather than an overwhelming desire on either side for deeper relations. Both the CIA and the JIC admirably resisted the temptation to interpret all events in the Middle East as the result of the looming Soviet hand, clearly attributing agency to Arab actors.[9] In the Arab–Israeli conflict the CIA wrote almost poetically that 'the Soviets are more a prisoner of Arab emotions than the architect of Arab policy'.[10] Their conclusions lend valuable credence to revisionist interpretations of the Cold War which would later suggest that the proxy nations, through which the superpowers flexed their geopolitical muscles, were just as capable of manipulating the Great Powers to their own advantage.[11] Specific estimates on the invitation thus accurately placed the initiative as lying with Egypt, rather than the Soviet Union.

From the documentary record available it does seem as if the Americans did not give due weight to the probability of Soviet intervention. However, the same cannot be said for their British counterparts. Indeed, this event demonstrates all too well the common problem of policy-makers ignoring or dismissing the wisdom of their analysts, who, in the British case, explicitly warned that Israeli deep penetration raids would provoke Soviet intervention in Egypt. When assessing the implications of the move, both Anglo-American analyses tempered the fears of policy-makers, highlighting that tense Soviet–Egyptian relations would limit the extent of political influence exerted by the superpower.

* * *

The War of Attrition

In the aftermath of the 1967 war, the Americans had no formal diplomatic representation in Cairo. Washington relied on a small team housed within the Spanish embassy led by Donald Bergus, a figure who was well known and liked by the Egyptian elite. In the American press, Bergus was described as a 'career diplomat with a penchant for talking soft and wearing loud shirts', and he declared himself to be 'an optimist' about the prospects of diplomatic progress on the Egyptian front.[12] The autumn of 1967 saw a hardening of Arab reactions to their collective defeat, loudly expressed in the fourth Arab summit conference held in Sudan earlier that summer. Despite vociferous proclamations at the Khartoum Conference of 'no negotiation; no recognition and no peace' with Israel, Nasser's reconciliation with the 'conservative' Arabs such as Jordan and Saudi Arabia hinted at a more realistic outlook. Instead of taking Nasser's statements at face value, the CIA recognised this shift, suggesting that 'the U.A.R. seems to realize that it must make some concessions in order to get Israel to withdraw from Sinai'. They noted that at the UN Egypt was willing 'to entertain a formula which would imply an end to belligerency in return for Israeli withdrawal'. Although Nasser would not tolerate formal peace negotiations with the Israelis, analysts estimated that he would 'strive for some accommodation which limits as far as possible the damage to his prestige'.[13] Their analysis presaged the later conclusions of scholars that no peace meant no *formal* peace treaty, no *direct* negotiations and no *de jure* recognition of Israel.[14] Just as the interplay between 'face' and 'rhetoric' had been a predominant factor in war, so it remained in peace.

The most vocal proponent of this view was the British ambassador in Egypt, Sir Harold Beeley. Beeley was a charming and experienced Arabist, specifically chosen by Foreign Secretary George Brown for his unparalleled record in winning Nasser's trust and respect. Beeley recognised that the possibility of a settlement 'imposed' by the Great Powers initially seemed the most likely option. Nasser, Ambassador Beeley assessed,

> could accept a settlement involving certain concessions to Israel, including above all the basic concession of admitting her right to exist, provided that the settlement was imposed on him by international authority. Any appearance that it was being imposed directly by Israel would oblige him to reject it.[15]

American echelons came to a similar conclusion. National Security Advisor Walt Rostow was an intellectual who had taught economics at Cambridge and Oxford before advising the White House and became well known for his pro-Israeli perspective. And yet he explained to President Johnson that, 'in the Arabs we are dealing with a different breed of cat than any others in the world. To them, face is more important than substance. It means more to them than to the Israelis or to us.' Belying overriding Cold War concerns, Rostow suggested, 'if we help them save face, we have the possibility, if we ac[t] fast, of getting a liveable settlement for Israel which would block Soviet influence out of the Middle East'.[16]

Israel was clearly not interested in Rostow's 'liveable settlement'. Prime Minister Eshkol's refusal to consider an 'imposed solution' and his insistence on direct negotiations reinforced Nasser's determination to pursue military action. He planned a series of assaults on the east bank of the Suez Canal alongside the painstaking discussions with UN Middle East peace envoy, Gunnar Jarring.[17] Egyptian sources suggest that Nasser always saw some military action as inevitable, believing that he could not negotiate with Israel from a position of weakness.[18] Numerous public speeches reiterated the importance of military strength in achieving a settlement.[19] As recent scholarship suggests, 'Nasser formulated a sophisticated strategy that attempted to combine (and sometimes to confound) military and political action.'[20]

Nasser's strategic thinking was not immediately evident. British diplomats interpreted reports of confrontations along the Canal in the summer of 1967 as indicating 'that the Government find it necessary to maintain the fiction that the fight is still on. With new military equipment arriving they find it physically easy and politically profitable for the U.A.R. forces to harass Israel positions in North Sinai.'[21] Nasser, however, made explicit to his military commanders that the UN resolution that he had accepted 'is not meant for you . . . What has been taken by force can only be recovered by force. This is not rhetoric.'[22] In February 1968, unprecedented student protests brought home the extent of domestic pressures on Nasser and reminded analysts that 'the Arabs could not negotiate in dignity while Israel is holding all the cards'.[23] President Johnson was informed that whilst Israeli occupation weighed heavily on Egypt's morale it was clear that 'the consequence is not [the] Anglo-Saxon notion of need to negotiate out of [a] situation. Rather Nasser's reaction is that this is time to show no weakness.'[24]

Nonetheless, during 1968, the prospect of war was regarded as slim – with rhetoric apparently substituting for action. In June the British embassy reported back to Whitehall that 'what sounds like war talk is in fact defensive and nervous, but with a very hard core'.[25] American analysts noted the 'frustration' and 'disgruntlement' occasioned by defeat but added that 'Nasser has no available course but the distasteful road of military restraint . . . His hopes, like those of most Arabs are pinned on the imposition of a settlement by the great powers.' They judged that Nasser would 'try to compensate for inaction with occasional bursts of aggressive rhetoric'.[26] It was a familiar pattern that analysts recognised from previous crises.

In the summer of 1968 Nasser visited the Soviet Union and allegedly received the go-ahead to escalate military action. Egyptian forces opened fire along the Canal, announcing a 'phase of deterrence'.[27] Beeley assessed that the Egyptians were 'not looking for trouble' but were 'apprehensive' about an Israeli attack, describing 'a nervously defiant mood reminiscent of that of late May 1967'. Estimating that the Egyptians would do no more, he warned that 'if the Israelis choose to press the issue there will be desperate reactions'.[28] The shadow of war was once again imminently cast over the Middle East.

Most significantly, however, Beeley stressed that Egyptian military aggressiveness did not necessarily signal rejection of a peaceful settlement. In October 1968 he reflected astutely that Nasser's 'basic idea has always been that a settlement can only be reached after a military balance of power has been established'. He was 'sceptical' that negotiations could 'obtain results until this balance has been created and demonstrated. I think it is in this context that the Egyptian part in recent incidents should be interpreted.'[29] Other diplomatic reporting struggled to disguise frustration with Nasser's actions: 'logically they should be deterred by fear of Israeli reprisals, but as experience shows, logic cannot be relied upon'.[30]

There were other factors informing Egypt's more aggressive posture. A combination of self-criticism and rigorous Soviet training had bolstered Egypt's military capabilities. [31] The British ambassador to Israel reported that Israeli Deputy Director of Military Intelligence Zeira claimed the weapons used in the attacks were 'if not under immediate Russian directions, certainly in accordance with Russian teaching and doctrine', and that 'the Egyptian standard of gunnery and professional efficiency in their use was an improvement on past performances'. He correctly assessed that 'some sort of strong action against is likely in the near future'.[32]

Yet Israel continued to seem intoxicated with victory. The final months of 1968 saw both Republican and Democrat American presidential candidates competing in their declarations of support for Israel, the rapid construction of the Bar-Lev line along the Canal and an Israeli attack on Beirut airport, all of which strengthened Nasser's determination to pursue a military solution.[33] Orders to prepare for battle were issued to the General Staff, a state of emergency was declared and the Popular Defence Army was placed on maximum alert.[34] On 8 March 1969, a massive artillery barrage was opened across the Canal, and the government announced that Egypt would no longer comply with the ceasefire.

Scholars have concluded that the by now fully fledged 'War of Attrition' was designed to address domestic concerns, convince Israel that the costs of occupation were too high and provoke Great Power intervention. One historian argues that analysts misunderstood the Egyptian position, ascribing 'the escalation to the contest between the military and civil establishments and not to Nasser seeking to achieve political objectives with a planned strategy'.[35] In fact, documents show that analysts were aware of the motivations later identified by scholars. They recognised Nasser's political objectives and the role that a greater military initiative could play in achieving a 'dignified' settlement. At the same time, there remained a sense in which the war demonstrated the illogicality of the Egyptians, driven to rhetorical escalation by a fatalistic obsession with 'honour' and 'face'.

The precedent of the 1967 war seemed to confirm the analytical premise that military capability (or lack thereof) and the prospect of military action had little relationship in the Arab world. In April 1969, the JIC reported that 'despite the Arabs' military inferiority it is by no means certain that this factor will remain sufficient to deter the Arab states from contemplating an attack against Israel'. Although 'united in their common fixation with the problem of Israel, the Arabs would seem to be in no fit state, politically or militarily, to take on Israel in the foreseeable future'. The Committee remembered,

> But as the events of May 1967 showed, Arab military and political intentions are not always based on realistic calculations or even deliberate decisions to get involved in hostilities. The Arabs' power of self-delusion is limitless, and they have a tendency to believe their own propaganda. Accordingly we cannot be confident that they will not again find themselves, however irrationally, in major conflict with Israel.[36]

The JIC could not hide their frustration and bewilderment at the delusional Egyptians, driven by their fatalistic concern for honour and trapped by their warlike rhetoric. The Americans expressed a similar frustration. Richard Parker was the Egypt desk officer in the State Department at the time, who later served as ambassador to Lebanon, Algeria and Morocco. He earned fame for his frank reporting on the Middle East and described himself as part of an elite club: 'Arabists who have been shit upon by Arab Kings'.[37] Reflecting on an inflammatory speech by Vice President Sadat, Richard Parker wrote:

> Of course, with the Arabs, words are often as important as deeds. Sometimes more so. Having uttered these warlike cries, Sadat can now go back to whatever it was he was doing, confident that he has done his duty for the war effort

He recalled that it was 'through a similar process of bluster that Egypt got itself into such a mess in 1967'. He assessed that Egypt's continued actions along the Canal was 'evidence of a longing for *gotterdammerung* which is recurrent. When the Egyptians say that if we don't play by their rules they are going out in the backyard to commit suicide, they are at least half in earnest.' There was, Parker concluded, an 'air of approaching apocalypse'.[38]

Yet the same assessments also recognised that there was a certain logic to the military offensive. Despite his frustration Parker recognised that, as Nasser saw it, 'what the Arabs must do is defeat Israel a little so the United States will abandon Israel and put its money on the Arabs'.[39] The JIC also saw the domestic considerations behind the decisions and the importance of 'an insurance against the abandonment of attempts to reach a political settlement'. It was primarily a defensive war, a means of improving their fortifications 'against Israeli reprisals and military action to which they are vulnerable'.[40] Analysts aptly noted that 'Cairo's policy along the Canal for the past two months gives ample evidence of being a concerted and considered effort to deny Israel the enjoyment of the East Bank of the Canal'.[41] Mr Sharara, first secretary at the Egyptian embassy in London, reminded diplomats that 'it was impossible for them to allow the situation on the Canal front to solidify since this might lead to Sinai being regarded as effectively Israeli territory. After all the state of Israel was built up within armistice lines'.[42] In July 1969, the CIA reinforced that the Egyptians were 'determined to keep the situation along the canal active whatever the consequences'.[43] Diplomats and intelligence analysts clearly presaged later scholarly conclusions that 'the principal Egyptian aim during this period was to prevent the front from "freezing" and Israel from consolidating her position in Sinai'.[44]

By the middle of 1969 the British embassy in Cairo was reporting back to Whitehall that in the absence of a settlement, 'we should expect the Egyptians, again half deliberately and half under the pressure of events, to slide rapidly into the kind of action which would provoke serious Israeli reprisals'. The result would be 'a state of affairs for which, whatever its precise form, war would be the only possible description'.[45] JIC agreed that, 'given the excitability of the Arabs and the fact that they are now again well-armed, it would be imprudent . . . to discount the possibility of Arab moves . . . provoking a fresh war with Israel'.[46]

Israel reacted to military incursions along the Canal with deep penetration raids in the Egyptian heartland. This drove home to analysts both the possibility of an escalation of the war and the primacy of 'dignity' for the Egyptian people as well as its leadership. Egypt's position was described as one of 'determined defiance'. Washington was informed that the 'Cairo regime is in less trouble than at any other time since the 1967 war' and noted that the rift between the regime and the military that characterised the immediate aftermath of defeat was healing: 'for the present at least, the regime and the military identify with each other more closely than at any other time since the 1967 war'.[47] Bergus reflected that:

> By any set of Western criteria, the Nasser regime should have long since disappeared, buffeted to death not only by the disastrous June 1967 episode in the Arab-Israel war but also by Egypt's built-in and perhaps insoluble social and economic problems. By the more exotic criteria of this area, however, the Nasser regime is doing quite well.

Nasser retained broad legitimacy among Egyptians, Bergus thought, because he continued 'to personify their most important aspiration – dignity'.[48] Challenging the JIC's thesis that the Egyptians had simply deluded themselves, Bergus wrote that Nasser was aware of Egypt's 'military shortcomings and discusses them frankly with his Arab allies'. Yet 'he also believes that he could not survive surrender of Arab territory'. Bergus assessed that Nasser would prefer a political settlement but only 'peace with dignity'.[49] Nasser's calculations were seen to be subject to a different cultural order of priorities.

Nor was he alone. The Egyptian people demonstrated an 'amazing ability [to] absorb military losses and blows to their infrastructure when they feel their dignity is at stake', Bergus cabled back to Washington. 'Egyptians feel they are at least doing something virile and dignified. Perhaps Israel will blink first, perhaps an unidentified "something" will occur "somewhere" to create a new situation favourable to Egypt. It is in the hands of Allah who must, in the fullness of time, reward his devoted servants.'[50] Hinting at the significance of Islam in popular feeling, Bergus also reported a demonstrable increase in the religiosity of the general populace which, he argued, reflected the regime's strength rather than weakness.[51]

By September 1969, both British and American analysts were warning about the dangers of Cold War escalation as a result of Israeli deep penetration raids.[52] As the Egyptian Chief of Staff claimed, 'we must take some action to defend the honour of the armed forces'.[53] The newly inaugurated British ambassador, Sir Richard Beaumont, was a quintessential Foreign Office Arabist, well versed in the politics and culture of the Islamic world. Wasting no time upon his arrival in Cairo, Beaumont urged a more active British response in Whitehall. 'I see the barometer set for the steady polarisation of the Middle East until there is no exception to the pattern of Israel plus the West against the Arabs plus the Soviet Union.'[54] Meanwhile, American diplomatic reporting stressed the role that President Johnson had played in exacerbating the conflict, suggesting that the delivery of American Phantom jets to Israel 'was followed almost immediately' by the Israeli strike across the Gulf of Suez.[55] Indeed by December the Egyptian SAM-2 air defence system had been wiped out, along with a substantial proportion of her air force. The Egyptian regime was forced to consider an alternative and more drastic intervention.

The Soviet Invitation

It had become conventional wisdom within the intelligence community that whilst seeking to expand their influence and prestige in the Middle East, the Soviets generally practised caution in the Egyptian–Israeli conflict. Indeed, Richard Parker recalls an incident during the War of Attrition that underlined the extent of Soviet cautiousness. The CIA was in the privileged position of being able to read the car telephone traffic of Politburo members in the wake of an Israeli bomb attack in the leafy Cairo suburb of Maadi that killed several Soviet generals advising the Egyptians. Brezhnev faced the angry protestations of certain individuals in the Politburo who telephoned to insist that such an insult could not go unanswered, to which he apparently replied that: 'You don't go to war over scratches.'[56]

There was little doubt, however, that the Six-Day War had prompted a deeper Soviet–Egyptian relationship, and analysts recognised that the Soviet Union was 'now bent on restoring its influence in the Middle East'. They correctly predicted 'an influx of Soviet advisers, trainers, and technicians into the area' and suggested that there was 'likely to be increased use by the U.S.S.R. of Arab port and air facilities'.[57]

In the wake of the Soviet intervention in Egypt, however, the CIA were forced to question the presumption of 'caution' that had dominated previous assessments of Soviet intentions in a top secret and recently declassified American post-mortem. The CIA suggested that analysts should have given greater weight to the prospect of a more ambitious Soviet policy.[58] The weight of scholarly evidence in fact indicates that the assumption of Soviet caution was more accurate than analysts believed at the time. Recent scholarship asserts that the initial Soviet response to the request for intervention was negative and that only Nasser's threat to resign persuaded the Kremlin to give in. Moreover, Brezhnev insisted that the missiles and personnel should arrive covertly rather than openly as Nasser wanted.[59] Russian accounts also indicate that even whilst Soviet regiments were being deployed in Egypt, the Soviet ambassador Vinogradov was instructed by the Kremlin to pressure Nasser into a ceasefire.[60]

This unusual post-mortem (citing several documents that have not in fact yet been declassified) also reveals that the CIA in fact raised the possibility of a 'more direct sort of help to clients' as early as January 1968 and specifically addressed the possibility of a renewal of hostilities in February 1969. The CIA felt that, 'should renewed hostilities occur, the U.S.S.R. might be drawn into assisting the defence of the Arabs' but qualified that they 'would not want to run the risks of joining in attacks on Israel or actually threatening its survival'.[61]

In general, assessments of Soviet intentions in this period portrayed Moscow as drawn into the conflict reluctantly, a thesis which correlates with both the Egyptian perspective and later historical scholarship. [62] In April 1968, a Soviet–Egyptian treaty on military and naval privileges was agreed, a move the JIC described as 'a cautious probing exercise in the Mediterranean area'. They stressed to policy-makers in Whitehall that the Soviet installations could not be considered as 'bases' because they remained under Egyptian sovereignty. They judged that they were primarily designed to lift morale and impose restraint on Israeli behaviour.[63] Despite Nasser's increased dependence on the Soviets, the CIA took a similar position, maintaining that Egypt remained 'suspicious of foreign advice and intervention, and without more evidence we are not inclined to believe that Nasser is prepared to accept Moscow's dominance'.[64]

Nor did they estimate that the Kremlin was willing to risk their relationship with Nasser by flexing their political muscles too strongly. In August 1969, the State Department assessed that Moscow's 'first consideration, over and above their need for a settlement, is their desire to maintain the position of President Nasser'. Concerned with their reputation, and opportunities for further penetration, they were thus unlikely to pressure Nasser to accept formulations that would damage his internal position.[65] Moreover the Kremlin would be loath to associate with a 'likely loser' and provoke a military confrontation between the USSR and US. The JIC concluded that 'the Russians are likely to counsel caution whether or not peace talks are productive'.[66]

There was a caveat, however. Whilst the Soviet Union was demonstrating encouraging signs of a more conciliatory policy, it was possible, the JIC reflected, though 'admittedly speculative and would involve a major change in Russian policy', that the superpower might consider adopting 'a harder policy e.g. by using and perhaps increasing their military presence in the area to put pressure on Israel'. Analysts suggested that the Soviet leadership might make 'the dangerous calculation that if their military forces occupy critical positions in the area neither Israel nor the West will take the risk of making a move which might provoke a U.S./ U.S.S.R. confrontation'. Indeed, as early as March 1969, the JIC had stressed unequivocally that 'we think it right to draw attention to the possibility that in the circumstances envisaged i.e. failure to achieve a settlement, the Russians will be drawn into further support for the Arab cause'.[67]

In the summer of 1969, Israeli deep penetration raids over Cairo naturally imparted urgency to such fears. In September 1969, Bergus reminded the new Secretary of State, William Rogers, that 'the Soviet Union remains committed to the preservation of the Nasser regime'.[68] British diplomats reported to Whitehall a revealing message from a German Middle East correspondent, Wolfgang Hauptman, that: 'the Egyptians would sooner or later have to ask the Russians to fly defensive air patrols over Cairo and protect vital areas'.[69]

In January 1970, Soviet premier Kosygin presented President Nixon with the strongest indication yet of Soviet intentions towards Egypt. In a strongly worded letter to the president, he insisted that unless Israel ceased the raids, 'the Soviet Union will be obliged to see to it that the Arab states have at their disposal such means which would help them to give a proper rebuff to the arrogant aggressor'. The Americans were sceptical of the Soviet threat.[70] As Richard Parker later put it 'the almost universal reaction among the Soviet specialists in the Department of State and the CIA was that the Soviets were bluffing' and would limit their support to supplying more equipment to Egypt.[71]

However, the British interpretation of the threat was much more astute. The British ambassador in Moscow, Duncan Wilson, was an Oxford-educated historian whose posting in the Soviet Union was the culmination of a long and eminent career, after which he enjoyed a prestigious retirement as the Master of Corpus

Christi College in Cambridge. Wilson was known as something of
an idealist in the Foreign Office but was all too clear in his reporting back to Whitehall. He warned that the letter was 'a gesture of
maximum support for Nasser' and that the threat to intervene was
'a genuine warning, primarily addressed to the U.S. government,
and intended to be taken at face value'. He stated unequivocally,
'I will only repeat my belief that the Russians are fully capable of
carrying out the action indicated.'[72]

Other indications followed. A Russian-speaking contact
informed American diplomats that the 'next stage of Soviet escalation will be use of Soviet pilots in air defence'.[73] In February 1970,
luminaries in the State Department argued that Soviet intervention
was unlikely but conceded that this was a possibility if Nasser's
survival was at stake. Once more they elevated the issue of 'dignity' to the forefront of their analysis.[74] British analysts put themselves on the record as 'less inclined to rule out the possibility of a
bigger Soviet military commitment in the U.A.R'.[75]

Indeed, these warnings in the British archives about the threat of
Soviet escalation provide a pertinent example of how policy-makers
dismissed the evidence presented to them by analysts. On the 19
February the Foreign Office wrote to Prime Minister Harold Wilson
of their concern over the deep penetration air raids on Egypt. They
stressed 'the danger of sharp retaliation by the Arabs leading to a
severe escalation of the conflict', resulting in 'the strong possibility that the Soviet Union may be driven to become more directly
involved in the defence of the U.A.R'.[76] They warned that Soviet
support 'would probably take the form of a more sophisticated air
defence system, manned by Soviet personnel or perhaps of short
range ground-to-ground missiles', and highlighted that:

> increased Soviet commitments in the area will make it harder for the
> Russians to avoid direct involvement in any crisis . . . we are bound
> to say that the U.S. government proposals have not successfully con-
> vinced the Arabs of the seriousness of their determination to pursue a
> political settlement.[77]

The secretary suggested an appeal to the US accordingly. A minute
was attached to the letter with the note, simply replying that 'the
Prime Minster did not agree with the FCO Secretary's submission'.[78]

Nor were American analysts oblivious to the motivations behind greater Soviet involvement. On 5 March 1970, the intelligence community stressed the importance of Egyptian defence requirements against Israeli deep penetration raids in Moscow's eyes:

> certainly Moscow does not like to see Cairo helpless in the face of Israeli air assaults . . . it would be fearful that a refusal to aid the U.A.R. in its hour of need would threaten to disrupt relations with Egypt and damage Soviet prestige throughout the Arab world.[79]

The analysis thus clearly revises recent scholarly claims that US intelligence 'failed to comprehend that . . . Moscow would be inextricably linked to the 1969 Arab defeat in terms of political prestige'. [80]

Ambassador Beaumont confirmed that the new system was 'purely defensive'. The Russians were undoubtedly 'driven by the compulsions on them to provide a more effective type of defence system against Israeli attacks on inhabited areas of the U.A.R. to accept the dangers which this increased participation could bring for them'.[81] In fact Beaumont took a relatively cool view of reports that the Soviets were manning the missile sites: 'It has been clear for a long time that they would have to take over radar control if the defence was to have any chance of success. On a missile site it is a relatively short step from giving the Egyptians advice to giving them the order to press the button.'[82]

American analysts evidently became frustrated with their more relaxed British counterparts. They noted that the JIC 'did not go quite far enough in underlining the seriousness of the situation which existed as a result of the present Soviet involvement in flights over U.A.R. territory'. They argued that the build-up of a Soviet manned air defence system was 'an evolving process and due weight should be given to the fact that the Russians had embarked upon a path from which it would be increasingly difficult for them to draw back'.[83] There was some discussion as to whether the move signified a more aggressive Soviet drive. British diplomats argued that 'either they have taken their new operational role with great reluctance and only because it was essential or they have been quite exceptionally skilful in giving that impression'.[84] Bergus agreed that it was a mistake to assume, as policy-makers such as Kissinger believed, that the

Soviets had decided on a more aggressive policy stressing that they had made their commitments in January when Phantoms were bombing the Egyptian heartland and 'U.S. silence was interpreted as acquiescence'.[85]

On 1 May 1970 Nasser gave a speech in the suburban town of Helwan commemorating International Worker's Day. The speech stressed yet again the importance of negotiations from a position of military strength.[86] Assistant Secretary of State for Near Eastern Affairs, Joseph Sisco, however, disagreed with Bergus's analysis of the moves as merely defensive: 'If we had seen anything in the last twenty years to suggest that the Arabs might push only so far and then have the self-control to abjure from further military force and get down to true political bargaining, we might have greater confidence in Arab intentions.'[87] There was clearly some reluctance in the White House to accept the conclusion of their 'man on the ground' in Cairo.

Some analysts were sympathetic to Nasser's predicament. They noted that 'even those Egyptians who are most frightened of a Soviet takeover and the first to blame Nasser for getting them into this mess are saying that as things stood he had no choice but to bring the Russians in'. They argued that his 'essential message to President Nixon was "save yourselves from the consequences of the next stage of polarisation in the Middle East and save me from the next stage of a Soviet takeover. I don't want it but I am going to do it if you cannot show me a way out."'[88] Analysts recognised that 'Egyptians do not want to be left alone with the U.S.S.R . . . Soviets provide the only shield against further humiliation at the hand of the Israelis.'[89] As Mahmoud Riad put it, Nasser had 'no choice but total dependence on the Soviet Union'.[90]

This understanding of Soviet–Egyptian dynamics also meant that analysts were much more sensitive to the likely implications of the Soviet invitation than their more alarmist policy-makers. Kissinger recalled that the introduction of military personnel into Egypt in March 1970 marked a 'unique turn in Soviet policy'.[91]

> Our intelligence community concentrated on trying to measure in precise hardware terms how the military balance had in fact been upset. All this missed the essential point . . . once the Soviets established

themselves with a combat role in the Middle East and we accepted that role, the political balance would be drastically changed, and the military balance could be overthrown at any moment of Soviet choosing.[92]

Similarly, on 6 July 1970, Foreign Secretary Sir Alec Douglas-Home, claimed in Parliament that 'It is not going too far to say that the policies of Egypt and Syria are today largely controlled by the Soviet Union.'[93] The prevailing belief amongst policy-makers was that the power of this decision lay with the Soviet Union and consequently the superpower would be the main beneficiary. Contrast then, the more nuanced reflections of Ambassador Beaumont:

> One of the salient lessons of Egyptian history [is] that any country which accepts a substantial military involvement here is led inexorably into increasing affairs in order to secure the requirements of its military. The first, although minor, signs of the Russian 'move-in' in this sense are now visible. If and when they consider that they have got to accept a still further military involvement, they may well be obliged to go some way towards taking over the effective direction of this country. True this might bring them even worse troubles and in the very long term have its advantages for the West but the consequences in the nearer future could obviously be very serious for us.[94]

Whilst the overall message remains one of concern, the ambassador nonetheless relayed a much more judicious set of assumptions within his assessment. His use of a passive verb to describe the Soviet role was consistent with the long established view that the Soviets had been 'drawn' into the Middle East, in comparison to the more alarmist interpretation of policy-makers implying Soviet initiation. Long-standing sensitivity to the nature of Soviet–Egyptian relations no doubt contributed to this. Ambassador Beaumont prophetically hinted that in the long term, Soviet involvement in Egypt was doomed to failure.

The assessments of the diplomats and the intelligence community thus played a fundamental role in proposing the likely implications of this move. In March 1970, the JIC reiterated 'that the U.A.R. can still not be considered a Soviet puppet'. Despite the large number of Soviet military advisers, the JIC seemed confident that 'they are in no position to direct or even significantly influence political attitudes in the forces'. In fact, they had received 'many reports suggesting that there is growing resentment in the U.A.R. armed forces about the measure of professional control which these advisors are already exercising'. The Soviets struggled to get along with their Egyptian counterparts. The JIC observed that:

> they are aloof and do not fraternise; they show up the inadequacies of Egyptian officers in the sight of their other ranks; and though they have done much for the efficiency of the U.A.R. armed forces, they have not done much for their morale.[95]

The overall balance sheet was not as favourable to the Soviets as policymakers feared.

Such analysis no doubt relied heavily the frequent diplomatic reports concerning the strained relations between the Soviet advisors and the Egyptian military. The Foreign Office files relate a particularly revealing anecdote of a British contact in Cairo who

> found himself sitting next to a Russian officer on the train from Cairo to Aswan. They had got into friendly conversation, and the Russian officer had at one point said: "Look – next time these Arabs fight the Israelis let us change sides: we will take the Israelis and you can take the Arabs. I am a serious soldier, and it is terribly frustrating having to try to get these chaps out of bed in the morning and teach them how to drive a tank."[96]

Analysts recognised that Soviet presence in Egypt was more likely to exacerbate the tensions already existing within patron–client relations. Such 'on-the ground' reporting would prove an important element to later successful assessments of the Soviet expulsion.

Indeed, when calculating likely implications of the Soviet invitation, analysts on both sides of the Atlantic evidently resisted the tendency to see the regional aspects of the Cold War exclusively as a battle for US supremacy over Soviet interests. They were able to look more empathetically upon the move, subtly asserting the implications for American national interests, outside the paradigm of Cold War rivalry. The CIA reminded its consumers that 'in spite of its dependence on the U.S., Israel has not been responsive to U.S. policy suggestions and has remained extremely sensitive to any situation of pressure'. It went on to suggest that 'the new situation the Israelis confront in consequence of the introduction of Soviet military forces might make the Israelis more inclined to accept U.S. advice, for example in moderating Israel's approach to the modalities of negotiation'.[97]

Whilst the White House regarded the invitation to be a fundamental setback from a geopolitical Cold War perspective, intelligence analysts pertinently recognised the move as portending a possible gain in the Arab–Israeli conflict, pressuring the Israelis to accept American advice and potentially pushing forward negotiations. Indeed, Nasser was to accept the Rogers ceasefire plan in July.[98] Perhaps most importantly, this analysis by the CIA reflects the variety and dissonance between the various perceptual frameworks of the American administration and the manner in which intelligence analysis could subtly guide and redefine ideas of national interest.

* * *

The War of Attrition provides a fascinating and under-examined case study of how the Anglo-American diplomatic and intelligence community perceived Nasser's regional role and his intentions in provoking yet another unwinnable war. On the one hand it is striking how frequently the 'cultural' beliefs explored in the first chapter permeated analysis. It is clear that the precedent of 1967 reinforced in the minds of analysts particular 'Arab traits' such as the primacy of 'dignity', the 'irrationality' of decision-making, the escalatory power of 'rhetoric' and increasingly, the 'fatalism' of the Egyptian people. At the same time, analysts (particularly diplomats stationed in Cairo) deconstructed an internal logic to Nasser's actions, recognising that he sought to deny Israelis use of the east bank of the Canal. They sympathised with the Clausewitzian quality in Nasser's worldview that ultimately war was an extension of diplomacy as rather than merely an alternative to a political settlement.

Nor does the Soviet invitation appear to have been as unanticipated as the historiography has suggested. Analysts recognised that the Soviets had committed themselves to restoring their prestige in the region after defeat and addressed the possibility of more direct involvement. They correctly regarded the shape and pace of the Soviet–Egyptian relationship as driven by the agency of the Egyptian leadership and saw the Soviets as reluctantly drawn into the Arab–Israeli conflict. The archives reveal several indications of deeper Soviet involvement from January 1970 and a specific warning from the British ambassador in Moscow and the Foreign Office that Israeli deep penetration raids were likely to provoke Soviet intervention. That such warnings were dismissed by policy-makers only reinforces the frequently large gap between incisive intelligence and sound policy. Perhaps most importantly, analysts were able to put the invitation into perspective, quelling the fear of policy-makers that the move signalled Egypt's transition to the status of Soviet client. Soviet–Egyptian relations had reached an uneasy peak, to be followed after Nasser's death by a slow and steady deterioration.

Notes

1. Simcha Diniz, 'The Yom Kippur War: diplomacy of war and peace', in P. R. Kumaraswamy (ed.), *Revisiting the Yom Kippur War* (London: Frank Cass, 2000), p. 104.
2. Televised address by President Nasser, 6 November 1969.
3. Mar'I, Awraq Siyasiyya [Political Papers], vol. II (Cairo, 1978), p. 520
4. A. Atherton, 'Arabs, Israelis – and Americans: a reconsideration', *Foreign Affairs*, 62: 5, 1984, p. 1198.
5. Interview with Richard Parker, 21 April 1989. Available at <http://adst.org/wp-content/uploads/2012/09/Egypt.pdf> (last accessed 1 March 2017), p. 476.
6. See, for example: R. B. Parker, *The Politics of Miscalculation in the Middle East* (Bloomington, IN: Indiana University Press, 1992); D. Adamsky, 'Disregarding the bear: How U.S. intelligence failed to estimate the Soviet intervention in the Egyptian-Israeli War of Attrition', *Journal of Strategic Studies*, 28: 5, 2005; Y. Blanga, '"Why are they shooting?": Washington's view of the onset of the War of Attrition', *Israel Affairs*, 18: 2, 2012.
7. Blanga, '"Why are they shooting?"', *Israel Affairs*, 18: 2, 2012, p. 161.
8. Parker, *Politics of Miscalculation*, p. 156.
9. Material from this chapter builds upon earlier research. See D. Rezk, *British and American Political and Intelligence Assessments of the Nasser-Sadat Transition*, unpublished MPhil thesis, Cambridge University, Cambridge, 2006.
10. NIE 11-6-70, 'Soviet policies in the Middle East and Mediterranean', 5 March 1970, FOIA Reading Room.

11. See, for example: A. Dawisha, 'Egypt', in Y. Sayigh and A. Shlaim (eds), *The Cold War and the Middle East* (Oxford: Clarendon Press, 1997), p. 45.
12. William Tuohey, 'America's man in Cairo expects anything these days', *Tuscaloosa News*, 12 September 1971.
13. SNIE 36.1-67, 'The situation and prospects in Egypt', 17 August 1967, FOIA Reading Room.
14. R. Stephens, *Nasser: A Political Biography* (London: Penguin, 1971), p. 523.
15. Despatch from Beeley to Stewart, 'Israel and the Arab states: is a settlement possible?', 9 July 1968, TNA, FCO 17/49. Beeley strongly believed that the Israelis should abandon their insistence on direct negotiations: 'I can only state my conviction that if the Israel government continue to insist on negotiating a treaty of peace with the United Arab Republic they will be turning their back on the first opportunity since 1948 of actually creating conditions of peace in the area.' He also criticised the Americans for not putting pressure on Israel to accept this.
16. Telegram from Rostow to President Johnson, 29 December 1967, FRUS 1964-68, vol. XX, no. 28.
17. Beeley's successor, Richard Beaumont, took a more sceptical view of the problems of an imposed solution. See memorandum from Ambassador Beaumont to Minister of State, 12 November 1968, TNA, FCO 17/638: 'One can't help seeing in this [an imposed settlement] (a) a reflection of the Soviet/French view of Power politics in the XXth century and especially on the Palestine question; (b) a solution which at one and the same time gives the U.A.R. (i) a justification to its own population – "it was imposed on us by the 'great powers', how could we resist it?" and (ii) possibly, a means of renouncing it later – "it was imposed on us, we never really accepted it."'
18. L. James, *Nasser At War: Arab Images of the Enemy* (Basingstoke: Palgrave Macmillan, 2006), p. 135.
19. Blanga, '"Why are they shooting?"', *Israel Affairs*, 18: 2, 2012, p. 157.
20. James, *Nasser at War*, p. 142.
21. Brief for Secretary of State, 11 July 1967, TNA, FCO 17/525.
22. James, *Nasser at War*, p. 134.
23. Memorandum from Saunders to Rostow, 'Conversation with the Egyptian Minister [Ashraf Ghorbal]', 16 February 1968, DDRS.
24. Memorandum from Smith in NSC to President Johnson, 'Nasser-Bundy conversation 3 July', 4 July 1968, FRUS 1964-68, vol. XX, no. 209.

25. Memorandum from Tesh in British Embassy Cairo to FO, 7 June 1968, TNA, FCO 17/48.
26. Special memorandum no. 8-68 by the Board of National Estimates, 'Nasser's limited options', 15 April 1968, CREST, NARA II.
27. Blanga, '"Why are they shooting?"', *Israel Affairs,* 18: 2, 2012, p. 169.
28. Telegram from Ambassador Beeley in Cairo to FCO, 15 September 1968, TNA, FCO 17/638.
29. Telegram from Ambassador Beeley in Cairo to FCO, 30 October 1968, TNA, FCO 17/757.
30. Telegram from Moore to Borroughs, 12 September 1968, TNA, FCO 17/638.
31. Information cable, 31 July 67, DDRS. Moheiddin reported 'our intelligence service is the most ignorant in the world. Whereas the Israelis knew the name of every Egyptian on relief and his wife's name too, we didn't even know where Moshe Dayan's home was'.
32. Telegram from Ambassador Hadow in Tel Aviv to FO, 11 September 1968, TNA, FCO 17/638.
33. The Bar Lev Line (named after Israeli Chief of Staff Bar Lev) was a sand wall with concrete support stretching approximately100 miles along the Canal, constructed by Israeli forces to defend against Egyptian assaults.
34. D. A. Korn, *Stalemate: The War of Attrition and Great Power Diplomacy in the Middle East* (Boulder, CO: Westview, 1992), p. 101.
35. Blanga, '"Why are they shooting?"', *Israel Affairs*, 18: 2, 2012, p. 165.
36. JIC memorandum (69) 16, 'The Arab Israeli balance and its political implications up to the end of 1973', 25 April 1969, TNA, CAB 186/2: 'They might again miscalculate the effects of a piece of political bravura, or they might be prompted by an exaggerated belief in the isolation of Israel, or by a misguided estimate of the effectiveness of Fedayeen action.'
37. R. Kaplan, 'Tales from the bazaar', *The Atlantic*, August 1992. Available at <http://www.theatlantic.com/magazine/archive/1992/08/tales-from-the-bazaar/305012/> (last accessed 1 March 2017).
38. Memorandum from Parker to Sisco, 'The Egyptian Weltanschuung', 16 April 1969, File Chron 1969, Office Memoranda, Records Relating to Egypt 1967-1975, Bureau of Near Eastern and South Asian Affairs, Office of Egypt Affairs, Box 11, General Records of the State Department, Record Group 59, NARA II.
39. Ibid.

40. JIC memorandum (69) 16, 'The Arab Israeli balance and its political implications up to the end of 1973', 25 April 1969, TNA, CAB 186/2. The JIC judged that 'the stronger each country becomes militarily, the less defensible will their "political" approach appear to domestic opinion'. They do not seem to have taken on board Ambassador Beeley's point that that military strength was *more rather than less* likely to make a political settlement possible but both diplomatic and intelligence analysis recognised the strong link between the political and military options.

41. Memorandum from Parker to Sisco, 'Contingencies in the Middle East', 7 May 1969, File Chron 1969 Office Memoranda, Records Relating to Egypt 1967-1975, Bureau of Near Eastern and South Asian Affairs, Office of Egypt Affairs, Box 11, General Records of the State Department, Record Group 59, NARA II.

42. Memorandum from Gray to Mallet, 1 July 1969, TNA, FCO 17/760.

43. CIB by the Directorate of Intelligence, 25 July 1969, FOIA Reading Room.

44. James, *Nasser at War*, p. 138.

45. Despatch from Stewart at British Embassy in Cairo to FCO, 13 June 1969, TNA, FCO 17/760.

46. JIC memorandum (69) 20, 'Soviet policy towards the Arab-Israeli problem', 19 March 1969, TNA, CAB 186/2.

47. CIB by the Directorate of Intelligence, 28 July 1969, FOIA Reading Room.

48. From USINT Bergus to Secretary of State, 24 September 1969, File UAR vol. II 1 Sept 1969–31 January 1970, Country Files Middle East, NSC Files, Box 635, Nixon Presidential Materials Staff, NARA II.

49. Ibid.

50. Ibid. Bergus described the 'classic Egyptian stance of standing pat, talking big, punishing enemy as much as he possibly can, and taking counterblows stoically.'

51. Telegram from Bergus to Secretary of State, 10 February 1970, File Pol Arab-Isr, 2-11-1970, Subject Numeric Files 1970-1973, Political and Defense, Box 2050, General Records of the State Department, Record Group 59, NARA II.

52. Adamsky, 'Disregarding the bear', *Journal of Strategic Studies*, 28: 5, 2005, p. 818. Adamsky rightly notes that Bergus was one of the few American analysts who recognised the threat of US and Israeli policy but that 'most of his telegrams went unanswered'. Similarly Richard Parker's warnings that Israeli deep penetration raids would

prompt a Soviet intervention 'ended up in the files with no notations whatsoever'.

53. James, *Nasser at War*, p. 158.
54. Telegram from Ambassador Beaumont in Cairo to FCO, 6 September 1969, TNA, FCO 17/760. Beaumont wrote: 'I do not believe that the present rate of progress towards a settlement accords with British interests' and suggested that the British role was to promote 'the best intermediate position' which is 'obvious to any objective observer', e.g. withdrawal from Sinai, UN presence at Sharm el Sheikh and Demilitarised Zones 'very much larger' on the Egyptian side than the Israeli side.
55. Memorandum from Parker to Sisco, 'Department of spilt milk: an historical footnote', 21 November 1969, File Chron 1969 Office Memoranda, Records Relating to Egypt 1967-1975, Bureau of Near Eastern and South Asian Affairs, Office of Egypt Affairs, Box 11, General Records of the State Department, Record Group 59, NARA II.
56. R. B. Parker (ed.), *The October War: A Retrospective* (Gainesville, FL: University Press of Florida, 2001), p. 196.
57. Memorandum from Kent at ONE to DCI, 'Nasser's prospects for survival', 15 June 1967, CREST, NARA II.
58. ONE memorandum for the Director, 'National Intelligence estimates on the Soviet role in the Middle East 1965-70', 20 July 1970, CREST, NARA II.
59. James, *Nasser at War*, p. 159.
60. Adamsky, 'Disregarding the bear', *Journal of Strategic Studies*, 28: 5, 2005, p. 823.
61. ONE memorandum for the Director, 'National Intelligence estimates on the Soviet role in the Middle East 1965-70', 20 July 1970, CREST, NARA II.
62. James, *Nasser at War*, p. 164. Citing several Egyptian sources, James concludes that 'the general trend of Soviet policy at this time was to restrain Egypt from aggressive action'.
63. JIC memorandum (68) 34, 'Soviet intentions in the Mediterranean', 20 May 1968, TNA, CAB 186/1.
64. SNIE 36.1-67, 'The situation and prospects in Egypt', 17 August 1967, FOIA Reading Room.
65. Memorandum from Moberley in British Embassy Washington to Tripp at FCO, 'Arab/Israel dispute: Soviet attitude', 8 August 1969, TNA, FCO 17/747.
66. JIC memorandum (69) 43, 'Outlook for the UAR: 1970-71', 13 February 1970, TNA, CAB 186/3.

67. JIC memorandum (69) 20, 'Soviet policy towards the Arab-Israeli problem', 19 March 1969, TNA, CAB 186/2.

68. Memorandum from Bergus to Secretary of State, 24 September 1969, File UAR vol. II 1 Sept 1969–31 Jan 1970, Country Files Middle East, NSC Files, Box 635, Nixon Presidential Materials Staff, NARA II.

69. Minute by Joy, 3 January 1970, TNA, FCO 95/882.

70. Telegram from Freeman at British Embassy Washington to FCO, 20 February 1970, TNA, PREM 13/3331: 'The United States assessment was that on the military side the Russians were limited in what they could do to relieve the pressure without substantial escalation involving the use of Soviet personnel in ways which the Americans did not think likely. It followed from this that if the pressure on Moscow and Cairo was not relieved, we could expect the Russians in time to make a further diplomatic or political move in the direction of a positive response to the two American paper, although this would not preclude measures to strengthen the UAR's anti-aircraft defence.'

71. Parker, *Politics of Miscalculation*, p. 156.

72. Telegram from Ambassador Wilson in Moscow to FCO, 4 February 1970, TNA, PREM 13/3331.

73. Cable from USINT Cairo to Secretary of State, Washington, 9 February 1970, File Pol 27 Arab-Israeli, 2-11-70, Subject Numeric Files, 1970-73 Political and Defense, Box 2050, General Records of the State Department, Record Group 59, NARA II.

74. Research memorandum by INR Director Cline to the Acting Secretary, 'USSR-UAR: at the brink of action', 11 February 1970, File Pol 27 Arab-Israeli, 2-11-70, Subject Numeric Files, 1970-73 Political and Defense, Box 2050, General Records of the State Department, Record Group 59, NARA II.

75. Telegram from Freeman at British Embassy in Washington to FCO, 20 February 1970, TNA, PREM 13/3331.

76. Letter from FCO to Prime Minister, 19 February 1970, TNA, PREM 13/3331.

77. Speaking notes attached to letter from Stewart at FCO to Prime Minister, 19 February 1970, TNA, PREM 13/3331.

78. Note by P. J.S.M., 21 February 1970, TNA, PREM 13/3331.

79. NIE 11-6-70, 'Soviet policies in the Middle East and Mediterranean', 5 March 1970, FOIA Reading Room. The American estimate also addressed the kind of aid the Soviets might be expected to provide noting the 'principal Egyptian problem is the lack of certain

more advanced weapons system and above all of qualified personnel to operate an integrated air defence system effectively' and that air defence of Cairo and Egypt's infrastructure would 'require the introduction of entire Soviet units involving many thousands of men'.

80. Adamsky, 'Disregarding the bear', *Journal of Strategic Studies*, 28: 5, 2005, p. 815.
81. Telegram from Ambassador Beaumont to FCO, 15 March 1970, TNA, PREM 13/331. Beaumont also argued that it was 'inconceivable that the Russians would hand over expensive and complex equipment of this type . . . into the hands of Egyptians who to judge by results (or lack of them) have proved themselves totally incapable of handling their existing missile system'. He warned against the risk of the conspicuous installations being detected by the Israelis and 'however illogical', thereby increasing 'pressure on President Nixon to agree to Israeli requests for Phantoms'. The prospect of Israeli aggressive action against the sites would run the further risk of a greater Soviet escalation.
82. Telegram from Ambassador Beaumont to FCO, 13 March 1970, TNA, PREM 13/331.
83. Telegram from Freeman to FCO, 30 April 1970, TNA, FCO 17/1317.
84. Telegram from Stewart in Cairo to FCO, 13 May 1970, TNA, FCO 17/1317.
85. Telegram from USINT Cairo to Secretary of State, 'Some random unthinkable thoughts', 5 May 1970, File UAR vol. IV, 1 May-31 July 1970, Country Files- Middle East, Box 636, National Security Council (NSC) Files, Nixon Presidential Materials Staff, NARA II.
86. James, *Nasser at War*, p. 162.
87. Telegram from Sisco to Bergus, 18 June 1970, File UAR vol. IV, 1 May–31 July 1970, Country Files- Middle East, Box 636. National Security Council (NSC) Files, Nixon Presidential Materials Staff, NARA II.
88. Telegram from Stewart in Cairo to FCO, 13 May 1970, TNA, FCO 17/1317.
89. Telegram from Bergus in Cairo to Secretary of State, 15 December 1970, File UAR vol. V. 1 August 1970–31 December 1970, Country Files- Middle East, Box 636, National Security Council (NSC) Files, Nixon Presidential Materials Staff, NARA II.
90. M. Riad, *The Struggle for Peace in the Middle East* (London: Quartet, 1981), p. 119.
91. H. Kissinger, *The White House Years* (Boston, MA: Little, Brown and Co., 1979), p. 569.

92. Kissinger, *White House Years*, p. 571.
93. Response to Parliamentary question of Goodhart, Soviet commitment to the defence of the UAR, by Foreign Secretary Hume, 6 July 1970, TNA, FCO 39/738.
94. Telegram no. 401 from Ambassador Beaumont in Cairo to FCO, 20 March 1970, TNA, FCO 39/738.
95. JIC memorandum (70) 25, 'Soviet prospects in North Africa and the implications for NATO 1970-1975', 19 March 1970, TNA, CAB 186/6.
96. Untitled minute from Bottomly to Hayman, 12 May 1970, TNA, FCO 39/73.
97. SNIE 30-70, 'The USSR and the Egyptian-Israeli confrontation', 14 May 1970, FOIA Reading Room.
100. Scholars question whether this move was the result of Soviet pressure, a tactical gesture to enable the movement of Soviet missiles or a genuine drive for peace. See James, *Nasser at War*, p. 165. The British ambassador argued that while there was a tactical element to the decision, it also represented Nasser's genuine commitment to a settlement. See telegram from Beaumont to FCO, 14 September 1970, TNA, FCO 17/1161: 'In general I remain convinced that the U.A.R. government is anxious to secure a settlement through Jarring on the lines of resolution 242, and it may be prepared to make some concessions to secure it but that in the mean time [*sic*] it does not wish to negotiate from a position of weakness if it can (even at the cost of breaches of the cease-fire) do so from a position of comparative strength with the Israelis.'

8   Early Years of Sadat's Presidency

There wasn't a lot of information about what kind of a person he [Sadat] was, how he would perform. Was he really just going to be temporary and overthrown by stronger forces trying to replace him? Well, as it turned out, Sadat was stronger and cannier than all of the others, but it wasn't immediately apparent.

Roy Atherton, 1990[1]

On 1 October 1970, President Gamal Abdel Nasser was carried to his grave after a sudden and fatal heart attack. The display of public grief and national solidarity at Nasser's funeral was unprecedented in Egypt and the event is still regarded as one of the largest public funerals in world history. It was symbolic of the 'moderation' with which Nasser had come to be regarded that his final act as international statesman was facilitating a reconciliation between King Hussein and the Palestinian Liberation Organisation in the bloody civil war that had raged in Jordan that summer. Analysts were faced with the challenging task of assessing Nasser's successor and his likely policies in a fragile Arab–Israeli climate.

Most historians have intimated that Nasser's death was welcomed by the West. William Quandt, for example, recalls that Sadat was viewed in Washington 'as a considerable improvement over Nasser'.[2] Similarly, erstwhile Egyptian Foreign Minister Mahmoud Riad writes in his memoirs that Nasser's death was met with relief by the Americans, who regarded him as a 'stumbling block on the road to peace'.[3]

The most recently declassified documents show either (or perhaps both) the power of retrospect in skewing historical recollection or the multiplicity of views on the new Egyptian leader.[4] In fact the new President was overwhelmingly seen as a weak, temporary figure occluded by Nasser's shadow. Moreover, Sadat's priorities were visibly different and as a result the leader was essentially regarded (particularly by British diplomatic analysis) as a considerably inferior statesman to his predecessor. This often manifested itself in an inconsistent political orientation, most evident in his relations with the Soviet Union.

Sadat's sudden expulsion of the Soviet advisors in 1972 was an exemplary expression of the new Egyptian leadership's unpredictability. As the late Fred Halliday put it, 'this Soviet experience was to play a role in the end of the Cold War itself', marking the beginning of Soviet disillusionment with their investment in third world socialism.[5] Intelligence and diplomatic analysis proved presciently aware of the motivations and implications of this move. There was tactical warning in the Presidential Daily Brief that the Soviets were going to be expelled. Moreover, in the years preceding the expulsion, analysts clearly identified key strategic considerations contributing to Sadat's decision: nationalist sentiment; cultural tensions between the Russian advisors and the Egyptians; pressures from Egypt's new Arab allies; and most importantly, the frustrated limbo of 'no peace and no war' with Israel. Tragically, however, there was a marked analytical reluctance to consider that Sadat might have expelled the Soviets in preparation for the most dramatic Arab–Israeli war yet to come.

* * *

First Impressions of Sadat

Approximately one week after Nasser's death, DCI Helms made explicit the seminal consequences for American policy in a briefing to the President's Intelligence Advisory Board. The US would now have to 'look for some new leader with the strength to speak for the Arabs in peace talks'. The intelligence community described Sadat as a 'compromise candidate chosen for his weakness'. Whilst Nasser's strength and popularity had allowed him to make 'possibly unpopular decisions: his more cautious heir must take more pains to ensure public support'. In the broader regional context, the CIA predicted that Cairo's influence in inter-Arab affairs would be weakened 'and may continue to diminish'. By the time of his death Nasser had come to be regarded as almost a judicious figure without whom 'the already unstable Middle East is in for further fragmentation and polarisation'. Even Israel would miss their long-time adversary, predicting 'a narrative from Tel Aviv' that with the 'moderate Nasir gone, there is no Arab leader left with enough authority to make dealing with him worthwhile'.[6]

The US diplomatic representative in Cairo, Donald Bergus, reflected on the legacy Nasser had left behind in Egypt. He was struck by 'a truly morbid and fatalistic obsession with concepts of "honour" and "dignity"'. He noted that the build-up of Egypt's air defences alongside American diplomatic initiatives created 'an Egyptian vision of peace with honour and dignity'. Indeed, Nasser's death had only served to strength this vision, accentuating 'the Egyptian people's will to peace and Egyptian sensitivity to the "honour" and "dignity" factors'. In November 1970, speaking to the Arab Socialist Union, Sadat accused 'imperialist circles' in the American government of waging a campaign of psychological warfare with their ally Israel.[7] However, Bergus reminded policy-makers that the new Egyptian leadership still regarded America as the only source of peace with honour and dignity and suggested that the US government 'turn the other cheek' to Egyptian verbal attacks which were 'childish foot stampings rather than real blows'.[8]

The CIA were initially sceptical about the longevity of Sadat's succession. They did not see Sadat carrying 'much personal weight in Egyptian political circles' and thought it 'doubtful that he will fill the presidency for more than an interim period'. They believed that Sadat 'owed his position more to his loyalty to Nasir than to his political strength and acumen'.[9] Similarly, the British ambassador, Richard Beaumont, suggested that whilst 'fairly popular' he had neither the appeal nor the intelligence of Nasser. Rather 'his leading position in the 1952 revolution as well as the obvious trust which Nasser placed in him lent respect'.[10] The derivative nature of Sadat's leadership was evident. Initially riding on the wave of Nasser's popularity and legitimacy, Sadat's main task would be to match the charisma of his predecessor in order to consolidate his leadership.

Broadly speaking, the Anglo-American intelligence community recognised that Nasser's would be a challenging shadow to cast aside. Here the contrast of dry and colourless intelligence assessments produced by bureaucratic committees like the CIA and the JIC against more colourful, empathetic iterations produced by the diplomatic service (essentially human intelligence) was particularly marked. In his seminal work on the JIC, Cradock criticises the Committee for underestimating Arab nationalism, a claim which the following assessment just months before Nasser's death appears to substantiate:

> Over the last 15 years the regime has managed despite many external setbacks and internal vicissitudes, to retain at least the acquiescence of the broad mass of the population. This has owed much to the traditional passivity of Egyptians and to the lack of any obvious alternatives to President Nasser though there have of course been more positive factors such as the identification of the regime with the struggle to regain Arab land from Israel and to neutralise 'imperialist' influence in Arab affairs and with the goals of social and economic progress.[11]

The Orientalist tendency to attribute Nasser's popularity simply to 'traditional passivity' is evident. Moreover, the reluctance to credit the 'positive factors', the central features of what defined Arab nationalism and Nasser's ambitious social and economic reforms pale against the vivid assessments of Nasser's appeal produced by the diplomatic service. Describing Nasser's funeral, Ambassador Beaumont wrote,

> In the course of a consular and diplomatic career I have had ample opportunity to observe the disarray of families suddenly bereaved, but I cannot recall ever having witnessed a scene of bewilderment and disarray such as was to be seen in Cairo in the days following Nasser's death. It went from the bottom to the top of Egyptian society . . . Thus the first Egyptian Pharaoh was carried to his grave in an atmosphere of grief and devotion such as this country cannot have witnessed since the last of the priest-kings was carried by his awe-stricken subjects to his richly stocked resting place to confer with Horus, Isis and Osiris.[12]

Figure 8.1 Nasser surrounded by Egyptians demonstrating in Cairo, 1954. Photograph by DDP, Camera Press, London.

As Heikal recalled in an interview thirty-six years later, the response to Nasser's death demonstrated that, 'the sound of music does not lie'.[13] His Weberian allusion to the sentiments of the Egyptian masses towards the charismatic leadership of Nasser was becoming apparent to both Sadat's domestic and international constituency as a significant difference between the two statesmen, and it was one that analysts were quick to highlight to policy-makers.

Sadat demonstrated a different temperament and more importantly, different priorities to his predecessor. Egypt's newly appointed Country Director, Michael Sterner, was surprised to be invited to accompany Don Bergus to meet the new Egyptian president at one of Sadat's rest houses at the head of the Nile Delta. Sterner had been Sadat's escort officer during his first eventful trip to the US some years earlier in which Sadat dined with

President Johnson, visited Congress, and even journeyed to Disneyland. So upon arrival in Cairo in March 1971, Sterner already enjoyed something of a rapport with the new Egyptian President. He remembered,

> It was a lovely spring day. Sadat had a large topographical relief map of the Sinai tacked up on a board and without many preliminaries . . . he began to outline a deal for partial Israeli withdrawal in Sinai and reopening of the Suez Canal . . . We had certainly never heard anything like this from Nasser.

'Still', Sterner recalled, 'there was the question of how stable Sadat was.'[14]

Despite his later turn to the West, the CIA were not convinced that Sadat had the charm or the conviction of his predecessor. Although Sadat was 'smart enough to see that the only way out for Egypt is a settlement and is more prepared to make concessions than was Nasser', the new leader lacked 'Nasser's self-confidence and Nasser's incomparable ability for dealing with Westerners'. They noticed that in negotiations, Sadat had a tendency to get 'carried away with himself' and 'lose respect for the intelligence of those to whom he is speaking', culminating ultimately in 'a highly unattractive mish-mash of emotion and twisted fact. In short he falls back on the old Arab habit of playing a phonograph record.'[15]

Analysts observed such differences of temperament and charisma not only in Sadat's manner with the West, but also with his own people. In 1971, Ambassador Beaumont reflected that, 'by temperament he [Sadat] is a very different man from Nasser'. Beaumont identified 'a certain grim and obstinate determination in Nasser which to the very end encased him in the prejudices and objectives of his youth and tended to demand of the Egyptian people a similar grim dedication of which he himself knew them – as he admitted to me on one occasion – to be temperamentally quite incapable'. In contrast, Sadat appealed to 'the easy going side of Egyptian character' in order to 'in the short term at least both achieve popularity and at the same time establish his personal ascendancy'.[16]

Perhaps most interesting is the implicitly critical eye with which this seasoned British diplomat looked upon Sadat's early manoeuvrings. In his valedictory despatch, Beaumont wrote a thoughtful and tentative assessment of the differences between the two leaders.

> I would say that as a man – sincere as his purposes may be – Sadat has not the same vision and does not inspire the same trust. Whatever the twists and turns of Nasser's policies – and there were many – one always had the impression, and, what is more important, the major-ity of his countrymen had the impression – possibly wrong – that he was tending towards an ultimate goal and that that goal was to their benefit and not to his own. With Sadat the impression has not been the same.[17]

Analysts shared the sense that Sadat's primary concern was that of maintaining his own power. The tone of Beaumont's report reveals an unspoken respect for Nasser, and an admiration of the 'ultimate goal' to which his often turbulent decision-making was directed. Alongside this lay an implicit criticism of Sadat for diverging from what had for so long been a defining feature of Egypt's post-revolutionary leadership. Perhaps most interestingly, Beaumont's analysis has been validated by all the Egyptians interviewed first-hand. That British diplomats were able to see Sadat so accurately through the eyes of the Egyptian political elite is surely a notable achievement.

Sadat's leadership seemed notably less consistent than that of his predecessor. In January 1972 British diplomats watched with con-cern as student consciousness expressed itself in an unprecedented manner in public protests. The students had brought international attention to the contradictory nature of Sadat's Egypt, the 'con-tradictions between liberalisation and mobilisation, between call-ing for war and searching for peace, between military dependence on the Soviet Union and the reopening of links with the West, between placing Egyptian interests first and getting the Arabs col-lectively to put pressure on Israel'.[18]

Beaumont feared that the ideological inconsistency of Sadat's leadership was breeding an increasing sense of disillusionment amongst the Egyptian populace.[19] The State Department took a more optimistic view however:

Although Sadat is broadly criticised for his lack of consistency and amateurishness, there may also be considerable passive acquiescence in Sadat's overall approach, especially since no-one else seems to be coming up with a better idea. The broad lines of Sadat's policy of 'not selling out Egypt's rights,' of avoiding (so far anyway) rash military moves, and of trying to build up the country's strength over the long term, are probably in tune with the way most Egyptians feel. This factor, plus his manipulative skills in creating diversions and keeping his enemies out-manoeuvred, could give Sadat and his regime a longer life-span than the period indicated toward the end of Beaumont's report. But we would agree that Sadat faces formidable difficulties in this respect and that the outcome is by no means certain.[20]

American analysts believed that Sadat was taking a 'safe' line of rejecting the half-hearted offers of peace put forth by Israel while strengthening Egypt's military and economic might. Combined with his domestic cunning, Washington felt that Sadat might last longer than their British counterparts had prophesised.

Nowhere was Sadat's opportunism and inconsistency more visible than in his relations with the USSR. The incoherent policy he pursued since assuming the Presidency only seemed to confirm a leadership of 'tactics' as opposed to one conceived of any firm principles. The CIA noted that 'Sadat is an ardent nationalist who is reportedly opposed to domestic Communism' but that he realised 'the value of both political and military aid from the U.S.S.R.'. The Agency judged that 'like many Egyptian politicians, he is probably more opportunistic or pragmatic than ideologically motivated'.[21] In May 1971, this was born out by events when a plot was uncovered to overthrow Sadat and establish 'socialism in Egypt' under the leadership of Nasserite and 'Soviet man' Prime Minister al-Sabri. The chief plotters were arrested and the Soviet threat purged. Diplomats assessed that 'the manner in which the crisis was brought to a head and resolved bears the mark of hurried decisions by Sadat'.[22] Western observers argued that Sadat had asserted his independence from the Soviet Union. Yet only two weeks later he signed a Soviet–Egyptian Treaty of Friendship and Co-operation with President Nikolai Podgorny. In his memoirs Sadat claims that he was hoping to allay the fears of the Kremlin and persuade them that he was involved in an internal power struggle rather than a new foreign policy regarding the Soviet Union. Ambassador Beaumont shrewdly suggested that whilst 'on paper' the treaty offered opportunities for Soviet expansion, 'these opportunities have been available to the Soviet Union for some years and it is arguable that their reinstatement in a public treaty of this kind is only necessary at a time when relations between the two countries have run into difficulties'.[23] In July 1971, Sadat's hostility to Communism was confirmed by his response to a Communist backed military coup in Sudan. He claimed: 'I cannot allow a Communist regime to be established in a country sharing my borders.'[24] Only one year later Sadat was to take the most dramatic step yet in redefining Egypt's relationship with the Soviet Union – demanding the expulsion of 15,000 Soviet advisors.

The Soviet Expulsion

Just as the Soviet 'invitation' had fundamentally altered the geopolitical dynamics of the Cold War in the Middle East, the sudden expulsion of the Soviet forces was a similarly dramatic achievement. One CIA analyst later recalled that it 'was not anticipated, but it was one of the few times during the period leading up to the war where there was intelligence information prior to the decision'. He claims that the Agency provided three days' notice in the PDB that Sadat had reached the decision and it would be announced.[25] This is all the more interesting because Heikal, who was Information Minister at the time, writes that 'only two persons knew in advance of the decision to expel Soviet experts from Egypt in July 1972, and they learned of it only a few hours before the Soviet ambassador was informed'.[26] Other works have suggested that the 'conception of Egypt as an obedient, client state had previously prevented all observers from even speculating on the possibility that Egypt might ask the Soviet Union to withdraw its military advisers'.[27]

In fact, there was warning of the expulsion preceding the dates of all these accounts. In March 1972, the CIA noted 'recurrent reports that some or all Soviet personnel will be expelled from

Egypt'. Such rumours had been circulating in the Middle East press but 'no concrete evidence' of any such expulsion had 'yet surfaced'. Instead these rumours were seen to be the 'predictable product of the long-standing and massive Soviet presence in Egypt'.[28] Assessments before, during and after the expulsion reveal that analysts had a good sense of the frictions resulting from Soviet presence and thereby motivating Sadat to take this decision.

Analysts looked beyond the polarity of the Cold War to the contradictory nature of Soviet–Egyptian relations. It is remarkable, for example, that, despite the fact that of all Soviet aid between 1951 and 1961 just under half went to Egypt, intermarriage between the two cultures was unknown.[29] Even at the height of Soviet presence in 1970, the JIC recognised that, 'as a creed communism has never had much appeal to the Egyptian masses . . . ideological fervour in the country is confined to Arab nationalism, and does not support international communism'.[30] In the build-up to July 1972, the Anglo-American intelligence community identified four compounding factors contributing to the expulsion: a powerful sense of Egyptian nationalism; the cultural differences between the Russian advisors and the Egyptian military; the recent inter-Arab links Sadat had forged; and above all, the untenable state of 'no peace no war' prevailing in Egypt. Their observations not only demonstrate the sensitivity of analysts to important domestic and cultural factors determining Egypt's policy, but also anticipate the later conclusions reached by scholars writing with the benefit of hindsight.[31]

The CIA had always looked upon nationalism as a powerful force militating against Soviet domination of Egypt. It was natural that 'after centuries of foreign domination' individual Egyptians would be 'quick to resent foreign intruders of any sort'. Egyptian nationalism only exacerbated 'the natural difficulties inherent in any adviser-client relationship' and resulted in 'discord'.[32] The year 1972 saw a particularly fierce expression of such nationalism kicking off, with student demonstrations reiterating popular resentment at the 'Soviet occupation'. British diplomats quoted leaflets from 'The Egyptian National Front' calling for Egypt's leaders to 'dismiss the Soviet Imperialism from our lands and keep away the Soviet octopus lying on our breast'.[33]

Interpersonal relations between the Soviet advisors and Egyptian clients were less than satisfactory. British diplomats observed that the Russians were 'contemptuous and rude'.[34] The physical presence of more than 15,000 advisors naturally made more acute the cultural differences between 'the stolid and businesslike Soviet attitude', which tended to 'offend the more open Egyptians, who characterise their Soviet counterparts as "bull-necked, arrogant bullies"'.[35] One American diplomat recalls that the Soviet advisors all lived in a high-walled compound in Alexandria: 'They rarely emerged, except en masse, whether they were going to work, to shop, to the beach or wherever. You never came across a Russian by himself in the souks, the traditional market areas, nor at the museum, the antiquities sites, anywhere, but you could run into fifty of them.'[36]

Nor did the Egyptians think particularly highly of the Soviet Union. The superpower was educating thousands of Egyptian students but Egyptian universities would not accept Soviet PhDs as qualifying the holders for teaching assignments. An Egyptian neural surgeon and Harvard Fellow who had visited the Soviet Union bluntly informed his American contact: 'you Americans are just plain stupid . . . you're trying to turn us against the communists by sending us off to the United States, which is OK, but if you really wanted to influence us, you should ship as many as you can off to Russia'. The Egyptian 'was astounded to find that in comparison with the Soviet Union, Egypt, poor backward Egypt, is miles ahead. Their hotels aren't any good. The restaurants are awful. You can't buy anything. The people are all badly clothed, downtrodden and unhappy. It's a terrible place. You should show as many of us as you can how bad it is.'[37]

To add insult to injury, the Russians plainly looked down upon their Egyptian clients. This was particularly evident after the humiliating defeat of 1967 in which they believed that valuable Soviet weaponry had been wasted by the ill-disciplined and disorganised Egyptian military.[38] This sense of superiority was naturally badly received by the Egyptians, who resented the Soviet manner as reminiscent of a foreign occupying power. As Sadat poignantly recalled, 'the Soviet ambassador had assumed a position comparable with the British High Commissioner in the days of British occupation'.[39] The impact of these individual interactions in a political culture where personal relations were of such importance were aptly recognised to be a central factor in prompting the Soviet dismissal.

Analysts also observed that Arab nationalism had mutated somewhat in the era following the Six-Day War. Defeat bred a resignation in Egypt that its leadership of the Arab world (and the inter-Arab rivalry that accompanied it) had to take a back seat to Egypt's practical needs. Nasser had improved ties with Saudi Arabia and other oil-producing states in order to buy arms. Out of religious reasons or pro-Western inclinations, the nations on which Egypt was becoming increasingly dependent made no secret of their anti-Soviet stance. As Beaumont reflected,

> the paymasters from Saudi, Libya and Kuwait . . . have been able to call the tune in Egyptian policies to an extent they would not have dared and therefore would not have attempted, in Nasser's day. For example they certainly had a hand in Sadat's decision to ask for the removal of the Soviet military advisors.[40]

These inter-Arab realignments not only added to pressures already mounting from nationalist feeling and individual Egyptian/Soviet military and social relations, but also meant that some of the financial, military and moral support provided by the Soviet Union to Egypt could be substituted by these wealthy Arab states in a redefined sense of Arab solidarity.

Nowhere was the prevailing nationalist sentiment more pronounced than in the mounting frustration over the 'no peace, no war' Arab–Israeli impasse. In March 1972, the CIA noted that 'reports of Egyptian grumblings over slowdowns in the flow of spare parts and new equipment are frequent'. Such delays were increasingly viewed by President Sadat and the Egyptians at large to be an attempt by the Kremlin to maintain the political stalemate, perpetuating Arab weaknesses and therefore forcing continued dependence on the Soviets.[41] In April 1972, a petition was put forth to Sadat, demanding that Egypt

> devise a policy of national liberation on the basis that only Egypt's own forces, spiritual and material, are the pillars of that policy. Our honour has been sullied, our dignity wounded and our land occupied,

and honour, dignity and land will only be recovered by ourselves. Calculations about the battle of national liberation must be revised in the light of Egyptian potential alone.[42]

British diplomats accurately assessed that the trigger to Sadat's expulsion was Soviet refusal to supply Egypt with the offensive weaponry required 'to reopen hostilities or provide a deterrent against Israel'. Instead, Soviet policy was bound by a 'desire to avoid a military confrontation with the U.S.' There was a sympathy within the diplomatic community with the prevailing Egyptian belief, that the Arab–Israeli stalemate 'suits the Russians very well since it gives them a continuing opportunity to maintain their position in the Middle East – an opportunity which settlement would remove by ending Egyptian dependence on Soviet support'.[43] Indeed the Sadat–Brezhnev communiqué of May 1972, just two months before the expulsion, was noted as foreshadowing 'military related actions of some import'.[44] Ousting the Soviet Union would break the stalemate, prompting either a diplomatic or a military solution.

In July 1972, the head of the Near East and North Africa Department in the British Foreign Office, James Craig, reflected on the possible significance of the Soviet expulsion. Craig was an Arabist of the first order. His diplomatic despatches later in life had an eager audience beyond Whitehall, and were apparently read by the Queen.[45] Craig was evidently puzzled by the move and his detailed analysis showcases both the strengths and the weaknesses of strategic assessments on the Soviet expulsion. First he proposed that perhaps Egypt was 'clearing the decks for a renewal of hostilities'. What made this 'hard to believe' was that even with Soviet support, Egyptian military prospects against Israel were dismal. How therefore could they win without it? Craig suggested an alternative: perhaps the expulsion was an attempt to 'declare to the West that if they would support her [Egypt] a little more, she is ready for a rapprochement'. The flaw in this interpretation was the timing. As Kissinger was later to note, surely it would have been more tactical to make the offer in advance and make sure of a response? The final possibility, 'on a middle ground', was that the Russians were unable to restrain Egypt any longer and so would continue to provide arms but avoid the risk of superpower confrontation.

Nonetheless it was perceived as unlikely that the Soviet Union would agree to supply arms without any dividend in political influence or that she would accept the loss of credibility. Having found flaws in all of Sadat's possible strategic considerations, Craig concluded that there was 'so far no plausible explanation!'[46]

The strength of this British analysis lay in an ability to 'imagine' and understand the strategic dimensions behind Sadat's decision-making, i.e., Craig evidently formulated the individual pieces of what would later be recognised as a strategic puzzle. What analysts had failed to do was envision these pieces *together*, as complementary rather than mutually exclusive options. The 'either-or' approach perhaps demonstrated a rigid Western-centric appreciation of strategy as an explicitly delineated set of movements taken with a clearly defined goal in mind. The 'strategy' in Sadat's mind, however, was that the odds were on getting rid of the Soviet Union. He hoped that a favourable Western response might in turn facilitate a political settlement of the Arab–Israeli conflict, but in the event that this was not forthcoming, Sadat estimated that the Soviet Union would probably seek to salvage relations by continuing its arms supply. Indeed in February 1973, War Minister Marshall Ismail concluded the most substantial arms deal with the Soviet Union.[47] The restrictions that the Soviet presence (by this stage, fully committed to détente) could impose on Egypt's ability to plan a military initiative would be effectively removed.

Yet analysts seemed unwilling to attribute such a multifaceted dimension to Sadat's thinking. The British saw him as taking a rash and ill-planned gamble with his superpower patron, and in the process undermining both Egypt's political and military leverage. Diplomats concluded that the 'expulsion of the Russian advisors was not part of a strategic plan so much as an isolated act from which Sadat subsequently tried, vainly, to extract advantage'.[48] Instead of acknowledging the possibility that the expulsion might be part of a strategic vision, they believed it was 'much more probable that Sadat has allowed himself to be carried along by the force of events without thinking ahead very far or deeply about the consequences of what he has done'.[49]

The move seemed only to reinforce the image of a desperate man with no plan. The State Department agreed that 'Sadat's internal position seemed weaker . . . The military option was not open to Sadat now.' There were, however, some qualifications to this familiar picture: 'While Sadat might not have the steadiness and ruthlessness to succeed . . . it would be premature to count him out.' In what would clearly reveal itself to be a substantial understatement, analysts wrote: 'He had shown some skill for manoeuvre and he was willing to take chances.'[50]

Ultimately, however, it was judged that Russian presence had robbed 'the Egyptians of the ultimate right to decide whether to fight or seek peace'.[51] The CIA criticised the Russians for underestimating Arab nationalism and lacking 'sensitivity to the cultural peculiarities of Third World societies greatly different from their own'. They predicted that the Soviets would 'probably continue to deliver new military equipment already contracted for by the Egyptians' but estimated that 'to bestow lavish military or economic assistance . . . would be to reward them for their abuse and perhaps to encourage others to behave similarly'.[52]

Some months after the expulsion, Sadat sent a mission to the Soviet Union to 'exchange views on the coming stage'.[53] British diplomats noted that the leader had made no 'attempt to prepare public opinion for this sudden switch' after bitter exchanges some months earlier. Perhaps, they speculated, Sadat had realised 'Egypt's military nakedness', which of course, followed to its logical conclusion, would suggest that Sadat was even at this point thinking seriously about war.[54] Yet the British dismissed this as a serious option, believing that Sadat's manoeuvres with the Russians demonstrated yet another contradictory policy that was breeding resentment and disillusion, once more predicting that his leadership could be at stake.[55]

Washington proposed a considerably more favourable interpretation of Sadat's manoeuvrings. The State Department described British reporting as 'somewhat pessimistic'. They conceded that Sadat was no 'masterful leader' and that it was 'apparent to everyone that he has yet to come up with a consistent strategy to cope with Egypt's predicament. We would also agree that his position has declined in certain months. But we are not sure this decline is irreversible.'[56]

Ultimately, the State Department felt that it was his domestic authority that truly mattered. Sadat's policy towards the Soviets was impulsive but American analysts disagreed with how this was interpreted by Egyptian public opinion.

> We are not convinced, for example, that his policy towards the Soviets, although certainly impulsive, is seen by the average Egyptian as quite the bumbling flip-flop that this report suggests. It will occur to many Egyptians who think about it that Egypt today is getting about the same arms from the U.S.S.R. that it was previously when there were 15,000 Soviets present in Egypt, and Egypt had the reputation of being a Soviet base. We think Sadat's decision, in spite of the realisation that it means a loss of military capability in the short term, has fundamental popularity at the gut level that is likely to last for some time.[57]

Egyptian accounts validate the American assessment: 'Everyone wanted to get rid of the Russians', erstwhile junior diplomat Mohammed Shakir recalled.[58]

If the State Department was abler to appreciate the strategic vision that might lie behind Sadat's motives, British analysis was better disposed to recognise the need to respond to this development. Kissinger recalls that after the expulsion of the Soviets, a message was received from high-level Egyptian echelons that the government sought assurance that it would be met with 'open hearts'. In his memoirs Kissinger recalls woefully: 'I knew too little about Egyptian psychology then to respond with comparable humanity; somewhat less poetically, I stated that we were prepared to enter the talks "with an open mind to determine what useful role [we] can play in promoting a just settlement".'[59] On the British side, several covert messages from prominent persons, including the Minister of Information, Ashraf Marwan, were sent prompting the UK government to recognise the pro-Western nature of Sadat's initiative. Ambassador Beaumont sent a clear message to Whitehall accordingly:

> I am convinced that we should not let this opportunity pass unnoticed and that some positive step of encouragement is required to let the Egyptian government know that we realise that there has been a significant shift in their policy in an area which is of vital interest to us.[60]

Whilst the Nixon administration was immersed in Watergate and most likely considered events in Egypt a relatively low priority, British policy-makers were acutely aware of their increasing financial stake in the region. The need to acknowledge the Soviet expulsion was consequently more pronounced in British analysis, yet ironically it was not British acknowledgement that Egypt most wanted.

*　*　*

One scholar suggests that Kissinger's failure to understand Sadat's expulsion of the Soviets 'could be chalked up to cultural differences'. Beattie writes,

> in Egypt where the rules of the bazaar make bargaining commonplace, it is often considered distasteful and caddy to haggle over some matters. Good deeds or noble acts are performed unilaterally, but it is expected in such circumstances that the beneficiary will respond by rendering a service of commensurate magnitude.[61]

It is revealing that while not explicitly making reference to this as a 'cultural issue', British analysts clearly felt that a more substantial Western response was required. Once again Ambassador Beaumont proved remarkably astute at discerning and communicating the significance of the move and sent a clear message accordingly to policy-makers.

The Anglo-American diplomatic and intelligence communities had a remarkably good sense of the immediate tactical reasons for the expulsion. However, they simply did not take seriously the notion that Sadat might have taken this decision with a strategic plan to wage war on Israel in mind. This is a central question surrounding the July decision that as yet remains definitively unanswered. Sadat maintains in his memoirs that he expelled the Soviets with such a plan, others say the contrary and ultimately the 'truth' will only be revealed when the Egyptian archives are opened to the public. The historical reality is perhaps of less import than deconstructing why analysts demonstrated such a reluctance to regard Sadat as operating within a strategic framework.

This chapter has suggested that cultural differences did play a part, though not quite in the way Beattie suggests above. Analysts seem to have approached Sadat's moves with a Western-centric concept of strategy as a clearly defined, linear rationale with a specific end goal. When Sadat's actions in July failed to fit into the various strategic scenarios posed by analysts, they dismissed the move as an ill-conceived and impulsive decision.

Such a conclusion also supported their first impressions of the new leader. The declassified documents reveal in great detail how Sadat was perceived by Anglo-American analysts in these forgotten years. In general, it seems as if Sadat grew on American analysts faster than their British counterparts but the overall impressions were similar. Both believed he was a temporary figure; both were inclined to see him as an inferior statesman to his predecessor; and both were struck by his 'tactical' approach to domestic and foreign policy. One cannot help but conclude that these unfavourable first impressions of Sadat belied an unspoken, perhaps even unconscious, respect for his predecessor – as the final chapter reveals this would remain an element of assessments on Egypt long after Nasser's death. Considering their long-standing enmity with Nasser, it is perhaps ironic that this was a more prominent feature of British diplomatic assessments.

The extent to which British and American policy was influenced by such assessments cannot be known without access to a more complete record and the relevant policy papers. Nonetheless the prevailing beliefs about the new leader in the documents available may go some way to explaining why Anglo-American governments neglected to respond sufficiently to this repulsion of the Soviet presence and arguably failed to avert the most dramatic Arab–Israeli War that was soon to follow.

Notes

1. Interview with Roy Atherton, summer 1990. Available at <http://adst.org/wp-content/uploads/2012/09/Egypt.pdf>, p. 321 (last accessed 1 March 2017).
2. W. Quandt, *Decade of Decisions: American Policy Towards the Arab-Israeli conflict, 1967–1976* (Berkeley, CA: University of California Press, 1977), p. 123.
3. M. Riad, *The Struggle for Peace in the Middle East* (London: Quartet, 1981), p. 169.
4. Few scholarly works have explored first impressions of Sadat in these forgotten years. Admirers of the leader such as Kissinger note with regret that Sadat was so underestimated, moving the discussion rather quickly to his later achievements. See H. Kissinger, *The White*

House Years (Boston, MA: Little, Brown and Co., 1979), p. 1294. More frank accounts write that Sadat was seen at home and abroad as a 'stopgap leader', nicknamed 'Colonel Yes Yes' and mocked for his Sudanese ancestry (and thus dark skin). See D. Reynolds, *One World Divisible: A Global History since 1945* (London: Allen Lane, Penguin, 2000), p. 370. This chapter explores in greater depth the prevailing impressions of this new leader in Britain and America and from what these impressions derived, building upon earlier research. See D. Rezk, *British and American Political and Intelligence Assessments of the Nasser-Sadat Transition*, unpublished MPhil thesis, Cambridge University, Cambridge, 2006.

5. F. Halliday, 'The Middle East, the Great Powers and the Cold War', in Y. Sayigh and A. Shlaim (eds), *The Cold War and the Middle East* (Oxford: Clarendon Press, 1997), p. 15.
6. DDCI Briefing for PFIAB 9 October 1970, 'The Middle East', 7 October 1970, CREST, NARA II.
7. President Sadat's address to the ASU National Congress, 12 November 1970. Available at <https://sadat.umd.edu/sites/sadat.umd.edu/files/Address%20to%20the%20Fifth%20Ordinary%20Session%20of%20the%20ASU%20National%20Congress.pdf>
8. Telegram from Bergus to Secretary of State, 'Egypt after Nasser: the end of the beginning', 14 November 1970, File UAR vol. V. 1 August 1970–31 December 1970, Country Files- Middle East, Box 636, National Security Council (NSC) Files, Nixon Presidential Materials Staff, NARA II.
9. CIA memorandum, 'Nasir's death: the immediate aftermath', 29 September 1970, DDRS.
10. Telegram from Ambassador Beaumont in Cairo to FCO, 29 September 1970, TNA, FCO 39/737.
11. JIC memorandum (69) 43, 'Outlook for the UAR: 1970-71', 13 February 1970, TNA, CAB 186/3. P. Cradock, *Know Your Enemy: How the Joint Intelligence Committee Saw the World* (London: John Murray, 2002), p. 111. The JIC report reveals the extent to which the narrative of Nasser the troublemaker endured to months before his death: 'A recent apparently reliable report suggests that the UAR Presidency Office is planning to establish branches of the Arab Socialist Union in all Arab states, while another report suggests that the Egyptian Intelligence Service may treat the Persian Gulf as a priority target for penetration.'
12. Diplomatic report no. 108/71 from Ambassador Beaumont to FCO, 'United Arab Republic: Annual Review for 1970', 25 January 1971, TNA, FCO 39/961.

13. Heikal, interview with the author, Cairo, 1 March 2006.
14. Interview with Michael Sterner, 2 March 1990. Available at <http://www.adst.org/OH%20TOCs/Sterner,%20Michael%20E.toc.pdf>, p. 22 (last accessed 1 March 2017).
15. CIA memorandum, 'Nasir's death: the immediate aftermath', 29 September 1970, DDRS.
16. Despatch from Ambassador Beaumont in Cairo to FCO, 'Arab Republic of Egypt: annual review for 1971', 7 January 1972, TNA, FCO 39/1200.
17. Diplomatic report no. 161/73 from Ambassador Beaumont in Cairo to Secretary of State for Foreign and Commonwealth affairs/FCO, 'Sir Richard Beaumont's valedictory despatch', 18 January 1973, TNA, FCO 93/74.
18. Telegram no. 139 from Ambassador Beaumont in Cairo to FCO, 'Student disturbances', 17 January 1972, TNA, FCO 39/1203.
19. Despatch from Ambassador Beaumont in Cairo to the FCO, 'Egypt in the doldrums', 28 November 1972, TNA, FCO 39/1207.
20. Memorandum of State Department's comments on Ambassador Beaumont's despatch 'Egypt in the doldrums' from Moberly in British Embassy in Cairo to FCO, 28 December 1972, TNA, FCO 39/1207.
21. CIA memorandum, 'Nasir's death: the immediate aftermath', 29 September 1970, DDRS.
22. Telegram from Cairo to FCO, 'UAR internal', 17 May 1971, TNA, DEFE 11/883. Ambassador Beaumont was unconvinced by the 'plot' and suggested that Sadat's opponents merely sought to rein in his power: 'they mistook the calibre and determination of the president . . . it has always been in the logic of Egyptian politics that a strong man should emerge at the top and Sadat has shown by his effective handling of the crisis that he is determined to remain that man'.
23. Telegram from Ambassador Beaumont to FCO, 'Soviet/UAR treaty of friendship and co-operation', 1 June 1971, TNA, DEFE 11/883.
24. C. Andrew and V. Mitrokhin, *The KGB and the World: Mitrokhin Archive II* (London: Penguin, 2006), p. 156.
25. Heikal in R. B. Parker (ed.), *The October War: A Retrospective* (Gainesville, FL: University Press of Florida, 2001), p. 56.
26. S. Ayubi, *Nasser and Sadat: Decision Making and Foreign Policy, 1970–1972* (Washington DC: University Press of America, 1994), p. 16. Ayubi provides an authoritative account of the motivations leading up to these decisions based on published material and interviews with key figures such as President Sadat and Heikal.

27. M. I. Handel, *The Diplomacy of Surprise: Hitler, Nixon, Sadat* (Cambridge, MA: Centre for International Affairs, Harvard University, 1981), pp. 275–6.

28. Intelligence memorandum, 'Soviet Egyptian relations: an uneasy alliance', 28 March 1972, FOIA Reading Room.

29. Andrew and Mitrokhin, *Mitrokhin Archive II*, pp. 151–3.

30. JIC memorandum (70) 25, 'Soviet prospects for North Africa and the implications for NATO, 1970-1975', 19 March 1970, TNA, CAB 186/6.

31. Ayubi, *Nasser and Sadat*, pp. 131–97.

32. Intelligence memorandum, 'Soviet Egyptian relations: an uneasy alliance', 28 March 1972, FOIA Reading Room.

33. Memorandum from Goulding in Cairo to Holding in North Africa Department, 'The Egyptian National Front', 27 October 1971, TNA, FCO 39/969.

34. Memorandum from Craig in Near East and North Africa Department to FCO, 'Egypt and the Soviet Union', 18 July 1972, TNA, FCO 39/1264.

35. Intelligence memorandum, 'Soviet Egyptian relations: an uneasy alliance', 28 March 1972, FOIA Reading Room.

36. Interview with Richard Undeland, 29 July 1994. Available at <http://adst.org/wp-content/uploads/2012/09/Egypt.pdf>, pp. 235–6 (last accessed 1 March 2017).

37. Ibid.

38. Ambassador Shakir, interview with the author, Cairo, 3 March 2006.

39. Ayubi, *Nasser and Sadat*, p. 183.

40. Despatch from British Ambassador Beaumont in Cairo to Foreign Secretary, 'Egypt in the doldrums', 28 November 1972, TNA, FCO 39/1207.

41. Ayubi, *Nasser and Sadat*, p. 185.

42. Text of a petition, 'Baghdadi memorandum', presented to President Sadat on 4 April 1972, from British Embassy in Cairo to FCO, TNA, FCO 39/1207.

43. Report from Craig in the Near East and North Africa Department to FCO, 'Egypt and the Soviet Union', 18 July 1972, TNA, FCO 39/1264.

44. Research study by the Bureau of Intelligence and Research, 'The Soviet Egyptian communiqué: militant summitry and the long pull', 11 May 1972, File Pol 7 Egypt, 1-1-72, Subject Numeric Files, 1970-1973, Political and Defense, Box 2249, General Records of the State Department, Record Group 59, NARA II.

45. Andrew Bryson, 'John Major's gifthorse ... and other Foreign Office tales', 21 September 2012, BBC News. Available at <http://www.bbc.co.uk/news/uk-politics-19653492> (last accessed 1 March 2017).
46. Report from Craig in Near East and North Africa Department to FCO, 'Egypt and the Soviet Union', 18 July 1972, TNA, FCO 39/1264.
47. Handel, *Diplomacy of Surprise*, p. 277. Handel argues that in fact the expulsion was an attempt to strengthen rather than weaken Soviet–Egyptian relations.
48. Despatch from Ambassador Adams in Cairo to FCO, 'Sadat's long haul', 7 September 1973, TNA, FCO 93/236.
49. Ibid.
50. Memorandum of conversation, 'Current Egyptian developments', 14 August 1972, File Pol 2- Egypt, Subject Numeric Files, 1970-1973, Political and Defense, Box 2249, General Records of the State Department, Record Group 59, NARA II.
51. Intelligence memorandum, 'The expulsion from Egypt: some consequences for the Soviets', 29 August 1972, FOIA Reading Room.
52. Ibid.
53. Despatch from British Ambassador Beaumont in Cairo to Foreign Secretary, 'Egypt in the doldrums', 28 November 1972, TNA, FCO 39/1207.
54. Ibid.
55. Ibid.
56. Ibid.
57. Memorandum of State Department's comments on Beaumont's despatch, 'Egypt in the doldrums', from Moberly in British Embassy in Cairo to FCO, 28 December 1972, TNA, FCO 39/1207.
58. Ambassador Shakir, interview with the author, Cairo, 3 March 2006.
59. Kissinger, *The White House Years*, p. 1299.
60. Telegram no. 1118 by Ambassador Beaumont in Cairo to FCO, 'Call on Egyptian Foreign Minister', 31 July 1972, TNA, FCO 39/1265.
61. K. J. Beattie, *Egypt During the Sadat Years* (New York: Palgrave, 2000), p. 128.

9   Yom Kippur War

On that Yom Kippur one, we just had convinced ourselves that it didn't make sense. And it didn't!

William Colby, 1991[1]

I think we were surprised to some degree by the Egyptian's attack, but not totally.

Hal Saunders, 1993[2]

On 6 October 1973, Egypt and Syria coordinated a lightening surprise attack against Israel. Though short-lived, it was a war that would change the face of the modern Middle East. Launched at 2 p.m. on the holiest day of the Jewish calendar, the Sabbath of Yom Kippur, the momentum of the attack carried Egyptian armoured units several miles east of the Suez Canal. Within just three days the Egyptian military were blocked by Israeli retaliation, yet the initial achievements of the Egyptians marked a symbolic turning point in world history. In retrospect the war marked the first step towards a bilateral peace treaty between Egypt and Israel that would dramatically alter Egypt's seminal role in the international politics of the Middle East. Moreover, it was a conflict with strikingly international implications, bringing the world's superpowers to the brink of a nuclear confrontation in support of their respective allies and provoking the first global oil crisis in numerous European capitals. Arab states united in an unprecedented manner to impose an oil embargo that would visibly punish the United States for backing Israel.

Most scholars have explored the intelligence failure of the Yom Kippur War from the Israeli perspective, with the assumption that the CIA was complicit in this failure because of the close relations that characterised the American and Israeli intelligence communities.[3] Surprisingly few works have sought to explain how and why Britain and America were unable to foresee that Egypt was planning an attack on 6 October 1973.[4] A leading intelligence historian concludes that the attack on Israel was 'not foreseen by any of the world's major intelligence services'.[5] A recently declassified post-mortem by the CIA found that intelligence of an impending attack was 'plentiful, ominous and often accurate', if only they had put the pieces together.[6]

The charismatic figure of Henry Kissinger has dominated our understanding of this Western intelligence failure. In his memoirs Kissinger highlighted the role of 'culture' in this crisis, famously claiming that 'our definition of rationality did not take seriously the notion of starting an un-winnable war to restore self-respect'.[7] First hand accounts from the Egyptian side corroborate this narrative of a 'cultural divide': 'in the Egyptian view, none of the principal policy-makers . . . managed to read the true Arab picture – that the Arabs would not be dictated to on terms for the future . . . they would have to deploy every means including resort to arms to get back their lands and their rights.'[8] Only now, with access to Anglo-American diplomatic and intelligence documents, are we able to verify what aspects of the 'true Arab picture' analysts were in fact able to read, and which proved more elusive.

The relationship between intentions and capabilities has long been recognised as the ultimate determinant of strategic surprise. In a much cited article on intelligence failure, Avi Shlaim put forth the following equation to explain strategic misconceptions: 'Threat perception may be said to equal estimated capacity multiplied by the estimated intent.' Shlaim has suggested that analysts had a good understanding of Egypt's capabilities, but failed to anticipate war because they fundamentally misread Sadat's intentions.[9] It is a typically 'Western' intelligence failure, where technology has served better in 'observing actions than divining intent', that is, accessing the 'secrets' rather than the 'mysteries' of conflict.[10]

It is possible to turn Shlaim's equation on its head somewhat. In fact, the CIA and the JIC showed an impressive strategic understanding of Sadat's intentions. Rather it was their underestimation of Egypt's *capability* which resulted in a failure to take these intentions seriously, that is, to return to Shlaim's equation, when estimated intent was multiplied by estimated capability; it was the latter rather than the former which was misunderstood, which consequently resulted in a reduced threat perception. Cultural preconceptions played a role in this equation, but not quite in the way that Kissinger suggests.

Both sides of the Atlantic proved remarkably far-sighted in penetrating Sadat's mindset. They accurately identified that a limited military victory would suffice to achieve Sadat's political goal of regaining Egypt's honour and reclaiming her land, they repeatedly warned that in the absence of successful diplomacy Sadat would have no option but to embark on war, and they empathised with the domestic and military pressures on him to take action. Their experience in the War of Attrition and the importance of 'honour' were crucial to these assessments of Sadat's intentions. The real weakness therefore lay not in their assessments of the 'mysteries' but more unusually in their analysis of the 'secret' – Egypt's improved capability.

There was a near unanimous agreement within the Anglo-American intelligence community about Egypt's military bankruptcy.[11] Moreover, Orientalist thinking clearly informed assessments on this subject.[12] Official wisdom relied on a library of cultural preconceptions about the Arab world (reinforced by the Six-Day War and early assessments of Sadat's leadership) that pervaded analysis. In addition, the dramatic expulsion of Soviet advisors in 1972 appeared to confirm to analysts that without their superpower patron, the Egyptians had no real military option. This case study puts into serious question how well the discourse of 'failure' serves our understanding of intelligence analyses in this period. As we shall see, the 'intelligence failure' of 1973 requires some qualification.

* * *

Mystery No. I: Limited Military Action

Two years before the 1973 war, the British intelligence community made a strikingly accurate assessment of the key motivating factors that would determine the next Arab–Israeli conflict. The JIC asserted:

Sadat might calculate that the strengthening of Egypt's system of air defence with Russian backing would enable him at any rate to reopen limited military action . . . without making it certain Egypt would suffer unacceptable casualties and damage through Israeli retaliation. Politically he might be influenced by the hope that such action would relieve him of criticism, internally and elsewhere in the Arab world. He might also hope that it might galvanise the United States into taking action to restore the ceasefire or into bringing greater pressure to bear on Israel in relation to the achievement either of an interim arrangement or a comprehensive settlement.[13]

The British intelligence community correctly identified three fundamental motivational factors that would determine Sadat's decision-making: the sufficiency of 'limited military action' (rather than absolute military victory) to redeem Egypt's honour; the political need to respond to domestic pressure; and the realisation that in the absence of effective international diplomacy, only war could 'galvanise the United States' to break the political stalemate.

Identifying the sufficiency of 'limited military action' was an impressive feat. It is the central precept of Western military logic and Augustinian political theory of war that a high likelihood of success is the primary consideration of a responsible leader in leading a nation to the battlefield. Scholars claim that 'one of the most fundamental assumptions by all analysts assessing the prospect of war in 1973, supported by accepted theories of war, was that Syria and Egypt did not have the ability to win and therefore were unlikely to attack'.[14] In a classic example of self-Orientalising, Heikal argues that this pragmatic reading of Egypt's decision-making neglected the 'obstinacy of the Egyptian and Arab character'.[15]

Yet analysts had a number of precedents indicating that military superiority was no precondition to waging war. During the War of Attrition, the JIC warned policy-makers that 'despite the Arabs' military inferiority it is by no means certain that this factor will remain sufficient to deter the Arab states from contemplating an attack against Israel, which could either precipitate an Israeli pre-emptive strike or lead to an Arab attempt to strike first'.[16]

Rather than 'mirror-imaging' their rationale onto their Arab subjects, the Committee recognised that within this cultural milieu absolute military superiority was not going to be decisive. Instead they assessed the likelihood of conflict in the regional context and according to Arab priorities. In particular, analysts recognised the relationship between domestic legitimacy and foreign policy and correctly concluded that the primary rationale driving the Arab leaders to war would be retrieving the sense of 'honour' lost in the 1967 defeat.

In the spring of 1973, Sadat gave a dramatic interview to Arnaud De Borchgrave of *Newsweek*. Analysts observed that its 'general tone' was that 'the time has come for a shock. Diplomacy will continue before, during and after war'.[17] Such a grandiose statement could easily have been dismissed as meaningless. Yet diplomats demonstrated detailed and impressive analyses of Sadat's answers, deducing vital conclusions about the relationship between notions of national honour and the corollary prospects for peace and war. The FCO's attention was particularly drawn to

> the rather odd implication of his [Sadat's] answers to the twelfth and thirteenth questions – that although direct negotiations are out of the question at a time when effective peace reigns that will not be true when battle is resumed. For some inscrutable reason this passage was *only* carried by <u>al Ahram</u>. What I think the president means is that direct negotiations with the enemy while the latter is occupying Egypt's territory and Egypt is not even trying to recover it would be tantamount to the unconditional surrender demanded of Hitler by the Allies. If so it could be that Egyptian honour would be satisfied by a very small and controlled bout of hostilities across the Canal leading almost at once to 'direct' peace feelers.[18]

The reference to occupation and its implications is particularly important. A recent analysis of Arab perspectives of the October War notes that recognition that 'in spirit the Arab offensive was a response to Israeli occupation, has been largely ignored in the dominant October War historiography'.[19] In contrast, this sensitive and detailed analysis underlines the extent to which British diplomats were evidently in tune with this key psychological dimension of Sadat's decision-making, precisely anticipating the diplomatic strategising that would follow an attack. Rather than dismissing such open sources as mere propaganda, rhetoric or 'irrationality', Sadat's answers were examined and cross-examined with cultural awareness and empathy, to infer fundamental insights into the political pressures Sadat perceived himself to face and the means by which the prevailing desire for 'honour' might be satisfied.

The interview also caught the attention of Harold Saunders, a South-Asia expert from the NSC who was to become a key architect of the Camp David Accords. Saunders concluded from it that Sadat 'may seriously be considering initiating a limited military engagement along the Suez Canal'. He judged that Sadat 'seems to realise that Egypt will not achieve its goal of recovering Sinai by military means, but that an end to the ceasefire might stimulate powers to press hard for a settlement'.[20]

In May 1973, the Bureau of Intelligence and Research at the State Department reiterated their fears of war more strongly. They noted that although Sadat 'has no illusions that Egypt can defeat Israel militarily, he seems on the verge of concluding that only limited hostilities against Israel stand any real chance of breaking the negotiating stalemate by forcing the big powers to intervene with an imposed solution'. They clearly warned that if Sadat was to 'shed his last doubts about whether military action is essential to achieve this American shift, the only remaining decision would relate to the timing and scope of his move'.[21] Sympathy for Sadat's position within the State Department was something of an open secret. A 1971 edition of the Israeli newspaper *Ha'aretz* depicted the State Department Arabists in Lawrence of Arabia costumes. Michael Sterner humorously recalled: 'This is how the Israelis ridiculed us.'[22]

That a limited military initiative would suffice to achieve Sadat's goal of provoking a political solution was thus amply recognised. Analysts had a number of precedents and public declarations indicating that in the Arab cultural context, absolute military superiority was no precondition to initiating an attack. Ultimately, the decision to go to war would depend on what international diplomacy could (and could not) achieve.

Figure 9.1 President Sadat with Egyptian War Minister General Ismail on the frontlines in Sinai, June 1973. Private collection.

Mystery No. 2: International Diplomacy

The quality and timeliness of international diplomacy was therefore recognised to be a fundamental factor in Sadat's calculations. Analysts identified that Sadat regarded military moves as a complement to diplomacy and accurately assessed that he would only embark on war when diplomacy appeared to have failed. Erstwhile Egyptian Presidential Adviser for National Security Hafez Ismail recounted that 'Sadat wanted the heat of the battle to be the force behind the political decisions which had to be taken'.[23]

The British intelligence community demonstrated considerable foresight about the consequences of diplomatic failure. As early as 1969 the JIC had warned, mincing no words, that: 'in the absence of a negotiated settlement meeting the principal Arab political aims, no Arab leader is strong enough to abjure publicly an ultimate resort to force, as a means of exacting forcibly what Israel is not prepared to yield politically'.[24] Looking back in 1974, the new British Ambassador to Egypt, Phillip Adams, reflected upon Sadat's calculations. Adams was one of the leading Arabists in the Diplomatic Service, known for his calm, collected manner, and apparently enjoyed the dubious privilege of being received by President Sadat in his pyjamas during the 1973 war. Adams concluded that although 'military factors determined the date and time of the attack, international political developments over the previous year had reinforced Sadat's commitment to the war option'.[25] US policy on the Middle East failed to evolve following President Nixon's re-election. Fresh supplies of Phantoms for Israel commenced even after Ismail visited Washington in February 1973. Little attention was paid to the Middle East at the Nixon/Brezhnev summit in June and the US vetoed a UN Security Council Resolution on the Middle East in July calling for Israeli withdrawal from occupied Arab territories.

The Americans took a more relaxed view. In March 1973, the CIA's Middle East analysts claimed that, 'despite the gloomy prognosis being assiduously disseminated from Cairo, Sadat has not exhausted his diplomatic options'.[26] The State Department's INR was inclined to state the case on the risk of hostilities with a political purpose with a little more urgency. If the UN debate of next year produces no convincing movement in the Israeli-Egyptian impasse, our view is that the resumption of hostilities will become a better than even lot.[27]

Though differing in emphasis, there was an understanding on both sides of the Atlantic that in the absence of a feasible diplomatic alternative, Sadat would be forced to resort to a dramatic military initiative.

The British particularly stressed the importance of American action in influencing Sadat's motivations. In March 1973, the British defence attaché in Egypt remarked: 'If I were asked what major operation the Egyptian armed forces were capable of conducting against the Israelis with some measure of success I would have to answer none.' He nonetheless entertained the possibility that if by 'political necessity or by pressure on the leadership Egypt was forced to take military action her least damaging solution and one which might place her in a position for international negotiation would be to cross the Canal to a limited depth of about 12 kilometres'. The attaché recognised that the end goal was ultimately political and pointed towards America. He reported that 'from this position she [Egypt] would hope to provoke political intervention by the Big Powers and presumably to negotiate from a fresh set of circumstances'.[28] It was a remarkably astute analysis, clearly identifying the strategic priority of international negotiations in any military assault. The attaché accurately gauged not merely what was likely to happen but the more important issues of why and how, combining military strategising with cultural sensitivity in penetrating the workings of Sadat's mind.

This heightened acuity on the British side both to Egypt's plight, and the potential implications of international diplomacy engaged policy-makers at the highest level. On 15 June 1973 British Prime Minister Edward Heath made a personal appeal to President Nixon before impending American–Soviet talks:

> I do not think it is overstating it to say that, unless Israel can be persuaded to show a greater willingness to withdraw from the territories she occupied in 1967, vital Western interests will soon be at risk. In

the circumstances I very much hope, Mr President, that you will give
the most serious consideration to using the unique influence of the
United States with the Israelis to persuade them that they must change
their line – in their ultimate interest as well as ours.[29]

It seems clear therefore that analysts communicated the primacy of
diplomatic negotiations as a key factor in Sadat's strategic considerations. They recognised that whilst Sadat hoped that the threat
of war could act as sufficient leverage in such negotiations, he was
increasingly subject to domestic and military pressures to take
military action.

Mystery No. 3: Domestic Pressures

Sadat's fragile domestic position was the final pressure point. It
was no secret that Sadat struggled to assert his authority as a
statesmanlike successor to Nasser.[30] The CIA initially assessed that
he was weak, chosen to succeed Nasser because he could be easily manipulated and was unlikely to last long.[31] Within a year of
his presidency, Sadat was forced to contend with an internal coup
within his government, led by Nasserist Ali Sabri. The plot was
successfully foiled but Sadat seemed far from secure.

More worryingly, Sadat's much-lauded 'year of decision' had
resulted in naught. On 12 October 1972, an army officer led troops
into a mosque in central Cairo and called publicly for war with
Israel. This open challenge to Sadat reflected deeper unrest within
the military, relayed in a number of Egyptian accounts.[32] By late
1972, analysts reported that 'more and more Egyptians are speculating openly about how long Sadat can last and who will take over
from him'.[33] As British Ambassador Phillip Adams reflected:

> The continued loyalty of the armed forces remains crucial for Presi-
> dent Sadat's survival and, if he can see no other way of warding off
> a coup by younger officers against him he could well decide to hot
> things up by ordering some limited military action even though he
> knows that the Egyptians would suffer heavily: better for him a dev-
> astating Israeli reprisal than the loss of his position. A cynical view of
> President Sadat's motives perhaps, but I fear a realistic one.[34]

This 'cynical view' has since been validated by several Egyptian elites affiliated with Nasser who claim that Sadat's focal motivation in going to war was indeed to retain his flailing position.[35]

Military dissatisfaction with Sadat's leadership mirrored broader societal concerns. The period preceding the war saw an unprecedented degree of public protests. Student demonstrations, sectarian unrest with the Christian Coptic community and innumerable lamentations by the political elite culminated in a petition presented to Sadat in 1972. Diplomats reported the contents of the petition back to Whitehall recounting 'the calamities which surround Egypt' that 'threaten not only the land but her civilisation and inheritance, her ideology and values . . . her enemies seek her complete destruction'.[36] This all-encompassing, prevailing sense of desperation within the Egyptian body politic led Ambassador Beaumont to describe 'a general feeling of growing impotence and of disintegration of President Sadat's regime'. Evoking an interesting if Eurocentric historical analogy, Beaumont noted that a French colleague compared it 'to the atmosphere which reigned in Paris at the demise of the fourth republic'.[37]

Though less concerned, American analysts also reported Egyptian assertions that the no war, no peace situation was 'more dangerous for the future of Egypt than war itself'. They judged that such statements were most likely a 'pressure tactic' to evoke a response from the US, but concluded that 'it probably accurately reflects Sadat's feeling that the present situation is both an affront to his personal self-respect and ruinous of national morals, dignity and constructive purpose'.[38] Despite a deteriorating economic situation, American analysts expressed 'doubt' that Sadat was 'under significant domestic pressure to go to war'. They argued that 'Sadat and his advisers are aware that their military prospects are poor at best'. The danger was that 'disaster might well sweep away Sadat's regime than rescue him from his dilemma'.[39]

It was clear that Sadat faced unparalleled pressures to wage war. As a weak successor to Nasser, he was seen as particularly vulnerable to pressures from the military and dramatic public protests. Though analysts felt that a military disaster might portend the end of the regime, they accurately gauged the all-encompassing and detrimental impact of the no war, no peace situation on Sadat's calculations.

The 'Secret': Underestimating Egyptian Capabilities

If the Anglo-American intelligence community was able to gauge Sadat's intentions with a relatively high degree of accuracy, the same cannot be said for their assessments of Egypt's capabilities. As Kissinger put it, 'I have never seen a military estimate by anybody, prior to the war which indicated that the Arabs had any chance whatever of defeating the Israelis or of even staving off their own defeat for anything longer than six days.'[40] It is revealing that no NIEs (National Intelligence Estimates) or SNIEs (Special National Intelligence Estimates) on the prospects of war between Egypt and Israel were requested or undertaken between May and the end of September, no doubt reflecting 'the fairly relaxed view US intelligence had of the developing crisis'.[41] Similarly in March 1973, British military attachés spoke in no uncertain terms of 'the bankruptcy of the Egyptian military capability'.[42] Anglo-American assessments echoed the claim by the director of the General Intelligence Service (GIS), Ahmed Ismail, that, 'Egypt was not ready for war . . . any attack mounted or led by Egypt under present conditions might lead to disaster.'[43] It is notable that during Ismail's year long stint as GIS director he ran a back channel with the CIA before being appointed War Minister in October 1972.[44]

Yet there were some signs indicating an improvement in capability. British air attaché Barnicoat recorded his assessment of a clash between Egyptian and Israeli aircraft in 1972 and noted that:

The fact that these pilots closed with the enemy when out-numbered showed courage and a press on spirit even if it was suicidal. This type of determination in the face of the enemy has not been noticeable in the past. If this is any guide to the morale of other MIG 21 planes it could be an important change.[45]

The JIC also reported some improvements. Whilst acknowledging that the 'relative standards' of training, morale and equipment between Arab and Israeli military forces differed significantly, the Committee nonetheless identified 'steps taken to weed out unreliable elements' in the army and recognised 'the impact of Soviet equipment and training'. However, the JIC definitively concluded that 'Arab officer cadres will not succeed in the period under review in matching the highly dedicated and professional Israeli commanders in morale or ability' and that this would 'remain the over-riding factor to be set against Arab numerical superiority'.[46] The sheer conviction of the statement, with none of the hedging 'mays' or 'mights' for which JIC assessments are typically criticised, demonstrates the extent to which analysts were convinced that Egypt could never achieve anything resembling a military victory against Israel. Why were they so sure?

Two overarching factors influenced and distorted perceptions of Egypt's capabilities: the first was the precedent of 1967 and several cultural conceptions it contributed to forming and reinforcing. The second was the shift in the Soviet–Egyptian relationship, which not only lowered the guard of Anglo-American intelligence services but masked regional dynamics in a deceptively simplistic Cold War framework.

Arab Political Culture and the Precedent of 1967

There was an undeniable 'Orientalism' to analytic assessments of Arab military capability. A former head of the JIC, Sir Patrick Wright, recalled in an interview with the author that the two fundamental misconceptions the West held about the Egyptians was that they were 'bad fighters' and 'irrational'.[47] The CIA suggested that the Arab fighting man 'lacks the necessary physical and cultural qualities for performing effective military services'.[48] Former NSC staffer Robert Morris reflected that 'the worst common flaw in the reading of the intelligence was an abiding cultural, perhaps racial, contempt in Washington and Jerusalem for the political posturing and fighting skills of the Arabs'.[49] Even once the war had started analysts believed that 'Egyptian forces face imminent and perhaps catastrophic defeat and that the ability of the Egyptian state to survive the defeat (and further Israeli military actions) is questionable'.[50] How did such absolutist beliefs take hold as 'common sense' within the psyche of the Anglo-American intelligence community?

Past experience was the first clue. There was a tendency to believe that a future Arab–Israeli war would resemble its 1967 forerunner – confused and unplanned. This also derived partly from a reluctance to see Sadat as a strategic, political leader in his own right. Despite negative comparisons with Nasser, assessments nevertheless tended to mirror assumptions of the 1967 war. Kissinger would later recall, 'not knowing Sadat, I had to conclude that he was still playing Nasser's game'.[51] Anthony Parsons, a distinguished Arabist renowned for his frank opinions and disarming sense of humour, was the assistant undersecretary for the Middle East at the time. Parsons reflected:

> The danger is that, in seeking to restore his [Sadat's] credibility, he will not only convince himself that he must do something but will also create a momentum which he will be unable to check. He also seems to suffer from the dangerous delusion that, if he reopened hostilities on the Canal, he could keep them within acceptable limits pending some action by the Great Powers to bring about cease-fire and diplomatic progress toward a settlement. There is also the danger . . . that he will repeat the 1967 performance, i.e. he will provoke the Israelis into some form of pre-emptive strike.[52]

That Nasser's actions in 1967 had unleashed a Frankenstinian monster born of miscalculation and a dogmatic commitment to 'face' loomed large in the minds of analysts, many of whom were probably the same people in the same posts.[53] They feared that like his predecessor, Sadat was foolishly backing himself into a corner, which would once more put the onus of unrestrained action on Israel.

Implicit in the assessments of Sadat's personal and strategic inadequacies was a belief that Arab political culture was not inclined to objectively self-analyse and learn from past mistakes. The CIA had long argued that 'the concept of self-examination, whether for purposes of self-management or self-improvement, could not be accepted because of its conflict with the more honoured cultural requirement of blameless dignity'.[54] Though this analysis of the

Arab 'national character' was by now almost a decade old, there were other more recent indications that it was still useful.

Indeed, this apparently 'cultural' characteristic had practical security implications. The JIC observed that, 'so far as we are aware the Arab countries get virtually no hard intelligence on Israeli tactical moves or intentions'. They added that 'Arab contingency planning ... has been unrealistic and probably based on misleading information. This heightens the risk of miscalculation and precipitate action by the Arabs.'[55] The Egyptian intelligence services had a notoriously bad reputation among diplomatic circles. One American diplomat recalls being 'informed by a friend of mine at the American University that the Egyptian intelligence service officer at AUC had asked him, who he knew was a friend of mine, to tell me to please slow down because they were having a problem following me in the car that I was driving.'[56] Egyptians were remarkably forthright about their own inadequacies. American analysts reported one prominent Egyptian complaining in the aftermath of the 1967 defeat that 'our intelligence service is the most ignorant in the world. Whereas the Israelis knew the name of every Egyptian on relief, and his wife's name too, we didn't even know where Moshe Dayan's house was!'[57]

Yet as Kissinger commented during the course of war, the defeated Arab states had clearly learned more from the 1967 debacle than anyone had anticipated and this was the crucial determinant of their short-lived military success.[58] Prior to war, however, the notion that Arab political and military leaders might actually have undergone a process of self-examination with the aim of identifying and improving their weaknesses was ill-considered. In an interview with the author, Nasser's Secretary General, Abdel Maguid Farid, stressed that the last years of Nasser's life were dedicated to rectifying the military mistakes that had culminated in the '*naksah*' (setback) of 1967.[59] A British intelligence analyst many years later agreed, confirming that 'Nasser made a thorough examination of their failure in 1967 and ensured that Egyptian officers were trained accordingly'.[60]

The theology of Islam was regarded as an important contributor to the absence of a self-critical culture in the Arab world. The

CIA had observed that 'by definition and by profession, Islam is the surrendering of the self to the will of Allah', encouraging the belief that 'all human actions and their consequences are but the sequels of God's doing'.[61] Consequently there was an inherent passivity associated with the Islamic faith and Arab culture. During the War of Attrition, the US diplomatic representative in Cairo, Donald Bergus, had described the 'classic Egyptian stance of standing pat, talking big, punishing the enemy as much as he possibly can and taking counterblows stoically'. The Egyptians hoped, Bergus wrote, that 'perhaps an unidentified "something" will occur "somewhere" to create a situation favourable to Egypt. It is in the hands of Allah who must, in the fullness of time, reward his devoted servants.'[62] The valedictory despatch of Ambassador Beaumont alluded to similar themes of passivity, describing Islam as the people's

> lesson and their encouragement in their approach to the Arab Israel problem. For they recall, in particular, the extrusion from outré-mer of the Crusaders of the Western world, after 200 years of colonisation and they see in this the hope that Israel too will fade away or be absorbed. It is a reason for hope and also a reason for not trying too hard.[63]

The British naval attaché reinforced that the 'Muslim belief in Allah's Providence and Will' and an 'innate fatalism' enabled the Egyptian people 'to survive a prolonged no-fighting war, but was not particularly conducive to sustained competence under pressure'.[64] Recent research has shown that the British intelligence community was in the habit of emphasising the passivity of other races, but in the Egyptian case Islam seems to have occupied a particular pride of place as a factor inhibiting a competent military performance and strategic capability.[65]

The manner in which the underlying religiosity of the Egyptian people could be mobilised to fight a losing battle was evidently misunderstood. If indeed 'Islam' affected the nation's response to war, it evoked a widespread readiness to sacrifice life in such a way that was barely comprehensible to the secular political culture of the West. Diplomats were informed that 'most Egyptians were farmers and even if their sons joined the army they still regarded a decision of war and peace as being of little concern to them since whether their sons or relatives died was a matter entirely preordained by God'. All levels of society in Egypt shared a 'basic hatred of Israel'. This was 'not merely a national but a religious phenomenon. War would therefore be popular.'[66] The notion of individual sacrifice for the spirit of Egypt alluded to Islamic scriptural metaphors in which the personal defeats of individual men were transformed into collective victories.

There was something of a cultural schism here. Not only would a Western state rarely embark on war in the knowledge that they would probably lose on the battlefield, but even military victory did not always translate into political gain. In Egypt's recent history, however, the experience had been quite different. In 1956, President Nasser had lost on the battlefield in the Suez crisis but had reaped enormous political gain. Even after a spectacular defeat in 1967, he managed to retain the support of the Egyptian public and other Arab states. This was partly a result of Nasser's political acumen but was also facilitated by growing expressions of religiosity among Egyptians. Bergus observed signs of a religious resurgence from 1970. He reported that 'since Israel started deep penetration raids, we have noted lively sale by street vendors of plastic mottos inscribed "Allah" or "Allah with us." ... Mrs Yael Vered (Israel's Miles Copeland) will doubtless inform anybody who will listen that this is another sign that Egypt is cracking under Israeli pressure. Our conclusion is just the opposite.' [67] Sadat himself was more explicitly devout than his predecessor.[68] In 1971, Sadat gave a speech to the Al Azhar mosque, reminding his listeners that 'Man should not fear anything; for that which befalls him is only what is destined to happen.'[69] The ability of Nasser's more pious successor to appropriate and mobilise this underlying religiosity among Egyptians to translate a military defeat into a political and spiritual victory was thus clearly underestimated.

The final belief about Arab political culture reinforced by the 1967 war was the notion that the rhetoric espoused by Arab political leaders bore little relation to their actual capabilities. In January 1973, the British naval attaché reflected on the peculiar relationship between word and fact in Egyptian politics, writing: 'the present posture is ... a timely demonstration that in Egypt there is a bizarre relation between word and fact; further that fact is a rare commodity that must usually be substituted by deduction and probability'.[70] The CIA had long made a similar analytic observation about the alleged subjectivity of the Arab mind, noting that that 'the facts become what the Arab emotionally wants to believe is true'.[71] The implication was that the words spoken by Arab leaders bore little or no relation to military realities.

Ideas about the misleading nature of Arab rhetoric were reinforced by, or at least reflected in, the work of an anthropologist and Orientalist reviewed by the CIA's in-house journal.[72] In a detailed study of 'the Arab Mind', Raphael Patai argued that certain discursive features such as *mubalagha* (exaggeration) and *tawkid* (over-assertion) were anchored in the richness of Arabic language as well as a culture that prioritised 'face' or honour over other values. Patai suggested that verbal precision was largely a function of literate and industrial society. In contrast the personal independence that traditionally characterised the lives of Arabs allowed for greater discursive freedom as a form of communication. Patai argued, in long established industrialised society,

> You must be on time for work, you are tied to a machine which will not tolerate imprecision, you live in a world of impersonal relations, you must be precise in what you do and in what you say. But if you are independent, say, you are a fellah [farmer] who works in the field, you come and go when you want, you talk the way you want. Verbal exaggeration, expansiveness, imagination, make man more free.[73]

Moreover, Patai specifically linked the Arab tendency to exaggerate to 'a cultural phenomenon with socio-economic foundations', effectively serving as verbal compensation for a material deficit. Militarily, this was particularly significant. Patai wrote that 'the Arabs have a proclivity for substituting words for actions . . . in the Arab mentality words often can and do serve as a substitute for acts', suggesting that the Arab tendency towards rhetorical aggrandisement actually had a pacifying function. 'As long as what can be called the oral phase of action lasts, there is always the hope that the aroused passions will exhaust themselves within words and the swords remain in their hilts.'[74] The implication was that *talking* about war could actually replace *going* to war.

That the CIA reviewed this book in its classified in-house journal is revealing. Though the review is dated in 1974, it seems plausible to deduce that academic works such as this may have encouraged analysts to dismiss what Arab leaders (and Sadat in particular) had to say as a substitute for, rather than an indication of, meaningful action. Moreover, Sadat's own practices reinforced such beliefs about a dissonance between rhetoric and action in Egyptian politics. He had begun making periodic statements about the need to gain lost Arab territories by force, and the infamous 'year of decision', since 1970. It was not simply the West who believed his war-like rhetoric was sheer bluff. Estimates of Egyptian military capabilities were so low and such statements made so often without tangible consequences that these warnings were not even taken seriously in Egypt.[75]

Indeed, some Arab diplomats were suspiciously forthright about the tenuous link between rhetoric and action in any future Arab–Israeli conflict. Just two months before the war the Jordanian Foreign Minister, Zaid Rifai, explained to British ambassador Balfour Paul that 'governments in other Arab countries maintained two quite separate levels of policy – "the Declared and the Real"'. He suggested that Sadat and Asad [of Syria] were able to exploit "their restored partners" [Jordan's] military inability' to join in hostilities towards Israel, 'as a pretext for calling them off, or deferring them'.[76] Such diplomatic reporting confirmed the Anglo-American belief in the role of rhetoric as a substitute for action. Speaking to a post-Orientalist literature, it also demonstrates all too well the manner in which cultural stereotypes can be used or indeed advanced by the 'Other' to justify and perhaps even conceal a strategic goal. Whether this was a manifestation of a subconscious 'native Orientalism' or conscious strategic deception, it seems clear that these diplomatic interactions would have further complicated efforts to distinguish the 'signals' (indications of Egypt's intentions and capability) from the 'noise' of Arab rhetoric.[77]

Analytical conceptions of Arab political culture thus loomed large in estimations of what Egypt could achieve militarily. The stunning military defeat of the Six-Day War undoubtedly played a major role as a powerful and recent historical analogy but Anglo-American analysts also underestimated how much had been learned from this traumatic turning point. Simplistic recourses to Islamic 'passivity' misjudged how religiosity could be instrumentalised as an active weapon of war among an increasingly frustrated population and military. Intersecting through and exacerbating all these cultural preconceptions was the notion that Arabs often 'do not mean what they say'. Anthropological works like Patai's and Sadat's own professions only fortified the perceived gap between rhetoric and action. Indeed, there are even hints that Western cultural preconceptions about Arab culture and resultant capability may have been cultivated in order to facilitate strategic surprise.

The Shadow of Soviet–Arab Relations

In a paradoxical way, notions of Orientalism also informed assessments of Soviet-Egyptian relations and the impact the expulsion of Soviet advisors would have on the eve of war. It is peculiar that one of the most notable features of CIA and JIC reporting on Soviet–Egyptian relations during the Nasser period was the emphasis on Egyptian agency in the relationship, particularly when Soviet influence was strongest in the post 1967 period.[78] Analysts clearly sought to quell the widespread fears of policy-makers that Egypt was merely a Soviet client state. However, with the expulsion of 15,000 Soviet troops in July 1972, the caution with which analysts had approached Soviet–Egyptian relations also left. Ultimately the Soviet withdrawal served to confirm that in the absence of the superpower, the Arab world *could not* contemplate a successful military initiative against Israel. Alongside this implicit denial of strategic agency, the expulsion seems to have lowered the guard of analysts and particularly military attachés, obscuring the extent of Soviet operational influence in the Egyptian deception plan.

The 'relaxing' effect of the Soviet expulsion on intelligence gathering in Egypt was made explicit by the British military attaché. He wrote:

> While Soviet weapons systems and their performance in Egypt still constitute a worthwhile intelligence target, my Service Attachés' time is now increasingly devoted to the promotion of defence sales . . . No

longer are the Service Attachés regarded as potential spies to be hampered in their work as much as possible but as friends, trying to assist Egypt in equipping herself for her own defence.[79]

The psychological impact of more amicable relations between British and Egyptian officers that followed the Soviet expulsion meant important residual Soviet influences would be missed.

Egypt's war planners based their plans on Soviet doctrine stipulating that a primary way to conceal real preparations for war is to disguise them as an exercise –'*maskirova*'. The Egyptians sought to convince the Israelis that the information about military preparations they were collecting was connected to '*Tahrir 41*', a large-scale routine crossing exercise – yet another one in a series of similar exercises conducted twice a year since 1968.[80] The secrecy of operations was thereby maintained. Platoon commanders heard that they were to start a real war only six hours before the attack.[81]

The potential impact of these operational influences was undermined by the physical removal of Soviet advisors. After the expulsion, American analysts argued that Sadat 'seems to have recognised that the withdrawal of the Soviet units has weakened Egypt militarily and at least postponed if not abolished his military option'.[82] The assessment mirrored heated debates about the move within the Egyptian establishment. Chief of Staff, Saad al-Din al-Shazly implored Sadat: 'You must realise how dangerous this decision is . . . There is no question this will affect our capabilities. The Soviet units play such a large role in our defense and electronic warfare.'[83] Egyptian elites were clearly also concerned about the impact of the Soviet expulsion on military capabilities.

In March 1973, the British defence attaché concurred, although his analysis included a crucial caveat:

> Soviet military withdrawal has gravely weakened both Egypt's ability to defend herself and any limited capability the Egyptians may once have had to mount an attack against the Israelis across the Suez Canal . . . My Defence Attaché believes the Egyptian Armed Forces are no longer capable of conducting a major military operation across the Canal, *except as a suicidal gesture designed to provoke intervention by the big Powers and the imposition of a Middle East settlement.*[84]

Only in hindsight was it seen that 'the removal of the restraining hands of the Soviet advisers meant that the Egyptians were now masters of their own house, able to lay their own plans according to their own ideas'.[85] Moreover, it was only *after* the expulsion that rearmament to the scale desired by Sadat, really began. Nonetheless, weeks before war analysts assessed (with a discernible tone of smugness) that 'Sadat's experience with the Soviets appears to have taught him a pragmatism that has enabled him to set a course and a pace better suited to Egypt's capabilities'.[86]

The extent to which the Soviet–Arab dimension blurred assessments is most pertinently illustrated in a CIA memorandum prepared on the morning of the attack, confirming that 'as many as 1000 dependents' had suddenly left Egypt.[87] Two plausible interpretations of the Soviet evacuation were put forth. The first was that the Soviet Union had 'gotten wind' of plans to initiate hostilities and in protest were evacuating dependents and advisors. Analysts concluded that, 'in so far as advisors are included in the evacuation, the effectiveness of an Arab attack is likely to be somewhat downgraded and the risks of Soviet involvement will lessen'.[88]

The second interpretation and the one that, revealingly, was more 'in favour with the intelligence services' was that the remaining Soviet advisors were 'being expelled from both Egypt and Syria'. The CIA incorporated considerations of the regional, inter-Arab dimension; specifically, that Saudi Arabia's 'King Faisal has been pressing hard to convince Sadat and Asad to cut their ties with Moscow'. This was also consistent with the tensions that had characterised Arab–Soviet relations since Sadat's presidency. Interestingly the NSC staffer suggested that *despite* their assessment, certain actions should be considered in case of hostilities, for example the evacuation of US citizens, preparations for an oil boycott and consultations with moderate Arab leaders. There was in this short memorandum an almost intuitive, if implicit, reluctance to dismiss the prospect of war entirely.[89]

JIC assessments of the days preceding the war remain unreleased. However, in an interview with the author, the head of the Middle East desk of the Assessments Staff at the time, Colonel John Davies, recalled his personal (and disregarded) warning that war was certainly coming. By spring 1973 Davies had become convinced that Egyptian stockpiles along the Canal portended an attack on Israel. He issued a draft assessment accordingly that was torn 'to shreds' by his superior, Lieutenant-General Sir David Willison, in a JIC meeting, based on 'his supposed expert assessments of Israeli defences'.[90] The JIC's refusal to accept an Assessment Staff submission was 'almost unprecedented', Colonel Davies recalled.

In September, Davies was alerted to further indicators of war based on communications between the Egyptians and Soviets by a contact in GCHQ. By the first few days in October, the increase in signals traffic between the two had become 'so heavy that I became convinced that an attack was imminent'. He recalls that 'the pattern of SIGINT all that week was such as to leave me and . . . my GCHQ contact in little doubt that it was traffic and not deception'. The evacuation of the Russians confirmed his suspicions. Davies issued a Special Assessment, which was passed to the FO duty clerk on Friday afternoon. Perhaps recalling Davies' discredited draft submission in April, the clerk decided that the assessment could wait until Monday. It was not passed to the head of the JIC until war had broken out the next day.[91] An interview with another veteran diplomat suggests that Davies' was indeed a lone voice in the wilderness. Head of the Near East and North Africa Department, James Craig, remembers that 'we discussed thoroughly the evacuation of the Russians from Egypt and reached the conclusion that we didn't understand it but Sadat would not attack! I remember ringing the FO [sic] duty manager to tell him so.'[92] During an invitation to Langley, Davies recalls (with understandable pride) DCI Colby's admission that: 'I had been the only analyst in the Western world to have forecast the Yom Kippur war.'[93]

* * *

In effect, misjudgements about Arab capabilities, both as a result of rigid conceptualisations of Arab culture and the Soviet shadow, meant that although analysts had a good sense of Sadat's motivations and intentions, that is, the various forces driving his actions, they underestimated his capability to carry them out. Even once war had started, DCI Colby thought that the initiative lay with Israel.

271

In May 1973, Sadat himself accused the American intelligence community of overlooking Arab 'psychology'.[94] Yet a detailed examination of the archival record shows that this was simply not the case. The central intelligence bodies in both Britain and America demonstrated a conceptual and applied understanding of the psychological drivers of Sadat's thinking. They appreciated the importance of a limited military victory to regain Egypt's 'honour', the significance of international diplomacy in his strategic considerations and the domestic context upon which Sadat's decision-making would depend.

British analysts demonstrated particularly astute assessments of Sadat's state of mind. Perhaps Britain's more accentuated policy interests in the region influenced the rigour and sensitivity of their assessments. That the onus of action was on the US rather than the UK may also provide some explanation – it is always easier to criticise or stress the need for action when the obligation to act lies on another party. It is also likely that the closer diplomatic relations between Egypt and Britain that characterised the post-1967 period (in contrast to the lack of diplomatic relations between Egypt and the US until after the Yom Kippur War) enabled more sensitive and comprehensive diplomatic reporting back to Whitehall.

Although Sadat's intentions were broadly well understood, it seems clear that analysts failed to take his intentions *seriously* because they doubted his ability to carry out his goals. In effect the result was the same – an erroneously reduced perception of threat. There is a double irony to this underestimation of Egypt's capability. Beliefs about the specificity of Arab political culture were a major contributing factor to analytical strengths in reading Sadat's *intentions* in 1973, yet similar cultural beliefs culminated in a fundamental misreading of Egypt's military *capabilities*. The second irony surrounds assessments of the Soviet role in the crisis. In the years that Soviet influence was most pronounced in Egypt, analysts were uncannily conscious of the need to resist interpreting developments exclusively through the prism of the Cold War, rightly stressing the importance of regional dynamics. After the Soviet expulsion, however, analysts regressed to a simplistic assessment of Egypt's capabilities through a misleadingly basic Cold War framework: that without the Soviet backing, Egypt stood no chance of military success.

This dual underestimation of Egypt's capability by Anglo-American analysts also accentuates the psychological primacy of the intelligence process – particularly the power of stated and unstated preconceptions in masking even the 'facts', that is, the 'secrets' of a nation's capability. As one seasoned scholar of strategic surprise puts it, 'avoiding intelligence failures requires the elimination of strategic preconceptions', but at the same time, as humans, 'we cannot operate without some preconceptions'.[95] In the case of 1973 this problem was even more acute because the cultural preconceptions with which the intelligence community had faced the Arab world in the decade before had been substantiated as accurate in, for example, the analytical 'success' of 1967. Notions like 'the Arabs do not mean what they say' were validated on many occasions, but October 1973 was an exception. As Kissinger later observed, Sadat 'paralysed his opponents with their own preconceptions'.[96] Here Kissinger unwittingly raises an important point sometimes neglected in postcolonial readings: the role of Oriental agency in using, reinforcing and manipulating Western cultural preconceptions to serve strategic purposes in war and peace.

This instance of 'failure' is thus considerably more complicated and certainly less absolute than scholars have hitherto suggested. Clearly there were analytical pitfalls that drew heavily on Orientalist beliefs about the 'Otherness' of the Arab mind. However, this appears to have been more prevalent in assessments of Egypt's capabilities than her intentions. To dismiss political and intelligence analysis as having 'failed' to understand Sadat's intentions, as the historiography overwhelmingly does, is to misrepresent the role of these perceptions in their historical context. That war was not anticipated in October 1973 was not the result of an inability to understand the motivations of a leader in crisis, for which intelligence is often criticised, but rather a rarer failure to recognise an altered capability.

Nor was this an exclusively Western misconception. As Heikal and numerous others have indicated, no one was more surprised by Egypt's military achievements early in the conflict than Sadat himself.[97] To this day, it is impossible to know whether the 'signals' and 'noise' problem that analysts faced with Sadat's vehement professions in the 1971–3 period was the intentional result of a long-term deception campaign, sheer indecision or something in between. Is it therefore plausible and historically accurate to lament the inability of Western intelligence services to reveal an outcome that Sadat was himself unsure about and call it a 'failure' of intelligence?

A final thought regarding this notion of intelligence 'failure' is its complex relationship with policy. How useful would foreknowledge of the date and time of plans for war have been for the successful execution of British and American policy? Israeli intransigence in Arab–Israeli negotiations had been openly acknowledged in both political and intelligence assessments. Counterfactual speculation suggests that accurate foreknowledge of the crisis might arguably have made American and British policy more difficult, forcing them to endorse an Israeli pre-emption which would only have strengthened and perpetuated the stalemate of the Arab–Israeli crisis and anti-Western feeling in the Arab world. As Kissinger privately noted to colleagues, the surprise of war had created a welcome 'realisation on the part of the Israelis that this cockiness of supremacy is no longer possible; like other countries in history, they now have to depend on a combination of security and diplomacy to achieve their security . . . Our insistence on a more politically orientated policy cannot [now] go unheeded.'[98] How, therefore, do we define an intelligence failure? Is it judged by the accuracy of the assessment or by the policy outcome? As Garthoff has illustrated in his seminal study on the Cuban Missile Crisis, it is not always a prerequisite or indeed advantageous for a power to have the maximum information for the successful execution of policy.[99]

On the other hand, sometimes the policy-makers do not *want* the relevant information. Former State Department Intelligence Director Ray Cline defended his analysts' performance in 1973 thus: 'the reason the system wasn't working very well is that people were not asking it to work and not listening to it when it did work'.[100] Other insiders from the intelligence community have backed the claim that the failure of 1973 was one of policy rather than intelligence. American strategic diplomacy can indeed be criticised for failing to capitalise on the strains between Egypt and the USSR; failing to respond to Sadat's pro-Western overtures

Figure 9.2 Meeting in the Oval Office between President Nixon, Secretary of State Henry Kissinger, and Egyptian Foreign Minister Ismail Fahmy, 1973. Nixon Presidential Library, Yorba Linda.

and, above all, failing to recognise how American policy towards Israel was perceived by the Arab world. These failings that insiders have suggested as a way of absolving analysts of blame perhaps mask the fundamentally symbiotic relationship between intelligence analysis and policy-making. Moreover, they underestimate the potential role of the analyst in *directing* the policy-maker to ask the right questions and listen to the right answers. It seems clear that analysts in 1973 had much knowledge and understanding to contribute.

Notes

1. William Colby cited in R. G. Hughes, P. Jackson and L. Scott (eds) *Exploring Intelligence Archives: Enquiries into the Secret State* (London: Routledge, 2008), p. 269.

2. Interview with Harold Saunders, 24 November 1993. Available at: <http://www.adst.org/OH%20TOCs/Saunders,%20Harold%20H. toc.pdf>, p. 45 (last accessed 1 March 2017).
3. For a full account of this historiography see U. Bar-Joseph, *The Watchman Fell Asleep: The Surprise of Yom Kippur and its Sources* (Albany, NY: State University of New York Press, 2005), pp. 4–6. Studies conclude that despite the excellent information that was available to analysts of the Directorate of Military Intelligence (AMAN) prior to the war, a range of psychological, organisational and bureaucratic factors both common to cases of surprise attack and specific to the Israeli intelligence community, inhibited high quality strategic warning. The reasons identified include the difficulty of distinguishing between 'signals' and 'noise' in the build-up to war; the Egyptian deception plan which exacerbated this difficulty; the dogmatic Israeli reliance on a strategic 'Conception', to which crucial information at the tactical level was subordinated; over-reliance on a recently disclosed single source named Ashraf Marwan (son-in-law of President Nasser) who was allegedly a double agent; and the manipulation of information by a motivated hierarchy.
4. For an exception see M. Penney, 'Intelligence and the 1973 Arab-Israeli War', in *President Nixon and the Role of Intelligence in the 1973 Arab-Israeli War*, 30 January 2013, pp. 7–10. Available at <https://www.cia.gov/library/publications/international-relations/ arab-israeli-war/nixon-arab-isaeli-war.pdf> (last accessed 20 March 2016). Like this chapter, the study also reveals 'documents that show the Intelligence Community grappling with reports that war might, in fact, be coming'. Regarding organisational initiatives the authors explain that 'having disbanded the Office of National Estimates, Colby had begun to replace it with a system of individual National Intelligence Officers (NIOs), whose new procedures were not yet effective. A number of personnel changes had recently been made, and some of the most knowledgeable Middle East analysts had moved to other jobs.'
5. R. Aldrich, *GCHQ* (London: Harper Press, 2010), p. 290.
6. DCI memorandum, 'The performance of the intelligence community before the Arab-Israeli War of October 1973: a preliminary post-mortem', 20 December 1973. Available at <http://www.foia.cia.gov/ sites/default/files/document_conversions/89801/DOC_0001331429. pdf> (last accessed 20 March 2017).
7. H. Kissinger, *Years of Upheaval* (Boston, MA: Little, Brown and Co., 1982), p. 465.

8. Ashraf Ghorbal in R. B. Parker (ed.), *The October War: A Retrospective* (Gainesville, FL: University Press of Florida, 2001), p. 33.

9. A. Shlaim, 'Failures in national intelligence estimates: the case of the Yom Kippur War', *World Politics*, 28: 3, 1976, p. 362. Shlaim argues that 'had the [Israeli] intelligence chiefs not been influenced by the current views about Arab intent they might have given more weight in their evaluations to the demonstrable increase in Arab capabilities which preceded the outbreak of war'.

10. D. Adamsky, 'Disregarding the bear: how U.S. intelligence failed to estimate the Soviet intervention in the Egyptian-Israeli War of Attrition', *Journal of Strategic Studies*, 28: 5, 2005, p. 807.

11. Undoubtedly their assessments mirrored Israeli complacency in this regard. As the Director for the Bureau of Intelligence and Research (INR), Ray Cline claimed in a meeting just weeks after war broke out, 'we were brainwashed by the Israelis who brainwashed themselves'. Transcript, 'Secretary's Staff Meeting', 23 October 1973. Avaiable at <http://nsarchive.gwu.edu/NSAEBB/NSAEBB98/octwar-63.pdf> (last accessed 20 March 2017). British intelligence veterans have also intimated that Israeli influence was important: interview with the author, Colonel John Davies, London, 25 March 2014.

12. As the Franco-Palestinian scholar Camille Mansour puts it, the Israelis were 'seen as the experts, the 'Orientalists' of the Middle East in the sense defined by Edward Said: they are at once knowledgeable about the terrain and imbued with Western civilization. They are the ones who can claim to understand Arab mentalities, their political processes, their 'irrationality'. C. Mansour, *Beyond Alliance: Israel and U.S. Foreign Policy* (New York: Columbia University Press, 1994), p. 8.

13. JIC memorandum (71) 43, 'Future development of the Arab-Israeli crisis and its consequences', 3 November 1971, TNA, CAB 186/9.

14. Shibley Telhami in Parker (ed.), *The October War*, p. 297.

15. H. Heikal, *The Road to Ramadan* (New York: New York Times Books, 1975), p. 77.

16. JIC memorandum (69) 16, 'The Arab-Israel military balance and its political implications', 25 April 1969, TNA, CAB 186/2.

17. Memorandum from Gladstone in Cairo to Pike in Near East and North Africa Department, FCO, 'Sadat's interview with Arnaud De Borchgrave', 10 April 1973, TNA, FCO 93/235.

18. Ibid.

19. C. Beckerman-Boys, 'Assessing the historiography of the October War', in A. Siniver, *The Yom Kippur War: Politics, Legacy, Diplomacy* (Oxford: Oxford University Press, 2013), p. 26.
20. Memorandum from Saunders to Kissinger, 'Comment on Sadat's interview with de Borchgrave', 2 April 1973, Saunders memoranda sensitive, Egypt/Hafez Ismail 1973, Country Files, Middle East – Sensitive 1971-74 (RN), Henry A. Kissinger (HAK) Office Files, National Security Council Files, Nixon Presidential Materials Staff, NARA II.
21. Cline to Acting Secretary, 'Growing risk of Egyptian resumption of hostilities with Israel', 31 May 1973. Available at <http://www2.gwu.edu/~nsarchiv/NSAEBB/NSAEBB415/docs/doc%201%2031MAY1973_INR_RAYCLINE(3).pdf> (last accessed 20 March 2016).
22. R. Kaplan, 'Tales from the bazaar', *The Atlantic*, August 1992. Available at <http://www.theatlantic.com/magazine/archive/1992/08/tales-from-the-bazaar/305012/> (last accessed 1 March 2017).
23. H. Ismail, cited in K. W. Stein, 'Evolving a diplomatic legacy from the October War: the US, Egyptian, and Israeli triangle', in A. Siniver (ed.), *The October 1973 War: Politics, Diplomacy, and Legacy* (London: Hurst and Company, 2013), p. 218.
24. JIC memorandum (69) 16, 'The Arab-Israel military balance and its political implications', 25 April 1969, TNA, CAB 186/2.
25. Memorandum from Ambassador Adams to FCO, 24 January 1974, TNA, FCO 39/561.
26. Memorandum, 'Indications of Arab intentions to initiate hostilities', from NSC Staff, March 1973, NSA.
27. Cline to Acting Secretary, 'Growing risk of Egyptian resumption of hostilities with Israel', 31 May 1973. Available at <http://www2.gwu.edu/~nsarchiv/NSAEBB/NSAEBB415/docs/doc%201%2031MAY1973_INR_RAYCLINE(3).pdf> (last accessed 20 March 2016).
28. Despatch from Ambassador Adams in Cairo to FCO, 'The Egyptian armed forces in 1972', 12 March 1973, TNA, FCO 93/65.
29. Telegram no. 1269 from FCO to British Embassy in Washington, 'Text of Prime Minister's message to Mr. Nixon', 15 June 1973, TNA, PREM 15/1764.
30. D. Rezk, 'Seeing Sadat, thinking Nasser', in L. Freedman and J. Michaels (eds), *Scripting Middle East Leaders: The Impact of Leadership Perceptions on US and UK Foreign Policy* (London: Bloomsbury, 2012).
31. Ibid.

32. S. Shazly, *The Crossing of the Suez* (San Francisco, CA: American Mideast Research, 1980), pp. 192–5.

33. Despatch from Ambassador Beaumont in Cairo to FCO, 'Egypt in the doldrums', 28 November 1972, TNA, FCO 39/1207.

34. Memorandum from Ambassador Adams in Cairo to FCO, 20 March 1973, TNA, FCO 93/235.

35. Hoda Abdel Nasser, interview with the author, Cairo, 2 March 2006; Hassanein Heikal, interview with the author, Cairo, 1 March 2006.

36. Text of a petition ('Baghdadi memorandum' presented to President Sadat on 4 April 1972) from British Embassy in Cairo to Foreign and Commonwealth Office, TNA, FCO 39/1207.

37. Despatch from British Ambassador Beaumont in Cairo to Secretary of State for Foreign and Commonwealth Affairs, 'Egypt in the doldrums', 28 November 1972, TNA, FCO 39/1207. Beaumont's analysis was described as 'somewhat pessimistic' by the State Department, no doubt reflecting slightly more positive perceptions of Sadat's leadership expressed by American analysts.

38. Ray Cline to Acting Secretary, 'Growing risk of Egyptian resumption of hostilities with Israel', 31 May 1973. Available at <http://www2.gwu.edu/~nsarchiv/NSAEBB/NSAEBB415/docs/doc%201%2031MAY1973_INR_RAYCLINE(3).pdf> (last accessed 20 March 2016).

39. Undated memorandum, 'Indications of Arab intentions to initiaite hostilities'. Available at <http://www2.gwu.edu/~nsarchiv/NSAEBB/NSAEBB98/octwar-01.pdf> (last accessed 20 March 2016).

40. Ibid.

41. M. Penney, 'Intelligence and the 1973 Arab-Israeli War', in *President Nixon and the Role of Intelligence in the 1973 Arab-Israeli War*, 30 January 2013, p. 16. Available at <https://www.cia.gov/library/publications/international-relations/arab-israeli-war/nixon-arab-isaeli-war.pdf> (last accessed 20 March 2016).

42. Despatch from Ambassador Adams in Cairo to FCO, 'The Egyptian armed forces in 1972', 12 March 1973, TNA, FCO 93/65.

43. Shazly, *Crossing of the Suez*, p. 24.

44. H. Heikal, *Autumn of Fury: The Assassination of Sadat* (London: Andre Deutsch, 1983), p. 64.

45. Memorandum from Air Attaché Barnicoat to Ambassador Adams, 'Annual report for 1972', 9 January 1973, TNA, FCO 93/65. (Annex B to Adams's despatch.)

46. JIC memorandum (69) 16, 'The Arab-Israel military balance and its political implications', 25 April 1969, TNA, CAB 186/2.

47. Patrick Wright, interview with the author, 15 May 2008.
48. H. Ford, 'William E. Colby as Director of Central Intelligence, 1973–1976', in *President Nixon and the Role of Intelligence in the 1973 Arab-Israeli War*, 30 January 2013, p. 21. Available at <https://www.cia.gov/library/publications/international-relations/arab-israeli-war/nixon-arab-israeli-war.pdf> (last accessed 20 March 2016).
49. Ibid.
50. Intelligence memorandum, ' Soviet policies in the event of imminent Egyptian collapse', 6 October 1973, cited in *President Nixon and the Role of Intelligence in the 1973 Arab-Israeli War*, 30 January 2013, p. 45. Available at <https://www.cia.gov/library/publications/international-relations/arab-israeli-war/nixon-arab-israeli-war.pdf> (last accessed 20 March 2016).
51. H. Kissinger, *The White House Years* (Boston, MA: Little, Brown and Co., 1979), p. 1285.
52. Minute from Parsons to Prime Minister Heath, 3 May 1973, TNA, PREM 15/1764.
53. For more on the role of historical experiences in shaping the mentality of bureaucracies, see D. Reiter, 'Learning, realism, and alliances: the weight of the shadow of the past', *World Politics*, 46: 1994, pp. 490–526.
54. Peter Naffsinger, '"Face" Among the Arabs', *Studies in Intelligence* 8, 1964, FOIA Electronic Reading Room. Available at <https://www.cia.gov/library/center-for-the-study-of-intelligence/kent-csi/vol8no3/ html/v08i3a05p_0001.html> (last accessed 20 March 2016). This piece is discussed at length in D. Rezk, 'Orientalism and intelligence analysis: deconstructing Anglo-American notions of the "Arab"', *Intelligence and National Security*, 31: 2, 2016, pp. 224–45.
55. JIC memorandum (69) 16, 'The Arab Israeli military balance and its political implications', 25 April 1969, TNA, CAB 186/2.
56. Interview with Arthur Houghton III, 30 April 2001. Available at <http://adst.org/wp-content/uploads/2012/09/Egypt.pdf>, p. 565 (last accessed 1 March 2017). Houghton was the Political/Economic Officer in Cairo from 1971 to 1974.
57. Intelligence information cable, 'Views of deputy UAR Prime Minister Zakariyah Muhiy Al Din on his power status within the UAR', 31 July 1967, DDRS.
58. Transcript of Secretary's staff meeting, 23 October 1973, NSA.
59. Interviews with the author: Hassanein Heikal, Cairo, 1 March 2006; Abd-el Maguid Farid, Cairo, 4 March 2006.

60. Interview with the author, Colonel John Davies, London, 25 March 2014.
61. Naffsinger, '"Face" among the Arabs', *Studies in Intelligence*, 1964, FOIA Electronic Reading Room.
62. From USINT Bergus to Secretary of State, 24 September 1969, File UAR vol. II 1 Sept 1969–31 January 1970, Country Files Middle East, NSC Files, Box 635, Nixon's Presidential Materials Staff, NARA II.
63. Diplomatic report no. 161/73 from Ambassador Beaumont in Cairo to FCO, 'Sir Richard Beaumont's valedictory despatch', 18 January 1973, TNA, FCO 93/74.
64. Report by the Naval Attaché Marriott, 9 January 1973 (Annex A to 'Annual Report 1972 by Defence Attaché Lewis), TNA, FCO 93/65.
65. R. Cormac, *Confronting the Colonies: British Intelligence and Counterinsurgency* (Hurst: London, 2014).
66. Minute by Eastwood on his talk with Mustafa Kamil Murad, 7 December 1972, TNA, FO 141/1505.
67. Telegram from Bergus to Secretary of State, 10 February 1970, File Pol Arab-Isr, 2-11-1970, Subject Numeric Files 1970-1973, Political and Defense, Box 2050, General Records of the State Department, Record Group 59, NARA II.
68. A. Sadat, *In Search of Identity: An Autobiography* (London: Collins, 1978), p. 3: 'everything around me, was made by an overseeing God – a vast mighty being that watches and takes care of all.'
69. Address by President Sadat to Delegation of Ulemas, 16 May 1971. Available at <http://www.sadat.umd.edu/archives/speeches/AAFP%20Spch%20to%20Ulemas5.16.71.pdf.pdf> (last accessed 20 March 2017).
70. Report by the Naval Attaché Marriott, 9 January 1973 (Annex A to 'Annual Report 1972 by Defence Attaché Lewis), TNA, FCO 93/65.
71. Naffsinger, '"Face" among the Arabs', *Studies in Intelligence*, 1964, FOIA Reading Room.
72. Book review by L. F. Jordan, in *Studies in Intelligence*, 1974, FOIA Reading Room.
73. R. Patai, *The Arab Mind* (New York: Charles Scribners and Sons, 1973), p. 61.
74. Ibid. p. 239.
75. Hassanein Heikal, interview with the author, Cairo, 1 March 2006.
76. Memorandum from Balfour Paul in Amman to Craig in FCO, 27 August 1973, TNA, FCO 93/82.

77. For the classic study of the differentiation between 'signals' and 'noise' see R. Wohlstetter, *Pearl Harbour: Warning and Decision* (Stanford, CA: Stanford University Press, 1962).

78. D. Rezk, 'Anglo-American political and intelligence assessments of the Middle East: 1957–1977', unpublished PhD thesis, University of Cambridge, Cambridge, 2012, p. 167.

79. Diplomatic report no. 209/73 from Ambassador Adams in Cairo to FCO, 12 March 1972, TNA, FCO 93/65.

80. Bar-Joseph, *The Watchman Fell Asleep*, p. 26.

81. U. Bar-Joseph, 'Israel's 1973 intelligence failure', in P. R. Kumeraswamy (ed.), *Revisiting the Yom Kippur War* (London: Frank Cass, 2000), p. 24.

82. Telegram from USINT Cairo to Secretary of State, 'Whither Egypt', 25 August 1972, File Pol Egypt. Box 2249, Subject Numeric Files, 1970-73, Political and Defense, Record Group 59, General Records of the State Department, NARA II.

83. M. Gamasy, *The October War: Memoirs of Field Marshal El-Gamasy of Egypt* (Cairo: AUC Press, 1993), pp. 141–55.

84. Diplomatic report no. 209/73 from Ambassador Adams in Cairo to FCO, 12 March 1973, TNA, FCO 93/65 [emphasis added].

85. Memorandum from Ambassador Adams in Cairo to FCO, 24 January 1974, TNA, FCO 39/561.

86. Intelligence memorandum, 'New policy directions in Egypt', 25 September 1973, CREST, NARA II.

87. Memorandum from Quandt to Scowcroft, 'Arab-Israeli tensions', 6 October 1973, NSA.

88. Ibid.

89. Ibid.

90. John Davies, correspondence with author, 10 January 2014. Willison was Deputy Chief of Defence Staff (Intelligence). In a subsequent interview, Davies also alluded to personal rivalry between himself and Willison based on a prior altercation.

91. Ibid.

92. James Craig, letter to the author, 10 November 2011.

93. John Davies, correspondence with author, 10 January 2014.

94. Text of interview Sadat gave to Arnaud de Brochgrave in *Newsweek*, 9 April 1973, TNA, FCO 93/44. Sadat used the Vietnam conflict to illustrate his point: 'McNamara warned [President] Johnson that by feeding the wrong data into the computers he was getting the wrong answers. Well, McNamara was right and Johnson was wrong . . . You simply forgot to feed Vietnamese psychology into the computer . . . The U.S. has overlooked one factor – Arab psychology.'

95. R. Betts, 'Analysis, war and decision: why intelligence failures are inevitable', *World Politics*, 31, 1978, p. 63.

96. H. Kissinger, *Years of Upheaval* (Boston, MA: Little, Brown and Co., 1982), p. 460.

97. Hassanein Heikal, interview with the author, Cairo, 1 March 2006.

98. Kissinger, transcript of Secretary's staff meeting, 23 October 1973, NSA.

99. Garthoff persuasively argues that had the US administration known that there were nuclear warheads on the missiles, it would in fact have made the crisis more intractable. See R. Garthoff, 'U.S. Intelligence in the Cuban Missile Crisis', in J. Blight and A. Welch (eds), *Intelligence and the Cuban Missile Crisis* (London: Frank Cass, 1998), p. 19.

100. R. Betts, 'Analysis, war and decision: why intelligence failures are inevitable', *World Politics*, 31: 1, 1978, p. 67.

10 Aftermath of Victory

He just didn't really believe in his heart that his people were against him, that he was in danger, or if he did, he was very fatalistic about it. It was a sort of Islamic fatalism. If it happened, it would be God's will. I'm the president of the people, I'm the father of these people. He used to personalize everything. 'My canal.' 'My army.' He really was a sort of father of his people.

Roy Atherton, 1990[1]

The Yom Kippur War was a radical turning point in Egypt's history. Indeed, the successful surprise attack on Israel shifted the whole political and psychological balance of power across the Middle East and beyond. Irrespective of the military facts, it was from this plateau of 'victory' that Sadat came to be considered a veritable statesman. He was credited with inviting Western investment in Egypt's economy *(infitah)*, opening the Suez Canal to international navigation, and eventually embarking on an unprecedented trip to Jerusalem that culminated in an Egyptian–Israeli peace treaty. Following the war, Sadat pursued a contentious melange of domestic and foreign policies that came to define contemporary Egypt. A debate about Sadat the man and leader ensued.

Our historical understanding of these changes through Western eyes is understandably based primarily on the memory of those individuals present or involved in the post-1973 negotiations. Kissinger describes Sadat's actions as demonstrating 'the transcendence of the visionary'.[2] President Carter's recollection is a little more guarded, depicting Sadat as a character 'extraordinarily inclined towards boldness'.[3] Ismail Fahmy, Egyptian Foreign Minister between 1973 and 1977, attributes Sadat's achievements to an 'impulsive style' of 'split-second decision making' and a quest for personal fame.[4] The memoirs of General Gamasy and Heikal explicitly accuse Sadat of squandering Nasser's achievements domestically, and Egypt's international standing abroad in the aftermath of the 1973 war.[5] It is perhaps only a slight oversimplification to suggest that, broadly speaking, there is something of a 'cultural divide' between Western narratives which portray the personality of Sadat, his achievements and his legacy in a positive light, and their Arab counterparts which tend to do the opposite.[6]

Anglo-American analysts painted a more complex picture of Sadat, one that lies somewhat in between the pro-Sadat (predominantly Western) and anti-Sadat (predominantly Arab) narratives.[7] The war certainly seemed to give Sadat a new sense of self confidence domestically and internationally. The CIA suggested that Sadat had somehow shed his 'Arabness' to espouse a more mature, pragmatic and rational approach akin to the Western world. Yet revealingly, the comparisons with Nasser prevailed. Moreover, they noted that lacking his predecessor's charisma, Sadat would struggle to prove himself to his Arab constituents.

Nowhere was this to be more of a challenge than in his moves towards peace with Israel. As the first disengagement treaty failed to satisfy Egyptian demands for its occupied land in Sinai, both intelligence communities across the Atlantic feared the renewal of war in 1975 before the second disengagement treaty was signed. Israeli 'intransigence' came to be a recurring term in official discourse. Analysts stressed the dangers of a bilateral peace treaty as early as 1974 and the risk of Sadat's assassination as early as 1975.

The precarious nature of Sadat's domestic position was not lost on analysts. There was a slow but discernible shift in perceptions of Sadat, particularly on the part of the British, and increasing criticism of the social and economic implications of his rule in the build-up to the infamous 'bread riots' in 1977. Analysts highlighted the threat from the religious right well before the Iranian revolution. Indeed, by the time of his assassination, it is striking how much constructions of Sadat had come to resemble more closely the negative images of pre-1973 rather than the hero of the October War.

The 'Corrective Revolution': Finally Shedding Nasser's Legacy?

In July 1974, Henry Kissinger was about to depart for Egypt. Few at the time could have predicted that a Jewish refugee from Nazi Germany would develop quite such a close relationship with an Egyptian President. Before his first trip to the Middle East in November 1973, Kissinger had never been to an Arab country and never met with an Arab head of state. He had little experience in the region but 'he was a fast learner'.[8] The CIA's background briefing for the Secretary of State described the war as bringing 'changes of revolutionary proportions' to Egypt. Analysts informed Kissinger that Sadat was 'seldom taken seriously before the war, either by his own people, by other Arabs or by the world at large'.[9] Whilst he had previously lived in Nasser's shadow, the 'sense of pride' occasioned by the war gave Sadat a 'proper title in his own right to the leadership of Egypt and the Arab world'. Egyptian belief in victory, whatever the military facts, had afforded him 'a certain freedom to set policies for Egypt and for the Arabs that he could not have carried off before'. The familiar theme of dignity emerged repeatedly in the CIA's briefing: 'without the restored sense of self-respect the war brought with it, Sadat could not have pursued negotiations with Israel, could not have improved his ties with the United States, and could not have shifted his concentration from war to reconstruction'. They noted an emphasis of 'equality' both with Israel and the superpowers and suggested that the 'new sensation' of self-confidence would manifest itself in a different attitude towards the West.[10]

Some months earlier the British ambassador had come to similar conclusions.[11] Philip Adams was unabashedly one of Sadat's greatest admirers. He publicly remarked that he found him 'remarkable among Arab politicians . . . for his capacity to look forward and for his consistency'.[12] In his annual review of 1973, he described Sadat's achievements of that year as 'remarkable', reflecting a 'growing maturity and sureness of touch'.[13] He argued that 'as a direct consequence of Egypt's crossing of the Suez Canal the Arab oil weapon has been unsheathed for the very first time'. Adams suggested a new personal respect for Sadat. The themes of friendship, equality and interdependence with the West emerge rather more strongly and explicitly from such British reporting than the CIA's briefing for Kissinger:

> We must accept that this part of the world and our relations with it will never be the same again. President Sadat . . . wants our friendship on the basis of a partnership based on equality of status and interest. The Arabs have found that they can exploit us just as effectively as they claim we have exploited them. The era of patent interdependence has arrived.[14]

The ambassador's musings reflect not only a more complimentary portrayal of Sadat and the significance of his achievements, but also a certain anxiety about the future of the colonial powers. No longer could the West look upon this particular Arab leader as an inferior 'Other' since he had patently demonstrated a military and political strength worthy of equality. Theories of the 'so-called decline of the West' prevailing in the Arab world as a result of the October War were clearly also shared by Western political elites.[15] The JIC expressed similar fears rather less poetically: 'The Arabs now recognise their power to disrupt . . . their financial behaviour will have to be closely monitored.'[16]

In inter-Arab relations, Egypt's 'stock had risen to the point where she can again fairly claim the leadership of the Arab world', although, Adams qualified, 'she is now content to share that doubtful privilege with Saudi Arabia'. Crossing the Suez Canal 'proved to herself and the world at large that Egyptian patriotism can produce deeds as well as words and that the despised Egyptian army can fight with fervour and determination', alluding to the previous underestimation of Egypt's military capability. The ambassador concluded that 'Sadat is now undisputed master and looks like remaining so, provided that the process of Israeli withdrawal is not too long delayed'.[17] It was an insightful and necessary caveat to include.

Other British commentators were more cynical. The Egyptian leader's sudden transformation left them reluctant to renounce entirely their earlier negative assessments of Sadat. 'It is curious', wrote the newly appointed British counsellor in Cairo, Richard Faber, 'how he has blossomed into such a potentate; but there was not room for two potentates when Nasser was alive'. It was not clear that even the victory of Yom Kippur could provide enough fuel to sustain Sadat's presidency. He added, 'I would not like to guess how long he will bear the strain, mentally or physically. At least his past career has given him plenty of opportunities to develop self-control and he does not yet seem to have lost touch with reality.'[18] Faber was known for possessing a rather lachry-mose temperament but his pessimistic outlook also alludes to the denigrating descriptions associated with Sadat before the war: a fundamentally weak leader, lacking self-control and potentially delusional.

Interestingly, it was a recurring theme that Sadat's success in the war and the 'dignity' that ensued had allowed him somehow to shed his troublesome 'Arabness' in pursuit of a more 'Western' pragmatism. The CIA informed Kissinger that 'Sadat often admon-ishes the Egyptians to rid themselves of the "complexes" that have characterized and hindered Egyptian policy in the past.' They added: 'His admonitions are at once a sign of his own confidence in Egypt's ability to pursue its domestic and foreign policies on its own terms, and a recognition that others in Egypt do not share his self-confidence.'[19] Sadat himself repeatedly expressed these senti-ments in order to define himself as outside a political culture he depicted as regressive and backwards.

In rather a patronising tone, the CIA claimed that Sadat had 'never shared the extremism of Arab politics'. But

> even he came only gradually to accept the necessity for flexibility, to recognise that the furtherance of any state's interest depends largely on its own actions, and to compromise lofty goals to the realities and exigencies of world power politics – to see, in short, the gray areas rather than only the black and white.

They explained that 'Sadat has not acted or talked as an Arab is expected to act and talk, either by the non-Arab world or by the Arabs themselves'. The Agency quoted the Egyptian President tell-ing *Time* magazine that 'we are now using language and trying to convince our brothers to adopt methods that can be understood in the whole world'.[20] This idea that by virtue of being an 'Arab' leader one could only see the world in the simplest terms and fail to practice pragmatic politics, was of course an erroneous basis upon which to analyse Sadat, and one readily disproved by his predecessor, yet significantly it was one that he himself repeatedly encouraged. The CIA assessed that presently, Sadat's principal task was to 'overcome the rigidity and extremism that prevent other Arabs from following him readily'.[21] The 'Westerness' or 'Arabness' of Sadat's political behaviour was a theme often to recur in political and intelligence assessments, particularly in comparisons with his predecessor.

In April 1975, the CIA completed a major review of the Egyptian presidency entitled 'A Coming of Age: The Foreign Policy of Anwar Sadat'. It highlighted some continuity between Sadat and Nasser but developed the idea of Sadat's more 'mature', 'Western' approach. In the Agency's view, the main difference between the two leaders was that Sadat knew 'the limits of confrontation and the advantages of co-operation'. The CIA contrasted Sadat's 'flexibility' to Nasser's 'inflexibility', attributed to the latter's 'concern for appearances' and 'rigidity' which had precluded 'even an exploration of areas of compromise'. Moreover, Nasser's 'own tendency toward conflict ultimately caused him to overplay his hand', whilst Sadat was 'aware of the interests of other states' and cognisant that 'some accommodation must be made if Egypt's own interests are to be furthered'. Consequently, he has 'consciously eschewed the revolutionary tactics, the appeals to emotionalism, and the invocation of "principle" in defence of inaction that have heretofore brought popularity but few foreign policy successes for progressive Arab leaders'.

> Sadat's concept of foreign policy is unremarkable by pragmatic Western standards, but by the standards of the Arab world it is revolutionary. Sadat himself describes it as a new maturity. It is a positive policy undertaken on behalf of a people imbued with a negative attitude toward the non-Arab, non Islamic world. It is a planned, action orientated policy imposed where ad hoc essentially reactive decisions have been the norm.[22]

There is a clear contrast here between Sadat's rational, mature, practical, strategic and Western (both in nature and orientation) foreign policy and Nasser's youthful, impetuous, negative and reactive foreign policy. Not merely a comparison of two leaders, the loaded language used by the intelligence analysts provides a revealing insight into their political thought about the revolutionary Arab world – the discourse of a 'passive', 'reactive' Arab world, 'coming of age' to the political maturity of their Western counterparts, by adopting and conceding to Western rationale and moderation. It is again notable that they quote Sadat himself encouraging this comparison.

At the same time, there were some serious qualifications to this newfound admiration of Sadat. Of Egypt, the CIA clearly posited that Nasser had 'made it the leader and political centre of the Arab world by the forces of a personality that Sadat cannot equal and by tactics that he does not choose to match'. Nasser maintained his edge by being 'more radical than the radicals . . . whilst Sadat has adopted a style that is attuned more to the moderation of the outside world than to the radicalism of the Arabs'. However, Sadat faced a crucial challenge in this regard. The CIA knew that 'to win acceptance of his policies among the Arabs, he must present them in a language the other Arabs understand'. It was a barely disguised word of warning: the popularity that Sadat gained gave him the ability to frame negotiations as an extension of war. The 'Westernisation' of his politics should not alienate him from his Arab constituency. Analysts correctly predicted that Sadat's popularity would wane unless he could demonstrate 'to the Arabs by practical results that his pragmatic approach to leadership produces more than radicalism can'.[23] Negotiations with Israel would prove this only too well.

Arab Culture and Negotiations

The theme of Arab 'Otherness' also featured strongly in Western analyses of Arab–Israeli negotiations.[24] In August 1973, the State Department engaged in a fascinating debate about 'the Arab view of Negotiations and Agreements'.[25] Diplomats questioned the idea of a 'fundamental' difference between the Arab concept of an agreement and its Western counterpart, but noted 'some differences in approach' or 'nuances . . . worth keeping in mind'. These included the importance of the 'beneficial lubricant' of the inter-mediary: 'Being told no bluntly and directly involves loss of honor for an Arab, and the preservation of honor is perhaps the most important matter at stake in a negotiation for an Arab.' Other cultural differences included the 'indirect' form of negotiations, verbal explorations as opposed to written formulations, and the importance in engaging 'the man in ultimate authority'. However, the State Department concluded that:

> too much emphasis can be placed on the differences mentioned above. Many of them are shared by non-Arab nations that also have yet to develop the West's sophisticated and systematic approach to the conduct of international relations. There is no special 'cultural gap' that makes negotiating with the Arabs inherently impossible or especially difficult. A certain amount of sloppiness is to be expected, making it desirable to approach the reaching of agreements in a very thorough painstaking manner. And above all, the viability of any agreement will depend, in the long run, on the construction of incentives that make it in the interest of both sides to continue to observe it.[26]

Whilst the hint of Western superiority is detectable, the Director of Egyptian Affairs, Michael Sterner, put the role of culture in its place. Other cultures indeed had different procedural imperatives but ultimately *realpolitik* interests would determine the success of negotiations.

Nor was the influence of Arab culture on negotiations an isolated concern of the State Department. Quandt also notes that 'Kissinger frequently mentioned he feared the Arabs' "romanticism," their impatience, their desire for quick results.'[27] Kissinger himself privately admitted to the Israelis in negotiations, 'I have no illusions about Sadat. With most Arabs I've met, you can't tell where reality ends and the epic poetry begins. With him, he's at least in touch with reality.'[28] Indeed the Egyptians themselves were willing to advance the 'Otherness' of their culture if it served to pressure the West effectively.

The American ambassador, Herman Eilts, struck up a unique relationship with Sadat. According to William Quandt, 'no American knew Sadat better'; moreover, he was one of the few career diplomats that Kissinger trusted.[29] Eilts reported an Egyptian diplomat reminding him that 'Egyptian people are fatalists, for what they deeply believe they will fight with complete disregard of personal feeling. They know fate is in God's hands. It makes no difference whether they live or die.' And he claimed that 'Egyptians' emotions are at present so aroused that people are prepared to die to drive Israel out of occupied lands.'[30] Similarly, the architect of the Camp David Accords, Harold Saunders, recalled another expression of native Orientalism in a conversation with his Jordanian counterparts:

> I talked to one of Hussein's senior advisors; I repeated my view that the peace process was an on-going and extended process. He said to me that Jordanians were a desert people; they would never leave one oasis without knowing where the next one would be . . . the Jordanian culture and language did not incorporate the thought of an 'open end' political process.[31]

The 'Other' was thus clearly ready to utilise Orientalist stereotypes when it suited their political purposes.

Sinai I

The first disengagement treaty between Egypt and Israel was signed in January 1974. Israel withdrew its forces from territories it had taken west of the Suez Canal during the Yom Kippur War and retreated several miles east of the Canal on the Sinai front. Though a limited step, the preliminary Israeli withdrawal achieved the first formal Egyptian commitment to peace-seeking. Ambassador Eilts recalled: 'I remember when that agreement was signed. Every one of Sadat's advisers was bitter about it. They felt that what Egypt was gaining from it was incommensurate with the sacrifices that it had made.'[32]

At the time, analysts credited Sadat with making a leap in the right direction. It was seen as significant that Sadat had persuaded Syrian President Asad to follow suit with a similar disengagement agreement in May. The CIA reiterated Sadat's 'adroitness in carrying off a policy that is essentially foreign to most Arabs'. They recognised, however, that Sadat faced opposition from Arab states who saw his 'policy as inimical to their interests'.[33] They reflected that the limited achievements of the treaty had escaped criticism because 'memory of Egypt's accomplishments in war was fresh and no Arabs could raise their voices above the euphoria created by Arab success against the Israeli enemy'. The danger was that 'Arab memories have since shortened, however, in the face of Sadat's willingness to compromise with that enemy and his notice-able relaxation of Egypt's military posture'.[34]

The Agency also hinted towards the danger of an over-reliance on the US and its principal power wielder, Secretary Kissinger. 'Egyptian children are being named after Henry Kissinger. Egyptians have always, even at the lowest point in the relationship, felt an affinity for Americans that contrasts markedly with their feelings for the Soviets.'[35] The risk was that too much faith was being placed in this newfound alliance, with Egyptians expecting that a complete Israeli withdrawal from Sinai was 'ultimately assured, that reconstruction will bring an end to severe economic ills, and that the U.S. will be the salvation of Egypt'. It became clear that 'both Sadat and the U.S. will be in trouble if the promises are not fulfilled'.[36]

Disengagement also coincided with a more determined anti-Soviet stance in Egypt. In 1974 the JIC assessed that 'recent Soviet policy in the Middle East has not been conspicuously successful'.[37] Since the disengagement agreement on the Egyptian front, there was less 'dependence on the Soviets'. Analysts noted a break in arms deliveries in mid-April, following a 'deterioration in relations' between Moscow and Cairo.[38]

Here again Sadat was walking a tightrope. Although he had announced a program to diversify Egypt's source of arms, the CIA assessed that neither Sadat nor the Soviets wanted an outright break in relations. Soviet arms and spare parts were still essential 'to maintain a credible military posture' in service of a final peace treaty.[39] The Agency also warned that Israel could 'take Egypt's continued military weakness as a cue to delay further Sinai negotiations' although they would be 'likely to reassess their position' if it became 'clear that the Soviets have agreed to deliver to Cairo previously contracted equipment without obtaining a political quid pro quo'.[40] In the more temperate climate of détente, Ambassador Adams noted that some of Sadat's 'closest advisors and also the Americans doubted the wisdom of going as far as he did' despite the overwhelming sense of 'personal disillusionment with the Russians'.[41]

The stolen files of KGB defector and archivist Vasili Mitrokhin demonstrate all too clearly the desperation with which the Soviets viewed their declining position in Egypt. The KGB devised elaborate forgeries intended to convince Sadat that Kissinger would double-cross him and specific instructions from Andropov to the First Chief Directorate (FCD) in April 1974 'to devise active measures to prevent any worsening in Soviet Arab relations'.[42] Declassifications from the CIA's in-house journal *Studies in Intelligence* on 'political forgeries in the Middle East' provide several examples of Soviet forgeries of American reports in Egypt as late as 1978.[43] According to the world's leading intelligence scholar, 'no other Third World leader inspired as much loathing in Moscow as Sadat'.[44] The conclusion reached by analysts that 'the Soviets distrust Sadat – for good reason' thus appears in hindsight to be something of an understatement.[45]

The Rabat Summit

The most concerning aspect of Sadat's foreign policy in the quest for peace with Israel was ultimately Egypt's relationship with the Arab world. The CIA noted that Syrian disengagement was actually more significant for President Sadat than Egypt's corollary agreement with Israel. In the interim he had been portrayed both by the Soviets and by 'radical' Arabs as a 'traitor' seeking to further his own and US interests 'at the expense of the Arab cause'.[46] At the same time, the Agency believed that 'Sadat served the Arab cause as no other Arab has by starting a war and then a negotiating process that has regained Arab territories. This gives him immeasurable strength against his opponents.'[47]

In October 1974, the Rabat summit called for the Palestinian Liberation Organisation (PLO) to replace Jordan as the legitimate representative for the Palestinians in future negotiations.

Scholars have argued that by caving into pressures to recognise the PLO, Sadat was purposefully excluding the Palestinian issue from the negotiations to encourage his American ally to focus on a second disengagement treaty.[48] The American intelligence community interpreted the move differently, reporting to policy-makers that the 'Rabat watershed' proved that 'the Arabs have the collective power to enforce their demands if they stick together' and that Sadat sought 'to inform Israel and the U.S. that he will not break ranks'.[49]

The Rabat summit was a powerful symbol of the challenge the Palestinian question had come to occupy in negotiations and the subtle transition of the Palestinians from a factor to an actor in this process. Sadat had always insisted that a lasting peace would mean 'some account be taken of the Palestinians' but it was by this point clear that the Palestinians would 'not be satisfied with merely being taken account of'. The intelligence community seems to have recognised this shift in power, observing that the PLO were now putting Arab rhetoric to the test.

The nascent political organisation continued to be used as a tool by the Arab states. If the intelligence community misunder-stood Sadat's spirit of solidarity towards the PLO, they accu-rately regarded Syrian support for the PLO's position as a means of limiting Egypt's freedom to negotiate unilaterally with Israel. Analysts thus recognised that the danger of the summit was subse-quent action by the US and Israel that ignored Syria.[50] Meanwhile Israel unashamedly made explicit its determination to break up this newfound solidarity. In an interview with *Ha'aretz* in Decem-ber 1974, Israeli Prime Minister Rabin publicly announced that Israel's goals were 'to separate Egypt from Syria, to delay negotia-tions until after the 1976 U.S. presidential elections, and to delay talks until the West was less dependent on Middle East oil'.[51] The CIA warned that 'Sinai remains the most promising single option open, but in the end, movement there without similar movement in Syria could be counter-productive'.[52] They recognised early on that whilst Sadat was bound by the remits of Arab unity for an 'overall' settlement, he wanted to maintain for Egypt the prospect of disengagement from Sinai. Analysts sensed the possibility and potential danger of a bilateral peace treaty as early as 1974.

Sinai II

By January 1975, analysts observed the hardening of positions. A familiar situation appeared to be developing whereby Israeli intransigence was goading Egypt to believe that the only way to break the stalemate was through military action. It was clear that Sadat's popularity was waning and not even another disengagement agreement was likely to appease his critics.

> A further agreement in the Sinai would bring additional respite, but it would not bring the same degree of satisfaction or the euphoria that accompanied last year's disengagement. The average Egyptian expected peace and economic recovery momentarily at that time; he has now come to doubt that either the Egyptian government or the U.S. intends to work for these ends. Popular discontent with Sadat, although temporarily relievable by another disengagement, is likely to continue simmering until both goals are achieved.[53]

With a notably critical tone, analysts reported Israeli frustration that they could not turn their military superiority into 'an effective counter' to the Arabs' financial and diplomatic power. They warned that Egyptians were 'running out of patience'. A real danger was that, 'if the Israelis convince themselves that an imminent Arab military threat exists, they would act first and worry about the U.S. later'.[54] Kissinger's fruitless shuttle diplomacy in February and March led to a firm public statement that Washington was prepared to enter a 'reassessment' of American relations with Israel.[55] Privately Kissinger wrote that 'Sadat is conceding more than I ever thought possible, but if he goes beyond a certain point he will be destroyed'.[56]

In March 1975, diplomats confirmed a deteriorating situation reminiscent of the build-up to previous Arab–Israeli wars. Washington was informed:

> Yesterday we heard an alarming amount of talk about pride and dignity from a leadership we have generally considered one prone to measure carefully the political and military factors inherent in so major a policy decision as resumption of hostilities . . . When the Syrians start talking about right being on their side, their obligation

to fight, of their pride and honor, and the desirability of martyrdom, I think we must take seriously the thesis that they are rapidly pushing themselves into a very dangerous psychological corner.[57]

On 5 June 1975, Sadat took the dramatic step of re-opening the Suez Canal. This was described by Ambassador Adams as 'the most solid evidence imaginable that Sadat intends no future war with Israel'.[58]

The JIC seemed unconvinced. A few weeks later the Committee assessed, 'It is difficult to predict when Sadat might decide he has no option but to return to war.' One secret source had reported that Sadat's initial reaction to the breakdown of the Kissinger talks was to order preparations to be made for an Arab attack on Israel around 20 May. The source also suggested that the prospect for renewed negotiations correlated with the arrangement of a meeting with President Ford in Salzburg. The JIC feared that, 'another point of despair could be reached quite quickly if a further attempt at a step in Sinai was thwarted by Israeli intransigence'.

> The breaking point of Arab patience could come after a few weeks if the Israelis remained intransigent . . . The timescale could possibly be much longer; it is even possible that Sadat or Asad will be able and willing to spin out diplomatic option long enough to see what the next American administration has to offer them but we doubt it.[59]

There was something of an underlying sympathy for Sadat in the Committee's reporting. Now seen to be a man of 'action', their presumption was that hostilities would inevitably resume; it was a question of when not if. Arab 'patience' was favourably contrasted to Israeli 'intransigence', providing a crucial insight into perceptions and discourse surrounding the Arab–Israeli conflict within the intelligence community. Though sympathetic, their language also suggests that the JIC were less optimistic as to the long-term success of Sadat's strategy than their American counterparts. Sadat or Asad 'might' be able to make a diplomatic gain but they were inclined to 'doubt it'. An attached supplement to the JIC report noted American frustration with Israel and the possible avenues through which the American government could induce them to be more forthcoming. The Committee were informed that military supplies had been delayed, cooperation on intelligence had been reduced, and cultural and scientific exchanges were cancelled. Although pro-Israeli sentiment in Congress limited certain actions, they warned that:

> the Israeli government may come to realise that the United States administration can put subtle pressures on them in a manner which Congress will find difficult to prevent: e.g. by the continued withholding of intelligence co-operation or assistance in vital areas of military development.[60]

The historical precedent of Sadat's behaviour before the 1973 war was ever-present in the minds of analysts. In July 1974, DCI Bill Colby had reminded Kissinger that President Sadat was 'a two track strategist' who followed a diplomatic course of action in 1973 even as he was preparing for war, and that the same was possible again, possibly 'within the next few weeks'.[61] Sadat was 'not likely again to risk a reputation for empty posturing'.[62] The State Department's INR considered the assessment, 'excessively pessimistic'.[63] American Ambassador Eilts agreed that despite intelligence reports of Egyptian military preparations in August 1975, 'while such military contingency planning may well have been ordered, it should not, rpt [sic] not be assumed that it will necessarily be implemented'.[64] Analysts were by now familiar with the strong association of diplomacy and warfare in the Arab world and furthermore, the gap between the 'declared' and the 'real'.

On 1 September 1975, a second Sinai disengagement treaty was finally signed, forcing Israeli withdrawal to the Sinai passes and the oil fields. Yet the most recent declassifications reveal the depths of Kissinger's despair as he reflected on the outcome of Sinai II. He concluded that the Israelis were

> clearly using this agreement not as another step towards peace but as a means of strengthening their position to resist efforts to achieve an overall settlement in the long run on any terms the Arabs might accept. This agreement grudgingly achieved will not do what step-by-step diplomacy was designed to achieve – increase confidence and provide stepping stones towards peace.[65]

Kissinger's efforts clearly did not bear the fruits that he sought.

Intelligence analysts demonstrated similar cynicism, with increasingly negative undertones about Israel and the prospect of Sadat's isolation. Michael Sterner later reflected that:

> you could not carry this slice-of-territory for slice-of-peace concept any further. The Sinai II agreement was a victory but it had its costs for American policy in the form of an ill-considered undertaking never to deal with the PLO which plagued our policy for the next ten years. [66]

The JIC correctly suggested that Sadat would find himself increasingly isolated if the Israelis expressed that Sinai agreement as their last concession rather than a step to a final settlement. They predicted as early as 1975 that 'there is a heightened risk of Sadat's assassination', noting the PLO as a possible perpetrator. [67]

In January 1976, an intelligence overview was conducted to examine inter-Arab dynamics in the wake of Sinai II. Here again, the cultural exceptionalism of Sadat's political behaviour remerged as a prominent theme. The intelligence community concluded that 'moderation in foreign policy . . . unemotional pragmatism that permits tactical compromise in pursuit of long range strategic interests . . . is a fragile commodity in the Arab world and it must be nurtured if it is to be given permanency'. Analysts put the onus of responsibility on Israel and the West to deliver the rewards of this newfound approach. Such 'moderation' and 'unemotional pragmatism' would be 'institutionalised only if the Arabs see that pragmatism and flexibility are demonstrably productive policies and *only Israel and with it the U.S. can make this demonstration*'.[68] They explained that:

> The simple fact of being 'an Arab' exerts a subtle and to the Western mind an often unfathomable, psychological pressure for solidarity with other Arabs that no amount of domestic stability or political sophistication is ever likely to alter completely . . . pragmatism and the give and take of negotiations are still unfamiliar concepts to the Arabs and there remains a strong emotional resistance to making concessions to Israel. This has lately been evidenced by the Syrians' and the Palestinians' horrified reaction to Egypt's concessions in the Sinai agreement and by Egypt's own insistence that it in fact made no concessions.[69]

Although inclined towards this more 'Western' political culture, analysts questioned whether Sadat would be able to escape fully the implications of his 'Arabness'. They estimated that the Arabs were militarily, economically and emotionally incapable of making peace or war with Israel individually and that Sadat himself was 'emotionally bound' to the Arab cause. Moreover it was 'a matter of public shame and considerable political risk to stray too far from the fold'.[70] Analysts seemed to take Sadat at his word that he would not, indeed *could not*, settle for a separate peace.[71]

The Palestinian problem remained the primary obstacle to a peace settlement. The JIC reported 'evidence that more "moderate" groups within the PLO are attempting to launch operations outside the Middle East. The prospect is therefore for a considerable increase in terrorist activity.' They warned that 'Sadat will himself be an obvious target for assassination'.[72]

At the same time, from the limited material that has thus far been declassified, it appears as if the Palestinian issue was not taken seriously by analysts. In a rather dismissive assessment, shot through with Orientalist undertones, they described how the

> continuing land hunger of a group of unsophisticated peasants, the strong self-generating sense of bitterness, the shock of loss and sense of betrayal and the enduring frustration at their inability to do anything about it enforced and reinforced impulses towards emotionalism and scapegoating not merely among the Palestinians but among Arabs in general.[73]

Analysts concluded:

> given their traditional powerlessness, the Arabs of Israel are not likely to count as much of a factor in the formulation of Arab or Israeli policies or in an Arab-Israeli dispute itself. Other than as subjects of propaganda proving their wretched fate or happy lot, most are likely to remain passive observers.[74]

Interest in a secular democratic Palestine was 'further vitiated by the extreme vagueness, equivocations and tailoring for specific audiences which PLO leaders engage in when talking about the matter'.[75] Their analysis of the Palestinians as passive, subjective and rhetorical reveals many of the pejorative stereotypes associated with 'the Arab' explored earlier. Harold Saunders recalled a meeting with

> One of the West Bank leaders [who] was trying to agree with my argument, but all the others were talking about why it couldn't be done. At the end of the evening, that West Banker threw up his hands and said that the Palestinians were all sheep destined to follow and not to lead. He was very frustrated by the conversation.[76]

Neither had the Arab governments proved more effective. Analysts noted that the Arab states 'never acted effectively, unselfishly or in unison' and tended to use the Palestinians to serve their own interests.[77] They cited future Egyptian President Husni Mubarak's description of the Palestinians as 'traditional trouble makers', displaying little sympathy for their cause.[78] At the same time they recognised that no Arab country wants to appear to be turning its back on the Palestinians. Syria's 'emotional commitment' to the Palestinian problem was regarded by analysts as greater than that of Egypt. 'By allying itself with the Palestinians, Syria had guaranteed the purity of its Arab credentials.'[79] Sadat's forthcoming trip to Jerusalem would be criticised for doing just the opposite.

Journey to Jerusalem

This was surely the most contentious move of Sadat's political career. Scholars have long since debated whether it signified a determined strategy to carve out a separate Egyptian–Israeli peace, noting for example that Sadat mentioned the prospect of a separate peace to President Carter early that year. Stein writes that 'the administration, which had its laser beam aimed at getting to Geneva at virtually any cost, did not see Sadat's Arab context and his frustration. Nor did they understand where he was headed.'[80] Others suggest that Sadat did not go to Jerusalem for a separate peace, arguing that both his public and private declarations indicated his commitment to a comprehensive settlement.[81] Sadat himself always advanced the thesis that the decision was made to break a psychological barrier that he felt was impeding peace.

Figure 10.1 President Sadat and President Carter in the White House, 1977. US NARA Carter Presidential Library, Atlanta.

Philip Adams's successor as British ambassador to Egypt was Sir William Morris. Willie Morris was a somewhat 'grumpy looking' but seasoned Arabist who had previously served in Saudi Arabia.[82] Though not as enamoured with Sadat as Adams, he would later describe Sadat's journey to Jerusalem as 'the most courageous and constructive act of my time here – perhaps of the past thirty years in the Middle East'.[83] At the time, he noted 'much pride in the applause and renown the President has won in the outside world, and even among intellectuals normally antipathetic to him, there is grudging acknowledgement of his courage'. Embellished with the native Orientalism that was commonly embedded within such diplomatic despatches, Morris gave as evidence of this view a quote from an eminent Egyptian author: 'The grand old man of Egyptian letters, Tewfiq al Hakim, has written in *Al Ahram* that the President's gesture was an indication that the Arabs are growing up.'[84] Morris did not explicitly indicate whether he agreed with the Egyptian intellectual's infantilising of the Arabs but neither did he express disagreement.

Morris was evidently more cynical about Sadat than his predecessor. There was a notable tinge of anxiety to his diplomatic reporting at times. He described Sadat's political style as 'that of a trapeze artist, making impossible and spectacular leaps that leave everyone breathless, and could be fatal if misjudged'. Of the trip to Jerusalem, he wrote that, 'this latest leap is as unexpected and bold and dangerous as any yet. A serious danger must be a fanatic's bullet.'[85] Whilst it was 'evident' that the move had forced Prime Minister Begin and the Israeli government to think about the real issues, Morris questioned whether they would offer 'commensurate concessions'.[86]

Alongside scepticism about what the move would achieve, assessments of the historic Jerusalem visit evoked fears that the move was primarily a 'distraction' from domestic problems. In a despatch on the Jerusalem initiative Morris noted that 1977 had begun badly with bread riots leading to upheaval on the streets not seen since 1952. Thus Sadat 'could ill afford a major setback in his policy on the Middle East problem'.[87] But he also placed the 'bold initiative' in the context of Sadat's 'temperament' and 'political style which brought him past success', inclining him to the 'traumatic and risky course'.[88] He observed,

> With the unfolding of events, however, this practical motive has grown into a more elevated conception – a vision of himself as the apostle of peace, through whose supreme effort, and if necessary through sacrifice of himself, the course of 30 years' history will be dramatically changed, and swords will be beaten into ploughshares. A note of exaltation – grandiloquence, if you like has come into his language. [89]

The self-proclaimed image of Sadat as strategic pragmatist was increasingly being displaced by the spectre of a more messianic quasi-spiritual figure. But analysts did not seem entirely convinced about the motivations or outcome of the move. Even those most impressed by Sadat's trip to Jerusalem observed 'the theatrical element in his nature' which 'clearly responded to the extravagance of the plot'. Morris added with a hint of mischief that, 'Mrs Meir is reported to have accorded him an Oscar'.

Israel's response was to be critical. Though Sadat and Begin were formally credited with a Nobel Peace Prize the following year, American intelligence was suspicious that the Israeli leadership would play for time to let 'passions subside in Israel' while they devised 'a strategy and tactics for dealing with Sadat's gambit'.[90] Israeli reticence presented evident dangers to Sadat. Morris reported to Whitehall that 'the risk that President Sadat might be assassinated on his return to Egypt was on everyone's mind'. Whilst the 'hero-actor' had gained prestige and created new possibilities, there was also a 'debit side'. In Egypt, President Sadat's popularity rested on the illusion that peace was now inevitable: 'there could be a backlash if the illusion is destroyed, and he is unwilling to embark upon the dangerous course of a separate peace'. Morris could see the contradictory position in which Sadat had placed himself. The president 'had throughout been insistent and explicit in repudiating the motive of seeking a separate peace for Egypt'.[91] The CIA clearly established that whatever Sadat's professions, he had now clearly and irrevocably isolated himself from his Arab partners, most poignantly Syria's Asad. For the latter to align with Egypt now 'would demand more in the way of lost face than Asad is ever likely to concede and more in terms of concessions to Israel than he is probably prepared or politically able to give'.[92] The inter-Arab implications of the move were grave.

Analysts seemed increasingly torn by the question of a separate peace that seemed to be on the table. On the one hand it was an indication of Western rational maturity to pursue one's national interests at the expense of calls for an abstract and emotional Arab solidarity. At the same time an isolated Egypt was essentially an Egypt disempowered. In 1978, reflecting on the events of the past year Morris wrote that 'there is some mystery why Sadat failed to press harder at Camp David for "linkage" between the agreements'.[93] In November 1978, the Baghdad Summit announced the suspension of Egypt's membership of the Arab League, moving the League's headquarters from its historic position in Cairo, and declared a boycott on Egyptian products. Even the Americans had started to doubt their ability to negotiate alongside Sadat effectively. An American memorandum during the final stages of the

Camp David peace negotiations reveals the private frustration with Sadat's less appealing diplomatic qualities:

> We do not have a satisfactory political understanding with Sadat as we enter a crucial phase of the negotiations. The reason, in my view, is that he has little idea of how to proceed and counts on us to bail him out. His impatience with details is becoming a real problem, as is his reluctance to engage in sustained negotiations.[94]

The two-pronged 1979 peace treaty eventually signed was a far cry from the comprehensive peace both Carter and Sadat had sought. Egypt's official relations with seventeen Arab countries were severed and only half of Sinai had yet been recovered. Before departing from Cairo, Sir Willie Morris blamed the West for 'attaching greater importance to U.S. and Israeli political realities than to those of the Arab world. Sadat was praised, but asked for further concessions, which, reluctantly, he made.' The result was Egypt's complete isolation from the region it had once led.[95]

Domestic Disillusion, Bread Riots and the Threat from the Religious Right

Sadat always portrayed his desire for peace as driven by a patriotic quest for domestic reconstruction.[96] *Infitah* sought to attract foreign investment to rebuild a flailing economy whereas the recovery of the Sinai oil fields and the reopening of the Suez Canal bolstered Egypt's balance of payments.[97] Yet borrowing also increased dramatically – by 1976 the combination of imports and government subsidies led to a huge deficit in the Egyptian treasury. Capital accumulation failed to create reinvestment in Egypt's productive capacity and much of the gains were siphoned away to foreign bank accounts.[98]

Analysts described the economy as the 'Achilles heel' of Sadat's rule. Even Ambassador Adams, who relayed some of the most positive images of Sadat both privately and publicly, wrote that the economy was 'virtually back in the "no war no peace" situation of 18 months ago . . . There has been too much ballyhoo and not enough sound planning.' Inflation had served to make the poor poorer and highlighted the growing disparity between their deteriorating standard of living and the increasingly open display of wealth by those with money.[99] In the autumn of 1974, workers began to protest and on 1 January 1975 over 1,000 Helwan steel mill workers demonstrated against the rising cost of living and clashed with police. Demonstrators chanted, 'Where is our breakfast, oh hero of the crossing and where is Nasser?'[100]

Economic pressures became particularly acute after the Sinai II disengagement treaty. Expectations of immediate economic benefits from the agreement failed to materialise. The CIA were forced to concede that 'things were in fact better economically before Sadat came along'. They reported corruption, widening disparity between the rich and the poor, growing food lines, the proliferation of beggars and a noticeable drop in the standard of living of average Egyptians. There was for the first time 'a new class of conspicuously wealthy individuals'.[101] President Ford was briefed that 'lower class alienation was a fact of life in the days of Farouk and the monarchy, but is a new factor in republican Egypt'.[102] It was not an impressive balance sheet.

1n 1976, Willie Morris reported his first impressions of Sadat's Egypt back to Whitehall. He agreed that the 'serious dangers' to the regime were on the economic and social side:

> [The] brutal truth is that the new economic policy – the 'opening' of the economy to foreign investment in a liberalised and revitalised private sector, the expected inflow of Western technology and Arab oil billions for massive reconstruction and development – has so far produced little more than increased prosperity for a very limited group, inflation and a mounting balance of payments problem.[103]

The editor of *Al Ahram al-Iqtisadi* (the economic journal of the daily newspaper) wrote sarcastically in 1976:

> With every step I take my eyes are dazzled by the glitter of the open door policy. I need only to walk into any grocery store to breathe a sigh of relief and to thank God that he has compensated us so well for the long period of frustration and deprivation.

He was talking about the masses of unaffordable imported goods that crowded Egyptian products off the shelves.[104]

The sense of excess and corruption associated with the 'new economic policy' was aptly illustrated in a humorous anecdote relayed by the Saudi ambassador to his British counterpart. Rumours were abounding that shortages of chicken and milk could be explained by the fact that they were the main food supply for the silver fox farm of Sayed Marei (speaker of the People's Assembly and close friend of Sadat's). Diplomats wrote incredulously: 'When you said it would take a lot of silver foxes to affect the chicken supply and that anyway silver foxes belonged in the cold north and could not live in Egypt, the answer was: "but the farm is air-conditioned."'[105]

These illustrations of official decadence amongst the political elite only prompted yet more comparisons with Nasser:

> For all his faults Nasser represented for the majority of Egyptians an irreplaceable hero: he was the first Egyptian born leader of modern times to put Egypt on the map and to champion the cause of the working class against the rich. For many people the failures of his later years never obscured the euphoria engendered by his early successes. The fellahin, factory workers, artisans and small shopkeepers indentified with him to the end. Lacking Nasser's charisma, Sadat has been forced to follow a different path. Less able to appeal directly to his people's hearts, he has concentrated on their religious and social traditions, on their minds (in the case of the educated middle class) and on their more material interests, perceiving that most Egyptians were ready – indeed anxious – for a quiet spell after the excitements of Nasser's rule. [106]

It was becoming increasingly clear that Sadat's open-door economic policy was based more on political rather than economic calculations. Morris observed that his 'public pronouncements on economic matters are often almost puerile and an embarrassment to his colleagues, a result to which lack of interest and lack of understanding contribute'.[107] As erstwhile Minister of Planning Muhammad Mahmud al-Imam put it, 'Sadat had no clear economic strategy. He just begged for money; and this offered no solution to the structural problem. He didn't say, "Egyptians, sit down and build your own country!"'[108]

In January 1977, Sadat's economic and social failures manifested themselves most visibly in riots that marked the worst upheaval since the fall of the monarchy in 1952. An earlier announcement that cuts in government subsidies (required for IMF aid) would double the price of staples such as bread, flour, tea, sugar and gas culminated in a dramatic backlash against symbols of the privileged class empowered by Sadat's neoliberal reforms. Analysts criticised the government for failing 'to prepare the ground or cushion the blow'.[109] A Canadian delegation to NATO blamed the 'haphazard and slipshod implementation of economic liberalisation policies' for the 'serious dislocation'. They noted that economic grievances had been eroding Sadat's popularity for some time, and put the riots down to Sadat's 'over-preoccupation' with his role as international statesman and 'neglect of careful supervision of domestic economic management ... at his own peril'.[110] Presciently foreshadowing Egypt's January revolution thirty-four years later, the CIA suggested that, 'if widespread violence were to resume the danger would exist that the military leadership might move against Sadat in the belief that this was the only way to restore order'.[111]

Reflecting on the riots, Morris wrote,

> I think the disturbances will take their place with the Ali-Sabri affair of 1971, the expulsion of Soviet military personnel in 1972, the October War, and the Second Sinai agreement as milestones in the life of the Sadat regime: with an important difference. The previous milestones marked stages in the establishment of President Sadat's dominance of Egypt and predominant influence on the Arab scene; this one marks a set-back – how major remains to be seen. In the previous events, he was the Daring Not-So-Young Man on the Flying Trapeze taking our breath away, but landing on his feet; this time he has come a cropper, which is apt to be more serious for a trapeze artist than for an ordinary pedestrian who takes a tumble.[112]

He warned, 'we must now believe that the Pharonic role and personality cult have gone dangerously far towards cutting him off', although he cautioned against underestimating Sadat again: 'I do not believe his right hand has lost his cunning'.[113]

This performance metaphor increasingly used to describe Sadat's foreign exploits became equally applicable to his domestic policy. Morris was confident that Sadat, 'continuing on his show business way, displays no signs of worry about his position' despite Egypt's impending economic collapse.[114] Other diplomats reinforced the message of the Egyptian government in 'show business (or even three ring circus) terms'. There was growing disillusionment with 'the permanent circus of foreign travel and domestic publicity stunts' and sparse support outside of government for how the country was being managed.[115]

There was no doubt that the riots had 'shaken' Sadat and 'left their mark' on his credibility and prestige. As Morris put it, 'the show goes on; but there have been no spectacular and successful leaps to demonstrate that the technical mastery is still there and restore the image to what it was'.[116] The ambassador described in detail the portrait of President Sadat that was being increasingly prevalent in popular Western media. It was

> that of an amiable, garrulous buffoon, living increasingly in a private fantasy world, detached from the realities of Egyptian economics and public opinion, and from the politics of the Arab-Israeli problem. (It is no accident that Western journalists who call on Hassanein Heikal tend to form this sort of judgement.) There is enough truth in the caricature to cause discomfort; *there is some reassurance, however, in recalling that much of this new Sadat is an old Sadat,* he was written off as a lightweight before he became President; he has always been garrulous; in 1972 he got himself as far out on a limb with his 'year of decision' as he is now with a 'comprehensive settlement at Geneva in 1977 or 1978'; all of his major decisions on relations with the Russians (e.g. the expulsion of the Soviet advisers) and relying on the Americans (e.g. the Second Sinai Agreement) have involved overruling the misgivings of his advisers; so have some major decisions on domestic issues (e.g. allowing political parties).[117]

By the time of Sadat's assassination, even the Americans seemed to be perturbed by his 'unusual flair for the dramatic'. As a result of being 'supremely self-confident', he rarely consulted with others. The CIA felt that the Egyptian President had 'weathered remarkably well the controversy generated' by the peace treaty, but that 'risking isolation from reality', Sadat had 'surrounded himself with those who are reluctant to report unpleasant developments frankly'.[118] Among such developments was most evidently the growing strength of the religious right.

The first explicit signs of this threat in fact emerged in April 1974 with an attack on the Military Technical College in the wealthy Heliopolis district of Cairo. It was the first attempt to overthrow the Egyptian government in the quest to establish an Islamic State.[119] In June, ninety people were detained for distributing pamphlets calling for a return to rule by an Islamic caliph.[120] In 1975, analysts noted the threat of 'Semi-lunatic groups', probably funded by General Qaddafi of Libya, warning that 'Sadat must fear the unexpected – the madman's bullet or the secret conspiracy of fanatics'.[121] Since 1974, diplomats had observed that rapes and muggings, 'hitherto unknown – or at least unnoticed – in Egypt are now becoming almost daily occurrences and Egyptians are commenting with apprehension on what seems to be a new and unprecedented aggressiveness in their fellow countrymen'.[122]

In May 1976, British diplomats reflected on the revival of the Muslim Brotherhood as a political and religious force. They estimated that more Western influence had probably stimulated religious conservatism in Egypt, identifying also the impact of Saudi influence in Egypt and a more liberal attitude towards the religious right to offset leftist sentiments.[123] The following year extremist group *Takfir Wal Haijra* kidnapped a government official and killed him. Foreshowing later profiling efforts, analysts noted 'that receptivity to the fundamentalist version of Islam is particularly strong among urban, middle and lower middle classes rather than among the uneducated rural masses'.[124] The recourse to a more hard-line Islamism in Egypt appeared to be less a response to outright poverty than to dashed expectations.

In 1979, the Iranian revolution provoked further discussion about Sadat's relationship to Islam and the threat it posed to his regime. Despite Sadat's self-proclaimed position as '*al-rais al-mu'min*' (the believer president), Arabist Mark Allen, who was likely the SIS representative in Cairo under diplomatic cover at the time, reflected on the dilemma Sadat faced. He wrote:

310

The fundamentalists say that faith is the function of the spirit and Islam its outward expression in Man's everyday life in community. Islam is an avowedly communal religion and they argue that to make it a private or interior matter of conscience is to diminish it . . . the constitution of the Muslim community is given in the Koran and the Sunnah. If Muslims do not follow these divine injunctions, in a basic way they cease to be Muslims.

He went on to suggest that 'this argument was hard to counter in Islamic terms. Any appeal to common sense or practicality is seen as a denial of the universal and transcendent truth of the Koran.' According to Allen, Sadat was 'evidently sensitive to this theological problem' but was 'stuck for arguments with which to counter the fundamentalists on the ground which they choose for their attack'.[125] The CIA highlighted that the Shah had faced similar criticism. 'The Shah did not act like a Muslim, therefore he was not a Muslim, and his insistence to the contrary was sheer hypocrisy.'[126] Sadat's own approach, Allen wrote,

that it is the spirit and not the letter which counts, and his emphasis on love, is congenial to the European mind. But it makes little sense to people who increasingly rely on religious tradition as an anchor in time of change and economic stress. The fundamentalists, theology aside, offer a vision of a just (i.e. successful) society which is very attractive to thoss [sic] who doubt they will benefit from the economic free-for-all which they guess President Sadat has in mind.[127]

As his assassins criticised, even Sadat's interpretation of Islam was pragmatic and 'Western'. Roy Atherton, who succeeded Herman Eilts in 1979 as American ambassador to Cairo, recalled the reluctance with which Sadat faced the threats to his life. He remembers that

we had a good intelligence exchange between our intelligence people and the Egyptian intelligence people. The Egyptian intelligence and security people were in despair because Sadat really did not take kindly to be told that he had to be on his guard from the security point of view.[128]

Though the tactical details of Sadat's assassination were unknown, the most recently declassified documents clearly show that 'strategically' analysts recognised the danger of the Islamic right to Sadat's flailing regime.[129]

* * *

Upon his arrival at the British embassy in 1976, Willie Morris reported his personal impression of Sadat back to Whitehall:

> His personality still mystifies me . . . he has given the impression of a warm, engaging, mellow and rather simple personality, relaxed and confident – altogether too relaxed and confident considering the problems that face him – but without any philosophical depth or detailed grasp of economic questions: he paints with a very broad brush . . . He seems to be unaware of or unconcerned about, any ill effects that his and his family's rather monarchical lifestyle, contrasting so much with the ostentatious austerity of Nasser may have on his position. He can act and react emotionally – calculation seems sometimes to be subordinated to emotion.[130]

This naive, childlike portrayal of Sadat is strikingly reminiscent of some of the more negative images of Sadat before 1973. It is clear that the evolution of Sadat's domestic and foreign policy appeared increasingly unimpressive to the Anglo-American political and intelligence community, although the Americans were less readily disillusioned with their new Arab ally. True to their assessments of Egypt for several decades, for the most part their reporting of Sadat combined nuanced and astute judgements with a more simplistic recourse to Orientalist lenses on occasion.

Analysts were quickly aware of the tensions between a *realpolitik* and potentially bilateral approach to peace versus Egypt's obligations towards 'Arab solidarity' and a comprehensive settlement. If policymakers such as Kissinger set aside the risks inherent in a bilateral peace, the same cannot be said for political and intelligence analysts, although the records declassified so far suggest that they underestimated Sadat's ability and willingness to break from the fold.

Initially there appeared to be a clear drive between Sadat's drive for peace and the quest for domestic reform. By the end of the presidency, analysts were resigned to a cynical view, more pronounced in Britain, that regarded much of Sadat's foreign policy as a distraction from his domestic failures.

Although the documents on Sadat's assassination have not yet been declassified, the records immediately preceding it reveal a much less favourable picture of the West's most important Arab ally than suggested in the extant historiography. In many ways analysts' perceptions reverted to the more disparaging assessments of Sadat that had existed before the war. The Sadat of 'strategy' and 'flexibility' and 'pragmatism' came increasingly to be seen as an 'erratic' and 'inconsistent' showman, 'performing' for the international stage at the expense of the wellbeing of his domestic constituency. Despite all of Sadat's efforts to the contrary, the mythological figure of Nasser was never entirely dispelled and his image recurred frequently as a point of comparison. Nowhere was the comparison starker than at Sadat's funeral. The event was attended by a record number of foreign dignitaries but ordinary Egyptians stayed resolutely in their homes. One American diplomat stationed in Alexandria at the time cynically speculated that 'one of the reasons why there were not a lot of demonstrations, wailing and beating of breasts . . . was because it was a holiday. The people did not want to be done out of their holiday.'[131]

Interestingly, Morris's first impressions of Sadat's successor, Husni Mubarak, mirrored early impressions of Sadat, although this time British diplomats seemed more alert to the possibility of being surprised. Mubarak, Morris wrote in 1977, 'remains unimpressive'.

> There is something apt about the description of him invented by the January demonstrations – '*La vache qui rit*'. He is virtually always at the President's side but rarely says anything . . . No one sees him as a suitable future president – which is not to say that he never will be, or that, if he does succeed, he will not surprise us; but if he does the talent will have been much more deeply buried than in Sadat's case.[132]

It remains for future scholarly research to reveal whether Western assessments of Mubarak were as dominated by comparisons with Sadat as those of Sadat were dominated by Nasser. Hints in the records so far suggest that Sadat never quite matched the power of his predecessor's hold over collective memory at home or abroad.

Notes

1. Interview with Alfred Atherton, summer of 1990. Available at <http://adst.org/wp-content/uploads/2012/09/Egypt.pdf>, p. 410 (last accessed 1 March 2017). Atherton was the American ambassador to Egypt from 1979 to 1983.
2. H. Kissinger, *Years of Upheaval* (Boston: Little, Brown and Co., 1982), p. 647.
3. Jimmy Carter, quoted in I. Karawan, 'Sadat and the Egyptian-Israeli peace revisited', *International Journal of Middle East Studies*, 26: 2, 1994, p. 249.
4. Ibid., quoting Ismail Fahmy.
5. Ibid.
6. See, for example: I. Fahmy, *Negotiating for Peace in the Middle East* (London: Croom Helm, 1983); M. I. Kamel, *The Camp David Accords* (London: Routledge and Kegan Paul, 1986); S. Shazly, *The Crossing of the Suez* (San Francisco, CA: American Mideast Research, 1980); M. Gamasy, *Mudhakirrat Al-Gamassi: Harb Uktubur 1973* (Cairo: Al Hayat al 'Ammat l-il-Kuttab, 1998); S. Sharaf, *Sanawat Wa-Ayyam Ma'a Jamal 'Abd al-Nasir: Shahadat Sami Sharaf* (Cairo: Dar al-Fursan lil-Nashr, 2005–7). For an Arab defence of Sadat see M. Fawzi, *Al-Sadat: Al-Za'īm Al-Muftará 'Alayh* (Cairo: Dar al-Nashr Hatyīh, 1995). Most Western historiography emphasises primarily Sadat's peace initiative. See, for example: J. Finklestone, *Anwar Sadat: Visionary who Dared* (London: Frank Cass, 1996) and K. Stein, *Heroic Diplomacy: Sadat, Kissinger, Carter, Begin and the Quest for Peace in the Middle East* (London: Routledge, 1999). Exploring also his domestic policies, K. J. Beattie, *Egypt During the Sadat Years* (New York: Palgrave, 2000), provides a more comprehensive and balanced assessment.
7. While this chapter presents the most original research of the book utilising documents that have only been released in very recent years, these documents are also by virtue of their recent nature, the most heavily redacted or indeed retained. In comparison to numerous JIC reports on Egypt in the 1960s, thus far the national archives have made available a mere handful of JIC reports on Egypt for the period after 1973. No doubt this also reflects Egypt's transition from an adversary to an ally in the eyes of the Committee. Whilst diplomatic reports and 2008 declassifications from the Ford Presidential Library have compensated for this dearth in JIC material, the analysis which follows is particularly subject to the disclaimer

(all too familiar in the field of intelligence studies) that further declassifications will undoubtedly refine the conclusions which follow.

8. Interview with Alfred Atherton, summer of 1990. Available at <http://adst.org/wp-content/uploads/2012/09/Egypt.pdf>, p. 338 (last accessed 1 March 2017).

9. CIA Briefing Book on Egypt for Secretary Simon and Assistant Secretary Designate Parksy, 5 July 1974, CREST, NARA II: 'His inability to match Nasir's flair or to reverse Nasir's defeats, despite persistent promises to do so, made him a subject for jokes even among those who had not been enamoured of his predecessor.'

10. Ibid.

11. Diplomatic report no. 125/74 from Ambassador Adams to FCO, 'The Fourth Arab-Israeli War: political results', 16 January 1974, TNA, FCO 93/561.

12. See P. Adams, 'Sadat's Egypt', *Bulletin (British Society for Middle Eastern Studies)*, 3: 2, 1976, pp. 73–8. His successors William Morris and Michael Weir were considerably more reserved in their judgements of Sadat.

13. Despatch from Ambassador Adams in Cairo to FCO, 'Annual review for 1973', 23 January 1974, TNA, FCO 93/378.

14. Diplomatic report no. 125/74 from Ambassador Adams in Cairo to FCO, 'The Fourth Arab-Israeli War: political results', 16 January 1974, TNA, FCO 93/561.

15. F. Ajami, The *Arab Predicament: Arab Political Thought and Practice Since 1967* (New York: Cambridge University Press, 1992), p. 52.

16. JIC memorandum (74) 35, 'The Arab/Israel situation: dangers of deterioration', 15 November 1974, TNA, CAB 186/18: 'on a rational analysis we must conclude that the Arabs will find the financial weapon too difficult and risky to use . . . we must however make some allowance for the possibility of irrational Arab action in an emotive situation'.

17. Diplomatic report no. 125/74 from Ambassador Adams in Cairo to FCO, 'The Fourth Arab-Israeli War: political results', 16 January 1974, TNA, FCO 93/561.

18. Memorandum from Faber to Craig, 'Wielders of power in Egypt', 27 February 1974, TNA, FCO 93/79.

19. CIA Briefing Book on Egypt for Secretary Simon and Assistant Secretary Designate Parksy, 5 July 1974, CREST, NARA II.

20. Intelligence memorandum, 'The mood in Egypt', 3 June 1974, CREST, NARA II.

21. CIA Briefing Book on Egypt for Secretary Simon and Assistant Secretary Designate Parksy, 5 July 1974, CREST, NARA II.

22. CIA memorandum, 'A coming of age: the foreign policy of Anwar el Sadat', 9 April 1975, CREST, NARA II. The memorandum explained, 'like most revolutionaries he [Nasser] was unwilling to adapt his policies and concepts to changing circumstances around him ... unable to view the interests of the outside world except in terms of Egypt's interests, and more particularly in terms of his narrower vision of himself'.

23. Ibid.

24. This idea has received some scholarly attention. See R. Cohen, *Culture and Conflict in Egyptian-Israeli Relations: A Dialogue of the Deaf* (Bloomington, IN: Indiana University Press, 1990). In an overly culturally deterministic analysis Cohen suggests that Israeli and Egyptian cultures are somehow designed to misunderstand one another.

25. It is notable that the date and subject matter of this document correlates with a similar document produced by the British and discussed in Chapter 1. See memorandum from Balfour Paul in British Embassy Amman to Craig in FCO, 27 August 1973, TNA, FCO 93/82.

26. Memorandum from Sterner to Sisco, 'The Arab view of negotiations and agreements', 7 August 1973, File Political Affairs and Arab Relations, Box 2042, Subject Numeric Files 1970-73, Political and Defense, Record Group 59, General Records of the State Department, NARA II.

27. W. Quandt, *Decade of Decisions: American Policy Towards the Arab-Israeli Conflict, 1967–1976* (Berkeley, CA: University of California Press, 1977), p. 125.

28. Memorandum of conversation in Jerusalem, 10 March 1975. File March 7-22, 1975 Kissinger Trip, vol. I (4), Middle East Memcons and Reports, Box 3, National Security Adviser Kissinger Reports on USSR, China and Middle East discussions, Gerald R. Ford Presidential Library (hereafter GRFL).

29. D. Martin, 'Hermann F. Eilts, adviser to Kissinger on Mideast, dies', *New York Times*, 20 October 2006. Available at <http://www.nytimes.com/2006/10/20/obituaries/20eilts.html?_r=0> (last accessed 1 March 2017)

30. Telegram from USINT (Eilts) to Secretary of State, 'Call on Vice President Hussein Shafei', 4 December 1973, File Arab Republic of Egypt Nov 1973–Dec 31 1973, Country Files- Middle East, National Security Council Files, Box 639, Nixon Presidential Materials Staff, NARA II.

31. Interview with Harold Saunders, 24 November 1993. Available at <http://www.adst.org/OH%20TOCs/Saunders,%20Harold%20H. toc.pdf>, p. 89 (last accessed 1 March 2017).
32. Interview with Herman Eilts, 12 August 1988. Available at <http://adst. org/wp-content/uploads/2012/09/Egypt.pdf>, p. 584 (last accessed 1 March 2017).
33. Intelligence memorandum, 'The mood in Egypt', 3 June 1974, CREST, NARA II.
34. Ibid.
35. Ibid. Analysts wrote, 'there is presently a mood almost of euphoria in Egypt that is dangerous simply for its intensity and the high expectations it has created'.
36. Ibid: 'Egyptians are a warm people, bourgeois in outlook, with a sense of humor and an expectation that foreigners in their country will treat them as equals.'
37. JIC memorandum (74) 17, 'The Soviet threat', 6 May 1974, TNA, CAB 186/18.
38. CIA Briefing Book on Egypt for Secretary Simon and Assistant Secretary Designate Parksy, 5 July 1974, CREST, NARA II.
39. CIA Briefing Book on Egypt for Secretary Simon and Assistant Secretary Designate Parksy, 5 July 1974, CREST, NARA II.
40. Memorandum by the CIA's Directorate of Intelligence, OCI no. 0407/75, 'Prospects in the Middle East', 7 January 1975, CREST, NARA II.
41. Despatch from Ambassador Morris in Cairo to FCO, 'Egypt: Annual Review for 1975', 12 January 1976, TNA, FCO 93/846. This is a point that requires further research but on the face of it analysts do not seem to have endorsed the notion suggested by recent scholarship that the West encouraged a bilateral Egyptian–Israeli agreement to exclude Soviet influence from the region. See, for example, R. Khalidi, *Sowing Crisis: The Cold War and American Dominance in the Middle East* (Boston, MA: Beacon Press, 2009), pp. 132–4.
42. C. Andrew and V. Mitrokhin, *The KGB and the World: Mitrokhin Archive II* (London: Penguin, 2006), p. 167.
43. D. Crown, 'Political forgeries in the Middle East', *Studies in Intelligence*, 22: 1, 1978, CREST, NARA II.
44. Andrew and Mitrokhin, *Mitrokhin Archive II*, p. 167.
45. Memorandum from Oakley to Secretary Kissinger 'Egyptian/Soviet relations', 1 February 1975, File Egypt (2), Country File: Cyprus-State Department Telegrams To SECSTATE-EXDIS, Box 3, Presidential Country Files for the Middle East and South Asia, General Ford Papers, GRFL.

46. Intelligence memorandum, 'The mood in Egypt', 3 June 1974, CREST, NARA II.
47. Ibid. This report also made the interesting observations that Foreign Minister 'Fahmi's air of informality and his "Western" insensitivity to the Arab sense of decorum grate on Arab leaders'.
48. K. Stein, *Heroic Diplomacy: Sadat, Kissinger, Carter, Begin and the Quest for Peace in the Middle East* (London: Routledge, 1999), p. 171.
49. Intelligence memorandum, 'The Rabat watershed', 27 November 1974. File Peace negotiations chronological, 27 November 1974 – 8 January 1975, Declassified Documents: Documents from the National Security Adviser: NSC Middle East and South Asian Affairs Staff Files (December 2008 Opening) Box 9, Ford Library Project File of Documents declassified through the Remote Archive Capture (RAC) Program: Photocopies 1969-1977, GRFL.
50. Ibid.
51. Stein, *Heroic Diplomacy*, p. 174.
52. Memorandum by CIA's Directorate of Intelligence, 'Implications of the Arab summit', 3 November 1974, CREST, NARA II.
53. Memorandum by the CIA's Directorate of Intelligence, OCI no. 0407/75, 'Prospects in the Middle East', 7 January 1975, CREST, NARA II.
54. Ibid.
55. Stein, *Heroic Diplomacy*, p. 176.
56. Memorandum from Scowcroft to the President relaying a report by Secretary Kisinger, 18 March 1975. File March 7-22, 1975- Kissinger's Trip- vol. II (3) Middle East Memcons and Reports: March 7-22, 1975, Kissinger Trip vol. I (1) Box 3, National Security Adviser Kissinger Reports on USSR, China, and Middle East Discussions, GRFL.
57. Telegram from Murphy in Damascus to the Secretary, 'Your March 9 Meeting with Asad', 17 March 1975, File March 7-22, 1975- Kissinger's Trip- vol. I (5), Middle East Memcons and Reports: March 7-22, 1975, Kissinger Trip vol. I (1) Box 3, National Security Adviser Kissinger Reports on USSR, China, and Middle East Discussions, GRFL.
58. Despatch from Ambassador Adams in Cairo to FCO, 'Egypt: a valedictory review', 14 November 1975, TNA, FCO 93/629.
59. JIC memorandum (75) 18, 'Arab/Israel the prospects', 20 June 1975, TNA, CAB 186/20.
60. Attached UKEA supplement of 'the American position' to JIC memorandum (75) 18, 'Arab-Israel the prospects', 20 June 1975, TNA, CAB 186/20.

61. Memorandum from DCI Colby to Henry Kissinger, 'Possible implications of Egypt's action on UNEF', 19 July 1975, CREST, NARA II: 'He has said frequently that he will take his case to the UN before going to war again, and he may consider that his current resort to the UN constitutes that last step. We recall that the October War came about two months after the Security Council debate in July 1973 – Sadat's last serious effort at diplomacy before the war.'

62. Ibid. The estimate stressed that Sadat was 'proud of the fact that with the war he surprised the world with his seriousness – proved as he puts it, that the Arabs were not a "dead corpse"'. Colby judged that 'Sadat's action on UNEF *is* a gambit to gain attention and exert pressure for more rapid movement in negotiations, but he is not unaware that, if it is unsuccessful, he must either take further action or lose credibility and diplomatic leverage.'

63. Ibid.

64. Telegram from Ambassador Eilts in Cairo to Secretary of State, 'Reported Egyptian military preparations', 21 August 1975, Box 51 Peace Negotiations Chronological File, 22 July – 1 September 1975, Declassified Documents: Documents from the National Security Adviser: NSC Middle East and South Asian Affairs Staff Files (December 2008 Opening) Box 9, Ford Library Project File of Documents declassified through the Remote Archive Capture (RAC) Program: Photocopies 1969-1977, GRFL.

65. Memorandum from Scowcroft to the President relaying a report from Kissinger, 23 August 1975, File 21 August – 1 September 1975-Sinai Disengagement Agreement- vol. I (2), Middle East Memcons and Reports: March 7-22, 1975, Kissinger Trip vol. II (5), Box 4, National Security Adviser Kissinger Reports on USSR, China and Middle East Discussions, GRFL.

66. Interview with Michael Sterner, 2 March 1990. Available at <http://adst.org/wp-content/uploads/2012/09/Egypt.pdf>, p. 206 (last accessed 1 March 2017).

67. JIC memorandum (75) 23, 'Arab/Israel: the effects of the Sinai agreement', 12 September 1975, TNA, CAB 186/20. The JIC admitted that their intelligence on Syria was sparse in comparison to their knowledge of events in Egypt, where, for example, they knew that 'top level officers were instructed to draw up plans for attack in mid-September if there had been no diplomatic progress by then'. They wrote 'it is difficult to say how far Asad is susceptible to domestic pressures in favour of war', since 'we lack hard information about the strength of his internal position'.

68. NIE Working Paper, 'Trends in inter-Arab co-operation over the next decade and the implications for Israel', 19 January 1976, CREST, NARA II [emphasis added].

69. Ibid.

70. Ibid.

71. Ibid. Nonetheless analysts judged that the move had 'clearly weakened this Arab unity and sapped Arab political as well as military strength' but questioned the wisdom of Israeli reactions. They wrote with some derision that 'some Israelis now take satisfaction in claiming that for the first time in their history they are the reason not for unity among the Arabs but for serious division'. The draft clearly questioned the 'apparently prevailing Israeli belief that time is on Israel's side and that advantage can be gained by feeding on and attempting to fuel Arab division'. Analysts accused Israel of myopia in their perceptions of Arab division and unity: 'what is good or bad in Israel's short range terms is not necessarily also good or bad in terms of the long range prospects for Middle East stability'.

72. JIC memorandum (75) 23, 'Arab/Israel: the effects of the Sinai agreement', 12 September 1975, TNA, CAB 186/20.

73. CIA Research Study, 'The Palestinian Arabs', March 1976, Subject File Middle East Security Assistance- Palestinians, Box 37, Declassified Documents: Documents from the National Security Adviser: NSC Middle East and South Asian Affairs Staff Files (December 2008 Opening) Box 9, Ford Library Project File of Documents declassified through the Remote Archive Capture (RAC) Program: Photocopies 1969-1977, GRFL.

74. Ibid.

75. Ibid.

76. Ibid.

77. Ibid.

78. Telegram from USDAD Cairo to DIA, 'Comments by Coomander [sic] Egyptian Airforce (U)', 19 November 1974, Presidential Briefings File October 29 1974 – February 1975, Box 43, Declassified Documents: Documents from the National Security Adviser: NSC Middle East and South Asian Affairs Staff Files (December 2008 Opening) Box 9, Ford Library Project File of Documents declassified through the Remote Archive Capture (RAC) Program: Photocopies 1969-1977, GRFL.

79. NIE Working Paper, OCI no. 046-76, 'Trends in inter-Arab cooperation over the next decade and the implications for Israel', 19 January 1976, CREST, NARA II.

80. Stein, *Heroic Diplomacy*, p. 222.

81. J. Lorenz, *Egypt and the Arabs: Foreign Policy and the Search for National Identity* (Boulder, CO: Westview Press, 1990), p. 85: 'Israeli sources indicate that Sadat, both in private talks with Begin and in public, stressed that he had come to Jerusalem not to make a separate agreement but to discuss the Palestinian issue.' Fawzi also argues that Sadat had the Palestinian interest at heart. See M. Fawzi, *Al-Sadat: Al-Za'im Al-Muftará 'Alayh* (Cairo: Dar al-Nashr Hatyih, 1995), p. 65.

82. N. Barrington, *Envoy: A Diplomatic Journey* (London: Radcliffe Press, 2014).

83. Ambassador Morris's valedictory despatch, 12 March 1979, TNA, FCO 93/1925.

84. Despatch by Ambassador Morris in Cairo to FCO, 'President Sadat's peace offensive: Chapter 1: The Visit to Jerusalem', 8 November 1977, TNA, FCO 93/1277.

85. Memorandum from Ambassador Morris to FCO, 21 November 1977, TNA, FCO 93/1277.

86. Ibid.

87. Despatch from Ambassador Morris in Cairo to FCO, 'President Sadat's peace offensive: Chapter 1: The Visit to Jerusalem', 8 November 1977, TNA, FCO 93/1277.

88. Ibid.

89 Ibid.

90. National Intelligence Daily Cable, 25 November 1977, FOIA Reading Room.

91. Despatch from Ambassador Morris in Cairo to FCO, 'President Sadat's peace offensive: Chapter 1: The Visit to Jerusalem', 8 November 1977, FCO 93/1277.

92. National Intelligence Daily Cable, 25 November 1977, FOIA Reading Room.

93. Despatch from Ambassador Morris in Cairo to FCO, 'Egypt: annual review for 1978', 27 January 1979, TNA, FCO 93/1924.

94. Stein, *Heroic Diplomacy*, p. 250.

95. Ambassador Morris's valedictory despatch to FCO, 12 March 1979, TNA, FCO 93/1925.

96. Limitations of space inhibited a more comprehensive discussion of Western assessments of Sadat's domestic political and economic reforms.

97. World Bank report 2738 – EGT, 'Arab Republic of Egypt: recent economic developments and external capital requirements', 12 November 1979, p. 29. Growth figures were registered as above 10 per cent for 1975 and 1976.

98. Beattie, *Egypt During the Sadat Years*, p. 150.
99. Despatch from Ambassador Adams in Cairo to FCO, 'Egypt: annual review for 1974', 27 January 1975, TNA, FCO 93/628.
100. Beattie, *Egypt During the Sadat Years*, p. 159.
101. NIE Working Paper OCI no. 046-76, 'Trends in inter-Arab co-operation over the next decade and the implications for Israel', 19 January 1976, CREST, NARA II.
102. President Thursday Brief, 4 February 1976, Country File Egypt-Economic, Box 2, Declassified Documents: Document from the National Security Adviser: NSC Middle East and South Asia Affairs Staff Files (December 2008 Opening) Box 8, Ford Library Project File of Documents declassified by the Remote Archive Capture (RAC) Program: Photocopies, 1969-1977, GRFL.
103. Despatch from Ambassador Morris in Cairo to FCO, 'On first looking at Sadat's Egypt', 9 February 1976, TNA, FCO 93/847.
104. R. Baker, 'Sadat's open door: opposition from within', *Social Problems*, 28: 4, 1981, p. 380.
105. Memorandum from Ambassador Morris in Cairo to FCO, 'Egypt internal: Saudi Ambassador's view', 14 June 1976, TNA, FCO 93/847.
106. Ibid.
107. Despatch from Ambassador Morris in Cairo to FCO, 'Who rules Egypt', 16 July 1977, TNA, FCO 93/1041.
108. Beattie, *Egypt During the Sadat Years*, p. 218.
109. CIA research paper by the National Foreign Assessment Centre, 'Sadat's liberalization policy', June 1979, CREST, NARA II.
110. Memorandum from the Canadian delegation to NATO, 1 February 1977, TNA, FCO 93/1045.
111. National Intelligence Daily Cable, 21 January 1977, FOIA Reading Room.
112. Diplomatic report no. 128/77 from Ambassador Morris in Cairo to FCO, 'The disturbances of 18/19 January in Egypt', 31 January 1977, TNA, FCO 93/1045.
113. Ibid.
114. Memorandum from Ambassador Morris in Cairo to Weir in FCO, 29 May 1976, TNA, FCO 93/847.
115. Memorandum from Coles to Quinlan, 'Egypt: April', 1 May 1976, TNA, FCO 93/847: 'In April the show continued as before. Production and stage management were as usual skilful. But by now, for this audience the techniques are becoming familiar, the material is wearing thin and the show is progressively less impressive. The

significant point is whether this goes for the wider Egyptian audience too.'

116. Memorandum from Ambassador Morris in Cairo to FCO, 'Who rules Egypt', 16 July 1977, TNA, FCO 93/1041.
117. Ibid. [emphasis added].
118. Interagency intelligence memorandum by the DCI, 'Egypt: the domestic political outlook', December 1979, CREST, NARA II.
119. Beattie, *Egypt During the Sadat Years*, p. 165.
120. Ibid. p. 166.
121. Despatch by Ambassador Adams in Cairo to FCO, 'Egypt: the Dawn of Democracy', 28 July 1975, TNA, FCO 93/625.
122. Memorandum from Gladstone to Wogan, 30 September 1974, TNA, FCO 93/380.
123. Chancery memorandum to FCO, 'Muslim Brotherhood', 28 May 1976, TNA, FCO 93/847. Diplomats noted that Sadat himself had used the religious right to defeat leftists in 1971. The 1971 constitution made '*Sharia* the principal source of legislation and in 1972, the People's Assembly passed a resolution, since quietly shelved that hand-chopping should be introduced as the penalty for theft'. Although there has been no legislation on dress, 'there has been a noticeable tendency for Muslim ladies even of quite high class to wear the *Tarha* (veil)'.
124. Research paper by the National Foreign Assessment Center, 'The Egyptian press', January 1979, CREST, NARA II.
125. Teleletter from Allen to FCO, 28 August 1979, TNA, FCO 93/1965.
126. Research paper by the CIA's National Foreign Assessment Center, 'Islam in Iran', March 1980, CREST, NARA II.
127. Teleletter from Allen to FCO, 28 August 1979, TNA, FCO 93/1965.
128. Interview with Alfred Atherton, summer of 1990. Available at <http://adst.org/wp-content/uploads/2012/09/Egypt.pdf>, p. 410 (last accessed 1 March 2017).
129. Ambassador Michael Weir correctly assessed, however, that the prospect of an Iranian style revolution was not likely. See despatch from Ambassador Weir to FCO: 'Islamic fundamentalism in Egypt', TNA, FCO 93/2394.
130. Despatch from Ambassador Morris in Cairo to Callaghan, 9 February 1976, TNA, FCO 93/847: 'He enjoys relaxing in a variety of presidential residences, and watching films of an evening. (That at least is one thread in a continuity otherwise difficult to trace

between the young revolutionary and conservative president: he had to be fetched out of the cinema to be told the coup was about to be launched in 1952).'

131. Interview with James Bahti, 26 March 1990. Available at <http://adst.org/wp-content/uploads/2012/09/Egypt.pdf>, p. 223 (last accessed 1 March 2017). Bahti was Consul General in Alexandria from 1981 to 1983.

132. Memorandum from Ambassador Morris in Cairo to FCO, 'Who rules Egypt', 16 July 1977, TNA, FCO 93/1041.

Conclusion

Many Egyptians never forgave the British for the ignominious treat-ment which we had meted out to them. Apart from occupying vast areas of Egypt with British bases, where Egyptian law was ignored, at the other end of scale there were the signs in public parks which read, 'Dogs, nursemaids and Egyptians not permitted on these lawns.' I was never surprised at the way Egyptians lionized Colonel Nasser and the way he freed the country from foreign domination.

Walter Coleshill, 2012[1]

The diplomatic and intelligence documents over these two decades reveal vivid imagery of two very different Egyptian leaders who both exploited, indeed mastered, the art of political surprise. Com-paring Egypt's presidents several decades on, the notorious Arabist Sir James Craig reflected that Nasser

> was a fine man and if he had been more patient and if British minis-ters had understood that Arab nationalism was a completely natural thing, they might have worked together. But no, successive British governments held onto the view that Nasser was anti-British and pro-Communist. They patronised him and he didn't like that.

Sadat, he suggested,

> was of much smaller stature than Nasser . . . a much lesser man, less intelligent, vainer. Most of my Arabist contemporaries . . . agreed with me on that, but ministers thought that Sadat offered a chance to bring peace to the Arab-Israel dispute. How wrong they were.[2]

As the previous chapter demonstrates, the diplomatic and intel-ligence community proved significantly more sceptical.

Indeed, it is true to say that over the two decades following Nasser's dramatic nationalisation of the Suez Canal, intelligence analysis performed better than scholars have conventionally thought. In fact, at times it is striking how far-sighted contemporary analysis proved to be with the benefit of retrospect. Moreover, bringing the 'missing dimension' of intelligence to the forefront of international history, it becomes apparent that historians of intelligence and diplomacy can do more with these analyses than merely identify which predictions emerged as either right or wrong, although this is of course an interesting undertaking in itself. A deeper examination reveals how 'official wisdom' on both sides of the Atlantic thought about critical events in the region and the role of 'cultural Otherness' in their assessments. Chapter 1 certainly disproves the contention that the Anglo-American intelligence communities neglected or were unable to study foreign thought structures. Ideas about Arab culture such as the deceptive nature of Arab 'rhetoric', the pre-eminence of 'honour' and the comprehensive influence of 'Islam' proved to be a prevalent (if not always constructive or decisive) part of intelligence assessments in the decades under examination.

Intelligence perceptions of Nasser were diverse and nuanced. Analysts depicted many 'faces' of the nationalist which correlate with the Arabic perspective and thereby reveal the limitations of Western scholarship that has emphasised the images of a 'Hitler on the Nile' or 'Soviet stooge'. Egypt's union with Syria and, for a brief moment, the Iraqi revolution transformed the rhetoric of Arab unity into reality and brought the face of 'Nasser the imperialist' to the surface of assessments. At the peak of Nasser's apparent success in 1958, we see the JIC's complicity in reflecting and justifying the hostility towards Nasser expressed by British policy-makers on all sides of the political spectrum. No doubt the absence of diplomatic relations between Egypt and Britain in these years contributed to an exaggerated sense of Nasser's desire for domination over the Arab world. At this particular historical juncture, American analysts were often more balanced, recognising the anti-Communist motivations of the union and suggesting that increased responsibility abroad might moderate Nasser's pan-Arab ambitions.

The spectre of Nasser in difficulty indeed began to emerge with the Iraqi revolution, when it quickly became clear that Nasser was far from 'in control' of the transition in Iraq. The advance of the Iraqi Communist Party, upon whom General Qasim came increasingly to rely in order to maintain power, proved worrying to both sides of the Atlantic. Indeed, intelligence assessments of Qasim provide a revealing point of comparison with those of Nasser. The negative stereotypes of a deluded, inefficient and paranoid Arab that dominated representations of Qasim are striking when set against the more positive, and at times adulatory language that was used to describe Nasser and his achievements. Indeed, Nasser increasingly came to be associated with 'moderation' and 'stability', particularly by the Americans. There seems little doubt that the increasingly erratic behaviour of the Iraqi nationalist contributed to Nasser's perceptual downgrading (or perhaps promotion) from 'radical' to 'moderate'. Nasser's rift with the Soviets in the summer of 1959 also seemed to indicate a growing 'maturity'. The JIC's pertinent analysis of the Iraqi Communist Party and its limitations perhaps explains why they felt less urgency than their American counterparts to embrace Nasser wholeheartedly.

The secession of Syria was tactically unexpected but, like the Iraqi revolution, there was good 'strategic notice' of the political, economic and cultural tensions created by the union and exacerbated by Nasser's policies. Analysts did not predict the union's dissolution outright, partly because the secessionists themselves were uncertain of the outcome. A deprecating view of Syrian culture, as well as relatively high estimations of Nasser combined to suggest the absence of a viable alternative. Analysts proved particularly incisive at forecasting the implications of the secession. They realised that domestic politics in Syria would be destabilised, potentially exacerbating the Arab–Israeli conflict. They correctly judged that Nasser's position in Egypt would be unaffected and recognised that whilst Nasser might take the opportunity to focus on domestic reform he would not be able to resist calls to re-establish his ascendency in the Arab world. The secession therefore provoked a curious duality in analysts' perceptions of Nasser; on the one hand he was a statesman chastened, on the other, he was a leader more prone to potentially volatile behaviour if the occasion presented itself.

The Yemeni revolt of October 1962 provided just this opportunity. It was one of the few Arab revolutions in which there was
good tactical, as well as strategic notice. It was recognised that
the Imam's death would provoke a crisis of succession and that a
revolutionary situation of sorts existed in this anachronistic state.
Analysts depicted Nasser as generally supportive and informed but
by no means the master orchestrator. The Yemeni conflict played
out the intimations of analysts in 1958 that Nasser was as much
a 'prisoner' of Arab nationalism as its driver.[3] American analysts
shared with their Egyptian counterparts overoptimism about the
prospect of republican success but soon recognised that the stalemate would be difficult to break. They correctly assessed that the
prospect of peace was hindered by Nasser's paramount concern
for 'face' which trumped his pragmatic realisation that this was an
unwinnable war. Moves towards a disengagement agreement were
ultimately thwarted by the announcement that the British were
leaving Aden. It became clear that Nasser 'the opportunist' would
not resist the opportunity to claim credit for yet another expulsion of Western imperialism. Although Nasser's troublemaking
potential was increasingly stressed in analysis from 1965 to 1966,
British assessments on Aden occasionally reminded policy-makers
that it was an inherently unsustainable situation, nurtured by
British policy and only exacerbated by Nasser's machinations.

Nasser's intrigues abroad were arguably the most important
justification for Western enmity towards him.[4] In general, however, assessments of Nasser's foreign policy towards Syria, Iraq
and Yemen anticipated later scholarly conclusions that 'Nasser's
involvement in specific Arab controversies or crises was often initiated reluctantly, in response to external stimuli rather than as part
of a grand desire for regional dominance'.[5]

Nasser's natural propensity to 'react' was all too evident in the
Six-Day War. This crisis clearly illustrates the potential importance
of intelligence analysis to policy. Analysts applied their cultural
understanding of Arab rhetoric and the pre-eminence of 'face' to
reassure policy-makers that Nasser had no master plan to exter-
minate Israel. They were also able to interpret Soviet and Israeli
intentions and capabilities in order to direct policy-makers to limit
escalation of the conflict and resist Israeli pressures for greater

support. Yet the crisis also reinforced as 'truths' certain cultural beliefs that would prove difficult to vanquish in the future.

Informed by their analysis of the 1967 war, the Anglo-American intelligence community regarded the ensuing War of Attrition with concern. On the one hand it was another demonstration that the delusional Egyptians, driven by emotion and a fatalistic commitment to 'dignity', were provoking yet another unwinnable war. On the other hand, diplomats noted the logic of denying the Israelis comfortable use of the east bank of the Canal, provoking American intervention and putting some military might behind negotiations. The latest declassifications reveal that the British Foreign Office provided the Prime Minister with a strong and detailed warning of the risks of Soviet intervention in 1970 that was patently ignored. Moreover, analysts concretely framed assessments of the Soviet intervention as a result of unacceptable Israeli deep penetration raids rather than a desire on the part of either the USSR or Egypt to strengthen relations.

Analysis of Nasser's death and first impressions of Sadat demonstrated a similar acuity. A largely accurate assessment of the likely motivations and implications of the Soviet expulsion in 1972 was only compromised by a marked reluctance to regard Sadat as operating within a strategic framework. This was consistent with the mostly negative first impressions of Sadat as a tactical, inconsistent and inferior statesman to his predecessor. Ironically, admiration for Nasser after his death resonates especially through the British diplomatic reports. Indeed, this chapter demonstrates all too well the potential significance of perceptive reporting by human sources.

Such reporting also sheds considerable doubt on Kissinger's famous explanation of the intelligence community's 'failure' to anticipate war in 1973 that: 'our definition of rationality did not take seriously the notion of starting an unwinnable war to restore self-respect'.[6] In a reversal of the conventional explanation of intelligence failures, the recently released records have shown that analysts (particularly on the British side) were perfectly aware of the 'Otherness' of Arab rationale in motivating Sadat to war. However, their severe underestimation of Egypt's *capability* diluted their processing of these motivations. This revises and reconfigures the prevailing wisdom concerning Western analysts' superior abilities to assess 'secrets' rather than 'mysteries'. In the usually more successful realm of intercepting 'capability', the Anglo-American intelligence community's analysis was adversely influenced by two psychological barriers that undermined perceptions of Egypt's agency in this conflict. The first was a set of implicit and explicit cultural preconceptions with which they approached the Arab world. The second was the effect of the Soviet expulsion from Egypt, which nurtured a false sense of security and reinforced the idea that the Egyptians could not wage war without their superpower patron. The study of foreign thought structures, therefore, evidently did not suffice to preclude an incorrectly reduced perception of threat in October 1973.

Assessments of Sadat's foreign and domestic policy after the October War demonstrate the potential utility of intelligence analysis in peace as well as war. In negotiations with Israel, analysts were aware of the dangers of a separate peace and the need for Sadat's 'Western pragmatism' to accommodate his Arab constituency. They did not predict Sadat's visit to Jerusalem but they appreciated its motivations and likely implications. Less impressive analysis of the Palestinian dimension perhaps contributed to its neglect by policy-makers in this period. Sadat's domestic reforms were regarded with hope by American analysts, no doubt due to increasing levels of American aid bestowed upon the Egyptian government. The British were more cynical, ironically never quite convinced that Sadat had the same good intentions as his troublesome predecessor. Perhaps most striking in assessments of Sadat's post-war leadership is the frequency with which Nasser's shadow permeated analysis. By the end of his rule assessments painted a picture of Sadat that more closely resembled the unstable, erratic and inconsistent politician that took power after Nasser's death than the admirable, pragmatic and triumphant statesman of October 1973. Whilst Nasser had been a troublesome adversary, analysts demonstrated a begrudging respect for his principles and dedication to his country for many years after his death. It is notable also that many Anglo-American assessments of both Nasser and Sadat in fact correlate more closely with the Arabic narratives than current Western historiography. The recurring spectre of Nasser's image in the 'Arab Spring' protests is a testament to the durability of his legacy and the acuity of their analysis some thirty years ago.

Nonetheless, it cannot be denied that the West's attempts to understand both leaders were often framed in 'Orientalist' language about Arab behaviour. This seems to have been more marked in periods of uncertainty, transition or crisis. When faced with a frustrating or incomprehensible cognitive scenario, Western analysts relied more heavily on cultural preconceptions: the 'typical Arab' traits of 'rhetoric', 'emotion', 'passivity' or 'irrationality' as an explanatory factor for an otherwise inexplicable event. Nasser and Sadat, in different ways, both challenged, and at times confirmed, the West's Orientalist thinking. It has been suggested by one scholar that the Western 'grudge against Nasser stems from the fact that he upset ingrained beliefs about Arabs'.[7] As a British report put it in 1959, Nasser 'exploded the myth of Western invincibility and thus has at last done something to give the Arabs confidence in themselves'.[8] Sadat, on the other hand, explicitly advanced the idea that he was more 'Western' in nature and orientation than either his predecessor or other Arab leaders. In justifying his trip to Jerusalem he claimed, 'you know nothing of the Arabs. I know them only too well . . . contenting themselves with bluster and empty slogans as they have done from the beginning. They will never agree on anything.'[9] Indeed this book has unearthed numerous examples from archival research and interviews which reveal that *it was often the Arab political elite themselves which advanced the notion of a cultural divide and reinforced the West's cultural beliefs*. Their motivations for doing so varied: to excuse, explain, sometimes even to deceive.

This study thus reinforces two unmistakable truisms that have emerged from the most important literature about 'culture'. The first is that 'the temptations of particularism are not confined to "orientalists" for in suitably altered form, they constitute much of the self-image of Middle Eastern people themselves'. As the late Fred Halliday put it, 'No one could be more "orientalist" than the Arab nationalist vaunting the uniqueness and specificity of the "Arabs".'[10] Further comparative research might usefully examine how Western depictions of the Arab differed to their depictions of other cultures.[11] The second truism is the notion that 'culture is better approached not as a script for action, but as an ambiguous repertoire of ideas through which people make strategy'.[12] In other words, the notion of 'culture' and the complex systems of meanings that define it must be understood as a fluid rather than a static concept, changing over time and across contexts in how it is constructed and instrumentalised.

These findings thus revise Said's fundamental conclusions about Western perceptions of the Arab 'Other' in both the past and the future. The fact that the historical study of the 'Other' preceded, coincided with, and then was formed or defined by empire does not render these studies, or those that follow in this tradition, useless or worthy of abandonment. It does, however, raise important questions about the relationship between knowledge and power, specifically the intentions that precede (and actions or decisions that follow) the accumulation of such cultural knowledge. As Said puts it, 'the closeness between politics and Orientalism' and therefore 'the great likelihood the ideas about the Orient drawn from Orientalism can be put to political use, is an important yet extremely sensitive truth'.[13] The analyst (like the historian) is never entirely detached from the object of his study – bound and limited by the language, the society, the culture in which his/her thoughts are formed and expressed. The prevailing power structure of that culture is also important. But the non-objectivity of such work does not mean that the scholarship should be abandoned, nor does it mean, as Said implies, that ethnocentrism is the exclusive purview of the West. In gratitude to Said for reminding us of the potency of the age-old association of knowledge and power, we should nonetheless endeavour to continue such studies for a more (if never entirely) uncorrupted and self-conscious knowledge of 'the Other', upon which the foundations of peace and understanding, rather than empire and domination, can be built. As the first chapter argues, and the CIA made explicit in their 1974 post-mortem of assessments on Vietnam, perhaps the most effective analysis of 'Otherness' requires a self-conscious awareness of the particular assumptions with which the analyst approaches the world and from where these have derived. So frequently were cultural beliefs casually scattered throughout political and intelligence documents as natural or immutable truths, yet so rarely were such beliefs made transparent and explicit. Asserting our beliefs about another culture explicitly, however unsavoury to our politically correct ears, is surely the most effective way of subjecting these cultural suppositions to debate and criticism.

Above all we must recall that intelligence in its 'primary or generic sense is everywhere a property of the mind. It stands for the human being's inborn capacity to come to terms with life by engaging in thought and acquiring, developing and investing knowledge.'[14] It is the inherently 'human' nature of intelligence analysis that rises to the forefront of this study. This book has shown that sensitivity to both culture and psychology can be a profound source of strength in intelligence analysis. The role of diplomatic assessments in picking apart open-source material within a leader's speech in order to identify hidden codes of signification was clearly an invaluable contribution to the intelligence process. Diplomats in particular demonstrated a remarkable ability to combine psychological prowess and a good dose of empathy (some positive 'mirror-imaging') to see the events of this period through the eyes of the Egyptian people. Vivid descriptions of Nasser's death, their astute impressions of Sadat both before and after the war, alongside assessments of Soviet-Egyptian relations or the Iraqi Communist Party, reinforce the importance of 'on-the-ground' human intelligence analysis. Their insights certainly add a new historical 'voice' to the existing historiography of this period, one where the quest for Soviet containment reigned supreme, thereby exacerbating fundamental misunderstandings of regional dynamics. Assessments in this period clearly demonstrate that this was in fact rarely the case.

Yet the psychological, human dimension also has its pitfalls. We see all too clearly the unnerving dissonance between knowing, even understanding, and the more difficult task expected of analysts: drawing exactly the right conclusions. The prevailing assessments of the Soviet expulsion in July 1972 illustrate perfectly this dissonance. Whilst analysts identified with precision and sensitivity the immediate motivations leading to this decision, they were unable or unwilling to conceive Sadat as taking this step within a strategic framework. In part, this derived from their unfavourable perceptions of Sadat, alongside an unspoken Western concept of strategy as a series of articulated, planned and organised steps geared towards a clearly defined outcome. Sadat's leadership and actions in this period evoked rather the opposite conclusions. That is not to say that Sadat expelled the Soviet Union in July 1972 with the clearly defined aim of going to war in October 1973. Until Egyptian archival sources on this are made available we can only speculate as to the extent of his fore-planning, but that this was a possibility should have been more seriously considered by intelligence analysts and policy-makers alike.

These case-studies also fundamentally challenge the value of discourse such as 'success' and 'failure' in scholarly studies of intelligence. This book has sought to illuminate the nuances that this black and white dichotomy obscures in our historical understanding of this period. To take one example, if Sadat did not articulate a clearly defined 'strategy' as such, then how realistic is it to expect analysts to impose a strategic plan on their interpretations of his actions? Perhaps the simple answer is that even Great Powers should generally operate under the assumption that their adversary is *more* rather than *less* competent, for only this assumption can reduce the likelihood of such surprise. A similar argument can be made for Syrian secession which was in fact unplanned by the secessionists themselves. Is it perhaps more important for intelligence to be able to *make sense* of sudden developments than to be able to *predict* them? To take a more recent case, the 'Arab Spring' protests clearly acquired a momentum and trajectory that the protestors themselves could not have envisaged. And yet Western intelligence agencies were castigated for failing to predict the upheavals that continue to play out to this day.

It is commonly asserted that Western intelligence agencies have proved better at discerning the 'secrets' or facts than unearthing the 'mysteries' or intentions of their adversaries. However, this study tells a different story. Analysts often proved unable to predict precisely what was going to happen and when, particularly if offensive plans were well guarded and few were informed of the details or timing (during the Iraqi revolution or the Yom Kippur War, for example). However, with the benefit of all source analysis, particularly diplomatic reporting by those immersed in the politics and culture of the target country, analysts were usually able to present astute explanations of how and why certain situations might come about and could often suggest appropriate policies to mitigate the damage in response to such events.

The relationship between intelligence and policy is clearly a critical one, though it is for another scholarly work to explore this dimension in detail. In general, I think former JIC Chairman Cradock is right to conclude that the Committee looked upon the world 'coolly and realistically, with few illusions'. He argues that 'the pretences and evasions are there, but they belong to the realm of policy'.[15] Similarly, long-serving American diplomats have suggested that 'there were times when intelligence was out in front of policy and I would argue that quite often in the Middle East this was certainly the case'.[16] These case studies illuminate several instances where astute and far-sighted policy recommendations were dismissed or ignored: the implications of not recognising the new Yemeni republic, Nasser's desire to escape the grip of the Soviets, or warnings about the escalation of the War of Attrition and the prospect of unprecedented Soviet military intervention in the Middle East.

The evidence clearly indicates that more often than not analysts had the knowledge and insight to hand. Does the fault lie therefore with the myopia of policy-makers, rather than with the analysts, as Cradock implies? The complex relationship between intelligence and policy renders judgements of 'success' or 'failure' yet more troublesome, because of course the questions that the analyst is tasked to answer are essentially set by their policy-makers. The record of Anglo-American intelligence assessments of the Middle East in this period suggest that analysts frequently had the right answers – they could tell policy-makers that even at the peak of Soviet influence, the Kremlin's control over Egyptian policy was negligible, or that the united military might of the Arab world could not inflict but a dent on Israel. The weakness of assessments lay rather in the questions that were *not* asked – by analysts and policy-makers alike. Amongst the considerable achievements of Anglo-American analysis in this period, perhaps too infrequently or mildly did analysts direct decision-makers in Britain and America with sufficient imagination, purpose and (when necessary) criticism as to the likely consequences of their *own* power in the region – the situation in Aden is a case in point. Analysts might have stressed more strongly the 'winds of change' spreading to this last imperial outpost. Discreet references to the dangers of covert meddling, in Syria or Yemen, for example, were too few and far between. In many ways this seems to be the major and most consistent weakness of intelligence analysis. It serves as a stark reminder that intelligence agencies do a critical job of 'telling truth to power'. Often this demands interrogating the beliefs and assumptions shared by both analysts and policy-makers about what is in the national interest and how the assumptions that underlie policy are interpreted by, and affect the actions of, our allies and adversaries alike. Of all the intelligence assessments titled 'Consequences of Soviet influence in the Middle East' perhaps too few were titled 'Consequences of American or British policy in the Middle East'. Whilst the quest to identify, understand and appreciate the 'Otherness' of dynamics in the region was often an invaluable aid to intelligence assessments, a deeper and more critical look *inwards* may nonetheless have been lacking.

Notes

1. Interview with Walter Coleshill, 10 April 2012. Available at <http://adst.org/wp-content/uploads/2012/09/Coleshill-Walter.pdf> p. 26 (last accessed 1 March 2017).
2. James Craig, letter to the author, 10 November 2011.
3. SNIE 30-3-58, 'Arab nationalism as a factor in the Middle East situation', 12 August 1958, FOIA Reading Room.
4. Restrictions of space prevented the inclusion of an additional chapter on Anglo-American assessments of Nasser's domestic policy. In contrast to foreign policy, it was assessments of Nasser's domestic achievements that occasioned some of the most positive depictions of the nationalist.
5. J. Jankowski, *Nasser's Egypt, Arab Nationalism and the United Arab Republic* (Boulder, CO: Lynne Rienner Publishers, 2001), p. 9.
6. H. Kissinger, *Years of Upheaval* (Boston: Little, Brown and Co., 1982), p. 465.
7. N. Izzedin, *Nasser of the Arabs: An Arab Assessment* (London: Third World Centre, 1981), p. 438.

8. FO Steering Committee Paper no. 8, 'Arab nationalist and radical movements in Egypt, the Levant and Iraq', 1959, TNA, FO 487/13. At the same time Nasser: 'reflected the Arab inferiority complex in his insistence on dealing with the West on a basis of equality'.

9. J. Lorenz, *Egypt and the Arabs: Foreign Policy and the Search for National Identity* (Boulder, CO: Westview Press, 1990), p. 95.

10. F. Halliday, *Islam and the Myth of Confrontation* (London; New York: I. B. Tauris, 2003), p. 13: Halliday makes a similar argument for Western perceptions of Islam during the Khomeini revolution suggesting that 'the opponents and proponents of the Islamic movement were in agreement that "Islam" itself was a total, unchanging, system . . . [thus] the image of a timeless "Islam" is not just the fabrication of fevered Western minds.'

11. M. Parris and M. Bryson, *Parting Shots: Undiplomatic Diplomats – The Ambassadors' Letters You Were Never Meant to See* (London: Penguin Books, 2010), vividly illustrates how Western stereotypes about other cultures are by no means limited to the Arab or Middle East. While not an academic work, it presents an important comparative insight that could potentially benefit from greater scholarly attention.

12. P. Porter, *Military Orientalism: Eastern War through Western Eyes* (London: C. Hurst and Co., 2009), Introduction, p. vi.

13. E. Said, *Orientalism* (London: Penguin, 2003), p. 96.

14. A. Bozeman, *Strategic Intelligence and Statecraft: Selected Essays* (Washington: Brassey's, 1992), p. 1.

15. P. Cradock, *Know Your Enemy: How the Joint Intelligence Committee Saw the World* (London: John Murray, 2002), p. 302.

16. R. B. Parker (ed.), *The October War: A Retrospective* (Gainesville, FL: University Press of Florida, 2001), p. 206.

Bibliography

Primary Sources

Awraq Siyasiyya [Political Papers], Vol. 2 (Cairo, 1978).

Files from the series CAB, DEFE, FCO, FO, PREM: The National Archives of the UK (TNA), at Kew, London.

Foreign Affairs Oral History Collection, Association for Diplomatic Studies and Training, Arlington, VA, accessed online at: http://adst.org/

National Archives II (NARA II), at College Park, Maryland, USA.

CIA Records Search Tool (CREST), at the National Archives II at College Park, Maryland, USA (NARA II).

Freedom of Information Act Electronic Reading Room (FOIA Reading Room), accessed online at: http://www.foia.cia.gov/

Foreign Relations of the United States (FRUS), accessed online at: http://history.state.gov/historicaldocuments/

Declassified Document Reference System (DDRS), accessed online at: http://infotrac.galegroup. com/

The National Security Archive (NSA), accessed online at: http://www.gwu.edu/~nsarchiv/

OSS/State Department Intelligence and Research Reports (OSS/SDIRR), The Middle East 1950-1961 Collection accessed at SOAS Library, London.

Gerald R. Ford Presidential Library (GRFL), Ann Arbor, Michigan, USA.

Personal interviews and correspondence with British and Egyptian diplomats.

Secondary Sources

Books

Abdel Nasser, H., *Abdel Nasser: El Sigil Bel Thowar* (Cairo: Al Ahram, 1996).

Abu-Lughod, I., *The Arab-Israeli Confrontation of June 1967: An Arab Perspective* (Evanston, IL: Northwestern University Press, 1970).

Ajami, F., *The Arab Predicament: Arab Political Thought and Practice since 1967* (Cambridge: Cambridge University Press, 1992).

Aldrich, R., *The Hidden Hand: Britain, America and Cold War Secret Intelligence* (London: John Murray, 2001).

Aldrich, R., *GCHQ: The Uncensored Story of Britain's Most Secret Intelligence Agency* (London: Harper Press, 2010).

Alexander, A., *Nasser: His Life and Times* (Cairo: Cairo University Press, 2005).

Allen, M., *Arabs* (London: Continuum, 2006).

Andrew, C. and Dilks, D. (eds), *The Missing Dimension: Governments and Intelligence Communities in the 20th Century* (Basingstoke: Macmillan, 1984).

Andrew, C. and Mitrokhin, V., *The KGB and the World: Mitrokhin Archive II* (London: Penguin, 2006).

Appy, C. G., *Cold War Constructions: The Political Culture of United States Imperialism, 1945–1966* (Amherst, MA: University of Massachusetts Press, 2000).

Ashton, N. J., *Eisenhower, Macmillan and the Problem of Nasser: Anglo-American Relations and Arab Nationalism, 1955–1959* (London: Macmillan, 1996).

Ashton, N. J., *Kennedy, Macmillan and the Cold War: The Irony of Interdependence* (Basingstoke: Palgrave Macmillan, 2002).

Ashton, N. J., *The Cold War in the Middle East: Regional Conflict and the Superpowers, 1967–73* (London: Routledge, 2007).

Ayubi, S., *Nasser and Sadat: Decision Making and Foreign Policy, 1970–1972* (Washington: University Press of America, 1994).

Badeeb, S. M., *The Saudi-Egyptian Conflict over North Yemen, 1962–1970* (Boulder, CO: Westview Press, 1986).

Bar-Joseph, U., *The Watchman Fell Asleep: The Surprise of Yom Kippur and Its Sources* (Albany, NY: State University of New York Press, 2005).

Baring, E., *Modern Egypt 1908*, 2nd edn (London: Macmillan, 1911).

Barrett, R., *The Greater Middle East and the Cold War: U.S. Foreign Policy under Eisenhower and Kennedy* (London: I. B. Tauris, 2007).

Beattie, K. J., *Egypt During the Nasser Years: Ideology Politics and Civil Society* (Oxford: Westview Press, 1994).

Beattie, K. J., *Egypt During the Sadat Years* (New York: Palgrave, 2000).

Bowen, J., *Six-Days: How the 1967 War Shaped the Middle East* (London: Pocket Books, 2003).

Bozeman, A., *Conflict in Africa: Concepts and Realities* (Princeton, NJ: Princeton University Press, 1976).

Bozeman, A., *Strategic Intelligence and Statecraft: Selected Essays* (Washington: Brassey's, 1992).

Brenchley, F., *Britain, The Six-Day War and its Aftermath* (London: Tauris, 2005).

Carter, J., *Keeping Faith* (London: Collins, 1982).

Churchill, R. S. and W.S., *The Six-Day War* (London: Heinemman, 1967).

Cohen, R., *Culture and Conflict in Egyptian-Israeli Relations: A Dialogue of the Deaf* (Bloomington, IN: Indiana University Press, 1990).

Coughlin, C., *Saddam: His Rise and Fall* (London: Harper Perennial, 2005).

Cradock, P., *Know Your Enemy: How the Joint Intelligence Committee Saw the World* (London: John Murray, 2002).

Dekmejian, R. H., *Egypt under Nasser* (Albany, NY: State University of New York Press, 1971).

Devlin, J., *The Ba'ath Party: A History of its Origins to 1966* (Stanford, CA: Hoover Institution Press, 1976).

Fahmy, I., *Negotiating for Peace in the Middle East* (London: Croom Helm, 1983).

Farid, A. M., *Nasser: The Final Years* (Reading: Ithaca Press, 1994).

Fawzi, M., *Harb al Thalath Sanawat 1967–1970* (Cairo: Dar al-Mustaqbal al Arabiyy, 1983).

Fawzi, M., *Al-Sadat: Al-Za'im Al-Muftará 'Alayh* (Cairo: Dar al-Nashr Hatyih, 1995).

Fernea, R.A. and Louis, W.R., *The Iraqi Revolution of 1958: The Old Social Classes Revisited* (London: Tauris, 1991).

Ferris, J., Nasser's Gamble: How Intervention in Yemen Caused the Six-Day War (Princeton, NJ: Princeton University Press, 2013).

Finklestone, J., *Anwar Sadat: Visionary who Dared* (London: Frank Cass, 1996).

French, D., *The British Way in Counter-Insurgency, 1945–1967* (New York: Oxford University Press, 2012).

Gamasy, M., *The October War: Memoirs of Field Marshal El-Gamasy of Egypt* (Cairo: AUC Press, 1993).

Gamasy M., *Mudhakirrat Al-Gamassi: Harb Uktubur 1973* (Cairo: Al Hayat al 'Ammat l-il-Kuttab, 1998).

Gerges, F., *America and Political Islam: Clash of Cultures or Clash of Interests* (Cambridge: Cambridge University Press, 1999).

Halliday, F., *Islam and the Myth of Confrontation* (London: I. B. Tauris, 2003).

Handel, M. I., *The Diplomacy of Surprise: Hitler, Nixon, Sadat* (Cambridge, MA: Centre for International Affairs, Harvard University, 1981).

Heikal, H. M., *Matar Bisaraha 'an Abd al Nasir* (Beirut: al-Dar al-Muttahida li al-Nashr, 1972).

Heikal, H. M., *The Sphinx and the Commissar: The Rise and Fall of Soviet Influence in the Arab World* (London: Collins, 1978).

Heikal, H. M., *Autumn of Fury: The Assassination of Sadat* (London: Andre Deutsch, 1983).

Heikal, H. M., *Sanawat al Ghalyan* (Cairo: Al Ahram, 1988).

Heikal H. M., *1967: Al-Infijar* (Cairo: Al Ahram, 1990).

Helms, R. and Hood, W., *A Look Over My Shoulder: A Life in the Central Intelligence Agency* (New York: Random House, 2003).

Heuer, R. J., *Psychology of Intelligence Analysis* (New York: Nova Novinka, 2005).

Hunt, L., *The New Cultural History* (Berkeley, CA: University of California Press, 1989).

Huntington, S., *Clash of Civilisations* (London: Simon and Schuster, 1996).

Ismael, T., *The Rise and Fall of the Communist Party of Iraq* (Cambridge: Cambridge University Press, 2007).

Izzedin, N., *Nasser of the Arabs: An Arab Assessment* (London: Third World Centre, 1981).

James, L., *Nasser At War: Arab Images of the Enemy* (Basingstoke: Palgrave Macmillan, 2006).

Jankowski, J., *Nasser's Egypt, Arab Nationalism and the United Arab Republic* (Boulder, CO: Lynne Rienner Publishers, 2001).

Jervis, R., *Perception and Misperception in International Politics* (Princeton, NJ: Princeton University Press, 1976).

Johnson, L. B., *The Vantage Point: Perspectives on the Presidency, 1963–1969* (New York: Holt, Rinehart and Winston, 1971).

Joll, J., *Origins of the First World War* (London: Longman, 1984).

Jones, C., *Britain and the Yemen Civil War, 1962–1965: Ministers, Mercenaries and Mandarins: Foreign Policy and the Limits of Covert Action* (Brighton: Sussex Academic Press, 2004).

Kamel, M. I., *The Camp David Accords* (London: Routledge and Kegan Paul, 1986).

Khalidi, R., *Sowing Crisis: The Cold War and American Dominance in the Middle East* (Boston, MA: Beacon Press, 2009).

Kissinger, H., *The White House Years* (Boston, MA: Little, Brown and Co., 1979).

Kissinger, H., *Years of Upheaval* (Boston, MA: Little, Brown and Co., 1982).

Korn, D. A., *Stalemate: The War of Attrition and Great Power Diplomacy in the Middle East* (Boulder, CO: Westview Press, 1992).

Little, D., *American Orientalism: The United States and the Middle East since 1945* (Chapel Hill, NC: University of North Carolina Press, 2002).

Lorenz, J., *Egypt and the Arabs: Foreign Policy and the Search for National Identity* (Boulder, CO: Westview Press, 1990).

Louis, W. R. and Owen, E. (eds), *Suez 1956: The Crisis and its Consequences* (Oxford: Clarendon Press, 1991).

Louis, W. R., *The Ends of British Imperialism: The Scramble for Empire, Suez and Decolonisation* (London: I. B. Tauris, 2006).

Louis, W. R. and Shlaim, A. (eds), *The 1967 Arab-Israeli War: Origins and Consequences* (Cambridge: Cambridge University Press, 2012).

McNamara, R., *Britain, Nasser and the Balance of Power in the Middle East, 1952–1967: From the Egyptian Revolution to the Six Day War* (London: Frank Cass, 2003).

Mangold, T., *Cold Warrior: James Jesus Angleton: The CIA's Master Spy Hunter* (New York: Simon and Schuster, 1991).

Matthias, W. C., *America's Strategic Blunders* (University Park, PA: Pennsylvania State University Press, 2001).

Mawby, S., *British Policy in Aden and the Protectorates, 1955–67* (London: Routledge, 2005).

Mutahhar, A., *Yauma Walada al-Yaman Majadahu: Dhikrayat' 'an Thaorat Sibtambir 1962* (Sana'a: Dar Nobal lil-tiba'a, 1990).

Oren, M. B., *Six-Days of War: June 1967 and the Making of the Modern Middle East* (Oxford: Oxford University Press, 2002).

Parker, R. B., *The Politics of Miscalculation in the Middle East* (Bloomington, IN: Indiana University Press, 1992).

Parker, R. B. (ed.), *The Six-Day War: A Retrospective* (Gainesville, FL: University Press of Florida, 1996).

Parker, R. B. (ed.), *The October War: A Retrospective* (Gainesville, FL: University Press of Florida, 2001).

Parris, M. and Bryson, M., *Parting Shots: Undiplomatic Diplomats – The Ambassadors' Letters you Were Never Meant to See* (London: Penguin, 2010).

Patai, R., *The Arab Mind* (New York: Charles Scribners and Sons, 1973).

Podeh, E., *The Decline of Arab Unity: The Rise and Fall of the United Arab Republic* (Brighton: Sussex Academic Press, 1999).

Porter, P., *Military Orientalism: Eastern War through Western Eyes* (London: C. Hurst and Co., 2009).

Quandt, W., *Decade of Decisions: American Policy Towards the Arab-Israeli Conflict, 1967–1976* (Berkeley, CA: University of California Press, 1977).

Quandt, W., *Peace Process: American Diplomacy and the Arab-Israeli Conflict Since 1967* (Washington: Brookings Institution; Berkeley: University of California Press, 1993).

Rahmy, A., *The Egyptian Policy in the Arab World: Intervention in Yemen: 1962–1967: A Case Study* (Washington: University Press of America, 1983).

Rathmell, A., *Secret War in the Middle East: The Covert Struggle for Syria, 1949–1961* (London: Tauris Academic Studies, 1995).

Reynolds, D., *One World Divisible: A Global History since 1945* (London: Allen Lane, Penguin, 2000).

Riad, M., *The Struggle for Peace in the Middle East* (London: Quartet, 1981).

Sadat, A., *In Search of Identity: An Autobiography* (London: Collins, 1978).

Said, E., *Orientalism* (London: Penguin, 2003).

Salah al Din Bitar, *Al-Siyasa al-Arabiyah bayn al Mabda aw al Tatbig* (Beirut: Dar al-Tali'ah, 1960).

Satia, P., *Spies in Arabia: The Great War and the Cultural Foundations of Britain's Covert Empire in the Middle East* (Oxford: Oxford University Press, 2008).

Seale, P., *The Struggle for Syria: A Study of Post-War Arab Politics, 1945–1958* (Oxford: Oxford University Press, 1965).

Sharaf, S., *Sanawat Wa-Ayyam Ma'a Jamal 'Abd al-Naṣir: Shahadat Sami Sharaf* (Cairo: Dar al-Fursan lil-Nashr, 2005–7).

Shazly, S., *The Crossing of the Suez* (San Francisco, CA: American Mideast Research, 1980).

Simons, Geoff, *Iraq: From Sumer to Saddam* (London: Palgrave Macmillan, 2004).

Stein, K., *Heroic Diplomacy: Sadat, Kissinger, Carter, Begin and the Quest for Peace in the Middle East* (London: Routledge, 1999).

Stephens, R., *Nasser: A Political Biography* (London: Penguin, 1971).

Trevelyan, H., *The Middle East in Revolution* (London: Macmillan, 1970).

Tripp, C., *Contemporary Egypt: Through Egyptian Eyes: Essays in Honour of Professor P. J. Vatikiotis* (London: Routledge, 1993).

Varisco, D. M., *Reading Orientalism: Said and the Unsaid* (Seattle, WA: University of Washington Press, 2007).

Vatikiotis, P. J., *Nasser and His Generation* (London: Croon Helm, 1978).

Vaughn, J., *Unconquerable Minds: The Failure of American and British Propaganda in the Arab Middle East, 1945–1957* (London: Palgrave, 2005).

Wohlstetter, R., *Pearl Harbour: Warning and Decision* (Stanford, CA: Stanford University Press, 1962).

Yaqub, S., *Containing Arab Nationalism: The Eisenhower Doctrine and the Middle East* (Chapel Hill, NC: University of North Carolina Press, 2004).

Chapters in Edited Books

Bar-Joseph, U., 'Israel's 1973 intelligence failure', in Kumeraswamy, P. R. (ed.), *Revisiting the Yom Kippur War* (London: Frank Cass, 2000).

Costigliola, F., 'Reading for meaning: theory, language, and metaphor', in Hogan, M. and Paterson, T. G. (eds), *Explaining American Foreign Relations History* (New York: Cambridge University Press, 2003).

Daniel, N., 'Contemporary perceptions of the revolution', in Fernea, R.A. and Louis, W. R. (eds), *The Iraqi Revolution of 1958: The Old Social Classes Revisited* (London; New York: I. B. Tauris, 1991).

Dawisha, A., 'Egypt', in Sayigh, Y. and Shlaim, A. (eds), *The Cold War and the Middle East* (Oxford: Clarendon Press, 1997).

Eilts, H., 'Reflections of Suez: Middle East security', in Louis, R. and Owen, E., (eds), *Suez 1956: The Crisis and its Consequences* (Oxford: Clarendon Press, 1991).

Garthoff, R., 'U.S. intelligence in the Cuban Missile Crisis', in Blight, J. and Welch, A. (eds), *Intelligence and the Cuban Missile Crisis* (London: Frank Cass, 1998).

Halliday, F., 'The Middle East, the Great Powers and the Cold War', in Sayigh, Y. and Shlaim, A. (eds), *The Cold War and the Middle East* (Oxford: Clarendon Press, 1997).

Khalidi, R., 'The impact of the Iraq revolution on the Arab world', in Fernea, R. and Louis, W. R. (eds), *The Iraqi Revolution of 1958: The Social Classes Revisited* (London: Tauris, 1991).

Khalidi, R., 'The 1967 war and the demise of Arab nationalism', in Louis, W. R. and Shlaim, A. (eds), *The 1967 Arab-Israeli War: Origins and Consequences* (Cambridge: Cambridge University Press, 2012).

Lesch, D., 'The 1957 American Syrian crisis', in Lesch, D. (ed.), *The Middle East and the United States* (Boulder, CO: Westview Press, 2007).

Louis, W. R., 'The Tragedy of the Anglo-Egyptian settlement of 1954', in Louis, W. R. and Owen, E. (eds), *Suez 1956: The Crisis and its Consequences* (Oxford: Clarendon Press, 1991).

Louis, W. R., 'The British and the origins of the revolution', in Fernea, R. and Louis, W. R. (eds), *The Iraqi Revolution of 1958: The Old Social Classes Revisited* (London: I. B. Tauris, 1991).

Osgood, K., 'Eisenhower and regime change in Iraq: the United States and the Iraqi revolution of 1958', in Ryan, D. and Kiely, P. (eds), *America and Iraq: Policy Making, Intervention and Regional Politics* (Milton Park: Routledge, 2009).

Podeh, E., 'The United States and the Baghdad Pact', in Lesch, D. (ed.), *The Middle East and the United States* (Boulder, CO: Westview Press, 2007).

Shamir, S., 'The collapse of Project Alpha', in Louis, R. and Owen, E. (eds), *Suez 1956: The Crisis and its Consequences* (Oxford: Clarendon Press, 1991).

Sluglett, M. and Sluglett, P., 'The social classes and the origins of the revolution', in Fernea, R. and Louis, W. R. (eds), *The Iraqi Revolution of 1958: The Old Social Classes Revisited* (London: I. B. Tauris, 1991).

Vaughn, J., 'Between Suez and the Six Day War: Israel and the Arabs, 1957–1967', in Hughes, R. G., Jackson, P. and Scott, L. (eds), *Exploring Intelligence Archives: Enquiries into the Secret State* (London: Routledge, 2008).

Journal Articles

Adams, P., 'Sadat's Egypt', in *Bulletin (British Society for Middle Eastern Studies)*, 3: 2, 1976.

Adamsky, D., 'Disregarding the bear: how U.S. intelligence failed to estimate the Soviet intervention in the Egyptian-Israeli War of Attrition', *Journal of Strategic Studies*, 28: 5, 2005.

Aldrich, R., 'H-Diplo/ISSF Roundtable review of: Special Issue on "the CIA and U.S. foreign relations since 1947: reforms, reflections and reappraisals"', *Intelligence and National Security*, 26: 2–3, 2011.

Ashton, N. J., 'The hijacking of a pact: the formation of the Baghdad Pact and Anglo-American tensions in the Middle East, 1955–1958', *Review of International Studies*, 19: 2, 1993.

Atherton, A. Jr., 'Arabs, Israelis – and Americans: a reconsideration', *Foreign Affairs*, 62: 5, 1984.

Baker, R., 'Sadat's open door: opposition from within', *Social Problems*, 28: 4, 1981.

Betts, R., 'Analysis, war and decision: why intelligence failures are inevitable', *World Politics*, 31: 1, 1978.

Blackwell, S., 'A desert squall: Anglo-American planning for intervention in Iraq, July 1958 – August 1959', *Middle Eastern Studies*, 35: 3, 1999.

Blanga, Y., '"Why are they shooting?": Washington's view of the onset of the War of Attrition', *Israel Affairs*, 18: 2, 2012.

Brown, W., 'The Yemeni dilemma', *Middle East Journal*, 17: 4, 1963.

Craig, J., 'A life with the Arabs', BRIMSES annual lecture, *British Journal of Middle Eastern Studies*, 28: 2, 2001.

Dawisha, A. I., 'Intervention in the Yemen: an analysis of Egyptian perceptions and policies', *Middle East Journal*, 29: 1, 1975.

Enein, Y. A., 'The Heikal Papers', *Strategic Insights*, 4: 4, 2005.

Gandy, C., 'A mission to Yemen', *British Journal of Middle Eastern Studies*, 25: 2, 1998.

Gerges, F. A., 'The Kennedy administration and the Egyptian-Saudi conflict in Yemen: co-opting Arab nationalism', *Middle East Journal*, 49: 2, 1995.

Ginor, I., 'The Russian's were coming', *Middle East Review of International Affairs*, 4: 4, 2000.

Guldescu, S., 'Yemen: the war and the Hardah conference', *Review of Politics*, 28: 3, 1966.

Jackson, P., 'Pierre Bordieu, the "cultural turn" and international history', *Review of International Studies*, 34: 1, 2008.

James, L., 'Nasser and his enemies', *Middle East Review of International Affairs*, 9: 2, 2005.

Joffé, G. H., 'Arab nationalism and Palestine', *Journal of Peace Research*, 20: 2, 1983.

Karawan, I., 'Sadat and the Egyptian-Israeli peace revisited', *International Journal of Middle East Studies*, 26: 2, 1994.

Quandt, W., 'Lyndon Johnson and the June 1967 war: what color was the light?', *Middle East Journal*, 46: 2, 1992.

Rathmell, A., 'Brotherly enemies: the rise and fall of the Syrian-Egyptian intelligence axis, 1954–1967', *Intelligence and National Security*, 13: 1, 1998.

Robarge, D., 'CIA analysis of the 1967 Arab-Israeli War', *Studies in Intelligence*, 49: 1, 2005.

Rotter, A. J., 'Saidism without Said: Orientalism and U.S. diplomatic history', *American Historical Review*, 105: 4, 2000, pp. 1207–17.

Seale, P., 'The break-up of the United Arab Republic', *World Today*, 17: 11, 1961.

Shlaim, A., 'Failures in national intelligence estimates: the case of the Yom Kippur War', *World Politics*, 28: 3, 1976.

Shpiro, S., 'The CIA as peace broker?', *Survival*, 45: 2, 2003.

Witty, D. M., 'A regular army in counter-insurgency operation: Egypt in North Yemen, 1962–1967', *Journal of Military History*, 65: 2, 2001.

Worrall, R., 'Coping with a coup d'état: British policy towards post-revolutionary Iraq, 1958–1963', *British Contemporary History*, 21: 2, 2007.

Unpublished Secondary Sources

Craig, A. J., 'The Joint Intelligence Committee and British Intelligence assessment, 1945–1956', unpublished PhD thesis, Cambridge University, Cambridge, 1999.

Ferraro, M., 'Anglo American relations and the Yom Kippur War of 1973', unpublished MPhil thesis, University of Cambridge, Cambridge, 2005.

Rezk, D., 'British and American political and intelligence assessments of the Nasser-Sadat transition: from the Six-Day War to Yom Kippur', unpublished MPhil thesis, Cambridge University, Cambridge, 2006.

Index

Page numbers in italics represent illustrations and those followed by 'n' notes.

EU representative:
Easy Access System Europe
Mustamäe tee 50, 10621 Tallinn, Estonia
Gpsr.requests@easproject.com

www.ingramcontent.com/pod-product-compliance
Lightning Source LLC
Chambersburg PA
CBHW050626280326
41932CB00015B/2536